Slavery in the Development of the Americas

Slavery in the Development of the Americas brings together new work from leading historians and economic historians of slavery. The essays cover various aspects of slavery and the role of slavery in the development of the southern United States, Brazil, Cuba, the French and Dutch Caribbean, and elsewhere in the Americas. Some essays explore the emergence of the slave system, and others provide important insights about the operation of specific slave economies. There are reviews of slave markets and prices and discussions of the efficiency and distributional aspects of slavery. As well, new perspectives are brought on the transition from slavery and subsequent adjustments. The volume contains the latest work of scholars, many of whom have been pioneers in the study of slavery in the Americas.

David Eltis is the Robert W. Woodruff Professor of History at Emory University. He is author of *The Rise of African Slavery in the Americas* (Cambridge, 2000). He also co-edited *The Transatlantic Slave Trade: A Database on CD-ROM* (Cambridge, 1999) with David Richardson, Stephen Behrendt, and Herbert S. Klein.

Frank D. Lewis is Professor of Economics at Queen's University in Kingston, Canada. He has published in numerous journals, including work on the U.S. Civil War with Claudin Joldin. Much of his recent research (with Ann M. Carlos) has concerned Native American history.

Kenneth L. Sokoloff is Professor of Economics at the University of California, Los Angeles, and research associate at the National Bureau of Economic Research.

Slavery in the Development of the Americas

Edited by

DAVID ELTIS

Emory University

FRANK D. LEWIS

Queen's University

KENNETH L. SOKOLOFF

University of California, Los Angeles

CAMBRIDGE
UNIVERSITY PRESS

PUBLISHED BY THE PRESS SYNDICATE OF THE UNIVERSITY OF CAMBRIDGE
The Pitt Building, Trumpington Street, Cambridge, United Kingdom

CAMBRIDGE UNIVERSITY PRESS
The Edinburgh Building, Cambridge CB2 2RU, UK
40 West 20th Street, New York, NY 10011-4211, USA
477 Williamstown Road, Port Melbourne, VIC 3207, Australia
Ruiz de Alarcón 13, 28014 Madrid, Spain
Dock House, The Waterfront, Cape Town 8001, South Africa

http://www.cambridge.org

First published 2004

Printed in the United States of America

Typeface Sabon 10/12 pt.   *System* LaTeX 2$_\varepsilon$ [TB]

A catalog record for this book is available from the British Library.

Library of Congress Cataloging in Publication data available

ISBN 0 521 83277 2 hardback

Contents

Appreciation: Stanley L. Engerman and Slavery

A fundamental principle of the new economic history, when it emerged more than forty years ago, was Adam's Smith's idea that individual self-interest guides economic actions, promoting the efficient allocation of an economy's resources, as if by an invisible hand. Associated with this principle was the notion that no one person, innovation, or even industry could have more than limited impact on the development of an economy. Such a perspective not only separated the new from the old, but also helped erect a dividing wall between the disciplines of economics and history, a barrier that stands to this day. Most historians with an economics background reject singular events as important to the course of development, and this view guides much of their work. By contrast, perhaps nine out of ten historians without such a background think this approach nonsensical.

Rejecting unicausal explanations has ramifications for all of life's endeavors. Applied to the world of scholarship, one might ask what possible difference can a single scholar make to a field of intellectual inquiry, given the pools of talent and widely available resources? New knowledge and new interpretations should evolve with or without the individual with whom such findings are commonly associated. Yet, if the logical basis for the current collection of essays, festschrifts in general and, beyond that, all recognitions of any kind, including Nobel prizes is unclear, economists and economic historians, who pride themselves on their realistic view of the world, still honor outstanding scholars, much as do the practitioners of other disciplines. Such apparent inconsistencies are the stuff of humanity, reflections at the micro level of the efforts of individuals and communities to strike a balance between their conceptions of what is right (principle) and the way the world works (expediency).

Studies of the past do not always acknowledge that the worldview of historical agents on the one hand, and the way those agents behave on the other, will to some degree always be at odds. Historians of slavery, in particular, have often preferred to apply the standards of our own day to the past, generating as a consequence easy moral judgments. For Stan Engerman, however, the nexus between the worldviews of historical actors and the economic outcomes is of central interest, as are the shifts in moral values over time. He has spent a good part of his career exploring societies that espoused freedom, yet practiced, and legally enshrined, extreme restraints on some individuals in the interests of improving the conditions of others. Cast more broadly, the study of slavery involves nothing less than the role of coercion in the development of the free labor and free enterprise societies of the modern world. And it includes Stan's focus on a capitalist system that came to reject slavery, which in the Americas was a profitable, viable, and highly flexible institution.

Stan has tracked the emergence of a modern labor force that responded to wage incentives, yet from the seventeenth century rejected the higher incomes associated with field labor on plantations, and continued to do so after slavery was abolished. The slave family life and culture that flourished in the Americas, in the face of masters' powers apparently greater than in any earlier slave society, have formed another of Stan's major preoccupations, as has the notion that demographic patterns were shaped more by environmental patterns shared across the slave–free divide than by the large gulf that separated slave and non-slave sectors. The recurring leitmotif of his work is the impossibility of any human action generating outcomes that are purely beneficial, or purely malevolent, even when those actions include the destruction and indeed the inception of slavery in the Americas. Class analysis and neo-classical economic theory both generate powerful insights into slavery, but understanding how a slave system could evolve and then disappear begins with realization of the complexity of the relationship between good and evil.

It is perhaps likely that the revolution in slave studies since the 1950s would have happened anyway, but no one has been closer to its epicenter, nor spent as much time there as Stan Engerman. His office at the Rochester Department of Economics (with its triple layer of books lining the walls) and home have functioned as a crossroads and clearinghouse for nearly four decades, not just for new ideas, but also of scholars – junior and senior, affiliated and unaffiliated, radical and conservative – seeking intellectual assistance and commentary. The finished output of those scholars has, as often as not, passed through this clearinghouse, first as a draft, second as a finished typescript, and third as a manuscript from a publisher (or journal editor) seeking advice on whether to publish. Each time through it has received informed and, above all, generous advice and, more specifically, a bundle of new references that its author had missed. Moreover, no one in the field (nor, we daresay, in either economics or history generally) has carried out more collaborative research. No one has more co-authors and co-editors. A few years ago at a plenary session of a large slave conference, Stan noted that he had been asked to co-edit the proceedings and asked his companion whether he should accept. "Why not," was the reply, "there isn't anyone else in the room with whom you haven't published."

Less well recognized is his role in finding and distributing primary materials. The revolution in slave studies was built, of course, on a widening interest in the subject on the part of both scholars and the general public, and on the micro-computer revolution and associated advances in quantitative work, but above all it was built on the exploitation of the remarkably rich primary materials that slave systems left behind. The real revolution in slave studies has been the quantum leap in what was available to know about slave systems in the Americas. No scholar has used a wider range of these materials in his own work than has Stan Engerman, and certainly no scholar has passed on so quickly to others both the documentary references and, where possible, what it was possible to cull from those documents. Thus, for example, anthropometric studies in slavery, indeed in history generally, began with an Engerman set of tables that appeared in *Population Studies* in 1976. All this activity has fueled a grasp of the core issues in so many different aspects of the field such that an outside reader for a multi-volume project that Stan was editing told the publisher, who had sought him out for an opinion, that not only was Stan Engerman a peerless editor, but also that if any of the contributors failed to come through with the commissioned essay on time, then the editor would easily be able to write it himself and deliver the manuscript on schedule.

The nature of the present volume is such that of all similar books published in the last two decades, this is the one that has passed through the Rochester clearinghouse the fewest number of times. After all, one could hardly ask a scholar to review his or her own festschrift. This leaves us with a particularly appropriate irony. To the extent that this collection falls short in any way, we regard such a shortfall in part as a testament to the quality of the scholar it is intended to honor.

Introduction

I

Between the fifteenth and the twentieth centuries, the center of gravity of global economic activity shifted from the Old World toward the New, and, within the Americas, from the tropical and sub-tropical to temperate areas. During most of this long durée – from the sixteenth to the nineteenth centuries – there evolved an intensive form of slavery supported by the largest mass migration of coerced labor in recorded history. At the center of both the growth process and the extensive coercion lay a relatively limited number of plantation regions that focused on the production and export of what was from the consumers' point of view a few luxury items: sugar, the various hard liquors that sugar made possible, coffee, and tobacco.[1]

The plantation complex was characterized by expansiveness, flexibility, and innovation; and because plantations relied on both sub-tropical climates and slave labor, the growth nodes of the New World remained largely outside the temperate zones, at least until 1850. Moreover, before 1800, the countries in the temperate areas that came closest to matching the economic performance of the sub-tropical slave economies were the ones that traded intensively with them. These included the colonial powers of the Old World that controlled the extensive plantation areas of the Americas. By contrast, after 1800 – following abolition of the transatlantic traffic in slaves and the

The authors would like to thank Stanley L. Engerman, Philip Morgan, David Richardson, Richard Salvucci, Mary Turner, and members of the Caribbean seminar of the University of London's Institute of Commonwealth Studies for comments on an earlier version of this Introduction.
[1] Sidney W. Mintz, *Sweetness and Power: The Place of Sugar in Modern History* (New York, 1985) argues that sugar provided a low-cost source of energy for workers before and during the industrial revolution that had the effect of increasing labor productivity. Any reasonable estimate of the share of sugar in the total diet and the incremental addition to physical activity that sugar made possible suggests that such an impact must have been trivial.

system of chattel slavery that it supported – rates of economic growth in the tropical areas lagged behind rates in the temperate zones.

In the late eighteenth century, Arthur Young remarked that coercive labor systems of varying intensity constituted the global norm everywhere outside the temperate North Atlantic region.[2] But there was no North–South economic development split of the kind that dominates modern discussions of global inequality. The mix of themes in the development of the Americas – wealth and poverty, coercion and freedom, shifts in the locus of economic power – have fascinated observers since Columbian contact. The research of the last forty years, in particular, much of it touched on and encapsulated in the papers in the present volume, has at once sharpened the paradoxes and offered new insights into understanding them.

The relative wealth of Central America and the Northern temperate zones, over the centuries since Columbian contact, was examined recently in several papers co-authored, appropriately enough, by Stanley Engerman who is the occasion of this volume. Engerman, Stephen Haber, and Kenneth Sokoloff drew attention to the fact that most European settlements in the New World began with the kinds of advantages that economic historians have traditionally seen as central to success.[3] New World migrants had access to "vast supplies of land and natural resources per person." Yet there was no doubt that, initially, the mainland possessions of the Old World latecomers – the English, the French and the Dutch – were of secondary, if not marginal economic interest. Indeed, before the arrival of Europeans these temperate regions supported a native population of much lower density than in the sub-tropical areas of the Americas.

The contrast in the economic performance of the tropical and temperate regions of the New World since 1700 is encapsulated by Sokoloff and Engerman's data shown in Table 1. Data for the pre-1700 period are necessarily sparse, but it is perhaps not unreasonable to assume that incomes in the early Spanish Americas were higher than elsewhere, that this Spanish American advantage eroded thereafter, and that the major shifts toward greater inequality, this time in favor of the British North American mainland and Canada, came after 1700 rather than before. As Engerman et al. explain,

[2] See the discussion in Seymour Drescher, *The Mighty Experiment: Free Labor Versus Slavery in British Emancipation* (New York, 2002), pp. 14, 16, 18–19.
[3] Stanley L. Engerman and Kenneth L. Sokoloff, "Factor Endowments, Institutions, and Differential Paths of Growth among New World Economies: A View from Economic Historians of the United States," in Stephen Haber (ed.), *How Latin America Fell Behind: Essays on the Economic Histories of Brazil and Mexico, 1800–1914* (Stanford, 1997), pp. 260–304. A revised version, with additions of political and educational material, is Stanley L. Engerman, Stephen H. Haber, and Kenneth L. Sokoloff, "Inequality, Institutions and Differential Paths of Growth Among New World Economies," in Claude Menard (ed.), *Institutions, Contracts and Organizations: Perspectives from New Institutional Economics* (Cheltenham, 2000), pp. 108–34.

TABLE 1. *Gross Domestic Product per Capita in Selected New World Economies, 1700–1997*

	GDP per Capita Relative to the USA			
	1700	1800	1900	1997
Argentina	–	102	52	35
Barbados	150	–	–	51
Brazil	–	50	10	22
Chile	–	46	38	42
Cuba	167	112	–	–
Mexico	89	50	35	28
Peru	–	41	20	15
Canada	–	–	67	76
United States	100	100	100	100
United States (in 1985 $)	550	807	3,859	20,230

Source: Kenneth L. Sokoloff and Stanley L. Engerman, "Institutions, Factor Endowments, and Paths of Development in the New World," *Journal of Economic Perspectives*, 14 (2000): 219.

while direct information on per capita incomes is lacking, patterns of migration, wages, anthropometric measures, and wealth-holdings all support the existence of this broad trend. In accounting for this pattern, many historians have emphasised differences in the institutions that settlers brought with them from the Old World. For example, the institutions that underpinned British colonial societies in mainland North America have been regarded as more conducive to economic growth than those brought from the Iberian countries.

By contrast, Engerman et al. focus on differences in factor endowments. They agree that political and economic institutions played a role, but argue that initial resource endowments in the various colonies of the New World were crucial in shaping the sorts of institutions that evolved and in accounting for relative economic performance over the long run. Thus, much of Latin America developed markedly unequal income distributions and social structures that gave elites a disproportionate share of power, as the environment favored latifundia and plantation agriculture. Inequality in turn inhibited economic growth. This emphasis on factor endowments, however, makes little distinction between the haciendas of Central America, on the one hand, which exported little across the ocean, and the plantation complexes, on the other, which for three centuries provided the cornerstone of trade in the Atlantic world. This approach is also broadly consistent with the view that from a twenty-first century perspective slavery had a malign impact on the long-run ability of societies to sustain productivity improvements and increase material welfare for all their inhabitants.

More has been written on the shape of New World societies as it was affected by the institutions the migrants brought with them and the environment in which they found themselves than about any other single theme in the history of the settling of the Americas by the peoples of Europe and Africa. It would be presumptuous of us to claim for this volume anything other than a more nuanced balance between the roles of imported institutions on the one hand and pre-existing endowments on the other; but before attempting a re-assessment, it is worth noting that in fact the central question regarding institutions and resource endowments may be even sharper than our opening summary suggests. It was not only that the Spanish pulled into their empire the richest and most powerful part of the Americas in the years after 1492, they had themselves just formed the most powerful nation in Europe and were able to draw on the most advanced capital markets and technology that the late fifteenth century sub-continent had to offer. It is hard to imagine the early Portuguese and Spanish transoceanic explorations and imperial ventures without a northern Italian financing and knowledge base. In effect, Columbian contact brought together what were probably the centers of economic gravity of both Europe and the Americas. In the three centuries after Columbian contact, it is even more remarkable that it was not just in the Americas that the economic center of gravity shifted to the temperate areas farther north. The same process occurred in Europe also as Spain, Portugal, and the northern Italian cities fell behind the northwest Europeans. South of the equator a parallel if less pronounced shift occurred as Brazilian coffee and later still, cattle-based activities gained at the expense of the older sugar sectors of northeast Brazil.

What was even more striking in light of the significance of slavery and the plantation complex in the seventeenth and eighteenth centuries was the fact that slavery was an integral part of the social fabric of both conquering societies – the Iberian nations – as well as those of their major victims in the Americas – the Aztecs, Incas, and the Tupinamba peoples of what became Brazil. By contrast, slavery was much less prevalent among both the native populations in most of the temperate zones of the Americas and the smaller Caribbean islands, and among the northern European nations that began to impinge on their lands many decades after the early Spanish and Portuguese initiatives in the New World. In the Americas, the incidence of slavery was greatest among those peoples who had moved farther away from hunter–gatherer, or at least a semi-settled status that was most common in the temperate regions. Slavery was probably most prevalent among the Aztecs, though in the settled, relatively densely populated and temperate northwest, the Haida, Tlingit, and Nuu-chah-nulth societies had more than 15 percent of the population in slavery.[4]

---

[4] Leland Donald, *Aboriginal Slavery on the Northwest Coast of North America* (Berkeley, 1997), pp. 17, 182–94; Orlando Patterson, *Slavery and Social Death: A Comparative Study* (Cambridge, MA, 1982), pp. 42, 52, 106–7, 123.

The Spanish could draw on the largest resources of any European power in the late fifteenth century thanks in part to their long struggle with Islam and the resulting greater familiarity with slavery compared to other western European nations. They were the first to arrive in the Caribbean, and the first to take advantage of the great riches they found. Among the earliest "commodities" that Columbus brought back to Spain was one hundred Indian slaves. How extraordinary at first glance then, that the Caribbean remained an economic backwater for a century and a half after contact, and that when it did develop it was in the face of Spanish opposition. Hispaniola exported no sugar to Europe until the late seventeenth century (and by then the exporting area was French); and Puerto Rico and Cuba exported none until the second half of the eighteenth century. Instead, the Spanish quickly came to treat the Caribbean islands as defensive bulwarks to their main imperial activities as they moved west to the most economically advanced and most densely populated part of the Americas. There they assumed control of pre-existing state superstructures. Indeed, the incidence of slavery was likely unaffected by the Spanish takeover. Why?

Part of the answer is transportation costs and, after that, factor endowments. For almost two centuries after 1492, the cost of moving goods from Central America and the Western Caribbean to Europe was so great that only the highest value products – gold and silver – could warrant the freight.[5] First looting and then mining precious metals characterized Spanish activities. The first produce sold in Europe from Central America that paid its own freight was probably exotic woods from what became Honduras.[6] These activities required labor, usually Native American and coerced; but the Spanish, like all Europeans, were certainly prepared to change the nature of coerced labor as it was practiced in the late fifteenth century, either in the Americas or Europe. Slavery may have been extensive in the pre-contact Central Americas, but the domestic and ceremonial uses of slaves by Aztecs and Mayas contrasts sharply with the intensive use of slaves as a source of labor which came after contact.[7] Yet, even though the Indian labor, which was

---

[5] By the late seventeenth century gold could be carried across the Atlantic twice – once from its source in Africa to the Americas and again from the Americas to consumers in Europe – for a shipping charge that amounted to less than one percent of its value in Africa. See David Eltis, "The Relative Importance of Slaves in the Atlantic Trade of Seventeenth Century Africa," *Journal of African History*, 35 (1994): 240.

[6] There were many other products carried to Europe from the Spanish Americas, but in all cases they were freighted in vessels whose main purpose was to carry high-value and low-volume metals. Freight rates for such items were inevitably low and few if any could have made the transatlantic crossing without "piggy-backing" on gold and silver.

[7] Robert D. Shadow and Maria J. Rodriguez–Shadow, "Historical Panorama of Anthropological Perspectives on Aztec Slavery," in Barbro Dahlgren de Jordán and Maria de los Dolores Soto de Arechevaleta (eds.), *Archaeologia del Norte y del Occidente de Mexico: Homenage al Doctor J. Charles Kelley* (Mexico City, 1995), pp. 299–323.

the mainstay of the silver mines, was coerced, it was not for the most part enslaved. Moreover, the fact is that the number of laborers – free and mita – employed in the production of silver in New Spain and Peru even at peak export periods was very small compared to the number of slaves that were to be found later on sugar plantations.

The work force in the mines of New Spain in the late sixteenth and early seventeenth centuries was below 10,000, and its counterpart in Potosi was perhaps double this in 1603, though a larger mita draft sustained this number.[8] The combined workforce of say 30,000 can be compared to the hundreds of thousands of slaves in the plantation complexes of the Americas a century after their establishment. Thus gold and silver deposits and a relatively abundant native population shaped the activities of the Spanish as they would have shaped the activities of any European group faced with the same options. It is hard to conceive of the English Elizabethan maritime adventurers behaving much differently from the conquistadors. The privateering activities of Providence Island, "the other Puritan colony," and later, early Jamaica, suggest that given the same opportunity, Francis Drake may have behaved no differently to Hernando Cortes (and a New England in Central America may have been no different from the historical New Spain).[9]

There is nevertheless a strong sense that Spain missed opportunities exploited by the English and French. Spaniards laid claim to all the Americas west of the line established by the treaty of Tordesillas, and they had the option of developing Barbados, which had no indigenous population, as well as what became St. Domingue. They already had an establishment in Trinidad and indeed there is a record of a slave ship with several hundred slaves on board disembarking its human cargo there in 1606.[10] The Spaniards were a major presence on all the Greater Antilles. They were even producing sugar in Cuba as early as the mid sixteenth century and, later in the century, had extensive sugar estates in New Spain, some staffed with African slaves.[11] Silver was perhaps the preferred option of all those coming to the New World, and as firstcomers, the Spanish found it easier to exercise that option. Yet

---

[8] Peter J. H. Bakewell, *Miners of the Red Mountain: Indian Labor in Potosí, 1545–1650* (Albuquerque, 1984), p. 182; Jeffrey A. Cole, *The Potosí Mita, 1573–1700: Compulsory Indian Labor in the Andes* (Stanford, 1985), pp. 15–17, 29. The mita labor was divided into three shifts each of which in the original formulation of Viceroy Francisco de Toledo, worked one week in three.

[9] Karen Ordahl Kupperman, *Providence Island, 1630–1641: The Other Puritan Colony* (Cambridge, 1993).

[10] Vincent T. Harlow (ed.), *Colonising Expeditions to the West Indies and Guiana, 1623–1667* (London, 1925), p. 125.

[11] Ward J. Barrett and Stuart Schwartz, "Comparación entre dos Economías Azucareras Coloniales: Morelos, México y Bahía, Brasil," in Enrico Florescano (ed.), *Haciendas, Latifundios y Plantaciones en América Latina*, (Mexico City, 1975); Ward Barrett, *The Sugar Hacienda of the Marqueses del Valle* (Minneapolis, 1970).

there was nothing obvious preventing the Spanish emulating the late seventeenth century Portuguese and encouraging the production of both precious metals and sugar in their possessions.[12] Instead the Spanish produced sugar in the Americas solely for local consumption. In the sphere of migration, over 200,000 Spanish arrived in the New World in the century and a half after Columbus, yet three times as many left the British Isles in a similar number of years after the mid seventeenth century, most of them heading to the plantation regions and under indenture – an institution particularly well adapted to long-distance migration and peculiar to French, German, and English migration.

Did the Portuguese seize the opportunity that the Spanish missed? The template for a New World sugar industry was well established in the Mediterranean for centuries prior to contact. The sugar complex (coerced labor, monoculture for long-distance export markets, and large capital inputs) moved out of the Mediterranean in the fifteenth century and over the course of two or three generations established itself first in Madeira and then São Tomé in the Bight of Biafra. In the middle of the sixteenth century the Portuguese island of São Tomé supplied most of the sugar consumed in Europe. As late as the 1640s Dutch vessels were bringing large quantities of São Tomé sugar into Amsterdam in apparently successful competition with sugar grown in Dutch Brazil. Sugar production for export to Europe was first established in northeast Brazil probably in the 1530s.

Transportation costs and factor endowments go some distance in explaining the trading patterns. For example, the location of northeast Brazil combined with the prevailing wind and ocean current systems of the North and South Atlantic meant that this region was the part of the Americas closest to African sources of labor and European markets for sugar. The voyages from Portuguese Bissau and Cacheu, in Portuguese Guinea, to Pernambuco, and from Pernambuco to Lisbon, were among the shortest of all transatlantic routes. However, others from Angola to southeast Brazil and Bahia, and later from the Bight of Benin to Bahia were far shorter than any routes from Africa to the Caribbean and North America. In addition, most of the Brazilian Atlantic coastline was on the preferred route from the East Indies to Europe. Two implications follow. First, as already noted, Brazil, not Spanish America, was the first locus of an American plantation complex. Second, slaves in Brazil would be cheaper than elsewhere in the Americas and, as Herbert Klein and Francisco Vidal Luna (Chapter 4) demonstrate, even in the nineteenth century they were to be found in a wider range of occupations than in other slave societies.

---

[12] An argument might also be made that the Spanish turned to sugar only after their silver-producing possessions won independence. Yet the major reforms to land tenure and opening slave supplies actually pre-date Latin American independence by more than 30 years.

Yet Portuguese, or more precisely, Brazilian dominance in sugar did not endure, although its economy did reemerge under different circumstances and with a different product – coffee – in the nineteenth century. Between 1650 and 1790 three additional sugar complexes appeared – the English, the French, and the Dutch – as well as two other plantation economies based on secondary crops. The Portuguese, who were supplying almost all Europe's sugar before the Dutch assault on Brazil in the mid seventeenth century, accounted for about 10 percent in 1770,[13] despite having had access for 250 years to the lowest cost African slaves and the most land suitable for sugar. Indeed, Brazilian sugar exports did not again claim an increasing share of world markets until first, the ex-slaves of St. Domingue removed the colony from competition for those markets, and second, the British abolished the slave trade to their colonies and then slavery itself, thus hobbling their own ability to compete.

The appearance of other plantation complexes also followed, in part, the logic of transportation costs and factor endowments. The first complex outside Brazil was in Barbados, the closest Caribbean island to Africa and Europe. Dominated initially by tobacco grown using white labor, the island switched to sugar between the early 1640s and 1660, and gradually began relying on black slaves. As early as 1655, Barbados planters were claiming to "ship out yearly as many Tunns of goods as ye King of Spain doth out of all his Indian Empires." The British plantation sector later expanded to the Leeward Islands (Nevis, Antigua, Montserrat, and St. Kitts), slightly further west, and then to Jamaica in the western Caribbean. By the early eighteenth century, before Jamaica had become the leading British producer of sugar, British Caribbean exports had surpassed those of Brazil as a whole.[14]

Under French control, the second plantation complex developed more gradually and followed the same westward shift, with Martinique playing the role of Barbados in the eastern Caribbean and St. Domingue, the role of Jamaica further west. Sugar dominated here also, although by the late eighteenth century, the plantations were producing more coffee, indigo, and cotton than any other polity in the Americas. If initial growth was slower, the end result was far more spectacular. The French islands out-paced both Brazil and the British Caribbean by the mid eighteenth century, and, at the outbreak of the rebellion in 1791, were likely producing more than the rest of the plantation Americas combined.

Three other smaller plantation economies emerged in this period. Lorena Walsh (Chapter 3) describes a vibrant export-oriented tobacco culture developing on the Chesapeake; and James Irwin (Chapter 9) documents the rise

---

[13] Seymour Drescher estimates the Brazilian share of Atlantic sugar markets c. 1800 at 10.8 percent (*Econocide: British Slavery in the Era of Abolition* [Pittsburgh, 1977], p. 48).

[14] Thomas Povey, "Book of Entrie of Forreigne Letters," British Library, Add. Mss., 11,411, f. 9; David Eltis, *The Rise of African Slavery in the Americas* (Cambridge, 2000), pp. 198–99.

in wealth in the region, which was based, as well, on an equally vibrant but less export-oriented mixed-crop economy. Far removed, initially, from the regions where transporting slaves from Africa was profitable,[15] the Chesapeake grew tobacco, relying at first on white indentured labor. But once supplies of these workers tightened and capital markets improved, transatlantic slave traders were able to extend their range north and west of the eastern Caribbean. In 1770, despite several decades of an active slave trade and natural slave population growth, the Chesapeake had only half the slave population of the British Caribbean, and produced less than one-quarter the value of exports of the island colonies. Another plantation economy, this under Dutch control, originated in Suriname, which was taken from the English in 1664. The complex spread westward, encompassing other parts of the South American mainland – Demerara, Berbice, Essequibo – and including a small eastern Caribbean foothold on St. Eustatius. As Pieter Emmer (Chapter 2) points out, Dutch preoccupation with much larger interests in the East and aggressive British and French pre-emptive moves in the Caribbean inhibited the Dutch plantation empire and the complex remained centered on the South American mainland producing at its peak, in the late eighteenth century, about one-quarter the output of the British slave system. In the eighteenth century a third complex appeared in the low country regions of South Carolina and, later, Georgia. Based on rice and, to a lesser degree, indigo – the latter thriving in a protected British market – this area was perhaps the most prosperous of the minor plantation complexes on the eve of U.S. independence.[16]

The relative importance and broad structure of the later plantation complexes are suggested by Table 2. The thirteen British continental colonies were exporting slightly more than their British Caribbean counterparts in 1770, but they were doing so with a population that was more than four times greater. If we take into account only the white population, per capita exports from the British Caribbean were thirty-seven times greater than those from the British mainland. Moreover, nearly 30 percent of the exports of the thirteen colonies went to the Caribbean, a much larger share than the sugar islands shipped to the mainland.[17] The Caribbean sugar islands could have found alternative sources for the provisions they obtained from the Northern Colonies far more easily than the Northern Colonies could have located a

---

[15] It is significant that the first African slaves to arrive in the Chesapeake were pirated from a Portuguese vessel heading for Spanish America and probably intended for work in the silver mines. See Engel Sluiter, "New Light on the '20 and Odd Negroes' Arriving in Virginia, August, 1619," *William and Mary Quarterly*, 54 (1997): 396–98.

[16] Russell R. Menard, "Slavery, Economic Growth, and Revolutionary Ideology in the South Carolina Low Country," in Ronald Hoffman et al. (eds.), *The Economy of Early America: The Revolutionary Period, 1763–1790* (Charlottesville, 1988), pp. 244–74.

[17] Calculated from James F. Shepherd and Gary M. Walton, *Shipping, Maritime Trade, and the Economic Development of Colonial North America* (Cambridge, 1972), pp. 94–5.

Introduction

TABLE 2. *Exports and Populations of Export-Producing Areas of Selected Areas of North and South America in 1770*

	Total Exports (million £ sterling)	Total Population (thousands)	White Population (thousands)	Per Capita Exports (millions £ sterling)	White per Capita Exports
Danish Caribbean	0.215	29	3	7.4	71.7
Dutch Americas*	0.573	100	5	5.7	114.6
British Caribbean	2.669	479	45	5.6	59.3
French Caribbean	3.819	458	46	8.3	83.0
All the plantation Caribbean**	7.276	1,066	98	6.8	74.2
New England	0.496	581	566	0.9	0.9
Middle colonies	0.609	556	521	1.1	1.2
Upper South	1.169	650	398	1.8	2.9
Lower South	0.534	345	189	1.5	2.8
All thirteen colonies	2.808	2,132	1,719	1.3	1.6

Note: *Excludes Curaçao, Saba. **Excludes the Spanish Caribbean.
Sources: Population data from John J. McCusker and Russell R. Menard, *The Economy of British America, 1607–1789* (Chapel Hill, 1985), pp. 103, 136, 153, 172, 203, 600, 712, except for St. Eustatius which is from Stanley Engerman and B. W. Higman, "The Demographic Structure of the Caribbean Slave Societies in the Eighteenth and Nineteenth Centuries," in Franklin W. Knight (ed.), *The UNESCO General History of the Caribbean*, 5 vols., 3 (Kingston, 1997): 49. Export estimates from David Eltis, "The Slave Economies of the Caribbean: Structure, Performance, Evolution and Significance." in ibid., 113–14, and James F. Shepherd and Gary M. Walton, *Shipping, Maritime Trade, and the Economic Development of Colonial North America* (Cambridge, 1972), pp. 95–6.

substitute market. Indeed, it is easier to imagine the dramatic growth of trade in the Atlantic region without the northern colonies, than without plantation America. A comparison with the plantation Caribbean as a whole reveals even more dramatic contrasts. In 1770 the Caribbean exported, in value, two and one-half times more than the North American mainland, with a population that was only half that of the thirteen colonies; and per capita exports for whites were £74, as opposed to £1.6 on the mainland.

These comparisons highlight the sharp difference between the Caribbean and mainland economies. The Caribbean was an export-based economy that used slave labor, where whites were in supervisory or entrepreneurial roles. By contrast, the continental colonies can be better characterized as a white farm economy with a significant, although subsidiary, plantation component producing for the export market.[18] Moreover, even in the Chesapeake,

[18] The mainland economies produced many crops other than plantation produce and had a smaller proportion of adult males in their workforce. If we were to include only the Upper

which in 1700 was less diversified than it was later to become and had a population whose age and sex structure was more in accord with that of Barbados, per capita exports were £2 to £2.25 compared to a Barbados figure of £7.3.[19]

Finally, we might note that the slave economies of eastern Brazil began to expand once more after the late seventeenth century, as sugar production in the traditional areas was supplemented by major gold discoveries in Minas Gerais. Unfortunately, there are no reliable estimates of gold output during this period, much less a per capita export estimate for either free or slave population. For Bahia, the leading sugar-producing area by this period, there is a crude 1700 per capita export estimate of between £3 and £4.[20] In a sense, Bahia shared elements of both the Chesapeake and Barbados. Like the former, it was home to a substantial white population, either not connected to the export economy, or producing tobacco; but like Barbados, Bahia's main crop was sugar. It is of interest, then, that its export ratio falls between that of the Chesapeake and that of Barbados, and, as we might expect, is closer to the ratio of the English area, which had more tobacco and greater crop diversity.

Per capita export differentials do not necessarily correspond to differentials in per capita income and wealth. Income and wealth estimates are much more problematic than the trade figures; nevertheless, the recent research suggests that trends in income and wealth in North America were broadly consistent with the trade patterns. Pre-nineteenth century income estimates exist only for the mainland colonies and one British sugar island, Barbados, albeit the dominant island in the Caribbean at the time. In 1774, per capita income in the southern mainland colonies is estimated to have been in the range of £10.4–12.1[21] – not very different from that calculated for the Middle Colonies and for New England. But, if the upper and lower South, and, indeed, the plantation sectors of these regions, could be separated out, the difference would no doubt be greater.[22] By contrast, per capita

and Lower South regions involved in the export economy and, in addition, standardised for age and sex, then the differences, though still striking would be somewhat less sharp.

[19] In terms of per capita exports and ratio of whites to total population, the Dutch Americas should, perhaps, be grouped with the French and British Caribbean. In terms of size, however, they belong with the minor systems of the Upper and Lower South.

[20] There are no population data for Bahia in 1700. A reliable census taken in about 1724 indicates a total population of 79,864. Slave arrivals at Bahia from Africa in the first quarter of the eighteenth century were at least 180,000, and free migration from Portugal was also strong, though perhaps most migrants, both slave and free, moved on to other regions (Stuart B. Schwartz, *Sugar Plantations* in the formation of Brazilian Society [Cambridge, 1925], 88, 343). If we assume a population of 60,000 in 1700, per capita exports are £3.79.

[21] Alice Hanson Jones, *The Wealth of a Nation to Be: The American Colonies on the Eve of the Revolution* (New York, 1980), p. 63.

[22] See the discussion in John J. McCusker and Russell R. Menard, *The Economy of British America, 1607–1789* (Chapel Hill, 1985), pp. 264–65.

income in Barbados in the late seventeenth century has been estimated at £16
in 1665–66. It grew at just under 1 percent per annum for the balance of the
century reaching £21 in 1699–1701 (1697 = 100). The 1699–1701 estimate
is £19 in 1774 prices. Thus, at the end of the seventeenth century average
income was already two-thirds greater in the leading Caribbean sugar island,
Barbados, than in either the southern mainland colonies or the thirteen continental colonies as a whole.[23] Needless to say, this income was not evenly
distributed. Philip Morgan (Chapter 10) describes the conditions of most
slaves in early America as typical of the European poor.

Per capita exports, which provide the foundation of the Barbados estimates, continued to grow strongly to 1770, and given the evidence in Table 1,
it seems unlikely that the income gap between the Caribbean and the mainland colonies narrowed in the generations prior to the American Revolution.
Richard Sheridan's per capita wealth estimates for Jamaica put that island
on a par with the mainland colonies in the early 1770s, but a recent rework-
ing of Sheridan's estimates suggests that per capita wealth in the island was
more than half as great again, even without including wealth holdings of
non-whites.[24] Inferring income from wealth has its pitfalls, but if this new
wealth estimate is accepted, Jamaica likely held the same position relative
to the mainland colonies in 1774, as Barbados held in 1700. Throughout
the New World, descendants of New World migrants were materially better
off, on average, than those who remained in the Old World; and while perhaps the Spanish American advantage had disappeared by 1774, the highest
per capita incomes were to be found in the Caribbean, not on the North
American mainland. Indeed, there is little evidence of income or wealth con-
vergence between the two regions before the 1770s.

II

In the nineteenth century, the plantation Americas were reshaped by revolution, a shift to less restricted trade, and abolition of the slave trade and
eventually slavery itself. Where in 1770 there had been six or seven colonial
systems producing a range of plantation output, by 1850 there were just

---

[23] David Eltis, "The Total Product of Barbados, 1664–1701," *Journal of Economic History*,
55 (1995): 321–36.
[24] R. B. Sheridan, *Sugar and Slavery* (Baltimore, 1973), pp. 229–32; Trevor G. Burnard, "'Prodi-
gious Riches': The Wealth of Jamaica before the American Revolution," *Economic History
Review*, 54 (2001): 516. Peter Coclanis had earlier argued that Sheridan's estimate overstated
the true figure by just under one-fifth ["The Wealth of British America on the Eve of Revolution," *Journal of Interdisciplinary History*, 21 (1989): 253–54]. For per capita exports,
see S. L. Engerman, "Notes on the Patterns of Economic Growth in the British North American Colonies in the Seventeenth, Eighteenth and Nineteenth Centuries," in Paul Bairoch
and Maurice Levy Leboyer (eds.), *Disparities in Economic Development Since the Industrial
Revolution* (New York, 1981), p. 50.

three major plantation complexes, each specializing in a different product. The U.S. South produced most of the world's cotton, Brazil a slightly lower share of the world's coffee, and Cuba a smaller share, but still about half, of all marketed sugar. All three still continued to have access to slave labor, but after 1852 only Cuba could import slaves from Africa via the transatlantic traffic. Early in the century, the richest slave colony in history, St. Domingue, had become independent Haiti via the world's most successful slave revolt, and the remaining French slaves had followed their British counterparts into freedom in 1848. Of the Dutch slave system, only a fragment survived to emancipation in 1863.

By the early 1820s no slave economy in the Americas could operate in the accustomed seventeenth and eighteenth century manner, free of restrictions on access to African slaves. At first, British naval patrols in the Atlantic did not fully prevent the transportation of slaves from Africa. However, as both Eltis and Richardson (Chapter 6), and Bergad (Chapter 7) document, attempts to suppress the trade helped increase the price of slave labor in Brazil, Cuba, and the French Americas – regions that still participated in the trade – as well as lower the price of slaves in Africa. By 1823 the British, along with the Danes and Americans, had effectively ended all slave trading with Africa, and the British imposed restrictions on owners' use of slaves. Britain abolished slavery itself in 1833, and other European nations followed suit later.

British West Indian sugar exports did not decline until slavery itself was abolished. Indeed, with the opening of new lands in Trinidad and British Guiana, exports actually increased slightly – but the British lost market share to Brazil and Cuba, the planters in both countries facing fewer restrictions on access to and exploitation of slave labor. Land reform in Cuba at the end of the eighteenth century encouraged the development of plantations by introducing something akin to freehold tenure; and at the same time, restrictions on the purchase of slaves from outside Cuba were greatly reduced. Prices of bozales slaves (new Africans) had been 50 percent greater in Cuba than in nearby Jamaica in the middle of the eighteenth century, but the differential disappeared by 1800.[25] Bergad (Chapter 7) shows Cuban slave prices after 1800 moving in tandem with slave prices elsewhere in the Americas. Development of a major plantation complex – that might have occurred in Cuba almost anytime after 1675 but for Spanish imperial policy – finally got underway; and by 1850 the Spanish Caribbean had assumed the position effectively abandoned by the British in world sugar markets.

How did these developments affect income in the Americas? Within the British West Indies, Jamaican sugar exports declined from 82,600 tons in

[25] Compare Eltis and Richardson (Chapter 6) in this volume, and the series in Laird W. Bergad, Fe Iglesias Garcia and Maria del Carmen Barcia, *The Cuban Slave Market, 1790–1880* (Cambridge, 1995), pp. 47–49.

1798–1807 to 78,500 in 1814–23 to 68,500 in 1824–33, then to 33,400 in 1839–46. In British Guiana, sugar exports more than doubled in the twenty years of slavery ending with abolition in 1833, and fell 30 percent, thereafter, before recovering with the arrival of Asian contract labor in the early 1850s.[26] After 1800, sugar prices were generally declining; yet in 1832, per capita income in British Guiana, still a frontier area, was £24.8, or about 40 percent above the U.S. level.[27] In long-settled Jamaica, which had faced growing restrictions on the use of slave labor, per capita product in 1832 is estimated to have been £13.8, or 23 percent below the U.S. figure.[28] Indeed, in the aftermath of the abolition of the slave trade the Jamaican slave labor force began to decline for the first time and most of those working in the fields in the largest British slave colony were female soon after 1807.[29]

British Guiana sugar production continued to expand to 1833 despite the British restrictions and in the face of slave prices that, by the early 1830s, were double those in the United States and Cuba (and more than double those in Barbados and Jamaica).[30] In fact, without the restrictive slave policies, per capita income in British Guiana might have been as far above that of the United States (and Britain) as Barbados per capita income had been 130 years earlier. By 1852, with slavery completely abolished in the British West Indies, per capita incomes in Jamaica and British Guiana had slipped to 50 percent and 85 percent, respectively, of U.S. levels.

Some narrowing of the gap between slave and the leading non-slave economies occurred by the mid nineteenth century, likely due to the gradual throttling of slavery and the slave trade. In 1850, Cuba still had substantial access to Africa for labor (albeit at higher prices than would have held with

---

[26] The best short survey of the impact of abolition is Herbert S. Klein and Stanley L. Engerman, "The Transition from Slave to Free Labor: Notes on a Comparative Economic Model," in Manoel Moreno Fraginals, Frank Moya Pons and Stanley L. Engerman (eds.), *Between Slavery and Free Labor: The Spanish Speaking Caribbean in the Nineteenth Century* (Baltimore, 1985), pp. 255–69, and for the British colonies, p. 261.

[27] Calculated from Thomas Weiss, "Economic Growth Before 1860: Revised Conjectures," in Thomas Weiss and Donald Schaeffer (eds.), *American Economic Development in Historical Perspective* (Stanford, 1994), p. 13; Michael Moohr, "The Economic Impact of Slave Emancipation in British Guiana, 1832–1852," *Economic History Review*, 25 (1972): 589; Barry Higman, *Slave Populations of the British Caribbean, 1807–1834* (Baltimore, 1984), p. 70.

[28] Calculated from Gisela Eisner, *Jamaica, 1830–1930: A Study in Economic Growth* (Manchester, 1961), p. 25; Higman, *Slave Populations*, 70.

[29] Higman, *Slave Populations*, 190.

[30] For price patterns in the British sugar colonies see Stanley L. Engerman, "Economic Change in the British Caribbean: The End of Slavery and the Adjustment to Emancipation," *Explorations in Economic History*, 21 (1984): 133–42. The high prices in British Guiana, as well as Trinidad, reflect the effectiveness of the ban on new slave arrivals in British Guiana and the confidence of British planters that they would be compensated should abolition of slavery itself (an issue in Britain since 1823) occur, as well as the open-land frontier in these colonies.

no restrictions whatsoever). Income estimates for Cuba are not as good as for the British Caribbean, but we do have estimates of the total value of exports, and if we assume that the ratio of such output to the production of all goods in the economy was the same as in Jamaica just prior to abolition, the result is a per capita income of £24.7 or 25 percent higher than the U.S. figure of £19.8. Juan Pérez de la Riva has estimated the 1862 per capita income of the western region of Cuba – the heartland of the sugar production – at $350, or more than twice the 1860 estimates for the United States and Britain, though per capita income for the whole of Cuba would be considerably below this figure.[31]

Within the United States, disaggregation of five major geographic regions allows comparison of slave and non-slave areas. In 1860, per capita income in the northeastern and southwestern states was higher than in any other region in the country, but after adjusting for the relatively large proportion of the northeastern population that was of prime working age, the differential between the northeastern and southwestern states is very small.[32] As noted, the highest per capita incomes in the U.S. South were in the southwest where all the U.S. sugar plantations were located. If the income gap between slave and leading non-slave economies closed in the nineteenth century, it probably closed first for those slave regions growing crops for which the economies of scale were less pronounced than in sugar cultivation.

There is other evidence that slave economies maintained their advantage over non-slave economies at least until the mid nineteenth century, and perhaps beyond. Prices of slaves rose through the eighteenth and nineteenth centuries, and prices of plantation output also increased from the 1730s on, but at a lower rate than slave prices. After the Napoleonic wars, however, the prices of sugar, cotton and coffee all began a steady descent.[33] Thus, before 1800, it would seem that increases in the demand for sugar, cotton, and

---

[31] Juan Perez de la Riva, "Aspectos Demograficos y su Importancia en el Proceso Revolucionario del Siglo XIX," in *Union de Periodistas de Cuba* (Havana, 1968), pp. 30–49, cited in Francisco Lopez Segrera, "Cuba: Dependence, Plantation Economy and Social Classes, 1762–1902," in Moreno Fraginals, Moya Pons and Engerman, *Between Slavery and Free Labor*, pp. 85–6. Another rough estimate for Cuba in 1860 puts per capita income 22 percent below the U.S. figure (Pedro Fraile Balbín, Richard J. Salvucci, and Linda K. Salvucci, "El Caso Cubano: Exportacíon e Independencia," in Leandro Prados de la Escosura and Samuel Amaral, *La Independencia Americana: Consecuencias Económicas* [Madrid, 1993], pp. 80–101).

[32] Fogel, *Without Consent or Contract*, 84–89.

[33] David Eltis, *Economic Growth and the Ending of the Transatlantic Slave Trade* (New York, 1987), pp. 283–7; Julia de Lacy Mann and Alfred P. Wadsworth, *The Cotton Trade and Industrial Lancashire* (New York, 1968), pp. 95–6; Noel Deerr, *The History of Sugar*, 2 vols., (London, 1950), 2: 530–32; John J. McCusker, *Rum and the American Revolution: The Rum Trade and the Balance of Payments of the Thirteen Continental Colonies, 1650–1775* (New York, 1989), pp. 1143–48; Great Britain, Parliamentary Papers, 1856, 55: 588–89. The argument in the balance of this paragraph is from Eltis, *Economic Growth*, 186–92,

coffee exceeded increases in supply, whereas after 1800, the situation was reversed. Throughout, but especially after 1800, the price of slaves was rising; and in all societies where slavery survived past mid-century, slave prices in real terms at least doubled in comparison with their 1800 levels.

Plantation records outside the United States have not been subject to the same analysis as those in the U.S. South, but it seems likely that the exploitation of new land, technological and organizational advances, and economies of scale in the marketing of crops account for the widening gap between prices of slaves and prices of the goods that slaves produced. Productivity improvements are addressed by Eltis and Richardson (Chapter 6), and Bergad (Chapter 7). Such improvements were of a magnitude comparable to those in British industry. The British cotton industry, for example, saw output per manhour increase at an average annual rate of 3 percent between 1830 and 1892, which compares to a 2.5 percent annual growth of sugar exports per slave from Cuba between 1827 and 1861, a period when the transatlantic slave trade to Cuba remained open.[34]

A basis for the high incomes generated by plantation economies was the economies of scale made possible by the use of human beings, whose wishes could largely be disregarded. The basic model explaining the relative efficiency of slave labor was first presented in *Time on the Cross*, debated subsequently in the *American Economic Review*, and restated in *Without Consent or Contract*. Field-Hendrey and Craig (Chapter 8) return to this central issue below with a stochastic production frontier approach. Their conclusions largely support Fogel and Engerman's original conclusions.[35] The economies of scale made possible by the use of gang labor were greater for some crops than for others, with, among plantation crops, tobacco deriving the least advantage, sugar the most, and cotton falling in the middle of this range. In fact, the severe decline, throughout the Americas, in the plantation economies following the abolition of slavery, lends support to the general proposition that the high productivity and high per capita incomes associated with certain crops were closely tied to taking the fullest advantage of slave labor.

To summarize, all early European settlements in the Americas were likely better off than their Old World parent communities; but, from the mid seventeenth to the early nineteenth centuries and possibly beyond 1850, the plantation regions, particularly those in the sugar-producing Caribbean, were the most prosperous of all. The evidence suggests that in sequence Barbados, Jamaica, St. Domingue, and Cuba had the highest per capita incomes in the

---

[34] Calculated from Eltis, *Economic Growth*, 189, and Mark Blaug, "The Productivity of Capital in the Lancashire Cotton Industry During the Nineteenth Century," *Economic History Review*, 13 (1961): 366.

[35] For continued skepticism, see Richard Sutch's comments in *The Newsletter of the Cliometric Society*, 16 (2001), pp. 8–9.

Americas and probably in the world. If the initial effect of the richest part of Europe taking control of the richest part of the Americas was a large-scale transfer of precious metals from the New World to the Old, by the early seventeenth century the main European economic interest had transferred to crop production. But, even though the locus of activity had moved from the old Aztec and Inca regions, the shift was not to the temperate regions, but rather to locations farther east in the same latitudes. From northeast Brazil in the south to the Chesapeake, it was the plantations along the Atlantic and Caribbean shores that preoccupied the Europeans, and led not only to the highest incomes of the time, but also to the largest forced migration in history. The temperate Americas, however, appear to have grown more slowly than other plantation regions, and would probably have grown more slowly still had they had not been able to trade with those regions.

III

Catch-up of the non-slave areas to high-income slave regions likely came with industrialization.[36] What has not been addressed, to any degree, is the role in this catch-up of the increasing restrictions on, and then the abolition of, slavery. Preliminary evidence suggests that the plantation economies of Cuba and the U.S. South grew at rates comparable to industrializing Britain, even though the structures of these economies were quite different.[37] It does seem, therefore, that without the abolition of the slave trade, nine-tenths of which had supplied the tropical Americas, and without the later abolition of slavery itself, the shift of the economic center of gravity toward the temperate zones would have occurred more slowly, if at all. The importance of the slave systems to the external trade of the temperate Americas supports such an assessment. Of particular interest is why, when the central supporting pillars of the plantation systems of the Americas – slavery and the slave trade – were removed, the advance eastward to the Atlantic and Caribbean shores of the Americas in high-income economic activity was not simply reversed. Why did the Spanish Americas not reassume their previous position as the economic heartland of the two continents?

It is possible to divine two routes to the high incomes of the mid nineteenth century: The first was through plantation agriculture based on a racial slavery that after 1800 was first restricted and then suppressed; the second was through industrialization based on waged labor, which has become inextricably associated with freedom.[38] At first sight these two routes to higher

---

[36] See the essays in John H. Coatsworth and Alan M. Taylor (eds.), *Latin America and the World Economy Since 1800* (Cambridge, MA, 1998) and the literature cited there.

[37] Fogel, *Without Consent or Contract*, 60–80.

[38] A third – free-labor agriculture in North America – generated incomes that were high by Old World standards, but remained behind those in the slave south and in industry.

rates of growth appear contradictory, a fact that may account for slavery not having received much attention in recent attempts to explain differentials in the long-term growth rates of American regions. The focus of recent work on the importance to growth of education, equality of income distribution, and wide participation in the political process seems to rule out consideration of slavery as a growth-enhancing institution, at least in the modern context. But while the above attributes will improve the quality of life for almost all members of society, contemporary China, the fastest-growing economy of the late twentieth century, lacks at least one and probably two of these three. As a corollary, while much more of the free than the slave population were literate in the U.S. South, literacy among slaves was sufficient to suggest that coercion was not automatically incompatible with education.[39] And of course throughout the Americas, skilled slaves were essential to the high growth rates that slave societies experienced. Many thousands of slaves worked in manufacturing, although most of the time it was more profitable to work slaves on plantations. At the same time Frank Lewis (Chapter 5) shows that, in the case of Guadeloupe at least, it was the skilled slaves who were in the vanguard of the transition from slavery. Many were able to take advantage of their high productivity by accumulating enough to attain their freedom through manumission.

In fact, examined against the broad backdrop of early modern global societies, western slavery on the one hand, and, on the other, the labor institutions in the West that evolved into free labor markets and sustained the industrialization process, were not at all incompatible. In sixteenth and seventeenth century Europe, employers assumed that the supply side of nascent labor markets was characterized by a backward-bending supply curve. Mercantilist attitudes to domestic labor ensured vagrancy laws and other coercive measures against the poor because it was thought that most people were not properly responsive to incentives. Slave labor in the colonies was predicated on the same set of beliefs, and was in some ways a logical adaptation of mercantilist attitudes for the land-abundant environment that Europeans came to control in the Americas. Further, at home, European masters hired servants for the same reason that slave owners overseas bought slaves – to

---

[39] Janet Duitsman Cornelius estimates that 5 percent of antebellum slaves were literate. (*When I Can Read My Title Clear: Literacy, Slavery, and Religion in the Antebellum South* [Columbia, SC, 1991], p. 9). Literacy was arguably higher in the eighteenth century prior to the passing of legislation banning the education of slaves. On the basis of advertisements for runaway slaves, Carter Woodson estimated a literacy ratio for slaves in the later eighteenth century U.S. South of one-third (Carter Woodson and Charles H. Wesley, *The Negro in Our History*, 11th ed. [Washington DC, 1966], p. 106; and Carter Woodson, *The Education of the Negro Prior to 1861* [New York, 1968], p. 228), though it should be noted that runaway slaves probably had higher literacy rates than the general slave population. The dramatic increase in literacy among the post-bellum black population is well known.

produce goods for sale, especially goods for export. Masters of both types of labor obtained what they needed from organised markets in which buyers and sellers responded to price changes. Free labor, in the modern sense, did not exist even in England, the North American colonies, and the early American Republic. A master–servant relationship gave masters a proprietal right to the extent that a servant's non-performance was a criminal offence equivalent to theft. At the same time, because choice of masters became increasingly possible, in comparison with slavery, the power of masters to exploit their workers was much more limited.[40]

The overlap between the condition of slave and free labor and the peculiarly western nature of both labor markets is most obvious if we remember that freedom to choose might also mean freedom to exploit others. In fact, by the sixteenth century, perhaps the key element in western exceptionalism was the vesting of property rights, especially those in human labor, to the individual rather than the group.[41] Kinship structures in the non-European world were extremely varied, but generally, status and rights in much of Africa and the pre-Columbian Americas derived not from autonomy and independence, but from membership in a kin group or some other corporate body.[42] Such a group would make collective decisions and hold, again collectively, at least some property rights in persons. By contrast, in the European Atlantic world, such rights would be held by individuals.

Europeans might purchase property rights in others (slaves) outright, or they might, as in the case of indentured servitude, temporarily give up some of their own rights, but in either case there was an individual owner of the rights in persons and a market transaction. To be a full citizen in much of the

---

[40] Robert J. Steinfeld, *The Invention of Free Labor* (Chapel Hill, NC, 1991), pp. 15–54; idem, "Changing Legal Conceptions of Free Labor," in Stanley L. Engerman (ed.), *Terms of Labor: Slavery, Serfdom, and Free Labor* (Stanford, 1999), pp. 137–67.

[41] Interpretations of the evolution of western economic dominance that stress the critical role of private property rights usually set up a polarity between private property rights on the one hand and common property resources on the other with the former being classed as "western." For a well-known example see Douglass C. North and Robert Paul Thomas, *The Rise of the Western World: A New Economic History* (Cambridge, 1973). In fact, group or corporate rights – a hybrid in terms of the above polarity – have been the global norm, a norm to which the western world has returned in a sense since the advent of widespread business incorporation in the nineteenth century. Most post-neolithic societies – western or not – must have drawn a very small share of their total income from common property resources.

[42] Philip Curtin, Steven Feierman, Leonard Thompson, and Jan Vansina, *African History* (Boston, 1978), pp. 156–71; Suzanne Miers and Igor Kopytoff, "African Slavery as an Institution in Marginality," in Miers and Kopytoff (eds.), *Slavery in Africa* (Madison, WI, 1977), pp. 3–77. For some interesting parallels in one context in the Americas see William A. Starna and Ralph Watkins, "Northern Iroquoian Slavery," *Ethnohistory*, 38 (January 1991): 34–57.

non-European world meant having more social bonds and less autonomy than would a marginal person without kinship ties. Freedom meant a belonging, not a separateness.[43] By contrast, in Europe and the European Americas, full citizenship meant ownership of property rights in oneself, and, from the eighteenth century at least, the ability to avoid giving up these rights in return for some payment. The basic unit of the expansionist societies of Europe in the early modern period was, or became, the individual; the basic unit of the societies with which they came into contact in the extra-European Atlantic world was some corporate entity comprising groups of individuals.

If, in the Western World, possessive individualism meant a recognition that one owns full rights in oneself, it also allowed for the accumulation of rights in others, as indeed happened in the slave societies of the European Atlantic. A market system per se, and the vesting of property rights in persons with an individual instead of the group, were thus perfectly consistent with both waged and slave systems. Indeed, it was perhaps the concept of rights, including rights to the labor of oneself and others, rather than slavery that better deserves the title "the peculiar institution."[44] The implications of vesting rights in the individual rather than the group played out along an ethnic divide. White servants, laborers, and women were not full citizens in the early modern West, but eventually became so. By contrast, many non-Europeans who fell under European control became the most thoroughgoing chattel slaves in human history.[45] But western systems of slavery and free labor had the same roots – the relative latitude allowed for individual action in Europe in the era of expansion.

Different types of labor were to some extent substitutes, and perhaps neither slave nor free labor per se was an essential prerequisite of sustained growth. Each had alternatives; convicts, indentured servants, and other forms of contract labor. Plantation output would have grown less strongly over the centuries and would have cost more, but sustained growth there would surely have been. Three out of four of those arriving in the Americas between 1492 and 1820 were African slaves, rather than Europeans.[46] In the

---

[43] Orlando Patterson, *Freedom*, 3 vols. (New York, 1991–), 1: *Freedom in the Making of Western Culture*, pp. 20–44.

[44] If slavery is defined more restrictively in terms of a "slave society" in Moses Finley's sense, then the description "peculiar" remains apt, because, as noted above, there have been only five such societies. See his "A Peculiar Institution," *Times Literary Supplement*, July 2, 1976, p. 819. But Finley also notes how unusual was the Greek practice of incorporating "peasantry and urban craftsmen into the community ... as full members" (p. 821).

[45] From present-day perspectives, of course, it was the new concept of "freedom" or more precisely, the new relationship between the individual and society, rather than the new concept of slavery that had, and is having, by far the larger impact on the non-European world.

[46] See David Eltis, "Free and Coerced Migrations from the Old World to New," in David Eltis (ed.), *Coerced and Free Migrations: A Global Perspective* (Stanford, 2002), pp. 73–81.

absence of abolition in the nineteenth century – in other words with a completely open transatlantic slave trade and with more extensive use of steamships – many of 50 million migrants who actually moved to the New World might have been African slaves rather than free Europeans. The essential institution facilitating such a flow was neither chattel slavery nor free labor per se, but the notion that property rights to labor were held by individuals and could be traded. In a land-abundant environment, this idea was conducive to the emergence of full chattel slavery.

This discussion may throw light on the emergence of labor regimes in the Americas, but it does nothing to explain the racial basis of slavery in the Americas. Given the western view that property rights to labor were held by the individual, why were slaves never white, whereas free workers could be of any origin? Seymour Drescher (Chapter 1) explores this issue, arguing that the unwillingness of Europeans to enslave other Europeans was a second imported institution that shaped the plantation complex. While the reason for the absence of white slaves may have varied across European societies, the unwillingness to enslave Europeans was apparently shared by all nations – at least from the time of Columbian contact. Whatever the reasons for this barrier, there is now close to consensus among historians on its existence. By excluding so many potential slaves, such an institution likely pushed up the cost of labor and plantation produce alike throughout the Americas.

As noted in the first section of this introduction, other institutions that immigrants brought with them did vary with the immigrant group, but adjustment took place to the point where in contrast to the earlier period, factor endowments do emerge as the dominant element accounting for differences in economic performance. By the late eighteenth century, the Spanish had introduced reforms in Cuba and Puerto Rico that allowed a plantation-based development of those islands that was even more rapid than that of Jamaica and St. Domingue. As Eugene Genovese pointed out thirty years ago, nineteenth century Cuban slavery appears little different from an earlier Anglo-Saxon variant. The contract labor arrangement that brought Chinese and Canary Islanders to Cuba in the mid nineteenth century was in essence identical not only to the British indentured contract servitude used in previous centuries but also to the contract system employed by the French, Dutch, and English to bring Asian labor to their nineteenth century sugar colonies. The flexibility of the European state system and social structures (perhaps the most important imported institution of all) ensured that institutions came together over time.

The different European slave systems appear to have been working with a similar set of institutions by the early nineteenth century. But no sooner was an equilibrium established than it was disrupted by a new set of imported rules for the ordering of society driven by a European abolitionist rather than a profit-maximizing impulse. If the motive was different, and the vehicle was primarily ideological rather than epidemiological and military, the impact was no less imperialist than earlier invasions.[47] Eventually all slave regimes were affected, leading to the reestablishment of a set of institutional constraints to which all regions were subject – a central feature of which was that slavery and the slave trade were not permitted. But for most of the nineteenth century the impact of abolitionism was regionally specific. As argued previously, because abolitionism affected the French and British slave systems first, its initial effect was to undermine French, then British preeminence in sugar – still by far the most important plantation crop in the early nineteenth century. Thus, by 1860, the leading British sugar colonies, Trinidad and British Guiana, together produced only one-third of Cuban output, even with access to Asian contract labor. This was an impact that no one could have imagined in the first centuries after Columbian contact.

We can now address the central questions of the significance of the mix of institutions and resource endowments for economic growth, and the position of slavery in the growth process. Measurements of early wealth are scarce but there is consensus that all European settler societies initially generated a level of material well-being in excess of what held in parent communities in the Old World. This was undoubtedly a result of labor having a higher marginal product in the land-abundant Americas. In effect labor had more factor input to work with.[48] But did overall (total factor) productivity increase as well? The highest income societies with the clearest evidence of productivity advance were those built around plantations, especially sugar plantations. In turn, northeast Brazil, then the mainly eastern English Caribbean, the mainly French western Caribbean, and the Spanish island of Cuba took the lead as the wealthiest societies in the Americas and probably the World. We have an estimate for seventeenth century Barbados and later slave societies, but nothing for early Brazil. Given the dramatic fall in Brazil's share of the world sugar market in the face of Caribbean competition, it is likely that English and French plantation innovations – perhaps in the form of gang labor – initially propelled the Caribbean ahead of Brazil.

The evidence of productivity growth in societies not dominated by slavery before the late eighteenth century is unclear. Estimates of long-term growth are best for the colonial United States, and these suggest modest growth in the range of 0.2 or 0.3 percent a year.[49] These rates may have been sufficient to make northern and mid-Atlantic colonies among the best performing non-slave economies, and to bring them up to the income of the southern colonies

---

[47] Howard Temperley, "Capitalism, Slavery and Ideology," *Past and Present*, 75 (1977): 95–118.

[48] The consensus does not appear well-founded empirically. No study that we are aware of attempts to compare systematically the effects of capital abundance in the Old World and land abundance in the New for the seventeenth century and earlier.

[49] McCusker and Menard, *The Economy of British America*, 51–59.

at the time of U.S. independence, but not enough to put them on par with the Caribbean. Rice and indigo notwithstanding, the U.S. plantation complexes were neither as extensive nor as wealthy as those in the Caribbean. Generally, family-based farming anywhere in the Americas and the urban and port activities that grew up to service them could not generate the productivity performance of slave societies.

It was apparently industrialization that allowed some closing of the income gap between the northeastern states and the Caribbean. If slavery was the first of the routes to productivity growth in the Americas, why was it that the second route revealed itself first in the northeastern United States? Such a large question is not far removed from the issue of why industrialization itself occurred, and cannot reasonably be addressed here, but at least we can comment on the association of growth with the initial factor endowments of the Americas.

The northeastern states, among the original thirteen in the union, exhibited greater equality of distribution of both income and political power than did the southern states. But, the greatest equality was to be found among frontier societies in North America, none of which led the way in industrialization or threatened to approach the level of income in slave societies.[50] More generally, greater equality of both income and political power is perhaps more properly seen as a result rather than a prerequisite of development. Outside the Americas, Britain, the first nation to experience industrialization, apparently did so with an elite whose political power was sufficient to conduct a series of successful and highly expensive wars before and during the growth process. Qualifications for participating in the political process were such that about 3 percent of the English population could vote in Parliamentary elections in 1831, somewhat more than in Barbados in 1857, but below that in most jurisdictions in the early Americas and tiny by modern standards. Participation did not increase much between 1832 and 1867, despite the first Parliamentary Reform, which enfranchised many tenants; but, by failing to provide secrecy in balloting, arguably increased the power of the landed elite.[51] Literacy in Britain was low compared to mainland North America, and economic inequality, while probably less than in most western European nations, was certainly greater than in any of the settlements in continental North America regardless of whether slaves are included in the comparison. None of these characteristics of British society before the last third of the nineteenth century apparently inhibited industrialization, yet they often appear as explanations for lack of development in modern Latin America and elsewhere.

[50] Stanley L. Engerman and Kenneth L. Sokoloff, "The Evolution of Suffrage Institutions in the New World," *Journal of Economic History* (forthcoming).
[51] David Lindsay Keir, *Constitutional History of Modern Britain Since 1485*, 9th ed. (London, 1969), pp. 402–403; Michael Brock, *The Great Reform Act* (London, 1973), p. 312–13.

Recent research on industrialization has focused on what has come to be called the "industrious revolution."[52] Indeed, the oft-cited comment of James Steuart, the Scottish economist, made before slavery in the Americas came under serious threat, that men must be slaves to wants or slaves to others, appears ahead of its time. Among non-slave societies the counterpart to the gang labor route to achieving greater output on plantations was likely the reorganized work schedule that the early factory system made possible. Power-operated machinery had much the same effect as a driver-driven work gang in the "factory-in-the-field," forcing laborers to work at a faster pace than they would otherwise have chosen. In addition, outside the factory and the field, there was a generalized productivity improvement. Service activities from transportation to financial intermediation became more efficient. Cuba, for example, was one of the leaders in the Americas in introducing railways – both on and off the plantation – and later the telegraph. Steamships and de-salination equipment were used in the final phase of the slave trade from Africa. Efficiencies in bringing together lenders and borrowers, and general scientific advances, made both slaves and waged worker more productive. The empirical evidence is overwhelming that such changes affected the pro-ductivity of slaves as well as the productivity of those workers dependent on wages.[53]

Such evidence leads directly to the issue of the long-term consequences of slavery and its implications for human welfare in the aftermath of abolition. This question has come to dominate the recent literature on the economics of slavery, and Robert Margo addresses it in Chapter 11. Abolitionists projected slavery as economically inefficient as well as immoral, even though few before the last quarter of the eighteenth century had ever viewed it as either. In one form or another this view of slavery as an economic system has survived down to the present day, though since the 1970s it has no longer formed part of the mainstream view of historians and economists. The prof-itability of slavery has become widely recognized, as have the managerial skills of the planters in running an oppressive system, but major elements of the abolitionist view survive including the "axiom" that, however profitable and flexible, slavery could not have endured into the late nineteenth and twentieth centuries.[54] Few U.S. historians take into account trends in the

---

[52] Hans-Joachim Voth, *Time and Work in England 1750–1830* (Oxford, 2001), especially pp. 242–76; Jan de Vries, "Between Purchasing Power and the World of Goods: Under-standing the Household Economy in Early Modern Europe," in John Brewer and Roy Porter (eds.), *Consumption and the World of Goods* (London, 1993), pp. 107–21.

[53] Fogel argues that productivity in the non-agricultural part of the southern U.S. economy was increasing much faster than in the northern non-agricultural sector (*Without Consent or Contract*, 101).

[54] One variant of this view is that in the U.S. case the demand for cotton could not have been sustained beyond 1860 and that the latter year was highly unusual in the level of planter profits sustained, [Gavin Wright, *The Political Economy of the Cotton South: Households,*

rest of the Americas where sugar and coffee expansion was keeping pace with cotton down to the Civil War, and demand for which expanded even more rapidly than for cotton thereafter. They also tend to ignore Lincoln's assessment of how long slavery would endure.

Perhaps the strongest remnant of the abolitionist view is the conviction that slavery could not sustain economic growth in the modern era. Thus, the slave system might encourage "economic growth" but not "economic development," though distinguishing between the two empirically is not possible. As Eugene Genovese has written, "empirically verifiable high growth rates are not the central issue. Rather, the issue concerns the structural constraints (political and ideological as well as economic) on economic development."[55] From a twenty-first century standpoint, the mix of moral reprehensibility and financial profitability that slavery embodied is extremely powerful. For those who cannot disentangle these elements (and Genovese is clearly not among their number), the argument that slavery, though profitable, had no future is attractive. Given that slavery came to be seen as evil in the Atlantic World between the mid eighteenth and the mid nineteenth centuries – after millennia when it was considered to be a normal institution – it is obvious that political sanctions against slavery were inevitable, whatever its capacity to sustain growth. The connection between the expansion of a system of free labor and the destruction of slavery has formed the basis of extensive debate in recent years and it now seems that it is more likely to exist at the level of ideological conviction rather than a drive to maximize incomes, national or personal.[56] But there is a difference between a position that sees slavery destroyed because it is reclassified as evil and one that sees slavery as an economic institution that could not survive in the American economies of

Markets, and Wealth in the Nineteenth Century (New York, 1978)]. Proponents of the insufficient demand hypothesis have yet to engage the response in Fogel, *Without Consent or Contract*, 96–102, first made in the *American Economic Review*, and restated in Fogel, *The Slavery Debates, 1952–1990: A Memoir* (Baton Rouge, forthcoming). Another variant is the older view that slavery destroyed the soil and could only survive as long as it had an open frontier to which it could move. Thus high Southern per capita income in the ante-bellum period was in part a function of the alluvial soils of the booming southwest and again could not have lasted. Both these positions have recently resurfaced in John Ashworth, *Slavery, Capitalism and Politics in the Antebellum Republic*, 2 vols., 1 *Commerce and Compromise, 1820–1850* (Cambridge, 1995), pp. 85, 89, though it should be noted that the main position of this book derives from a Marxist assumption that slavery is pre-capitalist.

55 *The Political Economy of Slavery: Studies in the Economy and Society of the Slave South*, 2nd ed. (Middleton, CT, 1989), p. xviii. Cf. Ashworth, *Capitalism and Politics in the Antebellum Republic*, 80–121, according to which slavery could not survive in a country dominated by a bourgeoisie intent on economic development – a position which on this issue is reminiscent of the work of Charles A. Beard and other scholars of the pre-World War Two progressive era.

56 Explored in the works of David Brion Davis, Seymour Drescher, Stanley Engerman, and Thomas C. Holt among others.

the late nineteenth and twentieth centuries. The papers in this volume testify to the striking flexibility that European-dominated slavery exhibited over the four centuries of its existence in the Americas after Columbian contact. They show slave owners responding to market signals little differently from employers of free labor. Their chattels were put to work in a comparably wide range of occupations, and there is no indication that slavery generated an income distribution or a pattern of consumption that inhibited growth at any stage in its existence. For three centuries plantation regions formed the growth nodes of the Americas until their source of labor was cut off, and the labor system around which they were built was destroyed. Of course, as slavery did not survive into the late or post-industrial era, there is no conclusive way of assessing its compatibility with the economic development of the Americas down to the present day. Nevertheless, arguments that slavery stymied the development of the Americas, both before and after its abolition, tend to rely more on hopeful constructions of social development than on hard empirical evidence of how slave societies functioned.

As for the institutions versus factor endowments issue with which this essay began, it would seem that much hinges on the time span examined. Before 1800, it was only slavery that generated consistently higher output levels per unit of input. All European nations established slave colonies, and these were located primarily in tropical and sub-tropical areas near the sea lanes to Europe and Africa. The high–income–temperate/low–income–tropical divide of the modern period is actually the reverse of what held in early modern era – at least in the Americas.[57] European nations also established colonies in the temperate zones of the Americas, but these relied primarily on non-slave labor, and none did as well in conventional economic terms as the slave colonies. The most exploitative form of slavery appears to have entered the Americas with the British. The adoption of the key techniques on the part of other Europeans was fairly rapid, with the French, not the British, holding the most productive colony of the slave era. While the tardiness of the Spanish and Portuguese does suggest some residual impact from imported institutions, by 1800 sugar, cotton, and coffee appear to have been cultivated in much the same way in all jurisdictions. After 1800, slavery was faced with a new set of institutional factors in the form of abolitionism that eventually brought about its demise. As this process unfolded, a new source of growth appeared in certain areas in the form of industrialization, based largely on free labor. The role of factor endowments in this second route to growth is much less clear than in the case of slavery. Factor endowments may

---

[57] Jeffrey D. Sachs, "Tropical Underdevelopment" (NBER Working Paper, No 8119, 2001), discusses the large and increasing income gap between temperate and tropical regions in the modern era, but his emphasis on the role of climate does little to explain why, in the pre-modern period, the sub-tropical regions that relied heavily on slavery had relatively high levels of income.

have encouraged social and political characteristics inhibiting growth such as elite control of the political process, unequal income distribution, and low educational levels. But such social characteristics were present in industrializing Britain, as well as the slave colonies of the Americas and modern Latin American societies. The first two of this triad developed high incomes in the eighteenth and nineteenth centuries, the last two (or their successors) developed relatively low incomes in the late nineteenth and twentieth centuries. No easy associations seem possible. There is a sense, however, that even though the inequality and institutions associated with slavery did not inhibit agricultural development in the subtropical regions, the property rights protection and broad participation in the commercial economy associated with England and the United States were keys to their early industrialization.

PART I

ESTABLISHING THE SYSTEM

White Atlantic? The Choice for African Slave Labor in the Plantation Americas

Seymour Drescher

I

During the course of the fifteenth century European navigators rapidly, and sometimes dramatically, conquered the Atlantic. The inhabitants of five continents were brought into the first continuous contact with each other. Over the next three centuries millions of Europeans and three times as many Africans were shipped across that ocean from their ancestral continents. Recent historiography has sought to understand these human flows both more precisely and more interactively. As we achieve increasing certainty about the timing and magnitude of the two migrations, a number of historians are making efforts to more rigorously specify the fundamental causal patterns at work in those migrations.

Although the creation of the early modern European Atlantic long received most attention, there has been a burst of interest in the African Atlantic that dominated transatlantic migrations for nearly two centuries after the 1630s. Assessments of demographic, political and cultural factors have been added to a traditional, and still prevailing, economic model of the development.[1] One historical project has been to determine why the differential

---

[1] The special issue of *The William and Mary Quarterly*, 3rd ser. 58 (2001), is the culmination of a long series of slave trade censuses first stimulated by Philip D. Curtin's *The Atlantic Slave Trade: A Census* (Madison, WI, 1969). For European migration see David Eltis, "Free and Coerced Transatlantic Migrations: Some Comparisons," *American Historical Review*, 88 (1983): 251–80; P. C. Emmer (ed.), *Colonialism and Migration: Indentured Labour Before and After Slavery* (Dordrecht, 1986); Magnus Morner, "Spanish Migration to the New World Prior to 1810: A Report on the State of Research," in Fredi Chiapelli (ed.), *First Images of America: The Impact of the New World on the Old* (Berkeley, 1976); Victorino Magalhaes-Godinho, "L'emigration portuguaise du XVème siecle à nos jours: Histoire d'une constante structural," in *Conjoncture economique – structures sociales: Hommage? Ernest Labrousse* (Paris, 1974); Leslie Choquette, *Frenchmen into Peasants: Modernity and Tradition in the Peopling of French Canada* (Cambridge, MA, 1997); Jan Lucassen, *Dutch Long Distance Migration: A Concise History, 1600–1900* (Amsterdam, 1991); David Galenson, *White Servitude*

---

flow of people made early modern migration history the story of a black
and slave Atlantic.[2] The prevailing explanation has had recourse to predominantly economic motives and forces. The opening of the Atlantic invited
the creation of a virtually unconstrained form of capitalism, whose benefi-
ciaries created and dealt in human chattels from Africa as their labor force.[3]
This model of untrammeled economic behavior has recently elicited a further question. Was African slavery really the optimal source of labor for the
rapid development of the Americas?

In *The Making of New World Slavery* (1997) Robin Blackburn hypothesizes a counterfactual scenario in which free Europeans became the prevailing
form of labor in the New World's tropics after the mid seventeenth century.[4]
In large part, Blackburn's benign counterfactual is a response to an earlier
hypothesis, first powerfully proposed by David Eltis in 1993, and elaborated
at greater length seven years later. Eltis challenges the prevailing model of
Europe's turn to African enslaved labor in the Americas as the epitome of
unrestrained profit-producing capitalism. He posits a still more profitable
option – Europeans enslaving Europeans. Had Europeans, particularly their
English component, enslaved themselves or other Europeans, the American
plantation system would have been still less costly and even more profitable
than it actually was.[5]

Both Blackburn and Eltis propose plausible "white Atlantic" alternatives
to the one that actually took shape. Both do what counterfactuals do best,

---

in *Colonial America: An Economic Analysis* (Cambridge, 1981); and Henry A. Gemery,
"Emigration from the British Isles to the New World, 1630–1700: Inferences from Colonial
Populations," *Research in Economic History*, 5 (1980): 179–232.

[2] See, inter alia, John Thornton, *Africa and Africans in the Making of the Atlantic World,
1400–1800*, 2nd ed. (New York, 1998); and Martin L. Kilson and Robert I. Rotberg (eds.),
The African-Diaspora: Interpretive Essays (Cambridge, MA, 1976). On a cultural plane see
Paul Gilroy, *The Black Atlantic: Modernity and Double Consciousness* (Cambridge, MA,
1993).

[3] See, inter alia, K. G. Davies, *The North Atlantic World in the Seventeenth Century* (Minneapolis, 1974), 211–15, and an exhaustive survey of the contents of articles listed under
"slave trade" in Historical Abstracts, an electronic index.

[4] Robin Blackburn, *The Making of New World Slavery: From the Baroque to the Modern
1492–1800* (London, 1997), pp. 350–363. Blackburn also suggests that seventeenth century
Europeans could have anticipated the indentured servitude of the mid nineteenth century and
signed up "Africans and Asians for freedom or indentured service with the right of return after
their terms of service." This moves the argument even further from any economic rationale
for the choice of labor in the Early Modern period.

[5] David Eltis, "Europeans and the Rise and Fall of African Slavery in the Americas: An Interpretation," *American Historical Review*, 98 (1993): 1399–1423, esp. 1422–23; and idem,
The Rise of African Slavery in the Americas (Cambridge, 2000), pp. 63–70. See 70, n.32, for
Eltis's economic critique of Blackburn's alternative. For another study premised on the idea
that African slavery in the Americas was not inevitable, see Russell R. Menard, "Transitions
to African Slavery in British America, 1630–1730: Barbados, Virginia, and South Carolina,"
Indian Historical Review, 15 (1988–89): 33–29.

engage the reader in a thought experiment that produces an "alternative history" by changing a single variable. In one respect Eltis's counterfactual is heuristically more challenging and rewarding than Blackburn's vision of a kinder and gentler America. Blackburn's scenario requires the reversal of what most scholars have taken to be the primary motive in the choices made by the planters and princes (and acquiesced in by peasants and proletarians) of Europe. Theirs were choices for maximized productivity, higher output, cheaper commodities and greater economic opportunities for Europe. Eltis repeatedly reminds us that, from the British Caribbean in the seventeenth century to the U.S. South into the second half of the nineteenth century, the slave plantation zone of the Americas was the site of some of the richest and most productive regions that have ever emerged in human history.[6]

Eltis simply proposes extending those very desires for wealth, efficiency, and opportunity still further. Our question will also be a simple one: Would the choice for a white and slave Atlantic have indeed maximized the profits of merchants and planters, the exports of the colonies, the flow of low-cost commodities to the consumer, and the standards of living and levels of income on both sides of the Atlantic? In conformity with his specifications, our analysis will consider the costs and benefits of this "whites-only" Atlantic migration as it would necessarily have affected the economic costs of that choice, both private and public.

Eltis has made a striking number of new points, which can be only briefly summarized here. He again places Europe and its long-term development at the center of the development of the Atlantic system. From a very traditional paradox in the history of the early modern world he draws bold and striking conclusions: European economic development prepared its inhabitants to reap disproportionate advantage from the naval mastery of Atlantic navigation after 1450. The development of freedom at home, including individual property rights, permitted Europeans to expand their rights in persons beyond Europe. European freedom at home was thus the prerequisite for European-directed slavery abroad. They could take fullest advantage of the opportunity to combine newly available New World lands with a new and more intensive system of coerced labor. Unable to dominate or even penetrate beyond the coastal lands of tropical Africa, Europeans tapped into the existing system of African social relations to produce crops more cheaply in

---

[6] See Eltis, *Rise of African Slavery*, pp. 203–4, 211–12; idem, "The Slave Economies of the Caribbean: Structure, Performance, Evolution and Significance," in Franklin Knight (ed.), *General History of the Caribbean*, vol. 3; *The Slave Societies of the Caribbean* (London, 1997), pp. 105–37, esp. 122–24; idem, *Economic Growth and the Ending of the Transatlantic Slave Trade* (New York, 1987), pp. 235–236; Robert W. Fogel, *Without Consent or Contract: The Rise and Fall of American Slavery* (New York, 1989), chs. 3 and 4; and idem and Stanley L. Engerman, *Time on the Cross: The Economics of American Negro Slavery* (Boston, 1974), ch. 6.

the Americas, and to deliver them to Europe more cheaply and massively than ever before.

A major novelty in this approach is its focus on Europe's non-economic development as well as its technological or military advantages. With such a focus Eltis offers an even more profound challenge to the traditional economically oriented historiography. He hypothesizes that, despite their more economically opportunistic propensities, which seemed to be driven to extreme limits in the Caribbean, the choice for African labor was ultimately limited, not by economic opportunity, but by European ideological self-perception. This line of argument, of course, has very significant implication for explaining why, by 1800, three out of four people landed in the New World had been Africans.

Eltis' explanation is straightforward. In 1500 Europeans were the most economically attuned people in the Atlantic world. In a broad band of the territories bordering that ocean, slavery was the cheapest and most efficient form of labor. Especially as developed by the English, the plantation became one of the most productive units of agriculture in the world. Its superiority was subsequently demonstrated in one area of the Americas after another between the late sixteenth and late nineteenth centuries. By 1660, for example, Barbadian exports per person exceeded anything to be found in any European country. It is doubtful whether any previous societies in history ever matched the output per slave of seventeenth century Barbados. Eighteenth and early nineteenth-century British Caribbean slaves at least matched the productivity increase of workers in early industrializing Britain. On the eve of the American Civil War the sugar region of Cuba "must have ranked among the top six of the world's leading national economies."[7]

Early modern Europe's turn to African slave labor was, therefore, eminently rational. Eltis, however, adds one crucial caveat to this conclusion. If slavery was the most rational choice for European capitalists in the circum-Caribbean and Brazil, were Africans really only a second-best choice? Once Europeans discovered that slavery was the optimal means of developing the plantation complex in the Americas, would it not have made still better economic sense for them to enslave other Europeans rather than Africans?[8] Time and money were needlessly lost in seeking cargos on the African coast. The costs of shipping European convicts to the Caribbean were similar to those from Africa. Using the "packing" ratios allotted to cargos of slaves instead of British convicts, merchants would clearly have further tipped the costs in favor of shipping Europeans. In other words there were no transportation-cost barriers to a European-slave substitution for Africans.

---

[7] See Eltis, *Rise of African Slavery*, pp. 7 and 203–203; and "Slave Economies of the Caribbean," 121–123, on Cuba. For the British West Indies, see J. R. Ward, *British West Indian Slavery, 1750–1834: The Process of Amelioration* (Oxford, 1988), p. 262.

[8] Eltis, *Rise*, 66.

Moreover, the movement of people from the coast of Europe was even more favorable to shippers than it was from Africa. If enslavement costs in Africa were trivial, the substitution of slave status for European prisoners and prisoners of war would have been neither difficult nor costly. There were well-established networks for moving convicts across every Western European state. The rapidly developing early modern canal systems would have made the cost per migrant per mile drop throughout the entire period before 1800 without costing a single extra shilling of public or private funds. Before 1830, the hypothetical cost of an outflow of migrants even four or five times their actual numbers would have been as sustainable for Europe, in demographic terms, as it was for Africa during the same period.

Indeed, from Eltis' perspective, other socio-economic gains would have tipped the scale even further in favor of a European slave trade. Europe's judges were already sending English, French, Portuguese, Spanish, German, Italian, Polish and other convicts to American plantations or Mediterranean galleys. The poorhouses and workhouses of England and the Netherlands could have been emptied, lightening the burden of poor relief. Europe's abundant and burdensome harvests of able-bodied prisoners of war could have been added to the Atlantic migration stream as ready-to-work laborers, as indeed they were during the English Civil Wars. Many seventeenth century contemporaries designated these plantation-bound workers as "slaves."[9] War added further justifications for coercion. One's own people were "impressed" into compulsory military service. The sixteenth and seventeenth centuries were chronicles of death, atrocities, rapine, war and civil conflict in Western Europe, and of enserfment and slavery in Eastern Europe. The absence of European slavery in the Americas seems paradoxical indeed. Why then did the migratory stream of coerced labor to the New World consist of enslaved Africans rather than enslaved Europeans? Eltis' short answer is

[9] See e.g. Peter Linebaugh and Marcus Rediker, *The Many Headed Hydra: Sailors, Slaves, Commoners, and the Hidden History of the Revolutionary Atlantic* (Boston, 2000), p. 123 on the Irish; Charles Carlton, *Going to the Wars: The Experience of the British Civil Wars 1638–1651* (London, 1992), pp. 327, 337 on the Scots, English and some foreign mercenaries, all (too) loosely characterized as having been sent as "virtual slaves" to Barbados. We note that the dichotomy European/non-European was never the sole determinant of policy vis-a-vis the limits of slavery. In early seventeenth century London, "Parishes included the poor soldiers and sailors who fought . . . with European and Ottoman rivals in the category of the deserving poor, out of gratitude and fear. . . . Manifestations of suffering exhibited by poor strangers and soldiers – physical marks of captivity, tongues cut out, brands, and assorted infirmities – punctuated their supplications. . . ." Fractures within Christian Europe, on the other hand, legitimated some affiliations between Protestants and Muslims. Some London parishioners supported the 'barbarryens' of Morocco who had been captured by Spaniards in 1615–16. John Rasheley, mariner, 'taken by a French Pirott & his tongue cut out,' received 12d. The Court of Aldermen also helped 'barbarians' by funding their transportation out of London and back to Barbary. See Claire S. Schen, "Constructing the Poor in Seventeenth-Century London," *Albion*, 32 (2000): 450–463.

that European cultural values more fundamentally determined its pattern of evolution than did its economic incentives or technologies. In a fundamental sense, early modern Europeans were culturally inhibited from enslaving each other, while uninhibited from, and even encouraged to, enslave others. As Eltis repeatedly says, ideology "at once shaped the evolution of African New World slavery and kept Europeans as non-slaves."[10]

It would indeed seem that, given the incentives to ensure coerced labor in the New World and the widespread indifference to human suffering in the Old, only a countervailing power of enormous psychological power prevented Europeans from crossing the line to enslaving each other. All of Eltis' references to that mental barrier are evocative of immense psychic power. The taboo against enslaving fellow Europeans was far greater than the lure of foregone wealth and power. European *values* "shaped the parameters of African New World Slavery," and kept Europeans free. These values constituted an "almost tangible barrier" against even the thought of enslaving fellow Europeans. Therefore, it was "of course, inconceivable that any of the potential European labor pools (convicts, prisoners of war, vagrants, etc.) could have been converted into chattel slaves."[11]

Eltis is less certain of the origins and nature of these psychological and conceptual inhibitions than of their presence. They were, he notes in passing, "shadowy" and "indescribable," as well as unthinkable by those they constrained. Perhaps, he hypothesizes, they emerged from the benign, pervasive, but limited, growth of European market behavior. That market may have "worked against slavery in the long run, but in the short run there was no imperceptible diffusion of non-enslavability." What is clear, however, is that the boundary between enslavability and non-enslavability was not measurable in the infinite gradations of market relations, but in sharp identity boundaries between groups – at least until a moment, c. 1770, when the boundaries suddenly came under sustained attack. Then they began to crumble even more dramatically than they had arisen. Eltis grounds his hypothesis in the silent, untraceable and unconscious long-term workings of the market on the psyches of individuals. Both European unenslavability (before c. 1750) and the subsequent extension of unenslavability to Africans, are embedded in the expansion and intensification of market relationships. Throughout the process European cultural constraints opposed the rigorous logic of

[10] Eltis, *Rise*, 2, 16, 83ff.

[11] Eltis, "Europeans and the Rise and Fall," 1408; *Rise of African Slavery*, 70. There is a substantial scholarly literature attempting to relate the rise and prevalence of antislavery in the West to economic change. See, inter alia, David Brion Davis, *The Problem of Slavery in the Age of Revolution 1770–1823*, 2nd ed. (New York, 1999); Thomas Bender (ed.), *The Antislavery Debate: Capitalism and Abolitionism as a Problem in Historical Interpretation* (Berkeley, 1992); and Seymour Drescher, "Review essay of *The Antislavery Debate: Capitalism and Abolitionism as a Problem in Historical Interpretation*," *History and Theory*, 32 (1993): 311–329.

European commercial rationality. Twice, in both the rise and fall of the African slave trade, psychological inhibitions carried the day against economic incentives. In an elegantly counter-economic inversion of Eric Williams' reasoning, "freedom, as it developed in Europe, first made possible the slavery of the Americas and then brought about its abolition."[12]

Eltis' perspective is interesting for more than the light it casts on the rise of African slavery, since it carries an implicit claim of the overwhelming victory of the libertarian dimensions of European history over its counter-libertarian dimensions during the course of modern history. Before looking more closely at the transition to African slave labor in particular, it may be useful to understand the limits of that claim. If by the sixteenth century it had become unacceptable for Europeans to enslave other Europeans, it was still quite possible to consider doing so in the mid seventeenth century (the definitive turning point toward Africans in Eltis' account). During the English Civil War, the Earl of Stamford suggested that royalist military prisoners who refused to join Parliament's forces be sold to the Barbary pirates as slaves. The proposal went nowhere, but one should be clear about its implications. Sale to North Africa meant sale into full chattel slavery, and at a time when British slaves in Africa still outnumbered African slaves in the British Americas.[13] Just 200 years later it was still possible for Anglo-Americans in North America to openly doubt the benefits of free labor. In the mid-nineteenth century one had only to open the books of George Fitzhugh or read public predictions by prominent U.S. Southern politicians in order for the impending social crisis of free-labor societies to compel them to institute some form of white bondage.[14]

More relevant to our own assessment, however, is the complete shattering of the taboo against the enslavement of Europeans by Europeans in the mid twentieth century. I would hypothesize that, under certain plausible conditions, such a breach was possible in 1640 as well as in 1940. Eltis

---

[12] See Eltis, *Rise of African Slavery*, 78–80; 272–74. Compare with idem, "The Volume and Structure of the Transatlantic Slave Trade: A Reassessment," *William and Mary Quarterly*, 58 (2001): 17–46, esp. 44. One can also envision the same anomaly in geographic terms: More territory in the Americas was put under slave cultivation in the century after 1750 than in the century before.

[13] Carlton, *Going to the Wars*, 253. An earlier English proposal to exchange captives in the custody of North African pirates for "harlots and the idle and lascivious portion of the female sect [sic]" met with no success [N. A. M. Rodger, *The Safeguard of the Sea: A Naval History of Britain, 660–1649* (New York, 1997), p. 384]. For early eighteenth century Britain, see Michael J. Rozbicki, "To Save them from Themselves: Proposals to Enslave the British Poor, 1698–1755," *Slavery and Abolition*, 22 (2001): 29–50. For the sixteenth century, see C. S. L. Davies, "Slavery and Protector Somerset: The Vagrancy Act of 1547," *Economic History Review*, 19 (1966): 533–49.

[14] See Eugene D. Genovese, *The Slaveholders' Dilemma: Freedom and Progress in Southern Conservative Thought, 1820–1860* (Columbia, SC, 1992), p. 106: idem, *The World the Slaveholders Made: Two Essays in Interpretation* (New York, 1969), pt. 2.

notes, but immediately denies, the relevance of Nazi German slavery to the enslavement of early modern Europeans. He argues that neither this, nor any other twentieth century case, resulted in "full chattel slavery for the purpose of maximizing profits."[15] Nevertheless, the German example seems more relevant to the discussion than Eltis allows. For the SS suppliers, who sold labor to German industrial firms, maximizing profits was not their priority, least of all for those laborers targeted for rapid destruction. But how did the SS differ in this from the behavior of some primary enslavers in Africa, two or three centuries before? Many Africans did not make war against their enemies primarily for economic reasons. For German armed units, as for their African counterparts, "enslavement costs were trivial." However, the German capitalists who purchased labor at 5 Zloty per day for their enterprises were explicitly acquiring and employing that labor at far below free (German) labor prices. That differential in returns to labor is among the rationales for the recent compensation settlements by some of those same industrial firms.[16]

---

[15] Eltis, *Rise of African Slavery*, 61 n.

[16] See, inter alia, Christopher R. Browning, *Nazi Policy, Jewish Workers, German Killers* (New York, 2000), pp. 62, 97; Ulrich Herbert, *Hitler's Foreign Workers: Enforced Foreign Labour in Germany Under the Third Reich*, trans. William Temple (Cambridge, 1997); Albert Speer, *The Slave State: Heinrich Himmler's Master Plan* (London, 1981). According to Ulrich Herbert, by 1944, one-third of the German workforce was forced foreign labor (the proportion in agriculture was more than half), many under conditions that occasioned charges of enslavement both at Nuremberg and in subsequent litigation. All occupants of conquered Eastern Europe were under legal obligation to work for the conquerors. Herbert estimates the total number of forced foreign laborers under the Nazis at 12 million. Another study estimates the number at 13.5 million: Mark Spoerer and Jochen Fleischhacker, "Forced Laborers in Nazi Germany: Categories, Numbers and Survivors," *Journal of Interdisciplinary History*, 23 (2002): 169–204. See also Michael Thad Allen, *The Business of Genocide: The SS, Slave Labor and the Concentration Camps* (Chapel Hill, 2002), ch. 5–7. Among the numerous discussions of the treatment of these laborers from an employer's perspective, see, inter alia, Reinhold Billstein et al., *Working for the Enemy: Ford, General Motors, and Forced Labor in Germany During the Second World War* (New York, 2000), pp. 54–57. In Stalinist Russia, perhaps 18 million people were incarcerated (between 1 and 2.6 million prisoners per year) in the period 1936 to 1953. See Edwin Bacon, *The Gulag at War: Stalin's Forced Labor System in the Light of the Archives* (New York, 1994), pp. 37, 125–126. It should be emphasized that, in the process of building their slave system, SS captors and others behaved more like the warriors or raiders at the African end of the Atlantic system than as planter capitalists. "[E]ntire villages were surrounded by press gangs." A Nazi official described such raiders as using "'the whole bag of tricks' used by Arab slave hunters among the Negroes of Africa in previous centuries." There is ample evidence that Hitler envisioned the area between the Vistula and the Urals as a zone in which any native would be classified as inferior to the lowest German stable boy. See Norman Rich, *Hitler's War Aims: The Establishment of the New Order*, 2 vols. (New York, 1974), pp. 326–32, 342–43. Within Germany itself, "the regime and the organization did not hesitate to lengthen the working week for foreigners to the limits of total exhaustion." See Tila Siegel, "Rationalizing Industrial Relations: A Debate on the Control of Labor in German Shipyards in 1941," in Thomas Childers and Jane Caplan (eds.), *Reevaluating the Third Reich* (New York, 1993), p. 147. On the preference

My primary reason for drawing attention to this example is not to argue for a complete analogy between Atlantic slavery and its Nazi German
variant. I note only that no insuperable psychological or cultural barrier to
enslavement or coercion-for-life was created by an even longer-term evolution of Europe than the one Eltis describes for the early modern period.
Moreover, in terms of the centrality of the coerced labor force to the economy as a whole, war-time Germany fulfills the conventional historiographic
definition of a "slave society."

Between 1940 and 1945 there were more than three times as many coerced European laborers in Europe as coerced Africans in the Americas two
centuries earlier. In terms of mortality, brutality, and sheer expenditure of
lives per unit of labor-time, twentieth century Europe also had no peer in
the slave Americas. Or, to put it slightly different, more Europeans were sent
to forced labor by other Europeans within a period of four years than were
Africans by Europeans in the Americas during the four centuries following the Columbian voyages. Germany's rulers clearly envisioned and imple-
mented a legalized hierarchy of free and coerced labor. Europeans certainly
did not find the idea of enslaving each other to be inconceivable or difficult to imagine. Tens of millions were designated as enslavable – potentially,
up to half of Europe's population. That twentieth century Europeans were
willing to act at least as brutally toward other Europeans as seventeenth
century Africans or Europeans toward Africans is patently clear. It is clearly
worthwhile to take a closer look at the full range of deterrents to the "Eu-
ropeanization" of American slave labor in the early modern period.

II

In order to properly assess the economic rationality of substituting European slaves for Africans in the early modern Americas we must begin by
outlining the parameters of question. First, slavery was not the only form
of labor available to employers of labor in the New World. Second, slavery
was recognized as particularly important to the production of only certain
outputs from mines and large-scale agricultural units. In these kinds of enterprises, other forms of labor would have been available only at much higher
prices. Third, the choices for labor in the New World developed within a
pluralistic political framework. There was no single political entity capable of allocating coerced labor throughout the Atlantic system. Fourth, it is
necessary to analyze the process of labor transition under various rubrics.
In addition to dividing population groups by geographic origin (Europeans,
Africans, Amerindians) or religion (Christians, Muslims, Jews, Pagans, etc.),

for bondage over death, see Raul Hilberg, *The Destruction of the European Jews*, 3 vols.
(New York, 1985), pp. 2, 529.

one must further subdivide the trade into various national groups as they
entered and dominated the Atlantic system (the Spanish, Portuguese, British,
French and Dutch). Because our analysis focuses on those who dominated
the transatlantic sea lanes, these intra-European regional and national sub-
divisions become very significant variables.

We therefore follow the traditional historiography in two major respects.
We divide the history of the early modern slave trade before the "Age of
Revolutions" into two major periods, the period of Iberian (especially Portuguese) domination before 1640, and the period of Northwestern European
intrusion between 1640 and 1815. We must further reduce these two regions
into national units, because most Europeans sailed to Africa under their national flags or participated in plantations subject to national sovereigns. Such
distinctions are therefore critical in any attempt to assess the viability of substituting enslaved Europeans for enslaved Africans in the Americas.

From Eltis's perspective a glance at Euro–African migration figures from
1500–1760 (Table 1) indicates that the shift to both African and slave labor
was far from obvious in 1580. Before 1580 more than two-thirds of migrants
crossing the Atlantic to the Americas were free Europeans, not enslaved
Africans. Only during the following century did the migration figures swing
decisively in favor of Africans. Especially in the half-century after 1492, the
proportion of slaves carried to the Americas "was little different than the
proportion of slaves in their own European or metropolitan areas."[17] Given
the dominance of Europeans in this first wave, the implication is that the shift
toward Africans and slavery was not as clear or predetermined during the first
century of the Atlantic system as it became in the second. From a "modern
perspective" (or at least in hindsight) it was the Northwestern European (and
more especially the Anglo–Dutch) relationships with Africans and Americans
that determined the demographic and legal contexts of race relations that
we confront in the twenty-first century. In any event, as relates to labor
choices, it was not the Iberians in the sixteenth century but the Anglo–Dutch
in the seventeenth who apparently determined the form of racial and labor
relations in the plantation Americas well into the nineteenth century.

We must engage Eltis's argument on his own favored ground (the English
imperium), and in his own chosen time (c. 1640–1700). But a first look at
the Iberian cases will show that both slavery and Africans were far more
integral to, if not as dominant in, the foundation of the Atlantic system
than Eltis's table might imply. Some historians of Latin America emphasize
that slavery was the very first labor system of choice for the conquering

[17] Eltis, *Rise of African Slavery*, 17. The division of carriers into separate, and usually conflict-
ing, European political economies is a fundamental frame of reference for the transatlantic
migration of Europeans as well as Africans. See, for example, the structure of Nicholas
Canny (ed.), *Europeans on the Move: Studies on European Migration, 1500–1800* (Oxford,
1994), passim.

TABLE 1. *European-Directed Transatlantic Migration, 1500–1760, by European Nation and Continent of Origin (in thousands)*

	(1) Africans Leaving Africa on Ships of Each Nation	(2) Europeans Leaving Each Nation for Americas (net)	(3) Africans and Europeans Leaving for Americas (Col. 2 + Col. 3)	(4) Col. 4 Plus Africans Shipped to the Atlantic Islands	(5) Percent African Migrants
(a) Before 1580					
Spain	10	100	110		9
Portugal	56	58	114	239	75.7
Britain	2	0	2		100.0
TOTAL	68	158	226	351	55.0
(b) 1580–1640					
Spain	0	90	90		0
Portugal	594	110	704		84.3
France	0	4	4		0
Netherlands	10	2	12		83.3
Britain	3	87	90		3.3
TOTAL	607	293	900		67.4
(c) 1640–1700					
Spain	0	76	76		0
Portugal	259	50	309		83.8
France	40	23	63		63.5

(*continued*)

TABLE I (continued)

	(1) Africans Leaving Africa on Ships of Each Nation	(2) Europeans Leaving Each Nation for Americas (net)	(3) Africans and Europeans Leaving for Americas (Col. 2 + Col. 3)	(4) Col. 4 Plus Africans Shipped to the Atlantic Islands	(5) Percent African Migrants
Netherlands	151	13	164		92.1
Britain	379	285	664		57.1
TOTAL	829	447	1,276		65.0
(d) 1700–1760					
Spain	1	92	93		1.0
Portugal	958	300	1,258		76.2
France	458	27	485		94.4
Netherlands	223	5	228		97.8
Britain	1,206	222	1,428		84.5
TOTAL	2,846	646	3,492		81.5

Sources: David Eltis, Rise, 9, as modified by Eltis, ed. Coerced and Free Migration: pp. 62–3. For Africans shipped to the Atlantic islands, Philip D. Curtin, The Atlantic Slave Trade: A Census, 20.

Europeans with Native Americans as the chosen. Economically speaking, residents on the spot in the Caribbean islands were cheaper forms of labor than were more distant Amerindians, Europeans or Africans. When demographic catastrophe ultimately made alternatives more attractive, there was resort to Africans. However, the first large coerced labor migrations in the early sixteenth century circum-Caribbean consisted of Indians. The isthmus of Panama and the larger Caribbean islands suffered drastic population depletion after 1500. Spanish conquering expeditions required large numbers of porters and servants. As soon as Central America was successfully invaded, it became the main center of a slave trade in Indians. Perhaps as early as 1515 Indian captives were sent to Cuba, and soon after to Panama and Peru. By the 1530s, slave trading was the basic industry in Nicaragua. At the height of that trade, 10,000 slaves were exported each year to Panama and Peru. A total of 200,000 Indians, perhaps one-third of the original population, had been enslaved by the mid sixteenth century, four times more than were landed in the Americas from Africa between 1500 and 1580.[18]

In such a milieu it is hard to see how Spaniards, urgently required for purposes of long-distance sailing and soldiering, would have been cheaper to transport to America and kept under discipline as slaves (even setting aside the costs of initial enslavement). In regions where Indians outnumbered Spaniards by 9:1, ratios as high as those ever reached by Africans to Europeans in the Caribbean, every European, and even some Africans, were needed for security. The highest priority of use for metropolitan Spaniards abroad was expanding and sustaining an empire. *Peninsulares* were regularly recruited to serve in the garrisons of Spanish Italy, from Naples to Lombardy; in the Netherlands and in Germany against rebels and heretics; in the Mahgreb against infidels; in the Atlantic, Mediterranean and Pacific oceans as naval crews; in conflicts with France and England. The state's cost per fighting man tripled over the course of the sixteenth century, with frequent mutinies over defaults in payment. The Spanish Army of Flanders, in particular, was "probably the most unruly" in Europe, with 45 mutinies between 1572 and 1609. Military loyalty was always a two-way street, even unto bondage. At Algiers, enslaved Spanish deserters expected to be well-fed and cared for until ransomed by Iberian charitable organizations, dedicated to rescuing Christians from bondage.[19]

Civilians bound for America in prosperous sixteenth century Spain almost never traveled individually as indentured servants. They crossed in groups through networks of family, clientage community and locality. Kinship ties in Spain, as in other areas of Western Europe, provided for coverage of

---

[18] See Murdo J. Macleod, *Spanish Central America: A Socioeconomic History 1520–1720* (Berkeley, 1973), pp. 48–56.

[19] Geoffrey Parker, *The Military Revolution: Military Innovation and the Rise of the West, 1500–1800* (New York, 1988), pp. 57–59.

the costs of transportation. This phenomenon of extended chains of relations on both sides of the Atlantic, in stark contrast to their virtual total
absence in the African migration stream, will be important to our final assessment of the potential economic costs of European enslavement. In the
post-conquistador period, various other forms of coerced Indian labor were
used. The most famous was the *Mita* for Indians at Potosí. In the highlands
of Peru their use appears to have been far cheaper for employers than that
of transported Africans and *ceteris paribus* for Europeans, whether free or
bonded. *Mita* Indians offered employers a steady reliable stream of labor,
reproduced, transported, and fed, at no direct cost to the employer. Epidemiology also seems to have favored local inhabitants over outsiders in
these highlands. Thus, even in some mines, with all the apparent advantages
of coerced labor, African slaves did not offer a competitive advantage in
the unskilled labor force. Where Indians remained plentiful enough, neither
African slaves nor Spanish convicts were cost-effective alternatives.[20]

The more important question to be addressed, for the "Iberian" period,
is Eltis's assertion about the relative preponderance of Old World sources of
migration in the first century following the Columbian voyages. His Table
I-1, in the *Rise of African Slavery*, seems to indicate that it was overwhelmingly Europeans, not Africans, who were on the move on the high seas until
the development of Portuguese-plantation Brazil toward the end of the sixteenth century. A slight adjustment, however, takes note of an undercounted
African presence. If we include the c. 125,000 Africans shipped to the Atlantic Isles (our Table 1) the picture changes. Africans, instead of representing
only 24 percent of the Atlantic's migrants before 1580, accounted for more
than 46 percent. More significantly, they represented fully three-quarters of
the combined total of African and Portuguese migrants. In other words, the
sixteenth century Portuguese profile of Afro–European migration was an
astonishingly precise forecast of the pattern of the transatlantic migration
between 1640 and 1760. In this respect Eltis's division of the early modern
period into a pre-1640 phase of Iberian contact, dominated by Amerindians,
and a second phase of Dutch–English interaction dominated by Africans, is

---

[20] Jeffrey A. Cole, *The Potosi Mita, 1573–1700: Compulsory Indian Labor in the Andes* (Stanford, CA, 1985), p. 4. Even in New Spain, where African slaves formed a small proportion
of the population, they outnumbered the Spaniards. See Colin A. Palmer, *Slaves of the White
God: Blacks in Mexico, 1570–1650* (Cambridge, MA, 1976), pp. 2–3. On the Spanish Atlantic migration network, see B. H. Slicher van Bath, "The absence of white contract labour
in Spanish America during the colonial period," in Emmer (ed.), *Colonialism and Migration*,
pp. 19–31, esp. 27–30. In the case of Africa, judicial enslavement of one's own subjects probably did not account for more than a few percent of total exports. Military action was by far
the most significant source of slaves. [See Thornton, *Africa and Africans*, 99; and Martin A.
Klein, *Slavery and Colonial Rule in French West Africa* (New York, 1998), p. 4.] Although
I consider both types of enslavement for Europeans, it is unlikely that their mix of captives
would have been notably different.

somewhat artificial. Portugal was the first country to cross the threshold of moving more Africans than Europeans on Atlantic ships.

As the first European nation to tap into African slavery, the Portuguese case is of particular interest. The first groups enslaved by the Portuguese in the New World were also Amerindians, obviously the cheapest and most accessible potential laborers. The Portuguese first choice of coerced labor in the Atlantic islands likewise was for captive labor in the vicinity – Canary islanders – followed by a mixture of enslaved Moors and African slaves. By the time Saõ Tomé began to develop as a sugar island, around the time of the Columbian explorations to the West, Africans had already become the labor force of choice. From the perspective of transportation costs this seems quite logical. It made far more sense to recruit a cane-cultivating labor force for Saõ Tomé from the proximate coast of West Africa than from the far more distant shores of Portugal. The implications of this choice for future developments are considerable. The epidemiological impact of African pathogens on Europeans at Saõ Tomé was as decisive as the almost simultaneous impact of Euro–African pathogens on the Amerindian populations of the Americas. The first attempts to settle that island were failures because of tropical diseases. In 1493 King João I of Portugal made a successful attempt, using a combination of *degredados* (convicts), black slaves from Africa, and young Jewish children seized from their parents in flight from Spain after the expulsion of 1492. The fraction of these who survived to maturity mated as free persons to Africans.

A number of points about the initial context of Portuguese settlement of the Atlantic are relevant to the Brazilian transition two generations later. From the perspective of transportation costs, Portugal, the pioneer of Atlantic slavery, could theoretically have been the pioneer enslaver of Europeans. However, aside from the potential costs of enslaving themselves, the Portuguese would certainly have faced enormous problems in meeting their global manpower commitments in Brazil, North Africa, sub-Saharan Africa, the Indian Ocean and Southeast Asia. Portuguese expansion began in the early 1400s in the context of a concern with underpopulation. The country had certainly not yet fully recovered from the ravaging effects of the Great Plague. Portuguese metropolitan outflows after 1450 were, to some extent, compensated for by an inflow of Africans slaves. These already enslaved laborers were brought to Portugal despite the additional costs of transportation. The Portuguese probably imported upwards of 50,000 Africans by 1550. Ten percent of Lisbon's population were then of African descent. No other European capital ever remotely approached that proportion of Africans or slaves in its population.[21]

---

[21] A. C. de C. M. Saunders, *A Social History of Black Slaves and Freedmen in Portugal 1441–1555* (New York, 1982), pp. 59–88.

Portugal's absolute net gain or loss is less significant than the fact that inflows of Africans were perceived as good capital investments for a century before the development of Brazilian plantations. One need take no position about whether Africans were imported to remedy a sustained, or only a perceived, demographic deficit. The more significant issues were economic rather than demographic. It would have been relatively easy for King João to have physically expelled all Jewish refugees from Portugal, or to ship them all to São Tomé. However, either choice would have been detrimental to his overall colonial and metropolitan interests. To establish a new colony dominated by adult Spanish Jews would have risked producing a colonial elite without any traditional loyalty whatever to the Portuguese crown. The very idea of opening the floodgates of Atlantic colonization to a Jewish majority was far more unimaginable than the idea of enslaving them. Such a deportation, whether free or captive, would also have deprived Portugal of valuable human capital at home. The Sephardic refugees of 1492 represented valuable urban mercantile and artisanal cohorts. Portugal had better uses for these detained and forcibly converted refugees than as an underutilized and rapidly dying remnant of field slaves off the coast of Africa.

Like Spain, Portugal began its slave system in the Americas at the very moment that it was consolidating the world's first truly global seaborne empire. The object of Portuguese statesmen and merchants in the world beyond Europe was to secure the economic benefits of their overseas networks without weakening the manpower available at home and abroad. A seaborne empire that had to recruit black slaves in order to meet shortages of manpower both in Europe and the Indian Ocean was hardly in a position to force its European subjects into field labor on islands in the Atlantic or on the colonial frontier of Brazil. In other words, sixteenth century Portugal was faced with the same constraints as Spain, with an even lower population base. A thin layer of Portuguese was spread across the world from Macao to Brazil, with particularly heavy manpower requirements along the shores of the Mediterranean, Africa, and the Indian Ocean. Portuguese exiles and *degredados* were sent forth to serve, not to hoe. The Portuguese seem to have arrived at the same rough soldier/slave division of labor that all Europeans were to follow before the age of the Atlantic Revolutions.

The lesson of early modern Muslim slave armies is relevant in this respect. Slaves often formed the core of Muslim armies from Indonesia to the Balkans and North Africa. However, most of the enslaved were recruited as children, often as tributary levies from conquered non-Muslim peoples. They were usually not kidnaped or conscripted captured adults.[22] For the Portuguese

---

[22] See C. R. Boxer, *The Portuguese Seaborne Empire, 1415–1825* (New York, 1969), pp. 52–57. The great majority of sixteenth century migrants from Portugal went to Old World destinations. For military needs, see Parker, *Military Revolution*, 125. It is significant that two thirds of the "New Christians" exiled to Brazil from Portugal were women. Many men

to have imitated the pattern of the Ottomans in the Balkans (i.e., kidnaping Christians) would inevitably have meant explosive conflicts with more powerful neighboring societies. After the mass roundup of Jewish children in Portugal, the next politically sanctioned mass kidnaping of other people's children by Europeans had to await the twentieth century – the *Lebensborn* project of a military-dominant Nazi Germany.

Considering the probable impact of a variety of Portuguese routes to the enslavement of Europeans draws attention to a fundamental principle of institutional economics. In any complex structure of social relations, one would not expect, absent total domination by one power, a once-for-all jump to full property rights in the bodies of human groups hitherto exempt from such treatment. The Portuguese monarchs would have had two major options, to either enslave their own subjects or to enslave captive Europeans. Either choice would have raised the cost of policing the new transatlantic settlements and of coping with the feedback of resistance from kin, class, community and foreign rulers. I will deal more explicitly with these costs with regard to the English slave system. Here, it suffices to emphasize that Portugal was an unlikely candidate for enslaving either prisoners of war or home-grown undesirables.

Any attempt to enslave European outsiders by one of Europe's smaller powers would most likely have been a formula for national disaster. It would have stimulated alliances designed to smash the power of any rogue prince attempting to initiate a violent appropriation of others' subjects. The Portuguese metropolis itself would certainly have become a target of retaliation. The proverbial Iberian rulers' fears of subversive Moors and Jews peopling their thinly policed plantation zones in the Atlantic islands, Brazil and the Spanish Main would have been intensified by the overseas presence of enslaved Christian Europeans. Their former rulers could pick off plantation areas at will, killing or even enslaving the Portuguese masters and shipping them to North Africa. In other words, the heaviest overhead costs would have been born by the innovator in the creation of property rights in Europeans. Europe's pluralistic state system guaranteed a steep rise in the frequency, ubiquity and intensity of violence against any attempt to deliver up to 650,000 European slaves to Brazil in its vulnerable formative period. Portugal's early pre-eminence in the slave trade and plantation slavery thus rested on the fact that its coerced laborers were Indians or Africans. For Portugal, a slave trade in Europeans was not just unthinkable. It was undoable.

---

were sentenced to forced labor in the Mediterranean galleys. Geraldo Pieroni, "Outcast from the Kingdom: The Inquisition and the Banishment of New Christians to Brazil," in Paolo Bernardini and Norman Fiering (eds.), *Jews and the Expansion of Europe to the West, 1450–1800* (New York, 2001), pp. 242–251, esp. 245–46. Even more significantly, of the very small number of Portuguese banished to Brazil for Judaizing (311), only four were sent to Brazil during the initial century of colonization.

Of course, it made economic sense for Portugal, as for Spain, to begin tropical cultivation of commercial staples by forced labor with the most proximate available populations. In Portugal's case this meant beginning with laborers-in-place on both sides of the Atlantic. When the epidemiological effects of intercontinental contact and coercion on Indians indicated a need for a new external source of labor in Brazil, it was most cost-effective to tap into the century-old network on the eastern edge of the South Atlantic system.[23]

An alternative strategy of enslaving their own countrymen would have been equally impractical at any affordable price. The overwhelming majority of potential "enslavables" (convicts and the poor) would have been "Old Christians." A large proportion of the merchants transporting them, perhaps a majority, would have been "New Christians." Ironically, the latter group, if also threatened with deportation as slaves, might have been tempted to buy time by announcing that they were crypto-Jews, subject to incarceration in Portugal by the Inquisition, and prohibited by law from residing in any Portuguese plantation. The Inquisition would have been threatened with the loss of one of its chief economic supports – confiscation of a heretic's property. A slave's former property, by contrast, would have been forfeit to the enslaver, that is, to the monarch. The Church would have had every motive to align itself with popular rage against both planter need and royal greed. Merely the contemplation of such a dangerous combination would probably have deterred any royal fantasy about "rounding up the usual suspects" – the poor and the criminals – from the ranks of the populace.

III

Under any plausible economic assumptions, the South Atlantic lowland plantation system would still have become slave, and increasingly African, during the century or more when Iberians dominated that system.[24] However, the

---

[23] See Stuart B. Schwartz, *Sugar Plantations in the Formation of Brazilian Society, 1550–1835* (Cambridge, 1985). Blackburn, in his *Making*, 356, imagines a scenario in which European powers would have ganged up on any initiator of slavery in the Americas. This seems highly improbable if Africans alone were the labor force. However, I find it more improbable that European rulers would not have acted, singly or collectively, against such an innovator when their own subjects were being enslaved.

[24] Eltis seems to hedge on the applicability of his European slave counterfactual as applied to the Iberian tropical lowlands: "The fact that African slavery in the Americas took longer to evolve than any European counterpart would have done – *at least in North America* – is accounted for by the greater cost of moving people from Africa as opposed to Europe" (Eltis, *Rise of African Slavery*, 70; my emphasis). Eltis does not offer any estimate of comparative potential costs in shipping European slaves from Lisbon to Brazil, as opposed to the route from London to Barbados, and both relative to the African alternative. I agree, of course, that the São Tomé African slave system was created for economically sound reasons. Eltis also seems to imply that Portuguese productivity gains in the movement of sugar from São

most critical phase of the transition occurred in the last two-thirds of the seventeenth century. During that period Africans definitely came to constitute the overwhelming majority of transatlantic migrants. The predominant terminus of that migration became that part of the Caribbean dominated by Northwestern Europeans. Within Northwestern Europe the English emerged as the principal carriers of slaves to the New World. It was this new interaction of Europeans with Africans that determined the profile of the transatlantic slave trade and the prevailing labor force for the next 150 years.

For many historians, the half century after Portuguese dominance of the slave and sugar trades was shattered in the 1630s and 1640s is a turning point in the Atlantic system. The Anglo–Dutch, with their combination of far more efficient economic institutions, superior organizations of credit and distribution, and their more rigorous use of slave labor, made New World slavery one of the most profitable, productive and dynamic forms of enterprise in world history.[25] The period of 1640–1700 also offers the best possible conditions for testing the potential of a plantation system hypothetically powered by European slaves. In the sixty years before 1640 more than seven out of every eight people shipped across the Atlantic by Northwestern Europeans were Europeans. In the sixty years after 1700 the proportion was exactly reversed. Seven out of every eight people shipped to the Americas, under French, Dutch and British flags, were from Africa (see Table 1). One can identify the crucial shift even more narrowly. Between 1580 and 1640, 97 percent of those carried to America in English ships were Europeans. Between 1700 and 1760, the European share fell to 16 percent. Inhabitants of the British Isles were the largest single European group to cross the Atlantic between 1640 and 1700. England appears to be the best possible case for imagining the substitution of coerced Europeans for Africans, and on a scale that would have been large enough to have made for a more efficient economic expansion of the plantation system in the Americas.

We accept the premise that, *ceteris paribus*, it would have been cheaper for European merchants to ship Europeans rather than Africans to the Caribbean and to ports in North America. The costs of transportation per capita would have become cheaper still by packing Europeans as tightly into carriers as were seventeenth century Africans in the Middle Passage. However, additional costs appear as soon as one has to consider how each segment

Tomé to Brazil in the 1540s were not as great as those entailed in the move from Brazil to Barbados in the 1650s (198 and n). Would this have further reduced Portuguese incentives to attempt to absorb the risk costs of switching from Indian to European rather than to Africans in the second half of the sixteenth century?

[25] See, inter alia, Pieter Emmer, *The Dutch in the Atlantic Economy, 1580–1880* (Aldershot, 1998), ch. 1, on the "Second Atlantic System." Most historians, including Blackburn and Eltis, view the periods of Iberian and northwest European domination of the Atlantic system as distinctive in important economic respects.

of the system would have operated under the assumption of an Atlantic Euro-slave system from the mid seventeenth century onwards.

Let us begin at the locus of the breakthrough – the Caribbean. Security concerns form a critical part of some explanations for the success of European slave plantations in the Atlantic basin. In order to establish and maintain high slave/master ratios working in gang labor conditions, the isolation of the labor force was highly desirable. Islands were more easily policed by European naval powers.[26] Eltis rightly insists on the importance of this insularity, but he writes of this naval power as a "European" force. European plantation systems, however, as all of his tables show, were national not "continental" units. They were established not by "Europeans" in general, but, successively, by Spanish, Portuguese, Dutch, French, English and Danish sovereigns. Slave trades likewise were sanctioned by political "powers," each with its own navy and merchant fleet.

What was the contextual situation of these plantation-founding states during the second phase of the Atlantic system? I note only three important conditions. According to a recent study of the incidence of war in European history, the years between 1500 and 1700 were the most warlike in modern times: in the proportion of years of war under way (95 percent); in frequency (nearly one every three years); in average duration; in extent and magnitude. Even more explicitly we must consider the relations between the three major naval powers of Western Europe: the Dutch, English and French fleets. Their governments sponsored the great non-Iberian flow of slaves to the sugar islands. During the founding period of their slave colonies (c. 1640–1713), when they were in rough military equilibrium, at least two of those three powers were almost constantly at war with each other. For the first time in world history, high seas' navies were capable of operating as long-range permanent fleets. Even when the balance of power was momentarily upset by a naval victory, the *guerre de course* made ample amends as a disruptive force. Between 1689 and 1697, for example, French privateers captured some 4,000 enemy vessels, despite the crushing defeat of France's major battle fleet in 1692. During this "savage and prolonged naval rivalry," armed ships could operate in the Pacific, the Indian Ocean and the Caribbean. This became the age, par excellence, of the privateer and the buccaneer.[27] The impact of this conflict on trade may be gauged not only from the litany of planter complaints but also from the freight rates per ton paid by the Royal

---

[26] See Arthur L. Stinchcombe, *Sugar Island Slavery in the Age of Enlightenment: The Political Economy of the Caribbean World* (Princeton, 1995), ch. 2; and Eltis, *Rise of African Slavery*, 161.

[27] See, inter alia, Parker, *Military Revolution*, 103. On the comparative level of European warfare from 1500–2000, see Jack S. Levy, *War in the Modern Great Power System 1495–1975* (Lexington, KY, 1983), pp. 88–91, 141–42.

TABLE 2. *Annual Average Freight Rates Per Ton for Homeward Shipment of Sugar Paid by Royal African Company*

	Barbados	Jamaica		Barbados	Jamaica
1678	£5.2	£6.5	1698	6.4	16.2
1679	4.0	6.6	1699	3.1	9.9
1680	3.5	5.8	1700	3.2	6.7
1681	3.5	6.1	1701	2.8	6.9
1682	4.0	6.1	1702	2.5	8.0
1683	3.6	5.0	1703	3.6	13.6
1684	3.5	5.1	1704	9.6	16.0
1685	4.8	4.6	1705	10.1	18.0
1686	5.2	4.2	1706	8.4	20.5
1687	4.4	4.0	1707	7.6	16.8
1688	4.2	4.0	1708	7.5	17.2
1689	6.1	5.6	1709	9.6	18.6
1690	10.1	7.8	1710	7.5	
1691	7.5	14.0	1711	6.0	
1692	7.8	16.9	1712	5.3	
1693	7.7	12.0	1713	5.4	
1694	7.2	12.0	1714	4.0	9.6
1695	9.5	17.5	1715	3.5	8.9
1696	11.2	18.0	1716	3.3	
1697	12.5	25.9	1717	3.4	10.0

Source: Ralph Davis, *The Rise of the English Shipping Industry in the 17th and 18th Centuries* (London, 1967), 283.

African Company. During the prolonged warfare after England's "Glorious Revolution" of 1688, annual rates often doubled, tripled and sometimes quadrupled (Table 2).

Another dimension of this maritime violence must be fully appreciated in order to consider the costs of Europeans enslaving Europeans. Most transported Africans were captives and prisoners of war. Like all other slave societies, Africans had boundary definitions of enslavability. Warfare in Africa might ensure a large flow of slaves. It could also severely disrupt such flows. The potential impact of war on the flow of slaves did not, of course, end at the African Atlantic coast. During the wars of the 1690s, deliveries of slaves from Anglo–Dutch shippers often dropped by more than 40 percent below their peacetime levels of the 1680s (see Table 3).

Any cost-benefit estimate, however, must go one step further. The actual volatility of slave transits from Africa to the Caribbeans is likely to underestimate the hypothetical impact of predation had slaves been loaded in *European* ports bound for the West Indies. Privateers operating out of their home ports in the offshore waters of Europe or the Caribbean would

TABLE 3. *Combined Anglo-Dutch Slave Trades in Peace and War, 1679–1712*

Peace/War	Period	Average Annual Transports	% Difference
Peace	1679–1688	11,198 p.a.	–
War	1689–1697	7,059 p.a.	−41
Peace	1698–1702	16,029 p.a	+127
War	1703–1712	10,529 p.a.	−34

Sources: For the English slave trade, David Eltis, "The British Transatlantic Slave Trade before 1714: Annual Estimates of Volume and Direction," in Robert L. Paquette and Stanley L. Engerman (eds.), *The Lesser Antilles in the Age of European Expansion* (Gainesville, 1996), 199–200; for the Dutch slave trade, Johannes Menne Postma, *The Dutch in the Atlantic Slave Trade 1600–1815* (New York, 1990), 35, 45 and 48.

have made the transhipment of Dutch, English, Irish or French captives more hazardous. A similarly heightened risk would have attended re-exportations en route from Guadeloupe, Jamaica, Barbados or Curaçao. The brutality of such naval encounters would have increased. Crews on slavers would not only have been fighting for their cargoes but also resisting their own appropriation as cargo.

As Eltis does for Africans, the costs of European resistance must be factored into the costs of Atlantic crossings. Europeans were far more familiar with, and less terrified by, their floating prisons than were their less experienced African contemporaries. Whereas African identities did not become subcontinental until after the ending of the slave trade, Europeans would have boarded slavers able to communicate almost immediately.[28] Prisoners of war would have been familiar with all of the weapons of their captors. If the cost of taking unwilling people from Africa was almost one-fifth higher than the costs of transporting consenting laborers, one can be sure that the cost of shipping enslaved over unenslaved Europeans would have been correspondingly enhanced.[29]

Much more significant than the costs of surveillance on board would have been the costs of policing the slave colonies themselves. Slave islands would have been converted from isolated prisons for Africans into permanent European targets of opportunity. The actual transatlantic slave trade depended on the combined inability of Europeans to project their domination into Africa and their ability to preserve the severance of African ties with their original communities. Just the opposite would have occurred between Europeans and Europeans. For example, when war broke out in Europe in 1666, the French seized the English part of the divided island of St. Christopher.

[28] Eltis, *Rise of African Slavery*, 231.
[29] Ibid., 159.

They appropriated 400 blacks and deported 5,000 white settlers.[30] In a world of enslavable Europeans it would have been far more profitable for the victors to appropriate the deported 5,000 as well. The implications of this incident are as clear as they are inescapable. Raiding Caribbean islands would have offered an abundance of seasoned slaves, cheaper to deliver to other islands or anywhere in the circum-Caribbean, in far shorter sailing times, at lower mortality rates, and in far better physical shape than could be matched by any slaver either from Africa or Europe. The smaller islands would have made ideal slave barracoons, just as they were ideal plantation zones. In venturing to the islands a prospective planter would also have had to consider that he was risking his liberty as well as his wealth. In such a situation he was virtual capital as well as an actual capitalist.

There are other probable security consequences to the enslavement of Europeans in the islands. In 1689 St. Christopher's Irish servants rose up in the name of deposed King James and sacked the English sector.[31] The French again invaded the English part of the island. Consider this picture: multi-ethnic islands, filled with French, English, Dutch, Irish, Scots or Spanish prisoners, each awaiting armed and mobile rescuers. At a minimum, such a prospect would have raised the overhead costs of preventing inter-island communication, whether in anticipation of foreign fleets or rumors of domestic plots. The same considerations that made Iberians rigorously exclude Muslims and Jews from their new colonies would have been intensified by slave populations consisting of hardened veterans of European warfare. Settled in African/European ratios, European slaves would have outnumbered their militarily inexperienced masters by ratios of up to eight or nine to one.

Even as indentured servants the Irish were considered to be entirely untrustworthy as militia. The degree of unreliability might rise in direct proportion to the certainty of the coerced Europeans that theirs would be a lifelong condition. I will not lengthen the risk list with the probable extra hemorrhage of slave laborers in non-insular North America. Nor is it necessary to stress the precariousness of the British Isles themselves in the face of French military threats between 1689 and 1815. As we will see, military recruitment

---

[30] Richard S. Dunn, *Sugar and Slaves: The Rise of the Planter Class in the English West Indies, 1624–1713* (Chapel Hill, 1972), p. 124. On seventeenth century colonial dissatisfaction with convicts in North America, see A. R. Erkich, *Bound for America: The Transportation of British Convicts to the Colonies, 1718–1775* (Oxford 1990), 134–40. See a similar argument in Edmund S. Morgan's *American Slavery, American Freedom* (New York, 1975).

[31] Dunn, *Sugar and Slaves*, 133–34. For another glimpse at the probabilities, when Nevis was attacked by the Spanish in 1629 the planters were deserted by their English servants, "who swam out to the Spanish ships leaving cries of 'Liberty, joyful Liberty' blowing in the wind." John C. Appleby, "English Settlement in the Lesser Antilles during War and Peace, 1603–1660," in Robert L. Paquette and Stanley L. Engerman (eds.), *The Lesser Antilles in the Age of European Expansion* (Gainesville, FL, 1996), pp. 86–104, esp. 93–94.

against other Europeans, and European others, trumped the marginal utility of enslaving other Europeans.[32]

We must go beyond imagining the higher costs of containing slaves in place in the Caribbean to the far steeper costs of innovating. The islands would not have been the central problem for the seventeenth century innovators. Eltis rests a good deal of his case for the great success of the Northwestern Europeans on the fact that they had not only moved further along in developing a culture of civil liberty for their fellow citizens, but also had created the infrastructure for enhancing economic development. Here the Dutch were recognized pioneers. They had developed a legal and institutional framework which allowed them to maximize the organization of labor and capital afforded by staple production in plantations. The Dutch, c. 1640, had a distinct edge in economic organization, allowing for a rapid increase in sugar cultivation.

Yet of all the European slaving powers between 1450 and 1870, the Dutch were the least likely to have made a transition to any form of slave labor but African. This was because the Dutch, unlike all other Europeans colonizers in the Americas, began their plantation system with African slaves in place. When the West India Company conquered part of Northeastern Brazil in the 1630s they became rulers of a fully furnished plantation system, complete with European masters and African workers. In wresting control of most of the African coast from Portugal by the early 1640s, the Company was briefly assured of an immediate source of fresh slave labor. Whatever the relative cost of transporting people from Europe or Africa to South America, it is inconceivable that it would have been less costly, or more profitable, for the WIC to suddenly have reversed the ethnic composition of their Brazilian plantations, and launched a new European labor force, even one drawn from a Europe embroiled in the Thirty Years War.[33]

---

[32] See Dunn, *Sugar and Slaves,* 160, for Jamaica; and Hilary McD. Beckles, "A 'Riotous and Unruly Lot': Irish Indentured Servants and Freemen in the English West Indies, 1644–1713," *William and Mary Quarterly,* 3rd ser., 48 (1990): 505–22, for the West Indies as a whole. On the persistence of French and Catholic threats to British policy makers, see Linda Colley, "Britishness and Otherness: An Argument," *Journal of British Studies,* 31 (October 1992): 309–329. On antislavery as an aspect of British nationalism, rather than European humanitarianism, before the second third of the nineteenth century, see Linda Colley, *Britons: Forging the Nation: 1707–1837* (New Haven, 1992), pp. 350–360; and Paul Michael Kielstra, *The Politics of Slave Trade Suppression in Britain and France, 1814–1848: Diplomacy, Morality and Economics* (Houndmills, 2000), pp. 1–21, 261–67.

[33] In their search for servile labor neither the Dutch nor any other Northwest Europeans could have looked farther east to enserfed Central Europe for their supply. In areas depopulated by the Thirty Years War (1618–1648), lords were making every effort to immobilize their workforces by rigorously enforcing statutes against migration. It is highly improbable that the magnates of depopulated Bohemia and Hungary would have risked simultaneously undermining their own enterprises and increasing the probability and costs of peasant uprisings by depriving their own labor force of its primary reason for enduring serfdom (i.e., hereditary

After losing Brazil in 1645–51, the WIC began again in the Caribbean. For labor, they now had an African supply network in place with no place to deliver them. They also lacked one element which at least one of their successful colonizing competitors had in abundance – Europeans ready to make the transatlantic crossing as voluntary settlers. From the beginning, the Netherlands required non-nationals to sustain both its metropolitan development and its overseas empire. Unlike the Portuguese, the Dutch sought and found an abundance of Europeans willing to come to the Netherlands to work, to serve in its armies, and to move on to one part of the overseas empire. At times, 60 percent of the soldiers in the armies of the Netherlands were foreigners.[34] The Dutch, more than any other Northwest European nation, needed soldiers and sailors in the Old World far more than slaves in the New. The Dutch East India Company mobilized a voluntary overseas movement of up to a million Europeans. It is difficult to see the Dutch risking this efficient recruitment system by attempting to impose forced labor in order to help the Dutch West India Company successfully colonize Suriname. The WIC was a trading company that had to bargain, through intermediaries, even with Livorno's poorest Jewish refugees from Spanish North Africa to resettle in the Caribbean. Such an enterprise was in no position to kidnap foreigners in European ports to fill its colonial labor needs.[35] Enslaving foreigners would certainly have endangered the foreign voluntary networks which operated much like other European overseas voluntary migration chains.

What about Dutch home-grown convicts, their unemployed and the poor? The Dutch standard of living in 1650 was the highest in Europe. Their underemployment or unemployment was probably the lowest, and their pool of "usable" convicts for serious crimes far too few to stock colonies on the scale achieved by their competitors. In terms of carrying Europeans to the Americas between 1640 and 1700, the Dutch ranked a poor fifth among the five major colonizing nations. Between 1640 and 1700, for every European leaving a Dutch port for America twenty were leaving from Britain. The Dutch/English ratio for the two centuries before 1760 is 3 to 100.[36] Could the Dutch have cheaply multiplied the number of native-born serious offenders twenty- or thirty-fold in order to generate a full quota of slaves? We can

security of tenure). A "long-distance serf-trade" is not only, as Eltis notes, an oxymoron, but also a recipe for exploding innovation costs. See W. E. Wright, "Neo-Serfdom in Bohemia," *Slavic Review*, 34 (1975): 239–52, esp. 243; A. Klima, "Agrarian class structure and economic development in pre-industrial Bohemia," *Past and Present*, 85 (1979): 50–53; and B. K. Kiraly, "Neo-Serfdom in Hungary," *Slavic Review*, 34 (1975): 269–78.

34 J. L. Price, *Dutch Society, 1599–1713* (New York, 2000), pp. 192–193.

35 See Van den Boogaart and P. C. Emmer, "Colonialism and Migration: An Overview," in *Colonialism and Migration*, pp. 3–4. On Livorno's Jewish refugees, see Mordechai Arbell, "Jewish Settlements in the French Colonies in the Caribbean," in Bernardini and Fiering (eds.), *Jews and the Expansion of Europe*, pp. 297–98.

36 Eltis, *Rise of African Slavery*, 9.

address that question more closely when we turn to the more abundant English potential pool of coerced laborers. In the meantime, minting Dutch slaves for Suriname plantation gangs while foreigners voluntarily signed up for more pleasant, if unhealthy, service in the East, moves the counterfactual hypothesis of an exclusively Dutch domestic coerced labor force toward the bizarre.

Two more observations suffice to show the difficulties entailed in the "home grown" hypothesis. Eltis argues that Dutch resistance to enslaving each other did not primarily derive, as in the English case, from a societal concern for the individual. The Netherlands, he says, with its many non-Calvinists as well as non-Dutch residents had a more acute sense of the "fragility of the social compact."[37] I believe it would have been a good deal more fragile had native Netherlanders, like Portuguese "Old Christians," found themselves in the peculiar position of enjoying fewer protections against lifetime bondage than outsiders coming into their own land. In a decentralized nation like the Netherlands it is implausible to imagine that the same local authorities who afforded their communities the best welfare system in Europe could have been induced to allow a small sector of mercantile interests to reorder the labor relations of the Republic. Dutch "fragility" went far deeper than its domestic pluralism and its decentralization in the seventeenth century.

The Dutch Republic was frequently fighting for its very existence against the seventeenth century's two most formidable land armies – the Spanish army of Flanders before 1648, and the armies of Louis XIV after 1672. In such a situation the advantages entailed in accumulating coerced laborers for the West India Company rather than in mobilizing the citizenry for national survival must have been self-evident to every last West Indian investor and overseas planter in the Dutch Atlantic empire.

This already takes us far from our economic analysis, and the English case offers us the final and best candidate for supplying a plantation system with a white and coerced (recall the Earl of Stamford) European labor force. As previously indicated, only one out of three migrants to the English Americas was an African slave as late as the 1650s. By 1700 three out of every four arrivals were African. Until well beyond mid-century, English labor, much of it involuntary, was still available for long-term hire, with enough credit and institutional faculties available to deliver them at a profit. More than any other colonizers, British capitalists founded their plantation economy with a mainly European workforce. The exodus from England actually peaked just before the turn to Africa, with more than one hundred thousand people departing from England.[38]

---

[37] Ibid., 83.
[38] Ibid., 49. See also E. A. Wrigley and R. S. Schofield, *The Population History of England: A Reconstruction* (New York, 1989), Table A 3.1, pp. 528–29. For reasons why

In the 1640s and 1650s England produced the whole range of possible sources of bound and coerced labor: servants, prisoners of war, convicts, social undesirables, prostitutes, sturdy beggars and vagabonds. One must agree with Eltis that, if convicts and prisoners of war had been condemned to lifetime service or chattel slavery, planters would have paid a high price for them, probably competitive with what was being offered for Africans. At this premium "the British government and merchants might have found ways to provide more convicts" – presumably enough ways to raise the numbers of lifetime bondsmen to the annual quota of 10,000 laborers demanded by colonial planters each year by the beginning of the eighteenth century. All could have been shipped more cheaply than the Africans actually landed in the English Americas.[39] One should also bear in mind that Europeans' willingness to torture, rape, kill and incarcerate other Europeans in galleys occurred at a moment when England was more saturated by the "rhetoric" of liberties than was any other contemporary society.[40] The English Civil Wars of the 1640s and 1650s also produced a surge of prisoners of war, domestic and foreign, coinciding almost precisely with the peak of enforced migration to English America.

What restrained Englishmen from taking the extra step to creating a condition of hereditary servitude for many of the inhabitants of the British Isles, given the temptations of war-induced captives and religion-induced hatred on the one hand, and surging planter demand for cultivators on the other? Eltis ascribes it to a powerful internalized barrier. The line to slavery was not crossed primarily because of the fundamentally psychological inability of Europeans to cross it, or (the Earl of Stamford aside) even to contemplate

seventeenth-century France, with a far larger population than England, sent fewer than one-fifth the number of migrants to the Americas between 1640 and 1700, see Olivier Pétré-Grenouilleau, "Puissances maritimes, puissances coloniales: le rôle des migrations de population (vers 1792)," kindly provided by the author. In addition to the political and economic reasons emphasized in this essay, one may also note the enormous alternative demands on French manpower due to the wars of Louis XIV. The increase of the French army's size from 20,000 in the 1660s to 300,000 by 1710, was more than six times the total migration of Frenchmen to the New World during that period. Moreover, discharged soldiers were more likely to remain in Canada than former *engagés*. Once more, the less-likely group to be enslaved was the more likely to strengthen the colony. See Peter Moogk, "Manson's Fellow Exiles: Emigration from France to North America before 1763," in *Europe on the Move*, pp. 236–260, esp. 256–57.

[39] Eltis, *Rise of African Slavery*, 67.

[40] On rhetoric, see Jonathan Scott, *England's Troubles: Seventeenth Century England's Political Instability in European Context* (New York, 2000). In actuality, as Eltis emphasizes, the division between temporarily indentured white servants and black "perpetual servants" was made explicit in metropolitan registration regulations in 1664. The Barbados Servant Code of 1661 had anticipated this metropolitan distinction. See Sharon V. Salinger, *'To Serve Well and Faithfully': Labour and Indentured Servants in Pennsylvania* (Cambridge, 1987), pp. 9–10; Dunn, *Sugar and Slaves*, 239–240.

crossing it. It was a "shadowy," almost preconscious market-generated barrier.[41]

The decision to limit the boundaries of enslavability did not occur first, or primarily, within the consciences of individual English men and women, simultaneously and silently deciding to not to submit fellow islanders to the extreme forms of bondage that they observed across the Atlantic. Politics, of course, cannot be discounted. For decades England was wracked by violent upheaval and escalating ideological tensions. The polarized language of liberty and slavery permeated political discourse. Freedom from slavery was central to, if not the exclusive component of, discourse in the Civil Wars. Radical rhetoric against slavery reverberated from the early 1630s through the end of the century, and, until the peace of Utrecht, the destiny of England, as all of its Western European neighbors, hung on the outcome of military struggle.[42]

Yet ideology alone might not have sufficed. Englishmen were as aware of the fragility of their own political institutions *in practice* as were their Dutch neighbors. It was not just concern for individual rights that deterred a major negative redefinition of legal rights, but the concrete costs to the political and social fabric of such an innovation. At the level of labor flows, all potential streams of migrants flowing to the New World from the British Isles were not interchangeable. For indentured servants, overseas migrations represented only the last step in a sequence of options that ran from the local to the overseas markets. Mobility was tied to contract.[43] The extension of an alternative market, tied to coercion, would have brought disruption to the voluntary labor streams.

The history of impressment offers an inkling of just what might have occurred with a massive switch by rulers to coercive labor. Impressment was an extraordinary extension of (*not a substitute for*) the voluntary labor market. Very few volunteers in Cromwell's navy were willing to serve in the Caribbean once news about the mortality rates there filtered back. Outside the capital city "the press" faced enormous difficulties. Parish constables were often afraid to carry out their recruitment orders. When a government had to threaten recalcitrant constables with impressment for non-fulfillment, one can glimpse the sharply rising cost of enforcement even in, and for, a national public emergency like war. If planters had offered "higher prices" for the government to provide them with convicts on demand, shipping costs alone would not have interfered with the process. On the contrary. But

---

[41] Eltis, "Slave Economies," 108; idem, *Rise of African Slavery*, 83.

[42] Scott, *England's Troubles*, 274, and final chapter.

[43] B. S. Capp, *Cromwell's Navy: The Fleet and the English Revolution, 1648–1660* (New York, 1989), ch. 8. On the distinction between impressment and enslavement see Nicholas Rogers, "Impressment and the Law in Eighteenth-Century Britain," in Norma Landau (ed.), *Law, Crime and English Society, 1660–1830* (Cambridge, 2002), pp. 71–116.

what of "onshore" costs? Would they have been "trivial," in establishing what Eltis calls "a properly exploited system"? Could they have generated 10,000 forced migrants each year from localities without raising serious enforcement costs to the local magistrates who were supposed to implement the system? In the formula of North and Thomas, what would this new institutional arrangement, introduced to create new property rights for a very small group of private investors located on distant islands, have cost? At a time when royalists and parliamentarians were desperately competing for popular loyalty, locality by locality, could such an activity conceivably have brought the private rate of return close to the social rate of return?[44]

In many parts of England impressment brought near paralysis. Some magistrates deliberately failed to "press" a single man for Cromwell's navy. If the failure to enforce payment of ship money to the king had produced imprisoned martyrs for liberty, what would imprisonment or deportation for failure to produce English slaves for Barbadian planters have generated? The only alternative to local enforcement would have been bureaucratic expansion. Government press gangs arriving to pick up even legitimately convicted petty thieves destined for sugar gangs might find their prey gone and themselves in flight under a hail of stones. It was precisely the enduring strength of local self-government, a distinctive characteristic of English administration, that would have made the conversion of England into a zone of enslavement for its own citizens more expensive than almost anywhere else in Europe.[45]

Perhaps a glance at a New England incident in 1850 will cast light on the potential administrative costs entailed in introducing enslavement and coerced migration into England in 1650. The successful return of Thomas

[44] See Douglass C. North and Robert Paul Thomas, *The Rise of the Western World: A New Economic History* (Cambridge, 1973), pp. 7–8.

[45] Capp, *Cromwell's Navy*, 213–17, 265–291. The shift in European policy along the coast of Africa sheds light on the choices available for labor recruitment in the Plantation Americas. In Africa it was armed deterrence, not ideological or religious inhibitions, that induced Europeans to switch from their "raid-and-trade" policy in the Atlantic islands to an almost exclusive reliance on purchasing slaves. Within Africa, institutional power also influenced vulnerability to enslavement. Large warrior-dominated societies had no monopoly on enslaving, and many groups in small or decentralized societies developed their own niches on the predatory side of the slaving equation. The uneven distribution of political and military power, however, meant that the upper echelons of centralized states reaped disproportionate allocations of human chattel. See, inter alia, Thornton, *Africa and the Africans*, 38–39, 89–93, 108–109; Klein, *Slavery and Colonial Rule*, 4; the articles by Walter Hawthorne, Andrew Hubbell and Martin A. Klein in the section "Decentralized Societies and the Slave Trade," *Journal of African History*, 42 (2001): 1–65; Klein, "The Impact of the Atlantic Slave Trade on the Societies of the Western Sudan," in Joseph E. Inikori and Stanley L. Engerman (eds.), *The Atlantic Slave Trade: Effects on Economies, Societies, and Peoples in Africa, the Americas, and Europe* (Durham, 1992), pp. 25–47; and W. E. Evans and David Richardson, "Hunting for rents: the economics of slavery in pre-colonial Africa," *Economic History Review*, 58 (1995): 665–686.

Sims, a black fugitive, from Boston to Georgia in 1851 cost the U.S. government $20,000. This must have been at least ten times Sims's market value in Georgia. Throw in the cost of all the unsuccessful attempts at deportation in 1851–1855, and a historian is forced to conclude that forced migration of large numbers of enslaved Englishmen would probably have been prohibitively expensive except in a permanently authoritarian state.[46]

Eltis may be correct in asserting that the impact of epidemiology on Europeans going to the Americas is less than most scholars assume. However, one cannot assume that disease played no role at all in Northwest European choices for African slaves. Differential mortality was probably decisive in the Portuguese choice of Africans for São Tomé in the late fifteenth century, and for Brazil in the late sixteenth century. It certainly increased the difficulties of the Dutch in recruiting migrants to the Dutch West Indies. Epidemiological concerns could hardly have weighed less on English decision makers, whether their labor migrants were coerced or voluntary. At the very least, a sugar island destination increased resistance at the initial point of enslavement in England. We already have evidence that resistance to impressment into Cromwell's navy increased dramatically when the West Indies was the

---

[46] Don E. Fehrenbacher, *The Slaveholding Republic: An Account of the United States Government's Relations with Slavery*, completed and edited by Ward M. McAfee (New York, 2001), p. 234. It is an open question whether some judges in late seventeenth century England might have been tempted by higher prices to favor rechanneling "capital" offenders to the plantations in huge numbers. "Hanging judge" George Jeffries was quickly reconciled into becoming a "shipping judge" by the Royal prospect of obtaining £10–15 per head for 800 captives, following the failed Monmouth rising against James II in 1685. One must, however, carry the hypothesis beyond the commercial calculations of courtiers and merchants. The overall rate of conviction for capital (i.e., also transportable) crimes per population remained the same in "transportation-friendly" eighteenth century England as it had been before the rise of transatlantic colonization. Convictions still required the acquiescence of judges and local jurors who reaped no profit from them. The close social relationships that characterized rural England were still embedded in structures of paternalism and deference that encouraged intervention on behalf of community members. Would efforts at wholesale convictions have satisfied the functions of such personalized justice? The social compact implicit in trial by jury was worth more than a mass of overseas slaves. On conviction rates, see Philip Jenkins, "From Gallows to Prison? The Execution Rate in Early Modern England," *Criminal Justice History*, 7 (1986): 51–71. On the context and function of convictions, see J. M. Beattie, "Crime and the Courts in Surrey 1736–1753," in J. S. Cockburn (ed.), *Crime in England, 1550–1800* (Princeton, 1977), pp. 154–186, esp. 179–182. At the very moment Chief Justice Jeffries was conducting treason trials for over 1000 prisoners, he himself accused the mayor of Bristol of kidnaping and selling local destitutes to the West Indies. Jeffries obviously drew the line of transportability between traitors and indigents. See Robert Clifton, *The Last Popular Rebellion: The Western Rising of 1685* (London, 1984), p. 237. Armed rebels were, of course, far less frequent than indigents in seventeenth century England. Enslavement was not even the issue. But Jeffries nevertheless was branded as the epitome of evil by the successful rebels of 1688. The convicts' utility overseas was unquestioned. They were pardoned by the new regime, but the colonial governors successfully lobbied for the power to force them to remain in the Caribbean.

anticipated destination for the fleet. When British convict transportation to the Americas was regularized in the eighteenth century, it was directed toward the Chesapeake, not the Caribbean. At a minimum there would have been an additional incentive for the British state to create a parallel (and necessarily larger) flow of African slaves to the Caribbean.[47]

Warfare within the British Isles might have offered a more promising path to coerced transatlantic migration. Battles generated prisoners. Perhaps as many as 12,000 Irish, English and Scots royalists were thus transported. This was not, however, an economically viable mode of recruitment. Armies raised in the Civil War were intended as short-term (because they were enormously expensive) human mobilizations. Deportation was almost always used as a deterrence (*pour décourager les autres*), that is, as a short-term terror tactic, not a long-term labor supply strategy. The prospect of deportation often accomplished the political aim of pacification as effectively as did its implementation. A long and expensive war of attrition in Scotland was brought to an end by just the threat to ship into "slavery in Barbados all those captured in arms."[48]

Had Cromwell considered enslaving those resisting naval recruitment he might still have rejected the idea out of hand. Too many British sailors escaped the press by fleeing to Dutch ships. Such volatile human capital was far too valuable to squander on clearing tropical islands or awaiting welcoming enemy fleets, which would welcome their sailing skills. Nor can one ignore the fact that foreign loans were needed to continue warfare within England, not very likely if the fellow citizens of Amsterdamers were being hauled off to harvest cane in the Caribbean. Finally there was the alternative of ransoming. Sending affluent captives to the tropics might well reduce their value by raising their chances of dying.

The war did generate a flow of prisoners to the West Indies. But the benefits to the planters were hardly commensurate with the costs of accumulation. England lost a higher percentage of its population between 1640 and 1660 (190,000) than in either of the twentieth century's two world wars. Scotland may well have lost 6 percent (60,000) of its population, and Ireland 41 percent (660,000). Civil wars are not good times for institutionalizing slavery, and often they are the opposite. The stakes are so high that contending parties often engage in competitive bidding in order to avoid defeat. Civil wars are thus times for large-scale military manumissions in slave societies, rather than for enslavements in non-slave societies. Calculations based on the opportunity costs of delivering English or African laborers to the Western Isles would have had to incorporate the high risks of wartime alienation. More important

---

47 For disease and the slave trade, see Philip D. Curtin, "Epidemiology and the Slave Trade," *Political Science Quarterly*, 83 (1968): 190–216. On the intensity of disease in Barbados c. 1650, see Dunn, *Sugar and Slaves*, 76–77.

48 Carleton, *Going to the Wars*, 327–28.

than the putative long-term appreciation for individual rights created by a
market society was the more tangible short-term risk of forfeiting loyalty in a
revolutionary situation. Brutality, far short of slavery, against white servants
in the West Indies raised fears in Parliament that "our lives will be as cheap
as those negroes."[49]

Consider the economic implications of the choice to use enslavement, not
as a one-off threat to induce pacification, but as an ongoing policy designed
to ensure an adequate flow of slaves to the Caribbean. Ireland and Scotland
would have become lands of marronage, perpetually awaiting, as they did
in the aftermath of the English Revolution of 1689, the arrival of French
armies and Stuart pretenders to stir insurrection on an ever-broader and more
virulent scale. A turbulent countryside in Ireland ran quite counter to English
landowners' needs for agricultural labor in a devastated and depopulated
country. Would the needs of proximate Ireland have been subordinated to
the needs of distant planters?

To these costs we must add those of reproducing the coerced labor of
Englishmen abroad. The problem of negative slave population growth in
the Caribbean would have had to be addressed. The ratio of females to
males in the actual convict flow across the British Atlantic during the eighteenth century fell far short of that reached with enslaved Africans during
the same period. The potential reproductive deficit of European bondsmen
in the Caribbean would therefore have been worse than that of the Africans.
Moreover, even if only lifetime service had been introduced, the natural reproduction rate of servile labor would have been nil, requiring still greater
imports than was the case with African slaves. It would have taken the Southern colonies of North America generations longer than it did for a natural
increase of slaves to make their slaves self-sustaining. Therefore, one can
presume that a much higher net flow of Europeans to the Americas would
have been required to ensure the same sized slave population in 1760 or
1800 as achieved by its actual African counterpart.[50]

This would not have been the only cost to the European colonization of
the Americas. English indentured servants bound for America would almost
certainly have been terminated. The Redemption system for foreigners would
have been stillborn. What European, without prior full funding for himself
or his family, could offer his labor in exchange for passage, outbidding slaves

---

[49] On Civil War losses, see Carleton, *Going to the Wars*, 341–42. On the Parliamentary comparison of Europeans and Africans as "slaves" in Barbados, see Linebaugh and Rediker,
The Many Headed Hydra, 134–35. By conservative estimate, the flow of British migrants
to Ireland between 1641 and 1672 was 200,000, far more than the flow to the British
Americas during the same critical period of transition from European to African labor. See
Nicholas Canny, "English Migration into and across the Atlantic during the seventeenth and
eighteenth centuries," in *Europeans on the Move*, pp. 39–75, esp. 61–69.

[50] Calculated from Eltis, *Rise*, 98.

who were being delivered to British docks at state-subsidized rates, and then packed into vessels at two or three to a ton? The slave trade would certainly have discouraged the waves of skilled Continental religious refugees, as well as the impoverished Continentals who otherwise found asylum in England or the Americas. The "best poor man's country" would soon have become the "worst white man's country." One can hardly imagine a Sir Josiah Child contrasting the failed colonization policy of Spain with that of England. In 1699 Child boasted that England had gained more subjects in its colonies by prosperity, freedom and religious tolerance in just fifty years, than had Spain in two hundred. When plantations belonged to "Mother-Kingdoms or Countries where Liberty and Prosperity is better preserved, and Interest of Money restrained to a Low Rate, the consequence is, that every Person sent abroad with the *Negroes* and *Utensils* he is constrained to employ... eight or ten Blacks for one White Servant... [so] *Every* England-man in Barbados or Jamaica *creates employment for four men at home.*"[51]

In short, the best that might be said for the enslavement of Britons, from even the narrowest commercial perspective, is that the Middle Passage, that is, the direct transportation of Europeans from Bristol to Barbados, would have been cheaper per capita than the shipment of the same number of African slaves from Bristol to Barbados via Benin, under the same conditions.

IV

One of the major contributions of Eltis' assessment of the early modern Atlantic is the degree to which he has brought Europe back into the story in strikingly new comparative terms. His account is fundamentally rooted in the evolution of European civil and economic relations during the centuries before and after the Columbian voyages. More systematically and cogently than ever before, he shows the plantation system to be an offshoot of European capitalism, and not vice versa. That system arose from the severe limitations imposed on European control of labor in either Africa or Europe, and the wider latitude allowed to Europeans over labor in the Americas. Eltis compellingly argues that European industrialization after 1750, like Caribbean slavery after 1650, owed its impetus primarily to economic patterns of behavior and capital amassed in Europe itself. *The Rise of African Slavery* puts the economic significance of New World slavery into a diminished perspective. Despite the outstanding productivity and per capita value of Britain's slave colonies, even their gross product equaled that of a small English county by 1700, and still only a larger single county by 1800. However, Eltis' assessment of the choice for Africans is still insufficiently Eurocentric.

---

[51] Josiah Child, *A New Discourse of Trade* (London: 1698), 190–191.

Contrary to the implications of his own premises about European centrality in the process, he reaches less deeply into Europe than he does into Africa and America. The agency costs and constraining conditions of Africa and the Africans are more carefully enumerated and quantified. The analogous costs and benefits of labor choices are left relatively underdeveloped for Europe.

I, therefore, conclude by focusing on two aspects of European development which are only separately addressed in Eltis' study, but which must be brought together for purposes of analytical clarity. The first concerns the fundamental distinction between the basis of European wealth compared with that of many other parts of the world in the centuries after 1500. Slaves were the principal form of revenue-producing capital recognized in African law. By contrast, in European legal systems, "land was the primary form of private revenue-producing property." Even in Iberia, slaves were a relatively minor form of property. Further north slaves were virtually or completely unrecognized in law. European property rights, especially in one's own labor, were vested in the individual, even in occupations still widely regarded as "servile." Control over labor was thus exercised through property rights in other means of production, in land or fixed capital.

This entailed different aims for collective violence. In Africa, wars and raids for slaves were equivalent to wars of conquest. European rulers of the seventeenth century aimed at conquering territory as a principal means of expanding their realm's wealth and power. A principal aim of conquest was to keep people productively *in place*. This was true despite the fact that warfare was endemic to the European continent during the sixteenth and seventeenth centuries, despite the fact that wars were frequent enough to have ensured an abundant supply of captives throughout that century, and despite the fact that the economies of Europe evolved "against all the obstacles that could be reared by war, hostility and jealousy between the rival nation states."[52]

In seeking territory, rulers assumed that the benefits of conquest could best be reached by keeping peasants and artisans on site and doing business as usual. When Louis XIV, the pre-eminent war lord of the second half of the seventeenth century, invaded the Dutch Republic in 1672, he distributed a message to all the communities he could reach: "His Majesty has been obliged, only with displeasure, to carry the War into the Lands possessed by the Dutch, and his design is only to punish those of the government, and not to ruin the populace...." His Majesty further promised "to pay his army punctually, to keep them in order, to have them feed themselves, to allow

---

[52] See Thornton, *Africa*, 74, 102; and Eltis, *Rise of African Slavery*, 21–65. Much later, in the first years of French rule in the Western Sudan, slaves represented 60–70% of the trade by value and probably most of the accumulated capital of the region. See Klein, "Impact of the Atlantic Slave Trade," 41.

civilians and their goods free passage into towns, to provide towns with inexpensive protection against marauders."[53]

The thrust of European war policy was toward the rationalization of civilian payments to armies and toward a minimization of civilian insecurity and mass flight. Even the pillaging and terrorizing of resisting towns by Cromwell's armies were deemed extraordinary disruptions of the everyday functions that should properly produce obedient subjects and taxpayers. States strove to lighten the burden of an acquiescent populace. Winning the compliance of one's own nationals was still more important to rulers, especially in regimes where active consent of the governed was assumed. Toward the end of the seventeenth century, the fate of the European powers was more dependent than ever before on a military struggle lasting for a full generation. England's costly and incessant warfare against Louis XIV required a "financial revolution," repeating the process of innovative state building first achieved a century before by the Dutch in their long war of liberation. As the unprecedented national debt of England attested, the war was best fought with a more rational mobilization of economic resources.

No group in England, mercantilist or otherwise, conceived of giving priority to the labor needs of remote island economies over the threat from Europe. When the jails of England were emptied it was in order to conscript the inmates for action across the Channel, not the Atlantic. National consent and domestic tranquility easily trumped the need for private coercion abroad. In the words of William Penn: "'tis the great interest of a Prince, that the People should have a share in the making of their own Laws . . . [because] it makes Men Diligent, and increase the Trade, which advances the Revenue: for where Men are not Free, they will never seek to improve, because they are not sure what they have, and less of what they get."[54] Such aims could hardly have been better achieved by dividing the nation into free and enslavable subjects.

Eltis' assertion that "hardening attitudes toward the poor were seen throughout Western Europe," and especially early in Protestant Europe, does not strike me as compellingly documented for the second half of the seventeenth century. It seems dubious as applied to England after 1655, when both population and voluntary overseas migration fell. Both developments coincided with a probable rise in wages, and with a wave of charitable foundations for the poor. Even voices demanding houses of discipline for the poor did not go unchallenged. As Dudley North noted, as early as 1691,

---

53 Myron P. Guttman, *War and Rural Life in the Early Modern Low Countries* (Princeton, 1980), pp. 61–62.
54 Scott, *England's Troubles*, 488. On military recruitment as a persistent priority in prosecutions and deterrence, see Peter King, "War as a Judicial Resource: Press Gangs and Prosecution Rates, 1740–1830," in Landau (ed.), *Law, Crime and English Society*, pp. 97–116.

workhouses were proving impossible of rigorous enforcement. Although they fell well short of slavery or bondage in exile, "our Natures" were "too soft and pittyful" to "hold one and another to hard labor." North proposed doing away with the entire Poor/Workhouse system, and allowing unfettered freedom of movement for labor. It was simply "not possible to force a free people to work for less wages than will produce sufficient sustenance for them and their families."[55] Introducing broad measures of enslavability into a system that no longer allowed for them would have created far more turmoil than did the purchasing of Africans. The costs of enslavement did not begin in the barracoons of Benguela. They could not have ended with barracoons in Bristol.

Even the line between enslavable Africans and unenslavable Europeans was not as clear as Eltis implies: "Clearly, the British viewed black slaves, including the few who lived in England, as British chattels rather than British citizens, if they saw them at all." Quite the contrary. As early as the end of the seventeenth century, Chief Justice Holt unequivocally held that, in England, "the law took no notice of a Negro." As far as I know, popular commentaries generally denied that any resident of England could be a chattel. The only consensual statement that one can make about black slaves brought to England was that even *their* status there remained disputed.[56]

Justice Holt's categorical statement for blacks remained contested because it threatened the legal framework of economic development on the other side of the Atlantic. Any attempt to widen the network of enslavables to incorporate freeborn Englishmen, however, would probably have produced a clear decision, reaffirming the metropolitan Common Law tradition "in favor of liberty," a full century before the Somerset decision of 1772. An analogous debate over Aryan–Jewish differentiation among Germans, in 1933–35, may again be relevant here. A "narrow" definition of Jewishness was favored by bureaucrats. It won out over a wider definition of pollution favored by Party ideologues. The bureaucratic argument was that the larger the proportion of the degraded, the lower was the likelihood of popular acquiescence.

The significance of countervailing power as an inhibitor is also illustrated by another choice of this same European power. Poison gas was massively used as a weapon for killing enemy soldiers between 1915 and 1918. Between 1939 and 1945 it was used by only one side, and against defenseless non-combatants. David Ben Gurion posed the relevant question to the allies: "If, instead of Jews, thousands of English, American or Russian women and

55 Andrea Finkelstein, *Harmony and Balance: An Intellectual History of Seventeenth-Century English Economic Thought* (Ann Arbor, 2000), p. 195. On the burst of philanthropic foundations at the end of the seventeenth century, see Joan Lane, *Apprenticeship in England, 1600–1914* (New York, 1996).
56 Compare Eltis, *Rise of African Slavery*, 16; and Drescher, *Capitalism and Antislavery*, ch. 2.

children and aged had been tortured every day, burnt to death, asphyxiated in gas chambers – would you have acted in the same way?"[57] *Mutatis mutandis,* the implicit answer to this twentieth century question offers one reason why Europeans were not substituted for African slaves in the seventeenth century.

If one views the possibilities from the perspective of European economic institutional development, (re-)introducing slave law into Northwestern Europe would have been, even for reasons of political economy alone, detrimental to European economic development. For the political and economic elites of 1650 to 1750, by what other criteria would European economic policy have been formulated? Is it accidental that Adam Smith, in 1776, justified both Europe's division of labor and its inequality of wealth by a comparison of Europe with Africa? At the end of the first chapter in his *Wealth of Nations* he concluded: "Compared, indeed, with the more extravagant luxury of the great, his [the very meanest person in a civilized country] accommodation must no doubt appear extremely simple and easy; and yet it may be true, perhaps, that the accommodation of a European prince does not always so much exceed that of an industrious and frugal peasant, as the accommodation of the latter exceeds that of many an African king, the absolute master of the lives and liberties of ten thousand naked savages."[58] It is not clear to me that many frugal peasants or laborers in Europe or the Americas would have disagreed with Smith, either in 1776, or two hundred years later.

To the bottom line then: Could most Europeans have done still better, economically speaking, by coercing other European laborers to, and in, America? My inclination is to paraphrase one of the late seventeenth century's

---

57 Yehuda Bauer, *Jews for Sale? Nazi–Jewish Negotiations, 1933–1945* (New Haven, 1994), p. 195. The closest approximation to domination over most of Europe prior to 1941–1944 was achieved by Napoleon Bonaparte at the beginning of the nineteenth century. He was certainly not averse to slavery, and re-enslaved the freedmen and women of France's tropical colonies in 1802. It seems extremely unlikely that he would have dreamt of replenishing the labor forces of those colonies with Europeans, even had he held on to St. Domingue in the bloody conflict which cost him that colony. By 1803 Europe's pre-eminent warlord was more conscious than any previous imperial ruler about the costs entailed in conscripting Europeans to the tropics. He was, moreover, as dependent on Europeans for his military ventures as were any of his predecessors during the previous three centuries. Fully half of the *Grande Armée* invading Russia in 1812 was composed of reluctant non-French "allies." Introducing a system of enslavement in restive central Europe, not to speak of the guerilla opposition in still unconquered Iberia, would have escalated policing costs on both sides of the French Atlantic empire. In Europe, such a policy would have subverted Napoleon's principal appeal to newly conquered areas of the Continent, where his new Civil Code promulgated individual equality and freedom of labor: "Contracts legally formed take the place of law for those who have made them" [Robert B. Holtman, *The Napoleonic Revolution* (New York, 1967), p. 90]. Napoleon's overseas colonies were even more completely vulnerable to enemy assaults than were his mainland territories.

58 Adam Smith, *An Inquiry into the Nature and Causes of the Wealth of Nations,* 2 vols. (Indianapolis, 1976), I, p. 24.

leading philosophers. From the perspective of economic development, Europeans were having the best of all possible New Worlds. Their imperial economic interests were well served by creating a house divided, with free labor at home and slave labor beyond the line, in the Americas. As long as the slave trade lasted the plantation slave societies were among the wealthiest and most productive areas of the world. The consequence was that the most optimal division of labor led to the Africanization of the plantation Americas. In the still longer run, Western European rulers of the seventeenth century also seem to have made a very judicious economic decision by not converting their home territories into zones of involuntary servitude for export. Extending the zone of enslavement throughout Western Europe would, at a minimum, have raised transaction costs, disrupted law and order, reduced property rights in one's own person and created a reign of terror, at least for a significant minority, and perhaps for all of Western Europe's inhabitants.[59]

Was it the peculiar culture of Europeans that led to this outcome – a culture that maximized economic gain and maximized moral or ethnic barriers to enslaving fellow Europeans? The institutional and political barriers to European enslavement seem to have been far more important. The virulent stew of religious and ethnic hostility within Europe during the century after 1550 offered an unprecedented possibility for intra-European innovation. A European polity, gaining supremacy on both sides of the Atlantic, might have been tempted to make a breakthrough to European enslavement (as happened during the past century), or at least to the lifetime servitude of Europeans in the New World.[60]

[59] At the beginning of the twenty-first century most countries located in the *Low Human Development* category of the United Nations Human Development index are in sub-Saharan Africa, the classic zone of enslavement in the Atlantic system. They remain the lowest twenty-five of the 170 nations recorded on the index. Those New World areas which relied heavily on slaves, but were not zones of primary enslavement, offer a more mixed picture. The United States, exceptionally, is among the top three on the index. The rest are all within the categories of *High Human Development* (from Barbados at #30) and *Medium Human Development* (down to São Tomé at #132). Haiti alone (at #150) is within the category of "*Low Human Development.*"

[60] One cannot assume that medieval developments created a once-for-all ideological boundary of unenslavability by 1500. Although extremely rare, "White slaves" (*esclavos blancos*) were listed in the records of the Archivo Nacional de Cuba. See Alejandro de la Fuente García, "Esclavos africanos en La Habana: Zonas de procedencia y denominaciones étnicas, 1570–1699," *Revista Española de Antropología Americana*, 20 (1990): 135–160, esp. 156–158. In fifteenth century Valencia, Christians were still buying and selling Greeks and Slavs. See David B. Davis, "Slavery White, Black, Muslim, Christian," *New York Review of Books*, July 5, 2001, 51–55, esp. 52. As late as 1600 there were some Greek and Slavic slaves in Cuba (from information kindly provided by Professor Davis). In a recent essay, Eltis concurs that European social structures and institutions also made an Atlantic plantation system worked by European slaves impossible. See "Free and Coerced Migrations from the Old World to the New," in David Eltis (ed.), *Coerced and Free Migration: Global Perspectives* (Stanford,

The political and economic constraints to such an innovation were clear in Europe's actual frame of reference. The balance of power and retaliation acted as a solid deterrent against bondage for Europeans (and often for Amerindians and Muslims) in the Americas. No power ever had sufficient omnipotence to ignore the risks of creating zones of Euroslavery in the Americas.[61] We get a faint echo of the significance of Europe's pluralistic constellation of power in faraway Virginia at the beginning of the eighteenth century. A 1705 Act Concerning Servants and Slaves declared, "that all servants imported and brought into this country, by sea or land, who were not Christians in their native country (*except Turks and moors* in amity with her majesty, and others that can make due proof of their being free in England, or any other Christian country, before they were shipped in order to transportation hither) shall be accounted and be slaves, and as such be bought and sold notwithstanding a conversion to Christianity afterwards." The cultural constraints against European servitude might or might not have sufficed to overcome the economic incentives to gang labor in the Caribbean. Europeans' choices remained more directly constrained by the actual and potential institutional limits on the uses of Old World laborers and prisoners of war than by taboos in Europe or economic opportunities in the Americas.

2002), 41–42 and n. One issue remains unresolved. Should we classify twentieth-century examples of intensive coercion merely as "anachronisms" in the "fuller integration of the world's peoples?" (Ibid., 3–4)

[61] See "The Virginia Slave Code, 1705," excerpted in Stanley Engerman et al., *Slavery* (Oxford, 2001), p. 119. Seventeenth century Europeans cut with equal ease through the European/non-European lines of otherness. For Dutch Protestants fighting for their independence a century earlier, "*liever Turcx dan Paus* (better Turkish than papist)" seemed self-evident. Half a century later, Amsterdam's Jewish merchants hardly needed to remind the settler-starved directors of the West India Company that "the more loyal of (sic) people that go to live" in New Amsterdam, the greater the economic benefits to both colony and Company [James H. Williams, "An Atlantic Perspective on the Jewish Struggle for Rights and Opportunities in Brazil, New Netherland and New York," in Bernardini and Fiering (eds.), *Jews and the Expansion of Europe*, 369–93].

2

The Dutch and the Slave Americas

Pieter C. Emmer

At the beginning of the seventeenth century no European country seemed in a better position to play a major role in establishing and profiting from the Atlantic slave economy than the Netherlands. Within a few years they were battling for control of Europe's largest source of sugar, and threatening to displace the largest national transatlantic slave trader. Yet a mere seventy-five years later the Dutch had lost their pre-eminence in the Caribbean and the North Atlantic to the British. Of all the American sugar-producing regions, they held only an enclave on the South American mainland. Why did the trajectory change? What went wrong? Had the Dutch chosen the wrong model for exploiting the Atlantic slave economy? Had they invested in those areas of the Atlantic with less favorable factor endowments? Had they brought institutions to the Atlantic that inhibited rather than stimulated economic expansion? Finally, were the consequences of this relative failure of significance for the economic development of the Americas?

It is difficult at first sight to give an affirmative answer to any of these questions. On the first, the Dutch had clearly avoided the Spanish emphasis on settlement, large-scale investment in the tropical Americas and exploitation of Indian labor and deposits of precious metals – an approach that was appearing increasingly unpromising by the late seventeenth century. They had instead opted for the route pursued by the English and French in the later seventeenth and eighteenth centuries of focusing on cash crops such as coffee and sugar and very intensive use of African labour. They initiated such a strategy with their conquest of Brazil and thereby became the first of the North European colonial powers to assume control of a plantation complex. After the loss of their Brazilian colony, the Dutch thereupon conquered part of the South American mainland bordering on the Caribbean Sea. Suriname, Essequibo and Demerara may not have been islands like Barbados or Jamaica, but they offered similar factor endowments. A tropical climate, easy access for seagoing vessels and sufficient trade winds to power windmills combined with good soil to provide an almost ideal environment for cane sugar. In the Dutch plantation colonies some of the fertile soil was situated below sea level and required an unusual amount of investment in sluices, digging canals, preventing silting and the like. On the other hand, plantations in tidal water areas could use their location to their advantage by harnessing the tidal differences in water levels to drive their sugar mills. In sum, there is no indication that the physical endowments of the Dutch plantation colonies in the New World were much different from those of other plantation colonies.

In order to exploit the soil, plantations needed labour, and by the second quarter of the seventeenth century the Dutch were experienced transatlantic slave traders with many trading contacts on the African coast. Unlike the Portuguese and the Spanish they saw little opportunity in employing Amerindian labour, which had in any event diminished considerably by the time the Dutch arrived in the New World. But the British and the French were faced by the same problem. In fact, the Dutch were the first of the Northwest Europeans to imitate the Portuguese by bringing large numbers of Africans to their plantations, and during the first half of the seventeenth century they also supplied the British, Spanish and French planters with slaves. This suggests that the productivity of the Dutch slave trade was higher than or on a par with that of the other Atlantic nations. That situation may have changed during the second half of the seventeenth century, but there is no reason to assume that the growth of the Dutch activities in the Atlantic was severely hampered by higher slave prices than those paid by their European competition. As for the institutions the Dutch carried to the Americas, most scholars have seen these as defining modernity in the early modern Atlantic world. If, according to Eric Jones, Europe was the area of the world with political structures least likely to inhibit growth, then the seventeenth century Dutch were to Europe what Europe was to the rest of the world.[1] The Dutch had no monarch who could have imposed policies that might have benefited the dynasty rather than the economy. The republican structure ensured that mercantile considerations always predominated. The government of the province of Holland – the most important of the seven united Low Countries – was made up of representatives of the cities, and city governments usually comprised members of the local merchant families.

The financial institutions of the Dutch seemed equally well equipped to further create a Dutch Atlantic slave economy. Establishing slave plantations and organizing Atlantic voyages required greater capital outlays and were riskier than most activities within Europe itself. But institutions that the Dutch had developed in Europe seemed well able to cope with these requirements. These included the practice of dividing the capital outlay for ships and their cargoes among a large number of participants, founding limited

---

[1] Eric Jones, *The European Miracle: Environments, Economies and Geopolitics in the History of Europe and Asia*, 2nd ed. (Cambridge, 1987).

companies with a large number of shareholders, borrowing money against low interest rates, and insuring maritime risks against reasonable premiums. Because of the high efficiency of their merchant marine, the Dutch had become the premier trading nation in Europe by the end of the sixteenth century. That provided a solid basis for branching out into the Atlantic. Around 1620 the Dutch probably carried more than half of the sugar harvest of Portuguese Brazil to Europe in addition to distributing products from Spanish America within the intra-European trade.

Finally, the religious toleration of the Netherlands is well known. After the Reformation, the religious institutions of the Netherlands came to accommodate religious diversity much earlier than elsewhere in Europe. In spite of the fact that Calvinism was the dominant religion, all other religious denominations were allowed to practice without persecution, though their members were not allowed to serve in governments. Remarkably for early modern Europe, at no time in Dutch history was there a reason to leave the country because of religious oppression. On the contrary, a sizeable influx of religious and political refugees came to the Netherlands with their families, capital and international networks of whom the Portuguese Jews, Christaos novos and the Huguenots are just the best known.

The contrast with England around 1600 is particularly striking. London was not the centre of the financial and insurance world, the English fleet operating in European waters was far smaller than the Dutch, between 1640 and 1660 the country was ravaged by a civil war, and religious unrest resulting in the exodus of both Puritans and Catholics continued much longer than in the Netherlands. From such an unpromising beginning, the English built a slave economy in the Atlantic that, except for the half-century dominance of St. Domingue after 1740, was pre-eminent for as long as it was allowed to continue. Such a reversal of fortunes calls for a closer examination of, first, the differences between the Dutch and British slave economies and, second, the diverging development of the Dutch and British metropolitan economies. But these paths continued to diverge beyond 1780. The contrast in importance of the two slave sectors was at its sharpest in the last years of the eighteenth century. Yet despite the enormous discrepancy in size at this late period, it was the Dutch system that survived longest after 1800. Counter-intuitively, by far the largest and most successful of the European-controlled slave systems – the British – jettisoned slavery first; the Dutch and the British were as far apart in their experience of abolition as they had been in their experience of slavery. This, too, calls for a closer look.

Dutch expansion into the Atlantic was always different from its English counterpart. First, the Dutch merchants broke the weakest link in the defences of the Iberian New World by illegally penetrating the production of and the trade in Brazilian sugar. Second, this peaceful, quiet policy of informal penetration was rather suddenly abandoned in favour of a frontal assault on Portuguese Brazil. The Dutch managed to conquer part of the colony, but had to withdraw completely just twenty-five years later. Between 1621 and 1654 the "Brazilian Adventure" cost the Dutch merchant community dearly. The disastrous history of Dutch Brazil shows that the original policy of interloping had made far better economic sense than attempts at outright conquest. While the Dutch were keeping the Iberians at bay in the South Atlantic, France and England took advantage of Dutch preoccupation to conquer a sizeable part of the Caribbean. The Dutch rivals started colonies of white settlement producing tobacco for the export market. Clearly, Brazil had lost the Dutch valuable time in obtaining their own Caribbean plantation colonies. It was not until 1667 that the Dutch conquered Suriname on the South American mainland. A special limited company was created in order to defend and administer this colony, as the Dutch West India Company (WIC) was in a virtual state of bankruptcy after the loss of Brazil. The weakened WIC no longer possessed enough resources to prevent the British from conquering New Netherland, the only Dutch settlement colony in the New World. Henceforth, the Dutch West Indian possessions would be dependent on the British mainland colonies for the supply of perishable victuals.

Dutch participation in the trade in sugar and slaves reflects this late access to the Caribbean. The Dutch slave trade had a history tainted with financial disaster. As early as 1640 the Dutch slave trade had become a losing proposition because the Dutch West India Company had delivered considerable numbers of slaves to the Portuguese planters in Dutch Brazil without receiving full payment. Profitability seemed to have increased again after the Dutch stopped selling slaves in Brazil and found new customers among the planters in the British and French Caribbean. In their attempt at creating a "second Brazil," the Dutch merchants helped some of these planters to switch from cultivating tobacco to sugar cane. Yet, it should be stressed that almost from the very beginning in the early 1640s the Dutch faced strong English competition for slaves on the African coast. Thus, the introduction of the Navigation Laws in 1652 did not revolutionize the Atlantic slave trade in the middle Atlantic as has been often suggested, but did curtail the Dutch carrying trade in slaves, sugar, provisions and European goods, including equipment for the sugar mills. By the early 1660s the English had succeeded in effectively barring the Dutch from their colonies. A decade later a similar process took place in the French Antilles. Some smuggling continued, but it did not pay for Dutch traders to extend credit to planters in colonies where their presence was illegal. After the conquest of Suriname, the Dutch finally started to develop their own plantation colony and to intensify the illegal trade with Spanish America. Relying on competitive prices for shipping and trade goods to generate trade in the Atlantic no longer sufficed. The growing commercial compartmentalisation of the Atlantic made it imperative for each Atlantic power to have its own infrastructure of colonies and trading forts. Between 1630 and 1665 the Dutch spent large amounts of money building such an infrastructure only to lose most of it as their competitors took away their colonies in both Brazil and in North America. During those crucial years the British (as well as French) were able to invest in plantation agriculture that offered many more opportunities for future development than the Atlantic investments of the Dutch.[2]

A second deviation from the pattern of the British activities in the Atlantic was the relatively large volume of the Dutch transit trade. Recent research has shown that the illegal trade to and from Spanish America in addition to the transit trade to and from the French Caribbean was worth more than the total value of the Dutch plantation produce. The Dutch preference for transit trade can be explained by the fact that it required much less investment than did plantation agriculture. The drawback was, however, that the Dutch had no control over the volume of that trade.[3]

A third difference between the British and the Dutch experience pertains to the way the two countries financed their West Indian activities. The British plantations received a steady inflow of investment, albeit much of it short term. Part of that inflow was the capital that a new planter took with him to the West Indies and another part was provided by merchant houses that had specialized in the importation and sale of plantation produce and that were used to advancing loans and mortgages to their West Indian customers. A similar pattern held for the Dutch Caribbean down to the mid eighteenth century, but then the nature of the financing changed. Small groups of Amsterdam investors began to offer large mortgages to West Indian planters in Suriname as well as in the newly acquired British "Ceded Islands." There was also a European-wide move away from buying government bonds and other low-risk instruments of investment toward high-risk "bubbles." Dutch investors were part of this pattern but were unusual in placing their high-risk investments in the West Indies. The result was disastrous. The value of mortgages advanced to the West Indian planters far exceeded planter ability to pay the yearly interest on these mortgages, let alone the principal. After 1773 this situation resulted in a wave of bankruptcies and soon the majority of the plantations came to be owned by the mortgage holders. As a result the level of investment fell dramatically after 1776, severely hampering the expansion and modernisation of the Suriname plantations. The Dutch were unable to develop a new plantation frontier, as the British, the French and even the Spanish were able to do. Only after the British takeover in 1796 did some ex-Dutch plantation colonies expand due to the influx of capital and planters from Britain.

Toward the end of the eighteenth century, the retarded development of the Dutch plantation colonies is best illustrated by the decline in slave arrivals. Before the crash on the Amsterdam stock exchange, planters used bills of

---

[2] P. C. Emmer, *The Dutch in the Atlantic Economy, 1580–1880: Trade, Slavery and Emancipation* (Aldershot, 1998), pp. 55–62.

[3] W. W. Klooster, *Illicit Riches. Dutch Trade in the Caribbean, 1648–1795* (Leiden, 1998).

exchange drawn on the merchant houses in the Netherlands (their source of mortgages) in order to pay the captains of the slave ships. That meant that slaving firms could obtain full payment for their slaves upon the return of the slave ship to its home port. After 1775 this method of payment ceased suddenly, as most bills of exchange were no longer honoured in the Netherlands. As a consequence, the shipping firms themselves were forced to collect the price of their slaves in cash or in kind from the planters. Full payment for a slave cargo often took many years. This explains why the Dutch slave trade declined by 80 percent during the last quarter of the 18th century, while the British slave trade was able to continue growing. In order to survive at all the Dutch slave trade needed government aid in the form of suspension of customary taxes and levies.[4]

The continuous growth of the British slave trade was in part based on an emerging superiority in productivity, a pattern suggested by the fact that an increasing number of British slavers were able to sell their slaves outside the British West Indies. Part of the viability of the British slave trade rested on the way in which those who bought slaves in the West Indies paid for them. In the Dutch case, the slave traders had to accept the bills of exchange directly from the planters and these bills were drawn on the merchant house in the Netherlands handling the commercial affairs of the planter. In the British case, the bills came from the agents of these metropolitan merchant houses residing in the West Indies. That provided the British slave traders with much more security than the Dutch slavers. "By comparison with their French and Dutch counterparts the Liverpool slave traders appear to have been much more independent of colonial credit and relatively unencumbered with the heavy indebtedness of the plantation economy."[5] Yet, the buying power of the planters in the British Caribbean must have also contributed to the relatively high profit rates of the British slave trade as the planters in the British West Indies enjoyed incomes that were in part based on the protective tariffs for their sugar on the British home market.[6] The British consumer not only bought more sugar than his continental counterpart, but also had to pay more for it than elsewhere. The figures are telling. In the 1720s Britain re-exported about 20 percent of its sugar to foreign markets and during the last quarter of the eighteenth century this percentage had fallen to less than 5 percent. The planters in the Dutch West Indies, on the other hand, did

---

[4] Kenneth Morgan, *Slavery, Atlantic Trade and the British Economy, 1660–1800* (Cambridge, 2000), p. 75.

[5] B. L. Anderson, "The Lancashire Bill System and Its Liverpool Practioners," in W. H. Chaloner and Barrie M. Ratcliffe (eds.), *Trade and Transport; Essays in Economic History in Honour of T. S. Willan* (Manchester, 1977), p. 59–97, esp. p. 80.

[6] Stanley L. Engerman, "British Imperialism in a Mercantilist Age, 1492–1849: Conceptual Issues and Empirical Problems," in *Revista de Historia Económica*, 16 (1998): 195–231, especially pp. 206–207. "Thus the protective provision of the Acts [of Navigation] led to some redistribution from British consumers to planters in the British West Indies...."

not receive such a subsidy and had to compete with the most cost-effective producers anywhere, resulting in relatively low profits in the slave trade as well as in plantation agriculture.[7]

The plantation slave economies in the New World received a new lease of life after the American War of Independence. As demonstrated by Table 1, in the Spanish Caribbean, Cuba finally became a major producer of sugar and coffee. In Brazil, exports of these items, particularly coffee, grew from the mid 1770s. The French Caribbean also experienced an upswing in plantation output due to the development of Tobago as well as further expansion in St. Domingue, and the British Caribbean increased its production by incorporating Trinidad, Berbice, Essequibo and Demerara. In response, the slave trade increased beyond pre-war levels. Even the smallest slaving nation, Denmark, carried more slaves, partly by exploiting its neutral position in the major wars of the period. The economic future of American South looked bright for those willing to exploit new areas and invest in cotton. "Aggregate slave imports into the Americas," it has been argued, "reached an all-time decadal high between 1781 and 1790.... Peacetime prices of sugar, cotton, indigo and tobacco continued to rise.... Clearly, the increase in demand exceeded the increase in supply, and demand pressures, previously felt by non-British and non-French areas only in time of war, now became steady and permanent."[8]

The Dutch alone proved unable to respond to this new Atlantic challenge. They failed to develop a new plantation frontier and they failed to take advantage of the increased demand for slaves outside their own colonies. Between 1785 and 1805 the value of the Suriname exports of sugar, coffee and cotton declined by 20 percent despite rising sugar prices, and the Dutch slave trade fell 75 percent.[9] Why were the Dutch such an exception? Usually, the reasons for this unique decline are attributed to international political factors outside Dutch control such as the loss of the Dutch neutrality during the War of American Independence and the Anglo–French Wars after 1795. However, the poor performance of the Dutch plantation sector and the Dutch slave trade during ten years of peace between 1784 and 1794 suggest that

[7] Seymour Drescher, *Econocide: British Slavery in the Era of Abolition* (Pittsburgh, 1977), pp. 52–53. David Richardson, "Profits in the Liverpool Slave Trade: the Accounts of William Davenport, 1757–1784," in Roger Anstey and P. E. H. Hair (eds.), *Liverpool, the African Slave Trade, and Abolition. Essays to Illustrate Current Knowledge and Research* (Liverpool, 1976), p. 80, mentions a profit rate of 8 percent. That is more than double the rate of the *Middelburgsche Commercie Compagnie* operating between 1732 and 1803 according to Roger Anstey, *The Atlantic Slave Trade and British Abolition, 1760–1810* (London, 1974), pp. 38–57, esp. p. 57.

[8] David Eltis, *Economic Growth and the Ending of the Transatlantic Slave Trade* (New York, 1987), p. 34.

[9] Van Stipriaan, *Surinaams contrast*, 35 (figure 2) and Johannes Menne Postma, *The Dutch in the Atlantic Slave Trade, 1600–1815* (Cambridge, 1990), p. 295 (Table 12.2).

TABLE 1. *Plantation Agriculture in the Caribbean, 1770–1850*

	Period	British Caribbean	French Caribbean	Cuba/Puerto Rico	Dutch Guianas
Surface in km^2	c. 1775	18,052	30,631	128,549	378,234
	c. 1850	238,109	2,881	119,819	163,265
Total population	c. 1775	410,849	462,091	200,883	95,000
Slave population	c. 1775	360,682	408,500	59,041	71,776
Slave population at emancipation		(1834) 541,130	(1848) 185,000	(1886) 240,000	(1863) 36,484
Sugar production	c. 1775	75,574	84,073	12,603	9,203
	c. 1850	137,235	36,195	327,280	14,786
Coffee production	c. 1775	900	42,833		9,427
	c. 1850	3,405	262	25,146	298
Value plantation output in £ 1000	c. 1770	2,669	3,819	220	573
	c. 1850	5,294	1,070	10,420	517
Average sugar output, kg per slave	19th century	242B/926G		(1860) 3,000	941
Average coffee output, kg per slave	19th century	187J/329G			105
Average cotton output, kg per slave	19th century	234G			87

Notes: B = Barbados, G = Guiana, J = Jamaica

Sources: Alex van Stipriaan, *Surinaams contrast: Roofbouw en overleven in een Caraïbische plantagekolonie 1750–1863* (Leiden, 1993), pp. 28, 29, 133, 139, 143; David Eltis, "The Slave Economies of the Caribbean: Structure, Performance, Evolution and Significance," in Franklin W. Knight (ed.), *The UNESCO General History of the Caribbean, vol. III, The Slave Societies of the Caribbean* (London, 1997).

the Dutch private sector was unable to cope with the new challenges of the Atlantic slave economy. It was in the slave trade that the failure of the private sector in the Netherlands showed most clearly. All other national carriers not only managed to transport more slaves but also to decrease shipboard mortality. Only Dutch slavers experienced a decline in number of slaves carried and an increase in mortality.[10] Dutch slave vessels supplied so few slaves to the Dutch colonies that the planters of Berbice decided to legally admit British and North American slavers in the colony until The Hague reversed the decision. Even the introduction of the Dolben Act restricting the number of slaves on board British vessels and, therefore, British ability to compete did nothing to increase the Dutch slave trade.[11]

In Suriname itself, the number of sugar plantations barely increased in this period and few sugar plantations were started in new areas of the colony between 1785 and 1805 in spite of the prospect such areas offered for increased output. The many new British planters in the Dutch colony of Demerara did much better: Their slaves produced on average twice as much cotton as those of their Dutch colleagues, as demonstrated by Table 1.[12] On the new slavery frontier, British planters were able to produce sugar without the protection of their products on the British home market. In addition, British planters were able to produce cotton more competitively than the Dutch without a protected domestic market of any kind. Thus cotton production in Demerara boomed as soon as the British had conquered this colony in 1796. It became the most rapidly expanding slave colony ever in the course of the next decade. Slave imports increased from an average of 397 per year in the period between 1785–1795 to more than ten times that number under British rule.[13] The Dutch response to the new stimulative environment was negligible by comparison.

With such a discrepancy in Dutch and British responses, it is, as already noted, striking that it was Britain that took the step of abolishing the slave trade and emancipating the slaves and not the Dutch. Of all the slave-trading nations in Europe, the Dutch could have abolished the trade with the least cost and dislocation because their traffic had virtually ceased to exist after the end of the fourth Anglo–Dutch war in 1784. Yet official abolition of the Dutch slave trade occurred only after Britain had brought pressure to bear on the Dutch government. And when the trade was abolished Dutch colonial

---

[10] Robin Haines and Ralph Sholomowitz, "Explaining Mortality Decline in the Eighteenth-Century British Slave Trade," *Economic History Review*, 53 (2000): 263 and Postma, *The Dutch in the Atlantic Slave Trade*, 252.

[11] W. S. Unger, "Bijdragen tot de geschiedenis van de Nederlandse slavenhandel. I, bekopt overzicht van de Nederlandse slavenhandel in het algemeen," *Economisch-Historisch Jaarboek*, 26 (1956): 165.

[12] Van Stipriaan, *Surinaams contrast*, 143.

[13] Drescher, *Econocide*, 172–173.

officials in Suriname did not even fully comply with the law. It was fortunate for slaves and abolitionists alike that Suriname was a colony without an expanding plantation sector and the demand for slaves could not even offset the decline of the slave population. The Suriname planters certainly had less buying power than their counterparts in Cuba and Brazil. Britain was able to put an end to imports into Suriname by forcing the Dutch government to institute a system of slave registration in 1826, effectively stopping further illegal imports. By contrast, Brazilian and Cuban planters were able to continue to buy large numbers of slaves direct from Africa in the 1820s and 1830s and the same would have happened in British Guiana and Trinidad had Britain not enforced compliance with the abolition laws on its own colonies.[14] Slavery itself continued in Suriname to 1863, thirty years longer than in the British Americas. Yet its continuation did not lead to an increase in total output of the Dutch plantations; at best it only prevented decline as shown in Table 1. Toward the end, Suriname planters were subjected to metropolitan pressures to increase food rations, improve slave housing and provide medical attention, particularly to pregnant women. The longer slavery in the Dutch West Indies lasted, the greater was the pressure to ameliorate conditions. Indeed the slave system in the Dutch Caribbean might well have been unique in the extensive protection it granted to slaves in the final years of slavery. Minimum standards for food, clothing and housing as well as a maximum number of working hours per week were defined, and the regulations were enforced. The colonial government even allowed the slaves to complain to the authorities in the case of non-compliance. Plantations had to close down when they could not afford the costs of the required improvements.[15]

During the post-slavery period after 1863 Suriname planters and slaves experienced the changes that had occurred in the British Caribbean thirty years earlier. At first, most plantations were able to continue operations because the emancipation law provided for an apprenticeship period of ten years during which the ex–field slaves had to remain on the plantations as opposed to four in the British Caribbean. In the Netherlands no influential abolitionist lobby capable of forcing the metropolitan government to abort the system of apprenticeship ever existed. Yet delayed slave emancipation in the Dutch colony could not prevent a repeat of the "flight from the plantations" that occurred in the rest of the Caribbean. In the British Caribbean in 1833 the abolitionists could still harbour the illusion that the liberation of the slaves would somehow coincide with an increase in income of both plantation owners and plantation workers. Thirty years later there could be

---

[14] G. Oostindie (ed.), *Fifty Years Later: Anti-Slavery, Capitalism and Modernity in the Dutch Orbit* (Leiden, 1995).

[15] Emmer, *The Dutch in the Atlantic Economy*, 167–179.

no doubt that an alternative workforce had to be in place before the period of apprenticeship ended.[16] The plantation sector in Suriname would have declined even more drastically if it had not had immediate access to an alternative labor supply in the form of Asian contract workers. British planters had no such option after the end of apprenticeship in 1838. British planters had initially continued to enjoy protective tariffs for their sugar, but they had no sustained access to Asian contract workers until 1850s, and of course there was no question of slaves arriving directly from Africa either before or after the abolition of slavery.

Parallels to British–Dutch differences in the slave Americas are apparent in nineteenth century Asia. As late as 1830 the Dutch instituted a taxation system on Java based on forced labour. The Dutch could perhaps institute such a system because free labour ideology had not yet gathered strength among the Dutch political elite. No doubt, a similar system of unfree labour would have greatly benefited the production of cash crops in British India. However, that would have been unthinkable in view of the abolitionist ideology prevalent in Britain and the country's self-appointed role as the foremost "moral" nation in the world. Without forced labour, the cultivation of sugar and cotton for export overseas at competitive prices in India was not possible and India never managed to compete with the New World in the production of sugar. By contrast, by the early 1830s Java was already producing more sugar than Suriname. Similar systems of forced or semi-forced labour were used in the colonies of the other continental colonial powers and the absence of forced labour in India demonstrates a British *Sonderweg* at this time. Thus the suppression of the slave trade, the subsequent abolition of slavery and the absence of forced labour in India increased the costs of producing tropical export crops in the British colonies. The British economy could absorb this disadvantage because it was growing in other areas both at home and internationally. Dutch policies did not completely fall into line with the British until after 1870. Only then was the British *Sonderweg* over.

How does this fresh look at Atlantic history affect existing interpretations of Atlantic history and the development of slavery in the Americas? First, the history of the Dutch Atlantic confirms the observation by Adam Smith that the wealth of the British colonies in the New World, and by implication the extension and intensification of slavery, "in a great measure" was based on "the great riches of England, of which part has overflowed . . . upon these colonies."[17] The Dutch entry into the slave Americas in the 1620s occurred when the Dutch economy was at its strongest relative to its main European competitors. That entry was highly aggressive in that it involved attempted

---

[16] Ibid., 143–165.
[17] Stanley L. Engerman, "France, Britain and the Economic Growth of Colonial North America," in John McCusker and Kenneth Morgan (eds.), *The Early Modern Atlantic Economy* (Cambridge, 2000), pp. 227–249, esp. p. 231 (citation Adam Smith).

conquest of the slave holdings of one of those competitors. The attempt ultimately failed and, as a result, the Dutch drive to establish plantations was set back several decades and put the Dutch behind the English and French in the establishment of Caribbean sugar colonies in the mid seventeenth century. Nevertheless, no other European power could have made such an effort in the first half of the century, and without the pool of capital from which to draw funds for military expenditures and investment in plantations, Dutch participation in the creation of the slave Americas would not have been possible. For several decades after it became Dutch, Suriname evolved much as did the other sugar colonies of the Caribbean. In the first half of the 1750s, slave prices were actually higher there than in St. Domingue and Jamaica, suggesting very high slave productivity.[18] In the late 1760s, slave prices had fallen behind those in the western Caribbean sugar-growing areas, but were still well above the average for the Americas as a whole. Thereafter, they were never again to reach such levels relative to the rest of the Americas. Nevertheless, as late as 1770, the value of total output in the major Dutch plantation colony was approximately one-third that of the very much larger British Caribbean and contributed nearly eight percent of the total value of plantation output in the Caribbean as a whole.[19]

In terms of the issue raised in the Introduction of this volume, it would appear that after their false start in Brazil and their conquest of Suriname, the Dutch behaved no differently to other European powers that had American slave colonies. If Suriname had remained English, or had become French or Portuguese after 1664, it is unlikely that its position in the hierarchy of the slave Americas would have been much different in 1770. The situation thereafter is less clear. By the late eighteenth century, however – a century and a half after the attempt to take Brazil – the corollary to the situation that had held between 1670 and 1770 had developed. Economic growth in the Netherlands peaked between 1580 and 1620. After 1670 a period of stagnation set in, lasting for about two centuries. Adam Smith, writing in 1776, was of the opinion that the Netherlands had "acquired the full compliment of riches which the nature of its soils and climate and its situation with respect to other countries, allowed it to acquire." The Netherlands had accumulated so much capital that profits were driven close to zero and the Dutch economy could advance no further.[20] The stagnation of the Dutch economy during the final decades of the eighteenth century had a strong impact on Dutch responses to new opportunities to further expand the slave Americas. While the Dutch West Indies outgrew the Dutch metropolitan economy in these years, it was only on the basis of exploitation of the Dutch

---

[18] See the Eltis and Richardson essay (Chapter 6) in this volume.
[19] David Eltis, "The Slave Economies of the Caribbean," 113.
[20] Jan de Vries, "Dutch Economic Growth in Comparative-Historical Perspective, 1500–2000," *De Economist*, 148/4 (2000), pp. 443–467 (Smith citation p. 451).

Caribbean by planters and investors who were not Dutch. As the Dutch fell short of exploiting their section of the Atlantic, barriers to foreign penetration of their plantation colonies crumbled. But even with foreign investors and foreign planters, the Dutch lagged behind the Spanish, Brazilians, as well as the British, and until 1791, the French, too. All these non-Dutch slave economies expanded dramatically, and the growth overall of the slave Americas was only temporarily checked by the successful rebellion of slaves in the largest slave colony of the New World.

The fact that until at least 1770, Suriname would likely have evolved in much the same way regardless of which European power was in control does not dispose of the argument that some institutions unique to the Dutch had a significant impact on the evolution of the slave Americas. Institutional considerations seem particularly important at the beginning and at the end of Dutch imperial activities. Prior to 1665, the history of the Dutch in the Atlantic shows how a purely mercantile expansion in the Atlantic differed from a policy spearheaded by a central state in shaping the foundations of a maritime empire. The policy of the English state, highly centralized by Dutch standards, was to direct shipping into trades that were relatively dangerous rather than to low-risk bulk trades. "Government action in the 1560s and 1570s helped to commit England to a relatively small fleet, relatively large ships, and relatively high costs of operating those highly defensible ships."[21] The Dutch had no comparable policy, a factor in their defeats in Brazil and North America. The Dutch elite were not willing to match the defence efforts of its opponents. Relatively low shipping costs were of no avail in the face of these policy differences, and in any event toward the end of the seventeenth century the Dutch advantage in the productivity of maritime transport had eroded.[22] Only the British built up a navy that not only could protect all possessions in the Atlantic, but could also harm or take away the overseas colonies of others – those of Spain, France and the Netherlands. What William III could achieve as king in Britain was not possible in his role as *stadhouder* in the Netherlands. Supported by a highly efficient internal revenue system, the British Navy by 1780 had four times as many ships and men as the Dutch.[23] A different government structure might have led to a different outcome in Brazil and an earlier Dutch move into the Caribbean.

In the aftermath of the onset of the relative Dutch decline in the slave Americas previously described, there emerged a second major institutional impact on the Dutch experience with slavery. As argued in the Introduction to this volume, abolition affected different regions in the Americas in very

[21] Richard W. Unger, "The Tonnage of Europe's Merchants Fleets, 1300–1800," *American Neptune*, 52 (1992): 259.

[22] David Eltis, *The Rise of African Slavery in the Americas* (Cambridge, 2000), pp. 114–136.

[23] Wolfgang Reinhard, *Parasit oder Partner? Europäische Wirtschaft und Neue Welt, 1500–1800* (Münster, 1977), p. 122.

different ways and may be viewed as an institutional constraint on a slave system that in 1800 was still expanding, and which could still draw on Africa for a labor supply. The Dutch Americas were among the first regions to feel the effect of the ending of the slave trade. Indeed because of the French wars, Suriname was largely cut off from Africa from the early 1790s. Moreover, the poor performance of the Dutch domestic economy meant that the Dutch abolitionists could hold out no hopes of replacing the slave trade by any alternative trade, be it inside or outside Europe. Suppressing the slave trade and banning slavery would diminish their overseas trade not reorient it as in the British case. Illegal arrivals after 1815 were trivial compared to those arriving in Cuba and Brazil, and while slavery itself endured to the 1860s, the Suriname labor force declined in absolute terms and was then, as we have seen, protected to some degree by Dutch amelioration policy. Both of these factors reduced labour input to the Dutch plantation sector. The long-run effect was to reduce the relative value of Suriname plantation output to less than three percent of total Caribbean output in 1850 – from nearly eight percent in 1770.[24]

One further powerful shaping factor on the Dutch role in the Americas was the absence of a supply of young, mobile people willing to work and settle overseas. The British and Portuguese probably accounted for over 80 percent of the shipping of migrants and at least two out of three of the migrants themselves before the nineteenth century. By contrast the Dutch and the French combined sent fewer migrants to the New World than the Spanish. Without such a supply of settlers, the Dutch expansion in the Atlantic took on a different character. Most of the Dutch viewed their stay overseas as a period of temporary exile, comparable to making a long voyage on a ship. However, differences between the Dutch and English migratory patterns are much less significant if we take into account Asia as well as the Americas. The Dutch could in fact command large numbers of young, mobile men to become sailors and soldiers overseas. Between 1600 and 1800 the Dutch East India Company was able to send more than 1 million of them to Asia, of whom only one-third returned alive. These figures indicate that the Dutch excelled in sending men to the tropics on a temporary basis. Their system of recruiting poor, young, unmarried men from Scandinavia, Germany and northern France was unrivalled. Dutch merchants exploited the lethal trade *niche* with the tropical zones in Asia, because they had enough men to do so.[25] If we include all overseas migrants, or at least migrants passing through Dutch ports, then the Dutch rank in numbers along with the British and Portuguese outflow much more closely than the previous comments might

---

[24] Eltis, "The Slave Economies of the Caribbean," 117–18.
[25] Jan Lucassen, "The Netherlands, the Dutch, and Long-Distance Migration in the Late Sixteenth to Early Nineteenth Centuries," in Nicolas Canny (ed.), *Europeans on the Move. Studies on European Migration, 1500–1800* (Oxford, 1994), pp. 153–191.

suggest. The three together probably account for at least nine out of ten of all European overseas departures.

Was the absence of Dutch settlers in the Atlantic a function of differences between Dutch and English institutions? This seems unlikely given that there was an underlying similarity in labor markets and land tenure arrangements in the two countries. The Netherlands was the first country to break the trend of lower real wages caused by rising populations and rising prices. After 1580 a widening difference between real wages in the Netherlands and England developed, lasting to the middle of the eighteenth century. During the first half-century after 1575, when the growth spurt set in, the nominal wage for unskilled labour increased from 0.28 guilders to 0.73 guilders. As prices rose much more slowly, the increase in real wages was at least 50 percent. The Netherlands was flooded with migrant labour from abroad. There was little danger that these migrant labourers would bring down wages as their numbers were more than matched by the rapidly rising demand for labour. The higher wages in the Netherlands made returns in the New World much less attractive to the Dutch than to the English whose wage levels long lagged behind those of the Dutch. This ensured a largely non-American destination for servants leaving Dutch ports. Indeed, most of those leaving for overseas destinations were not Dutch. Like the Portuguese, the Dutch dispatched mainly men, although they did not mix sexually with non-European populations as much as did the Portuguese. They also travelled much more to tropical and sub-tropical climates than did the British. Such a combination ensured that Dutch migration had much less demographic impact on recipient societies than did its British counterpart.

These considerations hint at a general conclusion on the factor endowments versus imported institutions debate. The major expansions and changes of direction in the economic development of the Americas coincided with shifts in the economic balance of power within Europe. The first century of European expansion saw the collision of the richest and most powerful parts of Europe and the Americas and the beginnings of the first transatlantic plantation complex. The emergence of the Dutch to commercial pre-eminence in the seventeenth century witnessed a large expansion of their overseas activity but one that was ultimately directed away from the Americas, because of Dutch failure in Brazil. This phase of European overseas activity was something of a hybrid between Spanish and later English activities. It generated high-value merchandise from the east that could stand the high transportation costs, though such goods were not quite in the same category as the precious metals from Spanish America. Yet unlike the latter, many of these goods were the result of agricultural activity – like the later exports of the major plantation systems of the Americas. In the course of the seventeenth century, transportation costs shifted lower and at the same time the demographic disaster that had engulfed the native population of the Americas continued to erode what was, from the European perspective, a potential supply of labor. By the time the English emerged as Europe's leading overseas commercial power to establish the leading plantation economies in Caribbean and mainland North America, the major sugar producers of the Americas had switched almost completely from Amerindian to African labor. For the English, as well as the French and several minor plantation powers that followed them, African slavery and all the characteristics of what Curtin has termed the plantation complex became possible in a way that was not possible before 1660 when the Spanish and Dutch were launching their overseas ventures. From this perspective, the Spanish, Dutch, and then English and French New World initiatives that followed in sequence over two centuries were shaped by the environmental and economic realities of the Atlantic and the Americas, rather than by the domestic institutions that these nationalities may have brought with them. To become a major player overseas, it was necessary for a nation to have a powerful European economic base, but once that was in place, institutional differences between these bases were not of central importance in influencing the economic development of the Americas. For the Dutch, the domestic economic miracle took place well before economic opportunities of the wider Atlantic became attractive.

It is nevertheless possible that a different Dutch policy in the 1620s and 1630s might have brought forward the sugar revolution of the Caribbean. The resources that the Dutch committed to Brazil for nearly three decades could perhaps have accelerated the establishment of the first Caribbean plantation complex if they had been committed to Barbados instead. It is, however, not at all clear if the decision to conquer Brazil can be traced back to Dutch domestic institutions. The Dutch commitment to a large chartered company as opposed to the scattered piecemeal settlement projects of the English is suggestive of differences, as are the variations between Dutch and English administrative and government decision-making structures. But these perhaps are not conclusive. At the other end of the slave plantation era, different policies might have staved off plantation decline (and thus aided higher economic growth in the Americas). The Dutch may not have embraced abolition of the slave trade and then slavery, but neither did they follow the Spanish and Brazilian strategy of encouraging, or at least tolerating, a virtually unimpeded slave traffic with Africa. The land frontier that existed in Suriname and the continued sugar production (on the basis of Indian indentured servants) after the abolition of slavery suggest that such a policy could have provided the basis of increased sugar output in the nineteenth century. A less drastic option would have been to follow the French example of allowing more limited slave arrivals, or more precisely slave arrivals for a more limited period. Even the refusal to introduce amelioration policies for the existing slave population would have helped the planters and therefore economic growth as conventionally measured. Again the question arises of whether the impossibility of such counterfactuals can be traced back to Dutch institutions or merely to the overwhelming pressures of the British Foreign Office and Admiralty. One more certain conclusion is that whatever the importance of imported institutions on the pace and timing of the economic development of the Americas, institutional considerations were important in determining which Europeans helped repeople the Americas as well as the distribution of power and resources among the European powers that colonised the Americas.

PART II

PATTERNS OF SLAVE USE

3

Mercantile Strategies, Credit Networks, and Labor Supply in the Colonial Chesapeake in Trans-Atlantic Perspective

Lorena S. Walsh

Everyone agrees that bound laborers were brought to the Chesapeake primarily for the purpose of raising tobacco. Consequently it is rather surprising that the eighteenth century scholars have neglected to examine in any detail the relationship between the supply of bound labor and the fortunes of the region's staple. Recently compiled databases on the Chesapeake slave and servant trades, and now information on staple prices, and on tobacco, slave, and servant traders allow us to explore the links for the first time.[1] This essay first reassesses the volume of imported bound laborers, the relationship between staple prices and labor supply, and the interplay between the trades in tobacco and bound laborers. It then examines in greater detail the strategies followed by merchants from Britain's major ports, and the

[1] The database is described in Lorena S. Walsh, "The Chesapeake Slave Trade: Regional Patterns, African Origins, and Some Implications," *William and Mary Quarterly*, 3rd ser., 58 (2001): 139–170. For merchants see Jacob M. Price, "One Family's Empire: The Russell-Lee-Clerk Connection in Maryland, Britain, and India, 1707–1857," *Maryland Historical Magazine*, 72 (1977): 1–44; "Sheffield v. Starke: Institutional Experimentation in the London-Maryland Trade ca. 1696–1706," *Business History*, 28 (1986): 19–39; Price, *Perry of London: A Family and A Firm on the Seaborne Frontier, 1615–1753* (Cambridge, MA, 1992); Price and Paul G. E. Clemens, "A Revolution of Scale in Overseas Trade: British Firms in the Chesapeake Trade," *Journal of Economic History* 47 (1987): 1–43; Edward C. Papenfuse, *In Pursuit of Profit: The Annapolis Merchants in the Era of the American Revolution, 1763–1805* (Baltimore, 1975); David Richardson, *The Bristol Slave Traders: A Collective Portrait* (Bristol, 1985); Richardson (ed.), *Bristol, Africa and the Eighteenth-Century Slave Trade to America*, 3 vols. (Bristol, 1986); Kenneth Morgan, "Bristol Merchants and the Colonial Trades, 1748–1783," Ph.D. thesis, Oxford University, 1983; Morgan, *Bristol and the Atlantic Trade in the Eighteenth Century* (Cambridge, Eng., 1993); W. E. Minchinton, "The slave trade of Bristol with the British mainland colonies in North America, 1699–1770," in Roger Anstey and P. E. H. Hair (eds.), *Liverpool, the African Slave Trade, and Abolition: Essays to illustrate current knowledge and research* (Liverpool, 1976), pp. 39–59; Minchinton (ed.), "The Virginia Letters of Isaac Hobhouse, Merchant of Bristol," *Virginia Magazine of History and Biography*, 66 (1958): 278–88; and David Hancock, *Citizens of the World: London Merchants and the Integration of the British Atlantic Community, 1735–1785* (Cambridge, 1995).

differing terms by which indentured servants, convicts, and slaves were sold in the Chesapeake. Finally it discusses some of the implications for the distribution of bound labor within sub-regions of the Tobacco Coast and among purchasers of varying wealth.

I

Slaves clearly predominated among bound laborers in the eighteenth century Chesapeake, although there is less agreement about the relative contributions of imports and of natural increase to this result. By the early 1690s slaves outnumbered servants by more than three to one even in Maryland, a colony which was less well supplied with slaves than Virginia throughout the seventeenth century. And by the 1720s indentured servants were no longer a significant component of the bound labor force in most of the region. Across the eighteenth century few free English men and almost no women chose to finance migration to the Chesapeake through indenture except for a spurt of emigration in the closing years of the colonial era. Southern Ireland and British prisons became the main sources for unskilled European laborers. Although no firm estimates of annual imports are available, historians agree that the supply of indentured servants was not enough to meet planters' needs for cheap labor. The transition to slaves in the skilled bound labor force did lag behind the transition in unskilled labor, and the Chesapeake continued to afford a market for both servants and convicts across the century. However many planters came to prefer slaves over British felons or Catholic Irish; these less desirable workers were increasingly relegated to the region's more marginal labor markets.[2]

Slavery and servitude continued to coexist up to the Revolution to an extent that has not always been appreciated. For the region as a whole, between 1698 and 1775, bound Europeans and involuntary Africans appear to have been imported in approximately equal numbers, about 100,000 of each. These different sorts of unfree workers were distributed unequally among various parts of the Tobacco Coast, and differences in destination lead to questions about the inter-relationship between sub-regional tobacco trades, merchants' strategies, and planters' preferences. Virginia planters moved closer to complete reliance on slaves for both unskilled and skilled labor than did Maryland planters. Data on slave imports are firmer than on imports of indentured servants and convicts. The available evidence does not permit much more than informed guesses about the numbers of indentured

---

[2] David Galenson, *White Servitude in Colonial America: An Economic Analysis* (Cambridge, 1981); Russell R. Menard, "From Servants to Slaves: The Transformation of the Chesapeake Labor System," *Southern Studies*, 16 (1977): 355–390; Farley Grubb and Tony Stitt, "The Liverpool Emigrant Servant Trade and the Transition to Slave Labor in the Chesapeake, 1697–1707: Market Adjustments to War," *Explorations in Economic History*, 31 (1994): 376–405.

servants and convicts brought into Virginia between 1698 and 1775. If one accepts the most generous estimates of imports of European laborers, then equal numbers of servants and slaves were likely brought into that colony, but there is reason to suppose that the more generous estimates for bound European migrants overstate servant migration to Virginia.[3] More information is available for Maryland, where many more European workers were imported than Africans. During the eighteenth century about three European servants or convicts were probably imported for every African slave, and between 1761 and 1775 the ratio rose to more than four to one.[4] However, because servants and convicts who survived their terms of service did eventually gain their freedom, whereas enslaved Africans and their descendants were retained in perpetual bondage, even in Maryland slaves were the majority of bound laborers. This is true despite the fact that servants predominated among imported workers. In 1755, the only year for which there is a census for Maryland, there were just over 63,000 unfree laborers in the colony. Indentured servants and convicts made up 14% of the total bound workforce with the majority concentrated in areas with mixed farming; these groups accounted for 19% of adult laborers, but only 6% of bound child workers.

---

[3] Estimates of net European migration, bound and free, to Virginia and Maryland between 1700 and 1775 are from 65,000 to 100,000. (Galenson, *White Servitude in Colonial America*, 216–17; Russell R. Menard, "Migration, Ethnicity, and the Rise of an Atlantic Economy: The Re-Peopling of British America, 1600–1790," in Rudloph J. Vecoli and Suzanne M. Sinke (eds.), *A Century of European Migrations, 1830–1930* [Urbana, IL, 1991], pp. 58–77). The estimates of European migration, especially that from the British Isles, are not well grounded empirically, and should be read as absolute minimums. Revised estimates for the mainland colonies as a whole and a critique of the existing literature are presented in P. M. G. Harris, *The History of Human Populations: Volume II, Migration Urbanization, and Structural Change* (Westport, CT, 2003), ch. 1. The most recent estimate of the number of imported convicts is about 40,000 [A. Roger Ekirch, *Bound for America: The Transportation of British Convicts to the Colonies, 1718–1775* (Oxford, 1987), pp. 115–16]. If convicts comprised 40% of transported bound European laborers sent to Virginia, as they did in shipments to better documented Maryland, then the total of servants entering the Chesapeake would be about 60,000. However in the available lists of emigrating indentured servants, significantly fewer chose to go to Virginia than to Maryland. (Galenson, *White Servitude in Colonial America*, 224–27; Bernard Bailyn, *Voyagers to the West: A Passage in the Peopling of America on the Eve of the Revolution* [New York, 1986], pp. 220–21). African imports are from Walsh, "The Chesapeake Slave Trade."

[4] These ratios are minimal ones calculated from the number of servants and convicts reported in extant Maryland Naval Office shipping lists with the number of Africans appearing in the Chesapeake slave trade database. The latter supplements extant Naval Office records with data on additional shipments of slaves found in other sources. There are gaps in the Naval Office records, especially for the Potomac, Patuxent, and Pocomoke Districts, and no attempt has been made to compensate for missing returns by collecting supplemental information on servant imports from other sources. In addition, the Naval Office records mention only three ships as carrying redemptioners, but there were clearly more. Newspaper notices appear in the *Maryland Gazette* advertising the sale of redemptioners carried on other ships who were identified only as "passengers" in the naval office returns.

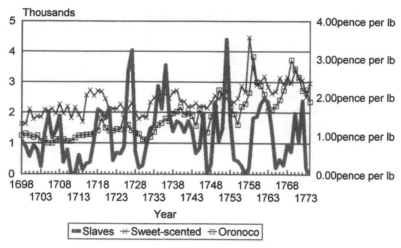

FIGURE I. Chesapeake Slave Imports and Tobacco Prices

II

The broad overall pattern is both clear and, in outline at least, unsurprising. Comparison of annual labor imports with tobacco prices demonstrates that labor imports were related to planters' greater or lesser ability to pay for additional workers (Fig. 1).[5] The relationship is, however, far from perfect. International warfare in 1702 to 1713, 1739 to 1748, and 1754 to 1763 disrupted both the staple and labor trades to varying degrees. War-induced shortfalls of new workers were followed by greatly augmented imports once peace was concluded. These additional workers contributed to subsequent surges in tobacco exports, leading to falling tobacco prices and a reduced demand for more labor. Such a pattern constitutes the familiar, Chesapeake-centered story well known to economic historians. Closer examination, however, suggests that other circumstances throughout the Atlantic trading system also affected the supply of servants, convicts, and slaves and did so differentially.

Among European migrants to Maryland, about 60% came voluntarily as indentured servants. The remaining 40% were convicts transported involuntarily. Forty-five percent of the voluntary immigrants came from Southern Ireland, and thirty-four percent left from London. Much smaller proportions came from Bristol, Liverpool, the outports, Northern Ireland, and Scotland. The supply of indentured servants was erratic, with peaks occurring in 1745, 1753–55, and in the 1770s, and troughs in 1747–50 and at the end of the Seven Year's War (Fig. 2). Conditions in Britain and Ireland rather than

---

[5] Tobacco prices are compiled from the author's research in progress on Chesapeake plantation agriculture. Annual slave imports are computed from the Chesapeake slave trade database.

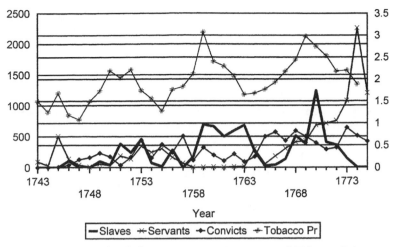

FIGURE 2. Maryland Slaves, Convicts, Servants, and Tobacco Prices

planter demand largely determined servant supply. Prospective servants, for example, most likely opted in the late 1750s not to risk an ocean voyage in the midst of war, or else found alternative employment in the army, navy, or in jobs abandoned by soldiers and sailors in Britain more attractive than emigration.[6] On the whole, upturns in servant migration lagged behind rises in the price of tobacco. This suggests that it took some time for prospective servants and servant recruiters to respond to economic shifts along the Tobacco Coast. The surge in voluntary servant migration between 1769 and 1775 occurred in a period of falling tobacco prices and reflected a spate of emigration fever in Britain rather than improved short-run prospects in the Chesapeake.[7]

The supply of convicts fluctuated less than that of indentured servants. This was doubtless because merchants who traded in this form of involuntary labor were usually paid a subsidy for transporting them, either by the British Treasury or by individual localities. London contractors shipped just over half of the convicts and Bristol dealers another third. As long as felons could be sold to Chesapeake planters for more than the cost of transport less the subsidy, merchants had an incentive to continue carrying them. And with only Pennsylvania offering a small alternative market for convicts, there were few options for switching to other regions when tobacco prices slumped. In economist's terms, the supply of convicts was much more inelastic than the

---

[6] This argument, advanced by Grubb and Stitt, "The Liverpool Emigrant Servant Trade," for Queen Anne's War, would presumably apply as well to the Seven Year's War. Since convicts continued to be brought to the Chesapeake during the Seven Year's War, shipping was likely available had servants chosen to emigrate.

[7] Bailyn, *Voyagers to the West.*

supply of servants or slaves. Prospective purchasers could thus count on a reliable supply of convicts being available, which was not the case with voluntary servants.[8]

III

Trans-Atlantic commerce in both labor and colonial produce became increasingly specialized during the colonial era. In the later seventeenth and early eighteenth centuries, the supply of unfree labor was closely connected to the tobacco trade. London merchants predominated, and many of the larger dealers invested in all facets of Chesapeake commerce, purchasing and marketing tobacco, extending credit, and supplying planters with both indentured servants and slaves. As Bristol, Liverpool, and Glasgow merchants began competing aggressively for shares of expanding Chesapeake tobacco and labor markets in the second quarter of the eighteenth century, specialization became the norm. In all the major British ports, the majority of merchants concentrated on only one or two facets of an increasingly complex trans-Atlantic trade. Most British tobacco merchants confined their dealings to the staple and occasional small shipments of indentured servants. London merchants were the primary suppliers of credit. The convict trade became the province of a few specialist London and Bristol contractors. The business of recruiting indentured servants in England also became concentrated in a few hands, and the trade in servants from Southern Ireland was conducted by an entirely different set of merchants who had few or no connections to tobacco. The transportation and sale of slaves fell largely to groups of Bristol and Liverpool merchants who developed complex trading networks between Africa, the Caribbean, and the North American mainland, and for whom the Chesapeake was not the main market. No English slave traders specialized solely in the Chesapeake. Glasgow tobacco merchants eschewed investment in the slave trade altogether, and were but marginally involved in transporting servants and convicts. Yet some interconnections remained, producing some unintended outcomes that had important implications for the development of Chesapeake society. The rest of the essay examines the marketing of first, slaves, and second, convicts/servants in an attempt to uncover hidden patterns of migration.

IV

The factors influencing the supply of slaves were the most complicated and trans-Atlantic in nature. In the Americas, other colonies offered larger

---

[8] Ekirch, *Bound for America*; Kenneth Morgan, "The Organization of the Convict Trade to Maryland: Stevenson, Randolph and Cheston, 1768–1775," *William and Mary Quarterly*, 3rd ser., 42 (1985): 201–227; Farley Grubb, "The Transatlantic Market for British Convict Labor," *Journal of Economic History*, 60 (2000): 94–122.

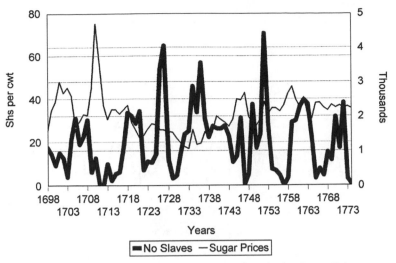

FIGURE 3. Chesapeake Slave Imports and Barbados Sugar Prices

markets for slaves than the Chesapeake. In addition to international wars, the trade in slaves was affected by changes within the British merchant community and in trading conditions in Africa, as well as in the course of the sugar and tobacco trades, and in the relative wealth of planters who grew these staples.

Conditions in the major West Indian slave markets strongly influenced the numbers of new captives sent to the Chesapeake. Until 1760 the pattern of Chesapeake slave imports inversely mirrors trends in Barbadian sugar prices, suggesting that slave traders shifted to the Chesapeake when demand for new laborers slumped in the islands (Fig. 3). Then the Chesapeake became an attractive alternative market, even if tobacco planters were not enjoying especially good times. In the later 1720s and early 1730s, for example, despite years of stagnating tobacco prices, substantial increases in the number of slaves brought to the Chesapeake occurred as a result of a dramatic decline in West Indian sugar prices.[9] Between 1698 and 1724 and again between 1753 and 1774, the West Indies was clearly the predominant market. Barbadian planters alone received three and a half times more slaves than did Chesapeake tobacco growers in the first and third quarters of the century, and Jamaica took even more. However, between 1725 and 1752 nearly as many Africans were shipped to the Chesapeake as to Barbados (Fig. 4).[10] Thus in the second quarter of the century, while the more recently

[9] Sugar prices are from John J. McCusker, *Rum and the American Revolution: The Rum Trade and the Balance of Payments of the Thirteen Continental Colonies* (New York, 1989), p. 1143.

[10] Annual African imports to Barbados were compiled from David Eltis, Stephen D. Behrendt, David Richardson, and Herbert S. Klein, *The Trans-Atlantic Slave Trade: A Database on*

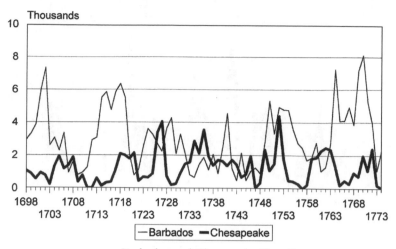

FIGURE 4. Barbados and Chesapeake Slave Imports

established sugar islands took the most imported Africans, the Chesapeake offered a significant alternative market to the oldest of the West Indian colonies.

The organization of the slave trade had a major impact on the timing and geography of the arrival of Africans within the Chesapeake, and some preliminary discussion of marketing and financing is called for. The preferred remittances were always bills of exchange, preferably readily negotiable ones drawn on London merchants. In the first half of the century specie was also accepted, albeit grudgingly, in part because the investors were loath to risk losing coin to shipwreck or capture on the return voyage to England. In addition, Virginia and Maryland rated the currency value of foreign coin above its sterling value in England. In theory agents should have found ways to discount payments made in real money to reflect the difference in value between coin in the colonies and in England, but in practice they apparently encountered difficulties. "The loss arising on Cash Remittances" remained a problem for investors.[11] Consequently agents were instructed to pay out

---

CD-ROM (Cambridge, 1999). The totals include imputed numbers. All voyages giving Barbados as the intended destination, including those whose later voyage history is unknown, were counted except for vessels known to have been captured or wrecked prior to delivering slaves. Assigning imports to a particular year when the vessel's date of departure from and date of return to England are known, but not the date of delivery in Barbados, sometimes necessitated a judgement call, as on the basis of the known chronology, delivery could plausibly have been made in either of two years. The Chesapeake series is from Walsh, "The Chesapeake Slave Trade." The number of Chesapeake imports was estimated somewhat more conservatively than those for Barbados.

[11] Trading practices are described in K. G. Davies, *The Royal African Company* (London, 1957); David W. Galenson, *Traders, Planters, and Slaves: Market Behavior in Early English*

locally as much specie received for slaves as they could for payment of duties, for costs of provisioning and repairing the ship, for payments to the ship's captain and for sailors' wages (part of which were paid in local currency in Chesapeake ports), and for the agent's commission. Agents then tried to buy bills of exchange with any remaining coin. Sometimes the investors had no option but to accept some tobacco as well (and in the most desperate cases even lumber and wheat), but usually only as a last resort when the most unpromising captives could be disposed of by no other means. Later in the century, specie was readily accepted, and sometimes as well sound Maryland paper currency or, in Virginia, well-established local merchants' notes. By then, the agents were using specie and local currency for direct purchases of tobacco, for which they received book credit in England, obviating the need to ship coin, and avoiding problems posed by the colony's over-valuation of hard money.[12]

America (Cambridge, Eng., 1986); Charles L. Killinger, III, "The Royal African Company Slave Trade to Virginia, 1689–1713," M.A. Thesis, College of William and Mary, 1969; Jacob M. Price, "Credit in the slave trade and plantation economies," in Barbara L. Solow (ed.), *Slavery and the Rise of the Atlantic System* (Cambridge, Eng., 1991), pp. 293–339; and David Richardson, "The British Empire and the Atlantic Slave Trade, 1660–1807," in P. D. Marshall (ed.), *The Oxford History of the British Empire, Vol. II, The Eighteenth Century* (Oxford, 1998), pp. 447–50.
    Some agents did make adjustments for differences in the valuation of coin. For example in 1727 Robert Carter discounted cash he received in payment for slaves at 20%, and in 1728 he purchased slaves with cash at a 15% discount. Carter to Pemberton, 23 August 1727, Robert Carter Letterbook, 1727–28, Robert ("King") Carter Papers, 3807, University of Virginia Library, Special Collections Department, Charlottesville, VA; Carter to [John Page] [21 May 1728], to Col. Braxton, 21 May 1728, to John Pemberton, 2 July 1728, Carter Letterbook, 1727–28, Virginia Historical Society, Richmond, VA. But in an account of a cargo of slaves sold in 1717, agent John Tayloe noted what sums were received in bills of exchange and what in cash, but apparently did not discount the cash. (Sales of the Charfield's Slaves, Stephen Loyde Account Book, MSS1T2118b1, Virginia Historical Society.) In 1720 some sailors on the London ship *Mercury* refused to take their wages in anything but sterling, even though the agents offered to increase sums paid in foreign coin by 10%. (Louis B. Wright (ed.), *Letters of Robert Carter, 1720–1727: The Commercial Interests of a Virginia Gentleman* [San Marino, CA, 1940] pp. 41–42). In 1737 John Carter was unable to buy bills of exchange with excess cash received for slaves sold for Cunliffe and Powell of Liverpool and purchased tobacco instead to avoid "the loss on cash remittances and on the contrary the saving of the Freight, Commission, and other Charges, as the Tobacco is your own." (Letter of 25 September 1737, John, Landon, and Charles Carter Letterbook, 1732–1781, Carter Papers, 4996, University of Virginia Library).
[12] Instructions to Chesapeake agents regarding forms of remittance to the Royal African Company are found in T70/58, PRO. Discussion of agency terms and forms of remittances actually sent appear in the Robert Carter Letterbooks, 1723–24, 1727–28, 1728–31, 1731–32, University of Virginia Library; Robert Carter Letterbooks, 1723–24, 1727–28, 1728–30, Virginia Historical Society; *Letters of Robert Carter, 1720–1727*; John, Landon, and Charles Carter Letterbook, 1732–1781; and Minchinton, "The Virginia Letters of Isaac Hobhouse." Terms of payment were published in advertisements of slave sales in the *Maryland Gazette* (Annapolis) from the 1750s and in the *Virginia Gazette* (Williamsburg) in the 1770s. On

English investors hoped to avoid selling slaves on credit, but here their interests diverged from the desires of both agents and planters. When credit sales could not be avoided, slave traders relied on their agents to sell only to purchasers who had sufficient reserves with British correspondents to back their bills of exchange, and obligated the agents to make good any bills that were protested. The Royal African Company ostensibly set the most inflexible terms. Slaves were to be sold for bills of exchange, and factors were obliged in theory to make good any protested bills within twelve months from the time of the sale. In practice, factors seem usually to have taken two to three years to collect outstanding debts from a given voyage, and some were never collected. Other traders, particularly those from the outports, explicitly authorized their agents to extend credit. When the number of slaves imported outstripped the number of buyers who maintained positive balances in Britain, or when ships arrived late in the season, slave traders allowed their agents to sell some captives on credit, accepting bills of exchange payable not at the usual sixty days after sight, but six to twelve months later. And often agents sold less desirable slaves on credit despite orders to the contrary, needing to shift the risks of death or escape of unwilling captives and the costs of their maintenance onto buyers as quickly as possible.[13] In addition, the agents had a further incentive to make credit sales because planters were willing to pay up to ten percent more for slaves sold on credit than for those bought for ready pay, thus increasing the amount the agent received in commissions.[14]

attempts to spend cash locally see especially Robert Carter to Chamberlayne and Sitwell, 26 July, 1720, *Letters of Robert Carter*, 41–43. (Chamberlayne and Sitwell, a London firm, are incorrectly identified as Barbados merchants by the editor.) On receiving book credit for cash the agent spent locally, see John Carter to Foster Cunliffe, 14 July 1737, John, Landon, and Charles Carter Letterbook. For acceptance of paper currency and sometimes tobacco see *Maryland Gazette*, 21 June 1753, 18 July 1754, 4 September 1760, 20 August 1761, 24 September 1761, 1 July 1762, 29 July 1762, 14 August 1762, 19 September 1763, 22 September 1763, 10 April 1764, 9 August 1764, 10 October 1765, and 31 August 1768. For acceptance of merchant's notes see *Virginia Gazette*, 16 August 1770, 30 August 1770, 13 September 1770, 7 May 1772, 9 July 1772, and 20 August 1772.

[13] The length of time agents had to remit proceeds and to make good on protested bills varied from one colony to another. For South Carolina see Price, "Credit in the slave trade and plantation economies," 310–11.

[14] John Carter to Cunliffe and Powell, 3 August 1738, John, Landon, and Charles Carter Letterbook. In slaves sales, prime men and women sold first and were usually purchased by large planters who seldom required credit. Less desirable slaves were sold toward the end of the sale, and more frequently on partial or full credit. To the extent that sale prices were adjusted to allow for the higher default risk of small buyers, a practice which David Galenson also identified in Barbados, "the observed decline in slave prices within demographic categories would tend to understate the true decline in the present value of the slaves – and hence in their quality – that occurred over the course of sales." (*Traders, Planters, and Slaves*, 201–02, n.38.)

V

Merchants trading in slaves in various parts of Virginia and Maryland followed somewhat different marketing strategies, some connected to and others little influenced by the tobacco trade. These will be examined on a port-by-port basis. Information on ship owners is spotty for the early eighteenth century, so conclusions about early investors, especially for London merchants who are the least well documented, is tentative.[15] In the seventeenth and early eighteenth centuries, Londoners dominated the Chesapeake slave trade, as they did the African slave trade overall. London was the headquarters of the Royal African Company and a major center of interloping activity. Although entry into the trade was unrestricted after 1698, London traders' greater knowledge of both African and Chesapeake trades was a crucial advantage. At the turn of the century, almost three-quarters of British ships carrying slaves to the Chesapeake were dispatched from London, and they transported 96% of captive Africans. Between 1704 and 1718, London merchants still sponsored over half of all Chesapeake slaving voyages, which carried three-quarters of the Africans imported. In the 1720s, however, Bristol displaced London as the Chesapeake's main supplier of enslaved laborers, accounting for about two-thirds of both ships and slaves entering the region. By the 1730s Liverpool merchants also entered the Chesapeake trade, financing a quarter of slaving voyages between 1731 and 1745, a third between 1746 and 1760, and half between 1761 and the close of the region's trans-Atlantic slave trade in 1774.[16]

For London slave traders, the Chesapeake remained a relatively minor destination compared to the West Indies. The chartered Royal African Company, composed largely of London investors, paid scant attention to mainland markets, between 1672 and 1689 contracting with and later licensing independent merchants, most of them tobacco traders, to handle Chesapeake consignments, rather than shipping slaves on the Company account. After 1698 most slaves were imported by separate traders who between 1698 and 1712 paid the Company a 10 percent duty on outbound cargoes to Africa. A few of the London separate traders (such as Humphrey Morice, Samuel

---

[15] Ship owners are enumerated in Chesapeake Naval Office returns, which survive (in part) for 1698–1703, 1725–1769, and 1771–1775, but they are not listed in other records reporting the entry of slave ships between 1704 and 1724. Sometimes all owners are enumerated, but when there were multiple investors, often only one name is given followed by the notation "& Co." Consequently the lists of investors are clearly incomplete. Additional evidence on investors was compiled from Eltis, et al., *The Trans-Atlantic Slave Trade Database*, which draws on British as well as colonial shipping records, and on the Chesapeake side from miscellaneous legal documents and private correspondence.

[16] A recent overview is Richardson, "The British Empire and the Atlantic Slave Trade," in *The Oxford History of the British Empire*, Vol. 2, *The Eighteenth Century*, 440–64. For the Chesapeake see Walsh, "The Chesapeake Slave Trade," 168–69.

Bonham, Richard Harris, and William Gerrish) operated on a large scale, financing multiple voyages from Africa to the West Indies as well as to the Chesapeake. Others were small investors of the sort who had participated extensively in the tobacco trade earlier in the century, and included ship captains, haberdashers, distillers, and pewterers. Most of the Londoners investing in Chesapeake slaving ventures early in the eighteenth century were merchants of one sort or another, and at least a quarter were also trading in tobacco. But few of the tobacco merchants were extensively involved in slaving ventures; rather most seem to have been occasional investors.[17]

A wave of bankruptcies among tobacco dealers early in the century, followed by more than a decade of stagnating trade, led to increasing concentration of the London commerce in fewer hands. The new generation of London merchants who dealt in Virginia tobacco were totally disinclined to invest in slaving voyages, and those who specialized in slave trading lost any interest in the Virginia labor market. Merchants handling Maryland tobacco continued to dabble in that colony's slave trade up to its end, but in the later eighteenth century it was primarily specialized London slave traders like Henry Bonham who supplied the Maryland market. From the 1720s London tobacco merchants' primary role in the Chesapeake slave trade was in extending credit to corresponding planters who drew on them for more funds than they had shipped tobacco to cover when they purchased slaves, and by acting as guarantors for Chesapeake planter–merchants, including those acting as agents for Liverpool as well as London investors.[18]

Bristol slave traders, in contrast to the Londoners, from the outset considered the Chesapeake an important market, as indeed it was in the second quarter of the century when the Bristol trade was aggressively expanding.[19]

---

[17] Price, *Perry of London*, 32–48; and Price and Clemens, "A Revolution of Scale." The wider trading activities of London merchants investing in the Chesapeake slave trade were traced in *The Trans-Atlantic Slave Trade Database*. The London slave trade remains little studied. The most recent surveys are James A. Rawley, "The Port of London and the Eighteenth Century Slave Trade: Historians, Sources, and A Reappraisal," *African Economic History*, 9 (1980): 85–100, and Rawley, *The Transatlantic Slave Trade: A History* (New York, 1981), ch. 10.

[18] Price and Clemens, "A Revolution of Scale"; Price, "Credit in the slave trade and plantation economies," 293–339. London separate traders may have more freely extended credit than the Royal African Company. However Price finds that during the wars of 1689–1713 when slaves were in short supply, long credits "were much less necessary or common than they had been before 1689 and were to be again after 1713." In 1720 Robert Carter remitted half the proceeds of one voyage originating in London shortly after the sale, and allowed buyers a year's credit for the remainder. *Letters of Robert Carter*, 41–42.

[19] For Bristol merchants see Richardson (ed.), *Bristol, Africa and the Eighteenth-Century Slave Trade*, I, xix–xxiii; Richardson, *The Bristol Slave Traders*; K. Morgan, *Bristol and the Atlantic Trade*, chs. 5 and 6; K. Morgan, "Bristol Merchants and the Colonial Trades," Appendix B; Minchinton, "The slave trade of Bristol"; Minchinton (ed.), "The Virginia Letters of Isaac Hobhouse"; and Madge Dresser, "Squares of Distinction, Webs of Interest: Gentility,

Bristol traders were more efficient than the London-based Royal African Company, delivering more slaves per crew than London slavers, and the smaller ships they typically employed were better suited to relatively small Chesapeake regional markets.[20] Another reason for their success in edging out London competitors in the Chesapeake seems to have been a greater willingness to extend credit to planter purchasers. By the late 1720s, Bristol traders required their Chesapeake agents to remit only half of the proceeds of slave sales with that season's returning tobacco fleet. The agents were given an additional year to remit the rest, and a further three months to make good on returned protested bills of exchange.[21] When both bills and specie were scarce, occasionally they also exchanged slaves for high quality, heavily prized tobacco.[22] Learning from the difficulties that agents for London slave traders experienced by accepting too many unsound bills of exchange, Bristol traders authorized agents to accept greater proportions of specie and to sell less desirable slaves on credit to buyers whom the agents judged most likely to successfully make deferred payments from subsequent tobacco sales. The legal protection afforded by the Colonial Debts Act of 1732, which made colonists' land and slaves liable for the satisfaction of debts due by bond, also encouraged the expansion of a credit-based slave trade.[23]

Scholars of the Bristol trade have noted little overlap between slave and tobacco merchants. Most of the investors in slaving voyages were specialized traders who financed scores up to more than one hundred voyages to the West Indies as well as to the Chesapeake and who were interested only in finding the best markets for captured Africans. Of 106 Bristol merchants sending slaves to the Chesapeake, 33 were identified by David Richardson

---

Urban Development and the Slave Trade in Bristol c. 1673–1820," *Slavery and Abolition*, 21 (2000): 21–47.

[20] David Eltis, *The Rise of African Slavery in the Americas* (Cambridge, 2000), pp. 121–22.

[21] Robert Carter to John Pemberton, 9 July 1728, Robert Carter Letterbook, 1727–28, f. 8, University of Virginia Library.

[22] Large planters producing sweet-scented tobacco took the lead in using big presses to prize more tobacco into hogsheads, especially in the first decade of the 1700s, when war at sea substantially raised shipping costs. Ordinary planters lacked the equipment to make such heavily prized tobacco. For example, in 1708 one Virginia merchant bought a cargo of tobacco in exchange for merchandise from small to middling Rappahannock and Potomac River planters; they delivered hogsheads averaging only 590 pounds net. Two years later, he sold a shipload of slaves to large planters living in the same area, accepting tobacco in payment. Their "choice weighty" hogsheads averaged 1,148 pounds net (Stephen Loyde Account Book). In September 1727 when Robert Carter feared he would be forced to sell many slaves consigned to him for tobacco, he stipulated that "I must have the Tobbo prized to at least Eight hundred neat and to be paid of mens own crops." Carter to Maj. George Eskridge, 21 September 1727, Carter Letterbook 1727–28, f. 70, University of Virginia Library.

[23] Price, "Credit in the slave trade and plantation economies," 309–10.

as leading agents who directly managed ten or more slaving voyages. These included John and Michael Becher, Henry Dampier, James Day, Thomas Deane, Richard Henville, James Laroche, and Noblet Ruddock. Only 16 investors were among those listed by Kenneth Morgan as ever dealing in tobacco, and for most of these, tobacco was clearly only an ancillary trade. Most were likely marketing minor amounts of tobacco remitted for slaves or carried as freight that they would rather not have received at all.

However a few of the Bristol slave traders (including Charles and Edward Harford, Abraham Hook, Elisha James, George Mason, and John Scandrett) had gained a firsthand knowledge of Chesapeake markets by trading there in tobacco and indentured servants at the turn of the century before they came to specialize in slaves. And in the mid 1730s and 1740s, some Bristol tobacco merchants, who hoped to gain an edge over London rivals in the trade of particular Chesapeake rivers, posted bond with Bristol slave traders guaranteeing payment for shipments of slaves consigned to favored Chesapeake correspondents. These planters sought the tobacco merchants' help in getting into the business of selling slaves, and in return, solicited their friends to consign tobacco to their merchant backers. Once Bristol tobacco traders ceased trying to expand their shares of York River and southern Maryland output, Bristol shippers sent few slaves to these areas, concentrating instead on the then prime labor market of the Upper James (Fig. 5). The Bristol tobacco trade became increasingly concentrated in a few leading firms, most of which shifted from the consignment method of trading to the cargo trade. Like the Londoners, Bristol merchants entering the tobacco trade in the third quarter of the century chose not to invest in Chesapeake slaving voyages. In addition, many of the agents who had dominated Bristol's slave trade in the first half of the century died or retired and were not replaced by immediate family members. The new managers were apparently more knowledgeable about West Indian markets than about these in the Chesapeake where they faced growing competition from Liverpool traders.[24]

Similarly there was scant overlap between Liverpool slave and tobacco traders. Of 73 investors in slaving voyages, only 8 also dealt in tobacco. Many of those with no connections to tobacco were major slave traders who were also involved in multiple ventures to the West Indies and to a lesser extent to South Carolina such as the Blundells, Charles Cooke, Edward Deane, Robert Hallhead, John Penket, Richard Townsend, and Thomas Seel. However, three of the four leading Liverpool tobacco firms – Backhouse, Cunliffe, and Gildart – had substantial investments in both trades, and

---

[24] K. Morgan, *Bristol and the Atlantic Trade*, ch. 6; Price, "Credit in the Slave Trade," 313–15; Lyde and Cooper v. Darnall, Attwood, and Digges, Chancery Record 8 (1746–67), ff. 9–75, Maryland State Archives; Price and Clemens, "A Revolution of Scale"; Richardson (ed.), *Bristol, Africa and the Eighteenth-Century Slave Trade to America, Vol. 3, The Years of Decline 1746–1769* (Bristol, 1991), pp. xviii–xxxi; Harris, *History of Human Populations*, II, ch. 2.

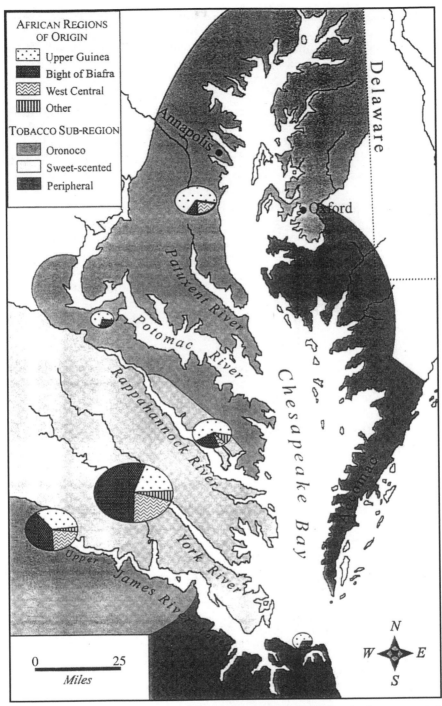

FIGURE 5. Coastal Origins of Africans Imported to the Chesapeake between 1698 and 1774, by Naval District. Map drawn by Gayle Henion with Rebecca Wrenn

Cunliffe and Gildart shipped indentured servants and convicts as well. These houses pursued integrated trading strategies, marketing slaves and servants in those parts of the Chesapeake where they were buying tobacco. If they changed the sort of tobacco they were buying, they also shifted the ports to which they sent servants and slaves. Because the Liverpool merchants dealt extensively in lower grades of tobacco for the re-export market to northern Europe, for a time Liverpool tobacco traders were important suppliers of slaves to more marginal tobacco growers. However, Cunliffe and Gildart, having extended credit too liberally in the late 1740s, wound down their trade in Maryland tobacco in the 1750s, and no Liverpool merchants dealing in tobacco on a similar scale replaced them. Between 1731 and 1760, tobacco merchants sponsored almost half of the slaving voyages leaving Liverpool for the Chesapeake, but only 16% of voyages thereafter. Liverpool slavers' interest in the smaller Maryland market then diminished, and after 1760 they sent most shipments to the Rappahannock and Upper James (Fig. 5). The stagnation or decline of both the Bristol and Liverpool tobacco trades in the later 1750s left the supply of slaves to the Chesapeake largely in the hands of specialized slave traders who concentrated on the larger, more profitable labor markets.[25]

Liverpool slave traders also allowed agents to sell some slaves on credit. Different firms apparently had different policies regarding the proportion of remittances that might be deferred, the kinds of payment accepted, and the length of time agents had to make good on all outstanding debts. At least into the 1730s, differing stipulations seem to have been made for each voyage. As with the Bristol merchants, Liverpool firms extended more credit, accepted more specie, and occasionally also took tobacco and other produce.[26]

VI

The shifting ownership structures and credit strategies of British merchants were central to immigration patterns of slaves, servants, and convicts. One major unintended effect was pronounced differences in the origins of

---

[25] For the Liverpool trade see Rawley, *The Transatlantic Slave Trade*, ch. 9; David Richardson, "Liverpool and the English Slave Trade," in Anthony Tibbles (ed.), *Transatlantic Slavery: Against Human Dignity* (London, 1994), pp. 70–76; Price and Clemens, "A Revolution of Scale"; and Harris, *History of Human Populations*, II, ch. 2. John W. Tyler, "Foster Cunliffe and Sons: Liverpool Merchants in the Maryland Tobacco Trade, 1738–1765," *Maryland Historical Magazine*, 73 (1978): 246–79, describes a shift of trading operations from one naval district to another, and Paul G. E. Clemens, *The Atlantic Economy and Colonial Maryland's Eastern Shore: From Tobacco to Grain* (Ithaca, NY, 1980), pp. 199–201, discusses the activities of the firms of Cunliffe and Gildart on the Eastern Shore. The patterns of Liverpool traders in the Chesapeake are from Walsh, "The Chesapeake Slave Trade." Activities of Liverpool investors outside the Chesapeake were compiled from *The Trans-Atlantic Slave Trade* Database.

[26] See John Carter's correspondence with Cunliffe and Powell in the John, Landon, and Charles Carter Letterbook.

Africans forcibly transported to different parts of the Chesapeake. Connections between the regional origins of enslaved Africans sent to particular Chesapeake ports and the marketing and investment strategies of English tobacco merchants depended more on trading patterns in Africa and shifting demand for various grades of tobacco in European markets than on conditions within the Chesapeake. Across the eighteenth century, about three-quarters of the Africans brought to the upper Chesapeake (Virginia Potomac basin and Maryland) and to the Lower James whose regional origins are known came from the upper parts of the West African coast, from Senegambia on the north, and south and east to the Gold Coast. In contrast, nearly three-quarters of the Africans disembarked in the lower Chesapeake tidewater (York and Upper James basins) came from more southerly parts of Africa east and south of the Bight of Benin, primarily from the Bight of Biafra and West Central Africa.

The patterns of importation and subsequent distribution of Africans of different origins within the Chesapeake largely coincide with the geographical divisions between sweet-scented, oronoco, and peripheral tobacco growing areas, an outcome unrelated to the crop itself, but rather the end result of complex interactions of African, British, and colonial trading patterns (Fig. 5). English merchants who had limited or no direct ties to the tobacco trade simply sought out the best markets for enslaved laborers – which happened to be those that produced high-grade tobacco and where planter wealth was most concentrated. For merchants whose principal business was, instead, tobacco, slave dealing was often part of a broader strategy for maintaining or expanding their shares of the tobacco trade on particular rivers. The cultural implications of the concentration of Africans from different ethnic groups within parts of the Chesapeake are taken up elsewhere.[27]

The predominance of Africans from the Bight of Biafra and Angola in southern Virginia does underscore planters' general inability to influence the ethnic composition of new arrivals. No Chesapeake planter is known to have expressed a preference for laborers originating in the Bight of Biafra, and indeed Igbo, and to a lesser extent Angolan, slaves were held in particularly low esteem in much of the Caribbean and in South Carolina. To the extent Chesapeake planters expressed any preference, it was for Gambian and Windward and Gold Coast slaves, as well as for predominantly adult male cargoes.[28] Until mid century when the Upper James became the prime outlet, British merchants judged the York basin the best slave market in the Chesapeake. Wealthy planters were most concentrated along this river, and

---

[27] Walsh, "The Chesapeake Slave Trade."

[28] Darold W. Wax, "Preferences for Slaves in Colonial America," *Journal of Negro History*, 58 (1973): 371–401; Wax, "Black Immigrants: The Slave Trade in Colonial Maryland," *Maryland Historical Magazine*, 73 (1978): 30–45; Douglas Brent Chambers, "'He Gwine Sing He Country': Africans, Afro-Virginians, and the Development of Slave Culture in Virginia, 1690–1810," Ph.D. diss., University of Virginia, 1996, pp. 250–55.

they were most likely to pay for slaves with sound bills of exchange drawn on well-known London houses or with ready cash. Conversely, planters living in more marginal areas more often paid with shakier bills of exchange drawn on less-established London or outport houses, or could buy only on long-term credit. For example, in 1687 a cargo of illegally imported Angolan slaves was put up for sale in the York River, "they being the ablest men to purchase for Money."[29] In 1723, John Tayloe, a Virginia planter and slave dealer, wrote Bristol merchant Isaac Hobhouse that he had undertaken to sell a cargo of Calabar slaves in the York "as being most for ye Owners Intrest, There being most money Stir[r]ing in that river." Tayloe's co-factor, Augustine Moore, advised Hobhouse that slaves were sometimes taken from the York to the Rappahannock only "after ye best [were] Sold, not for ye goodness of their bills but to gett rid of ye slaves in time."[30] By mid century, when the prices of upper James River tobacco began to equal and sometimes to surpass those offered for tidewater sweet-scented, the ability of large Piedmont planters to make good remittances rose in tandem with their rising need for additional laborers.

But why were British merchants sending the ostensibly least desired ethnic groups (which moreover typically included higher proportions of women and children than did the preferred groups) to the prime markets, while consigning slaves from the most desired groups to more marginal ports? The best explanation, advanced by Stephen Behrendt, is that British merchants employed ships of different tonnage (and hence slave-carrying capacity) in different African markets. Slave traders chose not only cargoes suited for a particular African region, but also ships. The navigational limitations of African ports; regional rates of slave delivery; the probable age, sex, and size of the slaves likely to be offered; and the probability that the captives would violently resist were all taken into account, as were crop cycles on both sides of the Atlantic. Ships going to the Upper Guinea Coast were smaller than those trading on the Gold Coast, Bight of Biafra, and West Central Africa. The merchants then directed the larger ships carrying the most captives to the biggest American markets where they were most likely to achieve quick sales. Although Behrendt's analysis focuses on the Caribbean, a similar policy seems to have prevailed in the Chesapeake.[31] Overall, ships arriving in the York and Upper James were of greater tonnage than those going to the more marginal districts. And while London, Bristol, and Liverpool traders each

[29] CO 5/1308, ff. 36–37, PRO.
[30] Minchinton (ed.), "The Virginia Letters of Isaac Hobhouse," 293–94, 297.
[31] Stephen D. Behrendt, "Markets, Transaction Cycles, and Profits: Merchant Decision Making in the British Slave Trade," *William and Mary Quarterly*, 3rd ser., 58 (2001): 171–204. As a Kingston, Jamaica, merchant firm later noted, "People from Old Calabar require a brisk market." Letter of Grove, Harris and Papps to Rogers, Mar. 10, 1793, C107-59, PRO, quoted in ibid., 196.

employed ships of differing tonnage, merchants from all three ports directed their largest ships (and hence more Biafran and Angolan slaves) to these two districts. Because most Liverpool slavers sent somewhat smaller vessels to the Chesapeake than did either London and Bristol merchants, they had more flexibility for choosing among destinations. Thus the distribution of different groups of Africans within the Chesapeake seems primarily an unplanned outcome of the marketing strategies of British and African merchants over which local buyers had little influence.

A second result of British ownership patterns and credit strategies was that those parts of the Chesapeake with scant connection to the tobacco trade – the lower Delmarva peninsula and the lower James River – received few shipments of Africans. So too did tobacco planters living along the Potomac River, because early in the eighteenth century English slave traders sent their cargoes to areas growing better grades of tobacco. The Scottish merchants who subsequently came to dominate the Potomac tobacco trade had no direct involvement in the slave trade, and English investors were highly reluctant to accept bills of exchange drawn on Glasgow, which were inconvenient and costly to redeem. For planters living in these places, lack of connections to English marketing and credit networks compounded the difficulties posed by lesser wealth.[32]

The backgrounds of the agents who marketed the slaves as well as the terms on which they were authorized to sell also had an impact on the distribution of enslaved Africans among Chesapeake planters. All English slave traders consigned slaves to local agents who agreed to sell them for commissions ranging from 5 to 10 percent of the gross proceeds. Good connections with English tobacco merchants were always essential, for the agents had to find merchants willing to act as "guarantees" who would post bond to make good any remittances the agent failed to collect.[33]

In the late seventeenth and first half of the eighteenth century the agents were invariably prominent planters – merchants like Robert "King" Carter or William Byrd II. At that time most prospective slave buyers were elite tidewater planters who shipped their tobacco to England on consignment rather than selling it in the country. Most professional merchants representing British firms in the Chesapeake dealt primarily with middling and small

---

[32] Walsh, "The Chesapeake Slave Trade;" and Walsh, "Summing the Parts: Implications for Estimating Chesapeake Output and Income Subregionally," *William and Mary Quarterly*, 3rd ser., 61 (1999): 53–94; Susan Westbury, "Analysing a Regional Slave Trade: The West Indies and Virginia, 1698–1775," *Slavery and Abolition*, 7 (1986): 241–56; Donald M. Sweig, "The Importation of African Slaves to the Potomac River, 1732–1772," *William and Mary Quarterly*, 3rd ser., 42 (1985): 507–24.

[33] Davies, *The Royal African Company*; Galenson, *Traders, Planters, and Slaves*; Killinger, "The Royal African Company Slave Trade to Virginia;" Price, "Credit in the slave trade," 293–339; and Richardson, "The British Empire and the Atlantic Slave Trade, 1660–1807," 447–50.

planters, and these traders were often not in a good position to evaluate the credit-worthiness of gentry purchasers. Hence slave traders instead employed agents who were themselves members of the planter elite. The risks agents incurred in collecting payments were high in the first half of the century, and the number of planters of fortune sufficient to be reliable agents was limited. These factors served to keep commissions in the first half of the century in the higher range. Some great planters like Robert King Carter would sell slaves only for a 10 percent commission, the rate offered by the Royal African Company at the turn of the century. Carter also refused to handle consignments if too many restrictive conditions were attached to sales, paid himself full commission on debts still outstanding, and at least once hinted that a 15 percent commission would be more appropriate. Other major slave dealers like Stephen Loyde and John Tayloe (who were not so wealthy or well-connected as Carter) actively competed for consignments by agreeing to sell for a lesser commission of 8 percent, and Loyde charged only 5 percent for slaves sold for tobacco.

Whatever the percentage they negotiated, the agents sought to maximize their personal profits by avoiding dealings with small buyers who had a higher risk of default and who were their social inferiors. Robert Carter, for example, refused to accept liability for a debt owed for a slave woman whom the ship's captain had sold to "one Killby an acquaintance of his" who was "a sort of a pilate" without Carter's approbation. Killby, who paid for the slave with a £20 bill of exchange on Glasgow and a personal note for the remaining £3 in cash, had subsequently sailed his boat by the agent's house several times, but had failed to call on Carter to pay the money; moreover, "his bills I am told are not worth a groat." Carter appeared as much troubled by the purchasers' inferior social status and failure to behave deferentially as by the questionable soundness of the tender.[34]

The practice of seeking payment for imported Africans in bills of exchange, as well as the preference of most agents for limiting their dealings to purchasers of high social and economic standing, tended to restrict the purchase of new Africans primarily to the planter elite. Those most able to buy were not only wealthier planters, but also well-connected, rich planters residing in the tidewater who maintained a correspondence with English and especially leading London merchants. Such men were also almost invariably members of the colonial political elite who were in the process of enacting legislation safeguarding their rights in human property. Influence and wealth conveyed other advantages in acquiring African slaves. At least

[34] *Letters of Robert Carter*, 93–95; Carter to John Pemberton, 15 September 1727, 19 December 1727, 9 July 1728, Robert Carter Letterbook, 1727–28, Carter Family Papers, Virginia Historical Society; Carter to Pemberton, 23 August 1727, 16 September 1727, to [John Page] [22 May 1728], Robert Carter Letterbook, 1727–28, University of Virginia Library; Stephen Loyde to Loving Brother, 8 December 1710, John Tayloe to Messrs [Samuel Jacobs and Company], 10 April, 1718, Stephen Loyde Account Book; Royal African Company to Willis Wilson, 16 December 1702, T70/58, PRO.

into the 1730s the agents took first pick of newly arrived slave cargoes. And relatives or close neighbors often made special arrangements with the agents to buy lots of twenty to thirty prime slaves for various family members with bills of exchange and ready cash in return for being allowed to choose the most promising of the captives before the slaves were exposed for sale to the general public.[35] Less well-connected planters were deterred from buying new Africans not only by their lesser ability to draw or purchase bills of exchange, but perhaps also by the knowledge that any slaves they might buy were likely to be captives who were too young, old, or unhealthy to interest elite purchasers. As a result, at least into the 1740s most newly imported Africans, and especially those who were healthiest and of prime working age, ended up living on large plantations owned by powerful men. There they were most likely to be subjected to dehumanizing regimens, gang labor, and harsh plantation discipline.[36]

The greater willingness of Bristol and Liverpool investors and agents to sell slaves on credit in the second quarter of the eighteenth century facilitated the spread of new Africans among non-elite planters who were less wealthy, less well connected internationally, and who had smaller plantations and fewer laborers than the great planters. Later-arriving Africans thus encountered more diverse forms of captivity than those transported at the beginning of the century. From 1745 on, the locus of most sales of new Africans shifted from the older tidewater to the Upper James and to more marginal tobacco areas. And agency shifted from great planters to local merchants. The main

[35] Carter to [Col. Page], c. 21 May 1728, Carter to Col. Braxton, 21 May 1728, ff. 85–86, Carter Letterbook, 1727–28, University of Virginia Library. The practice was apparently fairly common. Complaints were made to the Royal African Company in 1704 that agent Henry Fielding did not always advertise public sales, presumably because he was selling the slaves only to favored buyers (T70/58, PRO). In 1723 Carter advised London merchant Micajah Perry that "this year I know of no large Quantity have been sold together the Small folks and Middling people have been the only buyers." Carter letterbook, 1723–24, f. 14, Virginia Historical Society.

[36] Ira Berlin, *Many Thousands Gone: The First Two Centuries of Slavery in North America*, (Cambridge, MA, 1998), ch. 5. The fact that early in the 18th century males predominated on larger tidewater plantations, but that sex ratios were more equal on middling farms provides further evidence that rich planters had the first choice. Lorena S. Walsh, *From Calabar to Carter's Grove: The History of A Virginia Slave Community* (Charlottesville, 1997), pp. 29–30, 83–89; Philip D. Morgan, Slave Culture in Eighteenth-Century Plantation America," (Ph.D. diss., University College London, 1977), pp. 291–99. In the later 17th and early 18th centuries, in many parts of the Chesapeake, large slave holdings were far from common due to the limited supply of slaves and their high cost. However, whatever slaves were present were concentrated in the wealthier estates, those worth £150 or more. As Gloria Main observed, "The transition to slavery...was confined to the richest quintile of planters." [Main, *Tobacco Colony: Life in Early Maryland, 1650–1720*, (Princeton, 1982), pp. 101–06. See also Russell R. Menard, "Economy and Society in Early Colonial Maryland," (Ph.D. diss., University of Iowa, 1975), ch. 7, and David W. Galenson, "Economic Aspects of the Growth of Slavery in the Seventeenth-Century Chesapeake," in Solow (ed.), *Slavery and the Rise of the Atlantic System*, pp. 265–92.]

reason for these shifts in location and agency was that by the mid 1740s enslaved workers on large tidewater plantations had become self-reproducing.
Elite tidewater planters and many of their neighbors no longer had any need
to buy new Africans.[37] Then the agents most able to evaluate the credit
worthiness of prospective buyers became independent Chesapeake tobacco
traders or merchants affiliated with English firms who purchased tobacco in
the country from middling and small planters in both tidewater and the interior. Competition between merchants and reduced risks drove down the cost
of distribution. By the 1760s local merchants were accepting consignments
of slaves for only a 5 percent commission, the going rate for selling imported
goods and purchasing tobacco. And in the 1750s at least one well-funded
Virginia firm competed for consignments of "choice" slaves by promising
to remit half their estimated value immediately upon receipt of the captives,
and to transmit the remaining balance in good bills of exchange one to two
months later.[38]

The greater willingness to accept specie, local currency, and local commercial paper in the third quarter of the century promoted a further expansion
of slave buying among ever more ordinary planters spread throughout the
region who had only modest local connections. Probate inventories demonstrate the expansion of slave ownership among the less affluent. For example,
in one southern Maryland County, by the 1760s nearly half of probated decedents worth between £49 and £67 owned at least one slave, and two-thirds
of those with estates valued between £68 and £94 were slave owners. Many
of these slaves had likely been acquired through inheritance rather than by
purchase. However, once planters became slave owners by any means, they
were in a better economic position to acquire additional laborers. Moreover,
having gained some experience in managing black workers, they were more
likely to want to acquire additional slaves.[39] Finally, non-elite buyers had
greater chances for purchasing prime laborers once great planters stopped
buying by special arrangement prior to the general public sale.

VII

A combination of differing mercantile strategies and of differing local demand resulted in an unbalanced distribution of bound European laborers,
both geographically and among economic groups. As was the case with

---

[37] Walsh, *From Calabar to Carter's Grove,* pp. 134–44.

[38] For examples of 5% commissions see sales of the Little Sally, Othello, and Royal Charlotte,
Vernon Papers, box 2, folders 4, 8, and 11, Manuscript Department, New York Historical
Society. Charles Steuart to Blackman and Adams, 5 July 1751, Charles Steuart Letterbook,
1751–1763, Historical Society of Pennsylvania.

[39] Russell R. Menard, "The Expansion of Slavery in the 18th-Century Chesapeake: The Case of
St. Mary's County, Maryland," Paper presented at the annual meeting of the Social Science
History Association, Pittsburgh, October, 2000.

slaves, in the eighteenth century European indentured servants and convicts were also unequally distributed within the region. Some shippers of servants were primarily tobacco dealers who carried small numbers of servants as a way to increase profits by making use of otherwise under-utilized shipping space on the outward voyage and to better compete for the custom of local planters. Others were primarily in the business of transporting convicts or else combined the marketing of convicts with a retail store trade in manufactured goods exchanged for a wide range of produce.[40]

Unlike the slave trade, planters', farmers', and townspeoples' preferences for different kinds of European bound laborers played a more prominent role in determining the kinds of laborers brought to various Chesapeake markets. Lower tidewater Virginia planters had no use for convicts, and little desire to buy unskilled indentured servants, and few servant-carrying ships stopped in either the York or James Rivers. Nor did the relative poverty of peripheral lower Eastern Shore residents encourage any significant trade in either bound laborers or any other sort of merchandise there. The major destinations for both convicts and servants in Virginia were the Rappahannock and the Potomac Naval Districts, where poorer Northern Neck planters and back-country farmers provided a strong market for inexpensive laborers. The suppliers included London, Whitehaven, and Glasgow tobacco merchants, major London firms transporting convicts on contract, and a scattering of outport and Dublin merchants.[41]

In Maryland, wealthy Patuxent basin planters, like their counterparts in lower tidewater Virginia, were well supplied with African slaves and were apparently interested in purchasing only indentured servants who had skills. London merchants, often in partnership with their Maryland factors, were almost the sole suppliers. Few convicts or Irish servants were offered there, presumably because there was no market for them. Instead convicts were sold in the adjoining Potomac basin where there were more small and middling tobacco growers still in the market for cheap labor. North Potomac was probably the second most important Maryland destination for convicts.

[40] The 18th century indentured servant and convict trades are discussed in Margaret M. R. Kellow, "Indentured Servitude in Eighteenth-Century Maryland," *Histoire sociale-Social history*, 17(1984): 229–55; Galenson, *White Servitude in Colonial America*; Ekirch, *Bound for America*; K. Morgan, "The Organization of the Convict Trade to Maryland" and Grubb, "Transatlantic Market for British Convict Labor." On increased concentration of servant recruiting in London see James Horn, "Servant Emigration to the Chesapeake in the Seventeenth Century," in Thad W. Tate and David L. Ammerman (eds.), *The Chesapeake in the Seventeenth Century: Essays on Anglo-American Society* (Chapel Hill, 1979), pp. 51–95; Galenson, *White Servitude in Colonial America*, 97–98; and John Waring, "Migration to London and transatlantic migration of indentured servants, 1683–1775," *Journal of Historical Geography*, 7 (1981): 356–78.

[41] Ekirch, *Bound for America*, chs. 4 and 5; K. Morgan, "English and American Attitudes Towards Convict Transportation 1718–1775," *History*, n.s. 72 (1987): 416–31; database of Chesapeake servant imports compiled by Walsh from Naval Office shipping returns.

Its naval office records have not survived, but the 1755 Maryland census reveals large numbers of convicts in this area. As on the Virginia side of the Potomac, the suppliers likely included a mix of London, outport, and Scottish tobacco merchants and others who specialized in the transport of Irish servants or English convicts. On Maryland's Eastern Shore, the Oxford Naval District, which offered some tobacco of middling grade and also wheat and lumber, was supplied primarily by tobacco merchants.[42] A mix of London, Whitehaven, and Glasgow traders competed for this tobacco, along with the Liverpool firms of Gildart and Cunliffe, which were integrated partnerships dealing in tobacco, English and Irish servants, convicts, and slaves. These merchants supplied local planters and farmers with a limited number of Irish and English indentured servants.[43]

Annapolis was the main port of entry in Maryland for both indentured servants and convicts. Some were sold in or near the port, but local merchants marketed others initially arriving in Annapolis in Baltimore City, Chestertown, and other locations at the head of the Bay, as well as to back-country buyers. London and Maryland tobacco merchants transported and sold most of the English indentured servants. (An advertisement noting the arrival in Annapolis from Bristol of the schooner *Industry* with "a quantity of salt and a few servants, boys and girls" illustrates the nature of this trade.[44]) A combination of Irish and Philadelphia shippers and of English and Maryland tobacco merchants supplied Catholic servants from Southern Ireland, while Irish and Scottish traders transported the few servants who emigrated from Northern Ireland.[45] Over 7,500 convicts were carried from London by 45 different ship owners, almost none of whom dealt in tobacco, and only 15 of the 45 also transported indentured servants. Most were supplied by the major London specialist contractors James Armour, John Stewart, and Duncan Campbell, who also shipped convicts to Virginia. Nearly all of the 3,600 Bristol felons (as well as most of the some 500 Bristol servants) were transported by just two firms, Sedgley, Hilhouse, and Randolph, and

---

[42] Aside from 104 Scottish "rebel" servants imported in 1747, only 72 convicts were brought into the Oxford Naval District between 1743 and 1775.

[43] Clemens, *The Atlantic Economy and Colonial Maryland's Eastern Shore*, 199–205; Walsh, database of Chesapeake servant imports.

[44] *Maryland Gazette*, 22 December 1757.

[45] The most recent account of Irish migration is Marianne S. Wokeck, *Trade in Strangers: The Beginnings of Mass Migration to North America* (University Park, PA, 1999), ch. 5. Wokeck discusses the dual nature of Irish migration, with servants predominating among those leaving Southern Ireland, and free migrants among those from Northern Ireland. Most of the Northern Irish migrants chose to go to Pennsylvania, whereas most Southern Irish migrating under indenture went to the Chesapeake. No shipping records survive for the early 18th century, but the prevalence of Irish names among indentured servants appearing in Maryland court records and private papers around 1720 indicates substantial Irish servant migration in the first half of the century.

the subsequent partnership of Stevenson, Randolph, and Cheston. The latter firm cornered all convicts available for transport from the West Country surrounding Bristol and traded almost exclusively in Maryland. (These firms, however, also invested in slaving ventures to the West Indies, South Carolina, and Georgia.)[46]

The trade in convicts, like the trade in slaves, was highly seasonal, and often involved the use of specialized vessels. Timing of arrival was governed primarily by British court calendars; ships were dispatched soon after the spring and autumn sessions of assize courts with cargoes of convicts, dry goods, and occasionally a few indentured servants. Most convicts arrived in the Chesapeake in June and July, when they competed with shipments of new Africans, and again in October and November, at which time most slave sales had been completed. (Servant arrivals, in contrast, by the second half of the eighteenth century were more evenly spaced throughout the year.)[47] Specialist contractors who held the Treasury convict transportation contract earned higher profits per convict than did unsubsidized shippers, so it was not to their advantage to carry any indentured servants for whom their margin of profit was lower. Unsubsidized dealers in convicts, who often had to pay fees to jailers to get convicts released, were more likely to carry some servants as part of their freight because their earnings were similar for both kinds of laborers.[48] The larger London and Bristol convict transporters began using vessels with holds specially designed for human cargoes, and frequently employed the same ship for multiple voyages. Convicts, like slaves, were often shipped in irons, and although they were not as tightly packed as were Africans, convicts were not infrequently carried in vessels also used to transport slaves.[49]

Maryland servant buyers included a combination of middling to small planters who purchased cheap laborers primarily for raising tobacco, other planters who needed inexpensive plantation craftsmen, farmers at the head of the Bay who employed servants in mixed agriculture, industrialists, and townspeople in Annapolis and Baltimore who bought servants for their domestic or craft skills. Advertisements in the *Maryland Gazette* for the sale of servants and convicts demonstrate that these immigrants were marketed primarily for whatever skills they allegedly possessed, and only secondarily as unskilled agricultural laborers. This must have been especially true of those

---

[46] Ekirch, *Bound for America*; K. Morgan, "The Organization of the Convict Trade to Maryland"; Walsh, database of Chesapeake servant imports.

[47] K. Morgan, "The Organization of the Convict Trade to Maryland," 207; Walsh, database of Chesapeake servant and convict imports.

[48] Grubb, "The Transatlantic Market for British Convict Labor," 101–107.

[49] K. Morgan, "The Organization of the Convict Trade to Maryland," 206–07; Ekirch, *Bound for America*, 98–199. A number of vessels involved in the convict trade also appear in the *Transatlantic Slave Trade Database*.

arriving in the fall and winter when planters were less likely to buy new farm
hands. Often convict buyers had prior trade connections with the shippers,
and placed standing orders for workers with specific skills. The extent to
which, by the 1770s, convicts were sold to purchasers outside the tobacco
economy is indicated by one factor's comment that wheat rather than tobacco
prices governed local demand.[50] Buyers did expect that convicts, whom they
had reason to suppose were of flawed moral character, more unruly, and
more prone to running away, would be less productive than servants. Although the price of a convict was about 25% higher than that of a servant,
because they were sold for longer terms, their cost per year was 36 to 42%
below the annual cost of servants. Felons who had committed more serious
crimes or who had venereal diseases could be sold only at a considerable
discount.[51]

In addition to being significantly cheaper than slaves, purchase of convicts
and indentured servants remained attractive to small to middling planters
and farmers because of the more generous terms on which they were usually
sold. Although a few employers such as iron master Capt. Charles Ridgley
bought convicts in parcels, records of sales for the firm of Stevenson, Randolph, and Cheston show a preponderance of purchases of no more than one
or two convicts at one time.[52] Indentured servants were even more likely to
be purchased singly. Like slaves, most servants and convicts were sold at
retail on board ship within a few days of opening the sale, but unhealthy or
unskilled "residuals" were disposed of to secondary traders in a wholesale
lump.

Shippers of servants and convicts, like slave traders, also preferred remittances in bills of exchange, sterling, or current money. But, significantly,
tobacco was equally acceptable, and sometimes wheat, corn, and other produce as well (forms of payment more available to small planters than bills of
exchange or hard cash).[53] And some sellers also offered "a proper discount"
for ready money or for tobacco delivered at the time of purchase. Merchants
could then use any cash received for direct purchase of tobacco or wheat.[54]
However, because "reasonable credit" was almost always "allowed on giving
bond," most small purchasers, who were the preponderant buyers, bought
on credit. Some merchants tried to limit the period for repayment to four,
five, or six months so that remittances could be sent to England in time to

---

[50] Ekirch, *Bound for America*, ch. 4; for effect of wheat prices, ibid., 128–29; K. Morgan, "The
Organization of the Convict Trade to Maryland," and K. Morgan, "Convict Runaways in
Maryland, 1745–1775," *Journal of American Studies*, 23 (1989): 253–68.

[51] Farley Grubb, "The Market Evaluation of Criminality: Evidence from the Auction of British
Convict Labor in America, 1767–1775," *American Economic Review*, 91(2001): 295–304.

[52] K. Morgan, "The Organization of the Convict Trade to Maryland."

[53] Ibid.; Ekirch, *Bound for America*, chs. 4 and 5; advertisements for servant and convict sales
in the *Maryland Gazette* and *Virginia Gazette*.

[54] *Virginia Gazette* (Rind), 24 June 1773.

pay tradesmen's bills at home before the customary twelve-month credit period elapsed. But in practice most buyers took at least a year to pay off their bonds, and when tobacco and other produce prices slumped, failed to pay at all or could not do so for two or three more years.[55] Such free extension of credit enabled small planters, farmers, and rural and urban tradesmen who could not afford or did not want to buy slaves, to buy inexpensive skilled and unskilled bound labor. But the need to buy on credit probably limited most prospective purchasers to a choice of whatever laborers were offered locally. Should they travel to larger, more distant markets where they seldom traded produce and where dealers did not know them or their securities personally, it would be unlikely that they would be allowed to buy for anything other than ready pay.

The 1755 Maryland census, which enumerates indentured servants and convicts, as well as slaves, shows the extent to which the distribution of European bound labor was a result of both the nature of local economies and of local supply (Fig. 6). Convicts were concentrated in Baltimore, Anne Arundel, Queen Anne's, and Charles Counties, near the main points of sale – Baltimore Town, Annapolis, Chestertown, and Port Tobacco. Baltimore and Queen Anne's were mixed farming counties whereas Anne Arundel and Charles were major tobacco producers, and all but Queen Anne's were also well endowed with slaves. Hence, proximity to supply seems to have been the main determining factor in the distribution of convicts. Similarly, in tobacco-growing Prince George's County, adjacent to Charles, and in back-country Frederick County, served by Annapolis, convicts were fewer in number, but constituted a quarter of bound European laborers. All these counties also had large numbers of indentured servants, as did the mixed farming upper Eastern Shore counties of Cecil and Kent, which too were supplied through Annapolis. Lower down on the Eastern Shore, residents of Talbot and Dorchester Counties, who pursued a combination of tobacco and mixed agriculture and who were reasonably well supplied with slaves, used significant numbers of indentured servants, but almost no convicts. This distribution reflected the predominance of servants among laborers sent to the port of Oxford. In contrast, the tobacco-growing Lower Western Shore counties of Calvert and St. Mary's, the first wholly, and the second partly supplied through the Patuxent Naval District, relied primarily on slaves, and had fewer servants and almost no convicts. This reflects the smaller volume of voluntary, primarily skilled, European servants imported into that district, and perhaps as well a higher proportion of native-born slaves in this early settled area. The peripheral Lower Eastern Shore counties of Somerset and Worcester, which had few connections to trans-Atlantic trade and an economy geared more

---

[55] Ekirch, *Bound for America*, 123–24; K. Morgan, "The Organization of the Convict Trade to Maryland"; *Maryland Gazette*, 24 April 1766.

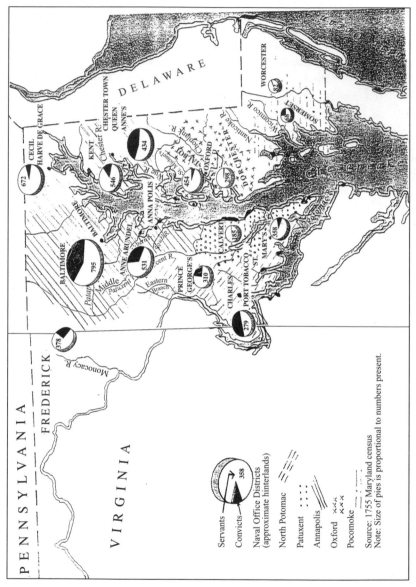

FIGURE 6. Bound Laborers in Maryland, 1755

Source: 1755 Maryland census.
Note: Size of pies is proportional to numbers present.

to self-sufficiency than to export products, had few bound servants of either sort.[56]

While access to supply seems to have determined the distribution of bound European male laborers in Maryland overall, the differing numbers of women servants in the various counties suggests that European workers were indeed acquired for different uses in mixed farming and in tobacco areas. Residents of the mixed farming counties at the head of the Bay and in back country Frederick purchased more female servants than did any of the tobacco-growing jurisdictions.

VIII

Despite the availability of cheap convict laborers, however, the goal of most tobacco growers remained the acquisition of slaves rather than servants. The attraction of permanently bound, self-reproducing workers dominated the strategies of most planters who sought to improve their own standards of living or to build up a family estate. And there were of course ways other than the African trade by which planters could acquire them. One important source was though inheritance. Because most Chesapeake planters divided slaves, like livestock and other personal property and unlike land, relatively equally among their children, inheriting slaves oneself or marrying someone who did were among the main ways that second- and third-generation creole planters acquired laborers.[57] Another was to buy slaves locally, most especially when they were sold to settle a decedent's estate or to pay the debts of a bankrupt planter. Here the terms of sale were quite different from those prevailing in the African trade. Purchasers could buy not only with bills of exchange, specie, or paper currency, but sometimes also with tobacco. Those who paid immediately received a five-percent discount on the selling price. But many buyers purchased slaves on credit. Accounts of local slave sales have yet to be systematically analyzed, but my impression is that the

---

[56] Kellow analyzed the census in terms of sub-regional economies and the proportion of slaves; Kenneth Morgan analyzed it in terms of sub-regional economies and supply. This characterization takes into account the three variables.

[57] Lois Green Carr, "Inheritance in the Colonial Chesapeake," in Ronald Hoffman and Peter J. Albert (eds.), *Women in the Age of the American Revolution* (Charlottesville, 1989), pp. 155–208; Jean Butenhoff Lee, "Land and Labor: Parental Bequest Practices in Charles County, Maryland, 1732–1783," in Lois Green Carr, Philip D. Morgan, and Jean B. Russo (eds.), *Colonial Chesapeake Society* (Chapel Hill, 1988), pp. 306–41; Carr, "The Effect of Inheritance on Slave-Holding Patterns: Maryland, 1700–1775"; and J. Elliott Russo, "'Did Devise A Negro Woman Slave': Patterns of Slave Acquisition in Eighteenth Century Somerset County, Maryland," both papers presented at the annual meeting of the Social Science History Association, Pittsburgh, 2000; and Russo, "'At Present Possessed of a Negro Man': Patterns of Slave Acquisition in Eighteenth-Century Somerset County, Maryland," Paper presented at the Institute for the Study of Slavery, Nottingham, Eng., 2002.

majority of purchases were credit sales. By the third quarter of the eighteenth century, newspaper advertisements for the sale of African or country-born slaves from local estates often stated: "Time will be given for Payment, on giving Bond with Security if required," or "Reasonable credit will be allowed to the purchasers, on giving bond on interest, with good security," or "A Short Time of Payment will be allowed for part, on giving Bond with Security if required." Those who purchased slaves repossessed on a defaulted mortgage or at an estate sale had at least six months and often an entire year to make full payment. And even if they failed to pay on time, sellers turned to repossession only as a distant last resort. More commonly they simply demanded interest from the day of sale if the money was not paid when due, and in practice might give a further period of "indulgence" in order to avoid suing the bonds in court.[58]

These terms made such local slaves as came on the market affordable to anyone who had land or other assets he or she could mortgage or who had a more affluent relative or patron willing to stand as a surety.[59] The buyer could then use the proceeds of the slave's labor to make payment. A major difficulty was, however, that the events which precipitated such sales could not be readily anticipated. Purchasing locally was thus a less predictable strategy for estate building than was the purchase of new Africans. (Hence the prevalence of annual hiring which permitted those in need of laborers to contract for them for a full growing season at a predictable time in the calendar year.) Local sales nevertheless facilitated an even wider expansion of slave owning, one sustained by more available local rather than trans-Atlantic credit. Moreover the slaves exchanged in such transactions included increasing proportions of seasoned and country-born slaves who were likely to be, or to be considered, more tractable than newly imported Africans. Most were somewhat to highly fluent in English and more conversant with European ways and local agricultural regimens, characteristics that would have attracted buyers reluctant to purchase unwilling workers with whom they could not communicate. The proportions of new African and of seasoned and creole slaves exchanged in local markets have yet to be assessed. But given that by 1770 fewer than 10% of Chesapeake slaves are estimated to have been born in Africa (and few of these were recent arrivals), the share of new Africans was clearly declining.[60]

---

[58] Examples appearing in the *Maryland Gazette* which mention sale of local slaves on credit include 6 December 1759, 17 December 1761, 22 April 1762, 8 May 1766, 7 September 1769, 25 October 1771, and 7 June 1774. For interest when bonds were not paid on time see the *Virginia Gazette* 12 and 25 March 1772.

[59] The correspondence of large Chesapeake planters mentions their posting bond for junior relatives and for their overseers who purchased slaves. For the spread of slave holding see Allan Kulikoff, *Tobacco and Slaves: The Development of Southern Cultures in the Chesapeake, 1680–1800* (Chapel Hill, NC, 1986), pp. 134–136.

[60] Philip D. Morgan, *Slave Counterpoint: Black Culture in the Eighteenth-Century Chesapeake and Lowcountry* (Chapel Hill, NC, 1998), p. 61.

Differing mercantile trading strategies, some closely connected to and others largely separate from the tobacco trade, thus had a pronounced impact on the distribution of bound laborers among different areas and classes of planters within the Chesapeake. Throughout the eighteenth century the supply of bound European laborers was insufficient to meet local needs. Skilled indentured servants remained in demand, but the supply was small and unpredictable. When they could not obtain enough skilled Europeans, planters turned to teaching the required trades to their slaves, eventually reducing the demand for servants. The supply of convicts was more reliable and the terms of sale advantageous, although some of the individuals offered were not particularly promising workers. Felons proved most attractive to buyers outside the tobacco economy. Although middling and small farmers, townspeople, and industrialists continued to purchase such bound European labor as was available, fewer and fewer Chesapeake residents came to view regular use of servant labor as a viable strategy for building a family estate.

Intersections of market conditions and market size in West Africa, the West Indies, and the Chesapeake influenced the volume, timing, and distribution of captive Africans across the Chesapeake, which was independent of preferences for Africans from particular African regions that planters on occasion expressed. Buyers' preferences had much greater impact on the distribution, if not the supply, of European laborers, but in those areas where tobacco was most important, demand for such laborers was declining. Neither the convict nor the servant trades long survived the severing of political connections between the colonies and Britain and the reorientation of trade networks that followed. The terms by which new Africans were sold initially favored their concentration on large plantations of the powerful planter elite where they were most likely to be subjected to a dehumanizing breaking-in, harsh discipline, and gang labor. Subsequently more liberal extension of credit and more varied methods of payment made it easier for ordinary planters throughout the Chesapeake to acquire African slaves. But more critical to the expansion of slave owning were the even more liberal terms by which seasoned African and creole slaves could be acquired through local sales. It was the growing impact of local rather than trans-Atlantic credit, in combination with inheritance, that propelled the Chesapeake along a trajectory toward a slave society.

4

African Slavery in the Production of Subsistence Crops; the Case of São Paulo in the Nineteenth Century

Francisco Vidal Luna and Herbert S. Klein

The use of African slave labor in America has traditionally been associated with the production of commercial export crops, above all sugar, cotton, tobacco, and coffee. Yet there was no regime where slaves were exclusively used for this activity, and even in the most export-oriented of such plantations, some food crops were produced for home consumption and possibly for local market sales. But in few cases was this activity as important as in the slave economy of Brazil and above all in the newly expanding coffee plantations which were evolving in the region of São Paulo in the first half of the nineteenth century. It is this unusual concentration of expensive slave labor in basic food crop production that we will examine in this essay. The role of slave and non-slave labor in the production of such staples and the relationship of this staple production to the growing of commercial export crops of sugar and coffee will be explored through an analysis of the São Paulo regional economy in this period.

Before examining this evolution, it is essential to understand the regional diversity of this province. The regions of the province were well-defined areas divided by a coastal mountain range (Serra do Mar), which separates a thin but fertile coast from a highland plateau, which in turn is defined by several river valleys and open plains. The "Litoral Region" extends approximately 400 kilometers and is dozens of kilometers wide. This was the first area occupied, but quickly lost its central position as settlement crossed the mountains. The first major interior plateau settlement was the town of São Paulo located on a natural route from the coast. Around the capital city grew several major agricultural regions, but the soils of this "Capital Region" were relatively poor compared to the virgin forested regions to the north, the south, and the west – all of which became the major centers of export agriculture. To the south were increasingly open plains ideal for grazing – the so-called "Region of the Southern Road"– a route going south to the border with the Spanish colony of the Rio de la Plata. To the northeast of the Capital Region was the

Paraiba Valley which extended into the northern border province of Rio de Janeiro. The Valley runs along the coast for some distance and is defined by the two mountain ranges, the Serra do Mar and the Serra da Mantiqueira. It was here that coffee had its beginnings, and its location close to the coast and to the mines of the interior of Minas Gerais also encouraged an active farming zone with several important counties producing a multiplicity of crops for export.

The "West Paulista" zone is due west and north of the Capital Region and remained mostly a forested frontier inhabited by Indians until the definitive penetration in the age of the railroads. In this period the frontier had extended some 200 kilometers inland and incorporated the richest agricultural lands of the province. This region was first to be the home of a major sugar industry, and then the center of the coffee plantations after the mid nineteenth century. Even today, the West Paulista region is the single most important agricultural region of Brazil.

The *paulista* rural economy through most of the period before 1800 had been based primarily on foodstuffs production for the home and internal market. Even after the growth of commercial sugar and coffee exports in this frontier region, the production of food staples remained a fundamental part of the economy and was also closely associated with the new export crops. From the earliest days, the dietary staples of corn, rice, and beans, and such meats as pork, were produced in every part of the province from the coast to the interior. There was also specialized production of such consumption items as tobacco, cane alcohol, and herbal teas, and a minor grazing industry which raised cattle and horses. Animal products such as lard were also important everywhere. Grown on family farms – often with the aid of Indian slave labor – most of this production went for self-consumption of the farm family, but over time more and more of the surplus was traded between regions and even beyond the borders of the province. This was especially the case in the period after 1700 when São Paulo became a major food-producing region for the newly opened gold mines in the neighboring province of Minas Gerais.[1]

Recent historiography has begun to reveal the ongoing importance of local small farm staples production in the Brazilian context as a counterweight to the emphasis on the plantations in the traditional literature.[2] Such production in most areas was both for subsistence and for sale within local and regional markets. It always involved the family unit, but often included

[1] For a more detailed study of this region see Francisco Vidal Luna and Herbert S. Klein, *The Evolution of the Slave Society and Economy of São Paulo, from the 1760s to the 1850s* (Stanford, 2003).

[2] On this theme, see Iraci del Nero da Costa, *Arraia–Miúda* (São Paulo, 1992). This theme is discussed in B. J. Barickman, *A Bahian Counterpoint: Sugar, Tobacco, Cassava and Slavery in the Recôncavo, 1780–1860* (Stanford, 1998).

servants and slaves, and in the case of pre-eighteenth century São Paulo, these were Indian slaves. This use of slave labor, at first Indian and then black, to produce these subsistence and local market goods has been one of the distinguishing features of Brazilian slavery. Few other American slave societies have made such systematic use of expensive slave labor in this area of production.

São Paulo is an especially good region to study this phenomenon. Initially without resources to enter the international economy and acquire the funds needed to import Africans, the Paulistas were forced to find internal market solutions to overcome their international market disadvantages. The combination of Indian captures and exploration opened up markets for their subsistence crops and provided a crucial additional labor force beyond the family. The occupation of Minas Gerais led to an active regional market, with the Paulistas supplying the transport animals and food essential to the mining economy. This market in turn was the major factor that permitted the Paulistas to shift from evermore expensive and difficult-to-capture Indian slaves, to African slave labor brought across the Atlantic.

The progressive domination of the local slave market by Africans after 1700 actually meant more rather than less use of slaves in the production of food crops. Although African slaves were most utilized in the sugar mills that exported to the international markets after 1800, they were also employed in the production of food crops for the local and regional markets from the beginning to the end of slavery in the province.

Using previously unpublished provincial census and production data, this whole market evolution of food crops from 1798 onward can be examined in some detail (see Table 1). Although sugar, even at this early date, accounted for two-thirds of all "exports" sold beyond the boundary of the county of production, a third was made up of these animal and subsistence products. In order of importance in terms of values came animals, cane alcohol, followed by the basic food products such as rice, beans, corn and manioc flour, and finally by lard. There was also strong regional variation in exports by products, with the animal and food products usually not coming from the sugar and coffee zones.

The export data, however, probably underestimate the value of food crop production. In the published Müller census of 1836, corn production alone represented a third of the value of all goods produced, exceeding even sugar and coffee, which were the dominant long-distance exports (see Table 2, p. 124). Corn and the other food crops produced for self-consumption or local sales were distributed unevenly across the province. Corn itself was most grown in the regions of the Paraíba Valley, the Southern Road, and the West Paulista plains, but was absent from the coast. Beans were also grown everywhere but on the coast. In contrast, rice was a major product of the coast but also produced in the Paraíba Valley. Thus even in the zones with the biggest sugar and coffee exports there was significant production of animals and food

TABLE 1. *Relative Importance and Regional Distribution of Exports from São Paulo in 1798* (1)

Regions	Sugar	Aguardente	Cotton	Tobacco	Coffee	Food-stuffs (2)	Animals (3)	Lard	Total
				I. Percentage by product					
Paraíba Valley	29.3	5.5	8.8	15.6	0.9	0.5	9.9	29.5	100.0
Capital Region	13.0	41.5	2.2	0.2	0.0	14.4	0.5	28.1	100.0
West Paulista	91.6	1.4	0.5	0.2	0.0	0.8	4.4	1.1	100.0
Southern Road	0.7	5.5	0.0	1.3	0.4	24.9	66.0	1.2	100.0
Coast	78.3	9.8	0.0	1.0	3.3	7.6	0.0	0.0	100.0
TOTAL	68.3	7.8	1.0	1.5	0.9	5.9	9.3	5.3	100.0
				II. Percentage by region					
Paraíba Valley	2.8	4.6	55.5	69.3	6.6	0.5	7	36.7	6.6
Capital Region	1.8	50.9	20.3	1	0	23.2	0.6	50.8	9.6
West Paulista	69.5	9.4	24.1	6.6	2.9	7.3	24.5	10.3	51.9
Southern Road	0.1	6.8	0	8.3	4.3	40.1	68	2.2	9.6
Coast	25.7	28.3	0	14.8	86.2	28.9	0	0	22.5
TOTAL	100	100	100	100	100	100	100	100	100

Notes: (1) Sales realized outside the municipios. (2) Rice, beans, manioc, and corn. (3) Cows, horses, and mules.
Source: Armenio de Souza Rangel, "Economia e riqueza – Formação da economia cafeeira no Município de Taubate – 1765/1835," (Ph.D. diss., FEA, Univerisidade de São Paulo, 1990), pp. 108, 364. The author used "mapas" on exports in the AESP for the year of 1798.

TABLE 2. *Relative Importance and Regional Distribution of Selected*
Agricultural Commodities Grown in São Paulo in 1836

| | Relative Importance of | | | | |
	Coffee	Sugar	Tobacco	Cotton	Aguardente
% of production value	17%	13%	0%	0%	3%
% by region					
Paraíba Valley	70.2	0.7	43.7	13.4	20.5
Capital Region	12.3	0.1	3.8	56.1	11.7
West Paulista	2.9	96.8	33.1	20.8	42.6
Southern Road	0.2	1.5	14.9	9.7	15.3
Coast	14.4	1.0	4.4	0.0	9.9
TOTAL	100.0	100.0	100.0	100.0	100.0
	Corn	Rice	Beans	Manioc Fl	Lard
% of production value	36%	9%	3%	1%	1%
% by region					
Paraíba Valley	11.0	41.2	35.5	34.1	73.2
Capital Region	16.7	3.9	18.1	20.4	0.0
West Paulista	45.8	9.3	31.5	5.5	0.0
Southern Road	26.5	5.2	14.6	21.7	26.8
Coast	0.0	40.3	0.4	18.2	0.0
TOTAL	100.0	100.0	100.0	100.0	100.0
	Cows	Pigs	Horses	Mules	Sheep
% of production value	6%	6%	3%	2%	0%
% by region					
Paraíba Valley	6.1	16.1	4.6	12.5	11.1
Capital Region	6.0	16.5	16.4	25.4	8.8
West Paulista	35.2	63.2	34.8	26.4	35.6
Southern Road	52.7	4.3	44.2	35.8	44.5
Coast	0.0	0.0	0.0	0.0	0.0
TOTAL	100.0	100.0	100.0	100.0	100.0

Note: These are the most important products of the region which represent 96% of all agricultural production during this year.

crops. In the Valley of Paraíba, for example, tobacco, cotton, corn, rice, manioc flour, and cane alcohol were produced. The same diversity of such products was also to be found in the West Paulista region. Thus even the most important sugar and coffee regions were not mono-crop areas. Only the herbal tea *erva mate* was totally concentrated in one region – that of the Southern Road.

It is important to note that the expansion of these food crops was related to the dynamics of the two principal commercial export crops, sugar and coffee.

The expansion of the economy was begun by sugar in the third quarter of the eighteenth century and complemented by coffee commercial production beginning in the second decade of the nineteenth century. Market conditions, including prices, as well as the production process itself, especially in coffee, provided the basic stimulus for the expansion of these two products, which in turn fomented slave importations and the other internal economic activities, including food production. Local food producers began selling their output to other regions, such as Rio de Janeiro, as well as to the expanding free and slave population of the province itself. It is also important to realize that the two export crops of sugar and coffee presented characteristics which differed from corn, rice, beans and even cotton production, in that they were perennial rather than annual crops. Coffee depended on a very long lead time for initial production, while sugar required large capital investments. These two crops, being of greater risk than the annual food crops, were less influenced by normal price fluctuations, which could stimulate rapid changes in local food production. The long-term trend in prices, however, did influence cycles of investment in these two commercial export crops, but did not influence production or the movement of workers into food crops. The production of sugar and coffee was relatively stable over time, with annual fluctuations more influenced by climatic factors. In the phases of very accelerated price rises there was a major stimulation of new investments, which encouraged new slave importations and eventually encouraged the transfer of labor from food to export production. Given that the export crops were relatively permanent, only a profound crisis, in which the producers definitively retired from this activity, would have led to a transfer of labor from sugar and coffee to food production. Nevertheless, this does not signify that there was not a movement of labor during the agricultural year into more than one crop. Taking advantage of the different timings of labor needs in the production of coffee and sugar, planters often shifted labor into the production of other crops during fallow periods, which explains why these export producers were also important producers of food crops. In the case of coffee this alternation between food crops and export production was fundamental in the initial development of coffee. Because coffee began to give results only after five years, in this initial phase the producers were able to maintain themselves through food production and the raising of animals for sale. This integration between export and food crops in coffee fazendas disappeared only in the second half of the nineteenth century, when the great producers of coffee reached a scale of activity completely different from that which we find in this period.

But the 1836 census of Müller also shows the relative unimportance of these products outside the province (see Table 3). Coffee and sugar together accounted for 80% of the value of external provincial exports. Of the remaining values, rice, *erva mate*, tobacco, and lard were the most important, though corn and all the other food products were also exported.

TABLE 3. *Volume and Relative Importance of Agricultural Exports from São Paulo in 1836*

	Value Exported	% of Value	Quantity Exported (arrobas)
Coffee (tons)	18,378	40.1	621,826
Sugar (tons)	17,379	37.9	998,123
Rice (tons)	6,878	9.1	69,868
Erva mate (arrobas)	169,607	5.4	84,768
Tobacco (rolls)	136,268	4.4	33,705
Lard (arrobas)	68,565	2.2	25,207
Beans (tons)	316	0.3	5,196
Manioc flour (alqueires)	11,761	0.4	8,269
Aguardente (casks) (pipas)	1,760	0.1	44
Corn (alqueires)	689	0.0	816
Other products		0.1	2,126
Total value	431,602	100.0	1,849,947

Source: Muller (1978).

Using the censuses of 1804 and 1829,[3] we get some detail about the nature of these food crop farms and a rough picture of the changing importance of all the economic activities geared to the local market. What is impressive is how universal food production was. In 1804 farms dedicated to the internal market absorbed some 86% of the agricultural slave owners and they controlled 70% of the slaves in this sector (see Table 4). Even as late as 1829, some three-quarters of the agricultural slave owners dedicated themselves to producing for the internal market and their slaves represented about half the servile labor force working in agriculture. In this same year, if we were to include all rural and non-rural slave owners, those dedicated to their internal market still made up half the slave owners and controlled 40% of the slave labor force.

As was to be expected, most of the food farms contained no slaves and were run by the families that owned them. Nevertheless the weight of slaves and slave owners in this sector is impressive. Close to a quarter of the food-producing households contained slaves, though the distributions were quite skewed. There were a very large number of farmers with just one slave – they represented a quarter of these food-producing farmers who owned slaves. These one-slave-owning units were probably quite similar to the family-run farms, and in fact most of the work was probably done by the family members in these same farms, and thus these small slave owners looked a

---

[3] A complete list of these population and production censuses for the state of São Paulo, which are housed at the Arquivo do Estado de São Paulo, will be found in Luna and Klein, *The Evolution of the Slave Society*, Appendix A1.

TABLE 4. *Characteristics of Slave Farms Producing for the Internal Market in São Paulo, 1804 and 1829*

% of farmers producing for the internal market in agriculture		
	1804	1829
% of heads of households	86%	74%
% of slaves	70%	49%
Slave owners		
% farmers with slaves	24%	25%
Average number of slaves	5	6
Standard deviation	6.8	7.2
Median	3	3
Mode	1	1
Gini of distribution of slaves among owners	0.52	0.52
Percentage of slave owners by size of holding		
1 slave	25%	24%
1–5 slaves	70%	67%
6–10 slaves	18%	19%
11–20 slaves	9%	10%
21–40 slaves	2%	3%
More than 40 slaves	1%	1%
Percentage of slaves by size of holding		
1 slave	5%	4%
1–5 slaves	32%	29%
6–10 slaves	25%	25%
11–20 slaves	24%	26%
21–40 slaves	11%	14%
More than 40 slaves	7%	7%

Notes: Group of 41 different localities.
Source: "Listas Nominativas dos Habitantes," Arquivo do Estado de São Paulo.

great deal like the non-slave owning farmers. In 1804, for example, one-fourth of the farmers with one slave were mulattos or blacks, whereas such non-whites were relatively insignificant among those owning more than one slave. Among the non-slave-owning food producers, mulattos represented a quarter of the farmers. However, in general, slave owners tended to be older and far more foreign-born than non-slave-owners, even among the one-slave-owning group. There was a high ratio of Portuguese and other Europeans among the slave-owning farmers, though less than there were among the slave-owning coffee and sugar exporters. In fact these Portuguese tended to be among the richest in terms of slave holdings.

Unlike coffee- and sugar-producing slave owners, those slave owners who produced food crops tended to be small holders of slaves. Those who held 5 slaves or less in this sector represented two-thirds of such slave-owning agriculturalists. There were, of course, a few large slave owners who held a disproportionate ratio of slaves, but on the whole 80% of the slaves working in food production were on units of less than 20 slaves and the Gini index of inequality among all slave owners in this area was a relatively low .52.

A more detailed examination of the structure of production in this sector can be obtained by a study of two typical food-producing counties, as well as the market for the three basic staples of corn, rice, and beans. The two counties we have selected are Jacareí and Cunha, both located in the Valley of Paraíba. The former produced numerous food and animal products for consumption in the market of the city of São Paulo and the capital city of Rio de Janeiro; and the latter was primarily producing corn as well as basic food crops also for the Rio de Janeiro market. Cunha is an especially interesting case because it was a major agricultural center with a very important slave labor force which never became a major coffee or sugar producer.

In the first thirty years of the nineteenth century, export crops made up less than 5% of production in the county of Cunha (see Table 5). Rather, a changing variety of food crops sustained the local economy, with corn and pigs – and their product lard – being always major factors in the local farming scene. In 1836, for example, Cunha produced 2,600 tons of corn, 177 tons of beans, 133 tons of lard (or *toucinho*), as well as significant quantities of rice and tobacco.[4] The total value of food and animal production for the internal market reached 81,000 mil réis in this year and represented almost the total value of production in the county of Cunha.[5]

The market orientation of the Cunha food producers enabled them to make intensive use of slave labor in producing these products. Most of the farmers without slaves probably dedicated more of their surplus to subsistence – few of these non-slave-owners listed output for sale and most often registered that they "*plantava para seu sustento*," that is they produced only for their own subsistence. Slave owners with more than 10 slaves in Cunha produced two-thirds of the corn, pigs, and lard that were marketed.

---

[4] For some unknown reason there is no listing of the raising of pigs in 1836, in contrast to what had been the norm in other years, despite the important production of lard in this same year. In some years, such as 1816 and 1823, the censuses list a large number of pigs, broken down into *leitões* and *capados*; but does not mention lard production. On the other hand, in 1836 there is no mention of the number of pigs raised, but on the contrary a very high output of lard is noted, whereas in the censuses of 1804 and 1810 both pigs and lard output are mentioned. In fact are these two indices complementary? It is obvious the animals in this case were simply not listed by the census-taker who listed only final output in most cases, rather than indicating the swine population in place. Could the corn also consumed by the pigs be omitted as well? It is impossible to know what the actual process was, but if this were the case, it results in an underestimation of both corn and swine production in the province.

[5] In the years 1816 and 1823 the production of corn was given in "cavalos." Unfortunately it has not been possible to convert this eighteenth century unit of weight into metric figures, as was the case with alqueires. Moreover we have found no census giving the price of corn in "cavalos," which might have permitted some type of estimate for conversion.

TABLE 5. *Profile of Agricultural Activity in Selected Products in Cunha, 1804–1836*

Quantity Produced	1804	1810	1816	1823	1836
Sugar (tons)	10				
Coffee (tons)					1
Tobacco (tons)	1				8
Corn (tons)	503	7		13	2,586
Corn (cavalos)			23,968	11,690	
Rice (tons)	7		11	8	34
Beans (tons)	44		71	33	177
Lard (tons)	70	189			133
Pigs (1)	368	440	3,767	2,024	
Piglets Leitões			2,592	689	
Value of production (in mil réis)	25,478	15,256	19,144	8,632	80,663
Percentage of total value (export products) (2)					
Coffee and Sugar	2.8%	0%	0%	0%	0.1%
Tobacco and Cotton	0.3%	0%	0%	0%	0.9%
Food crops and animals cereals and manioc	23.8%	0.3%	8.9%	16.6%	74.5%
Lard	32%	84%	0%	0%	23%
Animals	40.9%	15.6%	91.1%	83.4%	2.0%
Percentage of production by slave-owning households					
Corn (tons)	98%	87%			94%
Corn (cavalos) (3)			99%	100%	
Lard (arrobas)	97%	99%			98%
Pigs	100%	100%	100%	99%	

Notes: (1) Some of the pig output was listed in arrobas and these have been converted into units by estimating 5 arrobas per animal. In 1804 production was listed at 1,539 arrobos of swine, which corresponds to 308 animals.

(2) For prices and conversion rates used for weights and measures, see Francisco Vidal Luna and Herbert S. Klein, "Nota a respeito de medidas para grãos utilizados no período colonial e as dificuldades para sua conversão ao sistema métrico," and "Observações a respeito dos preços agrícolas em São Paulo (1798/1836)," both of which appeared in the *Boletim de História Demográfica*, Ano VIII, no. 21 (Março 2001) – [São Paulo].

(3) We could not find a conversion rate for "cavalos de milho," which makes it impossible to calculate the total value of corn in the years of 1816 and 1823. Given the importance of corn in total output, and our inability to estimate total corn production figures, both corn and total production is underestimated in these two years.

Source: Same as Table 4.

Almost a third of production came from the farms that owned 20 or more slaves.

What is impressive about these results is that Cunha was able to sustain and add to a major slave-labor force on the basis of wealth generated from traditional food crops. In contrast to Areias and Jundiaí, where coffee and sugar provided the income to purchase slaves and where food production was a supplement to these export crops, in Cunha it was only these very traditional food crops that served as the basis of the economy. This view from the censuses is confirmed by the nineteenth century French traveler Saint-Hilaire who visited Cunha and affirmed that in this county there was no sugar or coffee, but a very large production of corn and other food products destined for the market in Rio de Janeiro, which was shipped through the port of Parati.[6]

Approximately two-thirds of the households in Cunha were dedicated to agriculture, a figure one would expect from this type of county. But what is truly unusual about Cunha, aside from the type of goods it produced, was the very impressive penetration of slaves in this county. An astonishing half to 80% (depending on the census year) of the households in farming owned slaves – an extraordinarily high level by the standards of Brazil; and agriculturalists controlled more than 80% of the slaves owned in the county (see Table 6). In fact, close to half the total population were slaves in Cunha – some 1,500 out of some 3,000 persons – also an unusually high ratio by local standards.

Although Cunha had a large minority of poor households, the fact that slavery was so widely distributed meant that the Gini indices of inequality were quite low by nineteenth century standards. Among slave-owning households the Gini was .50 and even when all households are included it varied from 0.75 to 0.80 – low compared to other areas in contemporary São Paulo. This did not mean that there were no large owners, but rather that slaves were very widely distributed and most owners held close to the average number of slaves. Cunha, in fact, had slave owners who held between 60 and 70 slaves, a figure not insignificant even in the coffee and sugar zones. Unusual as well was the fact that the slaves were predominantly African. Some 50% of the servile labor force in the county were born in Africa, again a number quite comparable to the most advanced sugar and coffee counties. Given their origin, the sex ratio among the slaves was consistently above 160 males per 100 females and the average age was between 24 and 26 years. This stability of the labor force was matched by a stability of total population and the ratio of slave owners over time. Clearly from early in the century Cunha had become a thriving center of production for the internal

---

[6] Auguste de Saint–Hilaire, *Segunda Viagem do Rio de Janeiro a Minas Gerais e a São Paulo*, Belo Horizonte: Ed. Itatiaia (São Paulo, 1974), p. 102.

TABLE 6. *Profile of Slaves and Slave Ownership in Cunha, 1804–1835*

Population and Households	1804	1810	1816	1823	1829	1835
Number of inhabitants	2,887	2,781	3,018	2,860	3,375	2,574
Number of slaves	1,331	1,318	1,410	1,271	1,549	1,046
Number of free persons	1,556	1,463	1,608	1,589	1,826	1,528
Number of slave owners	189	183	185	165	189	132
% slaves in population	46%	47%	47%	44%	46%	41%
Number of households	346	348	368	346	407	373
% of households with slaves	55%	53%	50%	48%	46%	35%
% "poor"/total hshlds	5%	7%	4%	28%	5%	12%
Statistical indicators of slave ownership						
Average slaves owned	7	7	8	8	8	8
Std. dev.	7.8	8.6	8.8	9.1	9.1	9.6
Median slaves owned	4	4	5	5	6	5
Modal slaves owned	1	1	1	1	1	2
Gini for slave owners	0.52	0.52	0.50	0.51	0.50	0.53
Gini for hds household	0.74	0.75	0.75	0.77	0.77	0.83
Largest owners (no. slaves)	49	64	64	72	74	67
Slaves in agriculture	1,128	1,111	1,210	995	1,317	848
% of slaves	88%	87%	86%	83%	85%	82%
Slave owners	153	140	148	107	149	101
Average slaves on farms	7	8	8	9	9	8
% of households in agriculture	79%	63%	62%	50%	56%	60%
Slaves in other activities (1)	161	170	195	199	224	183
Slave owners in other activities (1)	30	36	33	28	37	29
Average slaves in other activities	5	5	6	7	6	6
Characteristics of the slaves						
% Africans	42%	51%	51%	53%	55%	21%
Sex ratio (m per 100 f)	158	159	170	164	168	160
Average age	25	26	24	25	26	26

Notes: (1) This includes artisans, merchants, liberal professionals, public officials, transport workers, and rentier persons.

Source: Same as Table 4.

market and it maintained its markets and its labor force and continued to grow in the midst of a province evermore committed to sugar and coffee exports.

The county of Jacareí, founded in 1652, was also located in the Valley of Paraíba, but at the southern end, just 90 kilometers from the capital. Like Cunha, it was essentially dedicated to production for the internal market, but at the end of the 1820s it also began to produce small amounts of coffee. Though its primary market was the capital of the province, there are some indications that it also shipped part of its surplus to Rio de Janeiro.[7] In the early nineteenth century Jacareí was in a phase of rapid expansion. Between 1804 and 1829 the value of its output grew six times to 68,350 mil réis, and in the later year it produced 1,962 tons of corn (see Table 7).[8]

But Jacareí was more than just a corn producer. In 1829 it also grew rice (192 tons) and beans (215 tons), along with 241 tons of coffee. Coffee production was growing, though even as late as 1836, its output was less than half of what Areias – the leading coffee county in the province – was producing. Despite this coffee output, Jacareí remained primarily a food producer for the internal market. The corn producers, for example, held a large ratio of the local slave labor force, and in 1829 more than half these producers owned slaves. By this date close to half the production of corn and beans occurred in households with slaves, and a third of the output was produced in units which held more than 20 slaves. The big difference of this county from Cunha was that these food crops were also produced in coffee estates. Coffee plantations produced about a third of the crops for the internal market.[9] The experience here was probably quite similar to that of Areias, in that corn and other food crop producers slowly got into coffee production

---

[7] Unfortunately there are relatively few instances of the censuses recording information as to the sale of products on the internal market. In these few cases, they usually cited the local county as the destination for such sales. In the case of food products, aside from the sales within the county, there is sometimes mentioned sales to the cities of São Paulo, Santos, and Rio de Janeiro, as normal destinations for the commercialization of these products.

[8] According to Müller, Jacareí in 1836 produced the extraordinary quantity of 1,071,400 alqueires. If this number is correct, it would mean that the value of agricultural production in this county was among the wealthiest in the province. Only Jacareí, Campinas (based on sugar, corn, and bean production) and Mogi Mirim (also sugar, corn, and pigs) produced more than 300,000 mil réis. But we very much doubt the correctness of this number. Although the 1836 "Listas Nominativas" are incomplete for Jacareí, we do have information on some 500 households. These households produced 3,501 alqueires of corn, as well as 18,707 *cargas* of this product. Assuming the conversion of 2 cargas = 1 alqueire, there was produced 12,854 alqueires of corn in the county of Jacareí in this year. This figure is very far from the extraordinary number given in Müller. Although our data are incomplete, between these figures and the more complete data for earlier years, it is evident to us that the very high Müller figure is incorrect.

[9] Thus 39% of the corn, 40% of the tobacco, 36% of the rice, 31% of the beans, and 44% of the swine came from the coffee plantations.

TABLE 7. *Profile of Agricultural Activity in Selected Products in Jacareí (1804–1829)*

Quantity Produced	1804	1829
Sugar (tons)	0.1	1
Coffee (tons)		241
Tobacco (tons)	0.2	13
Cotton (tons)	21	13
Peanuts (alqueires)	34	21
Corn (tons) (1)	590	1,962
Rice (tons)	21	192
Beans (tons)	81	215
Aguardente (canadas)	673	323
Sugar cane (cargas)	10	
Brown sugar (units)	6,100	
Flour (alqueires)	30	
Pigs	194	450
Value of production (in mil réis) (2)	11,277	68,350
Percentage of total value (export products)		
Coffee		50%
Tobacco and Cotton	13%	1%
Food crops and animals		
Corn	52%	31%
Cereals and manioc		
Aguardente	12%	1%
Animals	5%	3%
Percentage of production by slave-owning households		
Corn	30%	58%
Coffee		93%
Beans	35%	41%

Notes: (1) All "cargas" of corn converted into alqueiers at 2 to 1 ratio.
(2) All prices come from Table 5. We could find no prices for either peanuts or brown sugar. For metric conversion rates see conversion notes in Table 5.
Source: Same as Table 4.

and, while their trees were maturing (taking up to four years to produce their first beans), continued to maintain themselves through traditional exports.

Jacareí also differed from Cunha in its ratio of slave laborers in agriculture. Whereas it was similar in having 80% of the households of the county dedicated to agriculture, less than 20% of these agricultural households possessed slaves (see Table 8). Clearly a lot more of the food producers worked with only free workers, most of whom were members of their immediate family. Moreover they held on average fewer slaves than their Cunha counterparts. In Jacareí the average number of slaves in the exclusively food-producing sector by 1829 was only 3 per farm, compared to 12 slaves per coffee unit.

TABLE 8. *Profile of Slaves and Slave Ownership in Jacarei, 1777, 1804, 1829*

Population and Households	1777	1804	1829
Number of inhabitants	4,099	5,154	6,882
Number of slaves	305	494	1,298
Number of free persons	3,794	4,660	5,584
Number of slave owners	104	135	232
% slaves in population	7%	10%	19%
Number of households	772	971	1,355
Number of hshlds with slaves	104	135	232
% of hshlds with slaves	13%	14%	17%
Number of "poor" hshlds		111	10
% "poor"/total hshlds		11%	1%
Statistical indicators of slave ownership			
Average slaves owned	3	4	6
Std. dev.	2.5	4.2	8.9
Median	2	2	3
Modal slaves owned	1	1	1
Gini for slave owners	0.43	0.48	0.57
Gini for hds household	0.92	0.93	0.93
Largest owners (no. slaves)	12	33	66
Slaves in agriculture		371	1,154
% of slaves		81%	90%
Slave owners in agriculture		96	180
Average slaves on farms		4	6
% of households in agriculture		80%	85%
Slaves in other activities		87	132
Slave owners in other activities		30	45
Average slaves in other activities		3	3
Characteristics of the slaves			
% Africans		30%	63%
Sex ratio (m per 100 f)	94	94	155
Average age	27	23	23

Source: Same as Table 4.

Also, given the impact of coffee, the county held more Africans among its 1,298 slaves than did Cunha. By 1829, Africans represented two-thirds of the slave labor force.

To better examine this sector of the economy we will now study each of the major food products. To do this we have added to the counties analyzed above several other typical food-producing counties (or *municípios*). Our aim is to see how these crops were produced, by whom, and if there were any changes over time. Among the eight different counties investigated, some were deeply involved in the production of sugar, for example, Itu, Capivari,

Campinas, and Mogi Mirim; or coffee like Areias; and others like Cunha and Jacareí were much more involved in crops for the internal market.

Of all the crops consumed and produced for the local market, none was as ubiquitous or important as corn. This was a food consumed by humans and animals and as such was essential to the local economy. As the visiting German military officer Friedrich von Weech noted, corn was as important in the temperate zones of Brazil as manioc was in the more tropical zones. He noted that corn was "ground in mills until it is a very fine flour (called *fuba*) and is then boiled in hot water (*angu*), or dry, is an extremely nutritious food, completely replacing bread. To make bread with this corn flour, one mixes it with some wheat flour."[10]

Corn at the same time was served as subsistence to family producers, or commercialized either directly to the market or as sales for animal feed. It was fed to pigs and thus used in the creation of lard, another important provincial product, and it was a basic feed for the mules vital to the transport network.[11] As we have already noted in the study of coffee and sugar fazendas, corn was produced on farms exclusively dedicated to its production as well as being a byproduct on many plantations producing an export crop like coffee and sugar.

In 1836 Müller estimated that the value of corn production in São Paulo represented a third of the total value of agricultural production (refer to Table 2). Areias and Jundiaí clearly demonstrate a secular trend upward of growth in total product, average production, and average number of slaves per producer (see Table 9). Both also show the decline of non-slave and smaller producers. In Jundiaí for example, corn producers who owned no slaves dropped from accounting for 40% of corn production to just 27% by 1836;

---

[10] J. Friedrich von Weech, *A agricultura e o comércio no sistema colonial* (São Paulo, 1992), pp. 123–124.

[11] Without wagon roads or navigable rivers flowing in the direction of the coast, the majority of goods moved within the province on the back of mules in this period. Mules were a major consumer of corn. A partial agricultural census of São Paulo in 1854 listed a resident mule population on the sugar and coffee estates at some 36,000 mules [Dr. José Antonio Saraiva, *Documentos com que o presidente da provincia de São Paulo instruio o relatorio da abertura da assembléa legislativa provincial no dia 15 de fevereiro de 1855* (São Paulo, 1855), unnumbered table entitled "Quadro estatistico de alguns estabelecimentos rurais da Provincia de São Paulo"]. In this same period the custom house at Cubatão – which was at the entrance to the port of Santos – reported that some 166,000 cargo mules had passed through to the port in that year [Alves da Silva, "Abastecimento em São Paulo (1835–1877): Estudo histórico do aprovisionamento da província via Barreira de Cubatão," Master's Thesis, Departamento de História, Universidade de São Paulo (São Paulo, 1985), pp. 103–104, 162.] Thus the 36,000 mules was probably an underestimate of the total resident mule population in this period. In any case, using this population as probably a minimum resident in the province in the late 1830s and estimating their consumption of corn at 1 kilo of corn per animal per day would mean that this number of mules consumed 13,400 tons of corn, which would have represented 14% of the corn produced in 1836.

TABLE 9. *Characteristics of Corn Production in Eight São Paulo Counties 1816, 1822, 1829, 1836*

	Jundiaí	Cunha (1)	Areias (2)	Itu	Capivari	Mogi Mirim	Jacarei (3)	Campinas	Total
Quantity produced (tons) (1)									
1816	1,647	0	1,547	0	0	0	0	0	3,194
1822	1,123	13	1,527	0	0	0	0	0	2,663
1829	1,732	0	2,148	0	0	0	1,962	0	5,842
1836	2,420	2,586	1,233	2,357	1,118	749	389	1,708	12,559
Number of producers									
1816	502		677						1,179
1822	431	5	781						1,217
1829	448		973				986		2,407
1836	537	237	279	481	68	110	486	59	2,257
Average output per producer (tons)									
1816	3.3		2.3						2.7
1822	2.6	2.7	2.0						2.2
1829	3.9		2.2				2.0		2.4
1836	4.5	10.9	4.4	4.9	16.4	6.8	0.8	28.9	5.6
Value (mil reis)									
1816	16,897	0	15,865	0	0	0	0	0	32,762
1822	11,742	139	15,961	0	0	0	0	0	27,842
1829	18,562	0	23,023	0	0	0	21,034	0	62,619
1836	51,247	54,749	26,115	49,906	23,664	15,860	8,227	36,165	265,934

136

Number of producers with slaves

Year									Total
1816	137	218							355
1822	126	344	5						475
1829	164	459		163					786
1836	186	160	145	75	248	50	30	22	916

Number of slaves

Year						Total
1816	1,594					2,630
1822	3,110	133				4,360
1829	5,218	3,317	966	1,107		8,056
1836	2,001	1,343	173	440	432	10,760

Slaves per slave owners growing corn

Year						Total
1816	8					7
1822	9	27				9
1829	11	7	13			10
1836	11	9	6	19	6	12

Notes: (1) Corn production in Cunha in the years 1816 and 1823 was registered in "cavalos" – some 23,968 in the former year and 11,690 in the latter one. Given our lack of a measure for conversion of this colonial measure, we have not incorporated these numbers in the table. See Table 5 for conversion rates between pre- and post-metric weights and also for the structure of prices used.

(2) Bananal was taken from Areias in 1832; this affected production data in 1836.

(3) The census for Jacareí in 1836 is incomplete.

Source: Same as Table 4.

in turn, small slave owners (those who held 10 or fewer slaves) went from controlling over half of production to just 31% (see Table 10). The increasing concentration was also seen in size of output, with those producing 15 tons of corn declining from accounting for 80% of the corn harvest in the earliest period to less than two-thirds in 1836. This concentration process was made possible by the rise in the average number of slave workers per producer, which doubled in this period.

The same process can be seen in Areias during this period. The participation of non-slave-owners in the total harvest fell from 37 to 16% between 1817 and 1836. Small slave owners (those with 10 slaves or less) also went from accounting for over half to 37% of the crop, and dropped even further in 1836 to 29% of production. In turn smaller producers – those again accounting for 15 tons per annum or less – dropped from producing over two-thirds of the crop to just over half of production. At the same time average slave holdings of Areias's corn producers went from 7 to 13 slaves in this same period (see Table 9).

It should be recalled that these two counties were major exporters of sugar and coffee respectively. Thus all farms and plantations in these regions were growing larger over time and squeezing out the smaller producers and those without slaves. Nevertheless, the growth in the farms which produced only corn also experienced this same pattern of increasing size, increasing domination of slave-produced output and finally of ever-larger producers. In Jundiaí, for example, the average output of farmers who produced only corn went from 2.4 tons per annum to 3.8 tons in 1836, while the average number of slaves held by such corn producers went from 4 to 7 slaves. In Areias these same producers of just corn went from 1.7 to 2.7 tons and the average number of their slaves from 4 to 7 in this period.

The eight counties selected for our study of corn together contained more than 2,000 farmers who produced 12,500 tons of this product (see Table 9). Some 40% of these producers had slaves and accounted for 80% of total production. These slave owners averaged 11 tons per farm which was 6 times larger than the output on non-slave farms. Even among the slave-owning producers, the bigger owners produced the bulk of the corn. Those who owned 10 slaves or less accounted for over two-thirds of the slave owners but produced only some 41% of output (see Table 10). In turn, the largest slave owners accounted for half of total production, though they were just a fifth of the producers. Smaller producers (those whose output was three tons or less), though accounting for two-thirds of the farmers, accounted for only 13% of total production. Thus the growing tendency for slave-owning producers to control the harvesting of corn and increasingly larger producers and units to produce the largest share of that production was even more evident from this eight-county survey.

These eight counties were among the most commercialized producers. But it should be stressed that corn was produced in all regions of the province.

TABLE 10. *Characteristics of Corn Producers in Eight São Paulo Counties in 1836*

	0–3	3–7.5	7.5–15	15–30	30–60	60–100	100+	Total
1. Distribution of producers by size of output (tons)								
Quantity (tons)	1,319	2,276	2,012	1,815	2,534	1,061	1,541	12,559
Number of producers	1,354	515	195	95	75	16	7	2,257
Number of slaves	1,174	2,350	2,103	1,874	2,019	812	428	10,760
2. Distribution of producers without slaves by size of output (tons)								
Quantity (tons)	994	840	308	48	33	0	151	2,375
Number of producers	1,099	207	30	3	1	0	1	1,341
3. Quantity of these producers by tons produced								
Quantity (tons)	1,112	1,746	1,315	1,141	1,481	468	1,421	8,684
Number of producers	1,144	402	127	59	45	7	6	1,790
Number of slaves	446	1,083	704	755	631	141	328	4,088

4. Distribution of producers by size of slave holding

	No Slaves	With Slaves	1 to 5	6 to 10	11 to 20	21 to 40	41+	Total
				Number of Slaves				
Quantity (tons)	2,375	10,184	2,046	1,220	2,899	1,571	2,449	12,559
Number of producers	1,341	916	453	151	177	85	50	2,257
Number of slaves		10,760	1,178	1,168	2,593	2,408	3,413	10,760
5. Distribution of producers who did not also produce coffee or sugar by size of slave holding								
Quantity (tons)	2,220	6,464	1,750	929	2,078	519	1,188	8,684
Number of producers	1,218	572	351	94	98	20	9	1,790
Number of slaves		4,088	870	719	1,361	517	621	4,088

Source: Same as Tables 4 and 5 (for prices and conversion rates).

It was an easy crop to grow; it produced annually and required low-capital investments. As the provincial economy expanded from export crops and regional trade, so too did total output of corn. Moreover, even the largest slave plantation produced some of its corn for subsistence to feed its own workers and cattle. As we saw with Areias, corn was an easily marketed crop and clearly was fundamental in sustaining the new coffee plantations until their trees began to produce after several years. Finally most of this product was probably marketed within the region it was produced, or at most in nearby markets. Demand for corn was constant everywhere and any shortfalls in local production were met by producers within the region or at most in the next region over.

The same processes noted in the production of corn could also be found repeated in the production of rice (see Table 11). Rice was also grown primarily in slave-working farms and was even found on sugar and coffee fazendas. Our analysis of rice comes from these same eight counties. What is most evident from this data is that rice was rapidly expanding in most of these counties during the first third of the nineteenth century. Areias, for example, the largest rice producer of this eight-county sample, increased its production five times over from 1817 to 1829, and the number of producers almost tripled. Of these rice producers, half owned slaves, with a high average of 12 slaves per unit. Although 78% of rice production came from these slave-owning farms, many of which were export producers as well, each unit was a relatively small producer. Over three-quarters of the producers generated less than 701 kilos and these most probably went for home consumption. Unfortunately the zone par excellence of rice exports in this period, the county Igaupe, has no surviving data and therefore we cannot outline the patterns in a zone which saw a major commercialization of the crop beyond the boundaries of the county.

In 1836, these eight municípios had 1,200 producers of rice who harvested 652 tons in that year. Over half of rice producers owned slaves, with an average of a relatively high 13 slaves per farm, and they accounted for 80% of total production. As in the other crops we have examined, production was concentrated among the larger slave-owning producers. Half of production in these eight counties occurred in units that had more than 10 slaves. The average slave-owning producer grew four times as much rice as those who owned no slaves. Thus rice, like corn, a traditional food crop, was increasingly slave-grown in the nineteenth century. But unlike corn, rice tended to be grown in non-specialized units among a host of other crops, including the major export crops of coffee and sugar, at least in these eight counties. As we have noted several times, especially in the case of sugar, the São Paulo producers were unusual in dedicating themselves to a variety of crops, many consumed both locally and regionally. In 1836 more than half of the rice production came from farms that also produced coffee and/or sugar. But even without these export producers it is evident that rice was increasingly a slave-produced crop everywhere in the province. Considering

TABLE 11. *Characteristics of Rice Production in Eight São Paulo Counties, 1816, 1822, 1829, 1836*

	Jundiaí	Cunha	Areias	Itu	Capivari	Mogi Mirim	Jacareí	Campinas	Total
	Quantity produced (tons) (1)								
1816	8	11	136						154
1822	14	8	407						429
1829	35		661				192		889
1836	61	34	300	74	34	62	62	26	652
	Number of producers of rice (with and without slaves)								
1816	62	13	334						409
1822	54	10	514						578
1829	70		883				597		1,550
1836	178	73	254	158	57	183	225	44	1,172
	Average output per producer (tons)								
1816	0.1	0.8	0.4						0.4
1822	0.3	0.8	0.8						0.7
1829	0.5		0.7				0.3		0.6
1836	0.3	0.5	1.2	0.5	0.6	0.3	0.3	0.6	0.6

(continued)

TABLE 11 (*continued*)

	Jundiaí	Cunha	Areias	Itu	Capivari	Mogi Mirim	Jacareí	Campinas	Total
Number of producers with slaves									
1816	33	13	131						177
1822	27	10	253						290
1829	56		440				130		626
1836	106	64	143	117	43	81	55	27	636
Number of slaves									
1816	338	259	1,098						1,695
1822	417	138	2,757						3,312
1829	948		5,087				994		7,029
1836	1,484	811	1,874	1,667	864	629	385	566	8,280
Average slave holding									
1816	10	20	8						10
1822	15	14	11						11
1829	17		12				8		11
1836	14	13	13	14	20	8	7	21	13

Source: Same as Tables 4 and 5 (for prices and conversions).

just the three counties of Areias, Cunha, and Jundiai, for which we have good data for the years from 1816 and 1836, producers who owned slaves expanded their weight in production from 60% to 87%. Clearly this increasing use of slaves to produce rice meant that it was increasingly a commercial crop in nineteenth century São Paulo.

Along with rice, beans were probably the most important food consumed in São Paulo from the beginning of colonization. Like rice and corn, bean production was to be found everywhere in the province and was produced on the lands of the poorest squatter to the most capitalized planter. It was normal to find beans produced on ranches as well as sugar plantations. In Jundiaí there were a relatively stable 300 bean-growing farmers in the various census years (see Table 12). Of these, approximately 40% owned slaves and these slave-owning farmers accounted for some 80% of the beans produced. The average slave-owning farm in bean production possessed between 8 to 13 slaves, and grew eight times as many beans as those with no slaves. No farmer grew more than 10 tons per year and the overwhelming majority of producers grew less than 700 kilos. Smaller producers in fact accounted for 40% of total output.[12]

For the eight counties combined in 1836 there were more than 2,000 farms growing beans, of which close to half used slaves and these accounted for 84% of production. Here the average slave farm yielded six times as much as those without slaves. The large slave owners (with more than 10 slaves) accounted for 70% of slave-produced beans and 60% of the total crop. The average slave holding of these bean producers was again a rather high 12 slaves per farm in 1836, suggesting a multi-crop environment including some export crops.

If corn, rice, and beans formed the staple of human life, it was corn that was fundamental to the creation of pork and of its most important byproduct – lard. From the earliest export statistics and the earliest travelers accounts, lard was listed as a principal export from the province, being used universally in cooking and as a fundamental grease. As one early nineteenth century traveler noted:

In the provinces located close to the Equator, there is a large consumption of lard, utilized in the preparation of all foods. Many *fazendeiros* dedicate themselves exclusively to the raising of these lucrative animals, which, with some care, can become large and very fat. It has been shown that pigs grow fat rapidly when fed with corn, and their meat is extremely tasty and healthy and is even recommended for nursing mothers and sick persons, and the resulting lard is uniform. The lard is separated from the meat, salted, packaged and shipped. It is conserved for a long time. The meat is also salted and sold.[13]

[12] An unusual producer in this county was a women of 47 years of age who owned 96 slaves on her farm and grew 30 tons of corn, 1.5 tons of coffee, 9 tons of beans, and 1 ton of rice in an average year.

[13] Weech, *Agricultura*, pp. 165–166.

TABLE 12 *Characteristics of Bean Production in Eight São Paulo Counties 1816, 1822, 1829, 1836*

	Jundiaí	Cunha	Areias	Itu	Capivari	Mogi Mirim	Jacareí	Campinas	Total
Quantity produced (tons) (1)									
1816	127	71	223						421
1822	130	33	550						713
1829	154		367				215		736
1836	167	177	267	314	131	112	115	111	1,394
Number of producers of beans (with and without slaves)									
1816	336	46	61						997
1822	271	23	663						957
1829	291		783				908		1,982
1836	365	231	263	358	66	244	449	50	2,026
Average output per producer (tons)									
1816	0.4	1.5	0.4						0.4
1822	0.5	1.4	0.8						0.7
1829	0.5	0.8	0.5				0.2		0.4
1836	0.5	0.8	1.0	0.9	2.0	0.5	0.3	2.2	0.7

Number of producers of beans (with slaves)

Year							
1816	127	42	205	98			374
1822	117	22	331				470
1829	148		423	222	151		722
1836	159	144	151	51	76	31	932

Number of slaves

Year							
1816	998	536	1,539	769			3,073
1822	1,075	401	3,104				4,580
1829	1,703		5,061	3,344	1,070		7,834
1836	2,012	1,350	1,934	977	444	756	11,586

Average slave holding

Year							
1816	8	13	8	8			8
1822	9	18	9				10
1829	12		12	15	7		11
1836	13	9	13	19	6	24	12

Source: Same as Tables 4 and 5 (for prices and conversions).

The raising of pigs was thus an almost universal practice in all the regions of the province. The process of its creation was well described by the English traveler John Mawe who noted that:

They feed their pigs on Indian corn in a crude state, the time for confining them to fatten is eight or ten months, and the quantity of corn consumed for the purpose is eight or ten Winchester bushels each. When killed, the lean is cut off the sides as clean as possible, the fat is cured with very little salt, and in a few days is ready for market. The ribs, chine-bone, and lean parts are dried for home consumption.[14]

To analyze the structure of production of pigs and lard we have selected Cunha and Jundiaí as sample counties, situated relatively close to the city of São Paulo. Although both counties were major producers of pigs and corn – their basic food – only Cunha produced large quantities of lard, whereas Jundiaí sold only live animals to its urban market and produced little lard for export. It would appear that it was easy for Jundiaí producers to ship their animals live to the São Paulo capital market, whereas Cunha had to ship almost all of its exports to Rio de Janeiro by coastal shipping, which made the sale of live animals a much less viable proposition. In 1836, both counties averaged about 2,000 tons of corn per annum, thus guaranteeing their own animal feed.

For a pig-raising center such as Cunha, the primary form of marketing was the processing of pigs into lard. But this was a complex process alternating between raising and slaughtering animals.[15] Also the numbers generated by the census-takers and by Müller most likely underestimated production. The German traveler Baron Luis Guilherme von Eschwege has some suggestive comments on this theme. He noted that in the early decades of the nineteenth century, the province of São Paulo produced 358 tons of lard and commercialized 292 tons beyond the frontiers of the province, which left only 65 tons for local consumption, which is much too low a figure given the extraordinary quantity of lard consumed in Brazil in this period. In fact he argued that production probably reached something like 4,400 tons of lard, which in turn required the raising of 100,000 pigs – a figure also not found in the census numbers.[16] As for output, these nineteenth century figures suggest that from each pig could be extracted 44 kilos of lard. Finally the fact that Müller in his census of 1836 shows that Cunha alone produced more than two-thirds of the lard generated in the province (or

[14] John Mawe, *Travels in the interior of Brazil, particularly in the gold and diamond districts of that country, by authority of the prince regent of Portugal: including a voyage to the Rio de la Plata and an historical sketch of the revolution of Buenos Ayres* (London, Printed for Longman, Hurst, Rees, Orme, and Brown, 1812), p. 75.
[15] See above note 2.
[16] Cited in Affonso de E.Taunay, *História do Café no Brasil*, 20 vols. (Rio de Janeiro, 1939), II, p. 340.

130 tons)[17] seems to suggest a serious undercounting. Given the universality of pigs and the widespread use of lard, one would not expect such an unusual concentration of production in just one county.

But what of the output which was registered? The nineteenth century travelers Mawe and Eschwege estimated that each pig raised in 8 to 12 months consumed between 200 and 250 kilos of corn in their creation, and yielded 44 kilos of lard when slaughtered. Thus the output of lard registered in 1836 – some 132 tons – would have necessitated the raising and slaughtering of 3,000 pigs which would have consumed a total of 900 tons of corn. In this year the census registered a total corn production of 2,500 tons of corn – which would seem reasonable in terms of both human and animal consumption.[18]

The Cunha data also permits us to examine the structure of production. The total of 133 tons of lard came from 119 producers: 109 heads of these owned 1,111 slaves and they accounted for 98% of total output. There is little question, then, that export lard was produced essentially in slave-owning households. The average producer made 1,100 kilos of lard (the 10 farms without slaves averaged just 300 kilos). Thus we can see the same pattern of concentration of production in larger slave units with lard that we saw with all the other food crops. The 17 farmers who produced over 1,500 kilos made up 15% of such pig farmers and accounted for 40% of the lard processed in the county. The largest producer was a farmer of 60 years of age who registered an output of 4,700 kilos using 11 slaves. He also produced 33 tons of corn beside 1,400 kilos of beans. With his corn output this farmer was able to feed 130 pigs at 303 kilos per head, and each pig in turn produced 44 kilos of lard – thus his potential lard production was 5.7 tons – and he was registered as having produced 4.7 tons. Such data help corroborate the estimates of nineteenth century travelers used here.

What about the structure of ownership and production in the raising of live animals for export as seen in the numbers for Jundiaí in 1836? The county in this year produced 3,699 pigs, who were raised by 211 farmers, of which 114 owned slaves. These slave owners accounted for 80% of total production, raising on average 26 pigs, compared to just 7 pigs per non-slave household. Production was thus quite concentrated with those who raised 30 or more pigs being just 17% of the producers and accounting for two-thirds of production. The largest producer in Jundiaí was responsible for producing some 300 animals. He was 53 years of age, had 24 slaves and produced 9 tons of corn. He also refined 14 tons of sugar, 1,800 kilos of

---

[17] This figure is almost identical to what we obtained for the unpublished census for Cunha for 1836 which was 9,079.

[18] Given an annual production of 2,500 tons of corn and supposing a consumption of 900 tons used for raising production, we estimate 1,500 tons for human consumption, which given the local population, comes out to around 5 kilos per person.

beans, and 1,100 kilos of coffee. Given the ratio of corn to pigs, he would have required 95 tons of corn to raise the 300 pigs he produced and thus must have bought the corn he needed on the open market, or conversely did not declare the corn he produced for their consumption. However, given the number of slaves he possessed the former is more likely.

Within Brazil, especially in the northeast, the planting of manioc roots and their transformation into manioc flour was a very significant part of commercial food production. But in São Paulo, although some manioc was grown along the coast, the highlands concentrated on corn, a substitute for manioc.[19] In his 1836 census Müller noted that the average manioc crop was 89,000 alqueires, this compared to rice and corn which were in the 250,000 to 300,000 alqueires category.[20] This mandioc output represented only 1% of the value of production in that year. Our survey of the eight counties shows only Areias producing manioc, and then only Manioc flour. By the 1820s there were a steady 130 producers of manioc flour in the county with an average of 3,000 alqueires per annum. As in all other crops, the role of the farmers without slaves was on the decline. In 1822 such family-run farms produced almost half the crop, and in 1829 the remaining 35 producers who held no slaves accounted for only 10% of total output.

One last area worth examining in this survey of food production is meat production. Like all other parts of Brazil, cattle were raised in São Paulo, though nothing like on the scale in the far southern plains of Rio Grande do Sul, which shared an ecology similar to that of the Argentine pampas. But animals were raised on many farms, and there even existed ranches dedicated to raising cows for meat consumption. An unusual source of information for this sector of the economy is a detailed listing of ranches within the province in the published 1854 census of Oliveira. At this time in São Paulo there were 532 ranches (*fazendas de criação*) with 35,000 head of cattle, on which worked some 4,300 slaves and 1,700 servants (or *agregados*). Of the total number of animals raised, over two-thirds (24,000) were sold off the ranch in that year. In comparison with sugar and coffee farms, these ranches held few workers. They contained only 8 slaves per unit compared to the 20 per *fazenda* in coffee and sugar, and accounted for only 14% of the farm units, 4% of the slaves, and the same ratio of the value of production. But these ranches were unusual in their high ratio of *agregados*

---

[19] Buarque de Holanda has stressed that São Paulo was "a corn civilization" in contrast to the rest of Brazil. He noted that "... the region of the highlands ... corresponds traditionally to the area of corn meal, while manioc is above all a maritime coastal crop." Sergio Buarque de Holanda, *Caminhos e fronteiras* (Rio de Janeiro, 1957), p. 215. A French traveler referring to São Paulo in 1832 noted that "the principal cultivation is corn, one finds, on the other hand few plantations of manioc. The inhabitants of this province consider manioc flour to be bad, just as in the provinces of the North [of Brazil], it is corn flour which is so considered." Alcide D'Orbigny, *Viagem pitoresca através do Brasil* (Belo Horizonte, 1976), p. 178.

[20] Without a density estimate, we cannot convert manioc alqueires into kilos.

(accounting for 26% of such workers in the province) and of course in their large land holdings (comprising an estimated 43% of all agricultural lands). Regionally the greatest concentration of these large ranches occurred in the West Paulista area (68%), with the Southern Road second (17%). The West Paulista fazendas were unusual in the high proportion of slaves which they contained, which explains why they possessed four-fifths of all slaves in this sector. They also accounted for 64% of the animals raised and sold.

Thus, despite the growth of the commercial export agricultural sector, the traditional food and animal sector all remained strong and large numbers of these farms and ranches used slave labor. Some of this growth was tied to the export sector itself as the sugar and coffee estates both grew their own food and sold food crops into the market. The increasing tempo of the local economy also created demand for more food production as population increased and more traditional food producers entered more fully into the market. But the ever-increasing importance of sugar and coffee exports did lead to a relative decline of slaves within this food-producing sector. By 1829, although the slaves and slave owners in food production had increased considerably, their relative importance among farmers and slave owners was on the decline. The cause for this was the growth of the export crops of sugar and coffee that drew ever-higher ratios of slaves into the production of these crops.

But however much slaves were drawn to coffee in the rest of the century, the food-producing sector remained strong and continued to use slaves along with free labor. The bedrock of *paulista* agriculture remained food crop production, which expanded along with the export crops during the first part of the nineteenth century. Given the increasing importation of African slaves for sugar and coffee, even exclusive food producers, such as those planting corn, could have access to some slave labor. As the economy and population expanded, more and more of these crops were marketed locally and thus provided funds for slave purchases. Food producers selling into the market, of course, used more slaves than did subsistence farmers, and increasing slave concentration even among these farmers could be seen over time. But it is clear that African slaves entered even into the very traditional food-producing market of São Paulo and remained an important element in these non-export crops until emancipation.

5

The Transition from Slavery to Freedom through Manumission: A Life-Cycle Approach Applied to the United States and Guadeloupe

Frank D. Lewis

I

The transition from slavery to freedom in the Americas has been one of the central themes of Stanley Engerman's research.[1] This emphasis, which characterizes much of the research on slavery over the past fifteen years, represents arguably a natural progression in the historiography of slavery. The earlier work on the United States, culminating with *Time on the Cross* and *Without Consent or Contract*, was concerned mainly with the characteristics of the slave system and its effects. The focus was on profitability, productivity, the physical treatment of slaves, and the impact of slavery on economic development. Although Seymour Drescher and others have long been concerned with the question, economists and historians, among them Laird Bergad, Barry Higman, and of course Stan Engerman, have more recently turned their attention to why, after being a dominant form of labor organization in many regions, slavery came to an end, over a comparatively short period.[2]

I am grateful to David Eltis, Stanley Engerman, and Ronald Findlay for helpful comments. I also thank workshop participants at the Canadian Economic Association meetings and the Conference in Honor of Stanley Engerman.

[1] For example, Stanley L. Engerman, "Slavery and Emancipation in Comparative Perspective: A Look at Some Recent Debates," *Journal of Economic History* 46 (1986): 317–39; "The Economic Response to Emancipation and Some Economic Aspects of the Meaning of Freedom," in Frank McGlynn and Seymour Drescher (eds.), *The Meaning of Freedom: Economics, Politics, and Culture after Slavery* (Pittsburgh, 1992), pp. 49–68; and "Emancipation in Comparative Perspective: A Long and Wide View," in Gert Oostindie (ed.), *Fifty Years Later: Antislavery, Capitalism and Modernity in the Dutch Orbit* (Pittsburgh, 1995), pp. 223–41.

[2] In the New World full emancipation was achieved over the period 1834–1888. But if we exclude Britain and consider that free birth in Brazil and Cuba was enacted earlier, then the period 1847–1871 perhaps better reflects how concentrated emancipation was. See Stanley L. Engerman, "Emancipation in Comparative Perspective." For comprehensive discussions that

Most researchers of the transition from slavery to freedom have focused on the legislative actions that, within jurisdictions, emancipated all slaves at roughly the same time. There were, however, some slaves, although a very small proportion of the total, who secured their freedom well before the general abolitions. The manumission of these slaves has received little attention, hardly surprising given the small numbers involved, but the mechanism has not been ignored entirely. A special 1989 issue of the journal *Slavery and Abolition* is devoted to entirely to manumission; Drescher and Engerman's *A Historical Guide to World Slavery* includes an entry on manumission that lists quite a number of sources;[3] and we now have a variety of case studies to draw on, including those of Bergad et al., Libby and Paiva, and Brana-Shute.[4] Not surprisingly, the specific findings of these researchers differ; but some aspects of manumission are common to a variety of regions and time periods. These include the higher rates of manumission of females and those of mixed blood, the higher rates in urban areas, and the comparatively low rates among younger (adult) slaves. The more recent studies point to a strong economic motivation for manumission on the part of owners, and to the important role of the slaves themselves, in determining whether freedom was granted.

Recognizing that social and religious factors were at the root of many manumissions, the approach taken here is in the spirit of studies that emphasize the economic aspect. Specifically, manumission is treated as a life-cycle problem, involving a transaction whereby slaves purchase their freedom, either explicitly or implicitly. It is hoped that the analysis, while stylized, can shed light on the patterns of manumission, and how rates of manumission were affected by such factors as the productivity of workers, both slave and free, the access of slaves to borrowing, and the specific features of the emancipation process. The life-cycle model will be applied first to the U.S. South. The simulations developed using data from that region are suggestive of what factors were important in the manumission decision. The other case study is for the French Caribbean islands of Guadeloupe. The French colonies had in place a well-defined process by which freedom for slaves could be secured,

---

include the transition from slavery to freedom, see Seymour Drescher (foreward by Stanley L. Engerman), *From Slavery to Freedom: Comparative Studies in the Rise and Fall of Atlantic Slavery* (New York, 1999); Barry Higman, *Slave Population and Economy in Jamaica: 1807–1834* (Kingston, 1995); and Laird Bergad, Fe Iglesias Garcia, and Maria Del Carmen Barcia, *The Cuban Slave Market, 1790–1880* (New York, 1995).

3 Seymour Drescher and Stanley L. Engerman, *A Historical Guide to World Slavery* (New York, 1998).

4 Bergad et al., *Cuban Slave Market*; Douglas C. Libby and Clotilde A. Paiva, "Manumission Practices in a Late Eighteenth-Century Brazilian Slave Parish: Sao José d'El Rey in 1795," *Slavery and Abolition* 21 (2000): 96–127, and Rosemary Brana-Shute, "Approaching Freedom: The Manumission of Slaves in Suriname, 1760–1828," *Slavery and Abolition* 10, *Special Issue: Perspectives on Manumission*, edited by Frank McGlynn (1989): 40–63.

and the result, in the case of Guadeloupe at least, is an individual-level data set that may be the best available for analysing certain questions relating to manumission.

In the United States, emancipation through manumission was rare. On the eve of the Civil War, the number of free blacks in the United States, 488,000, was only 12 percent of the slave population of whom about half were in living in slave states.[5] Thus, roughly 6 percent of the black population in the South were freedmen or their descendants, and of the entire free population of the slave states only 3 percent were black. This record stands in contrast to the experience of nineteenth century slave colonies in other parts of the Americas. In these areas manumission was more widely accepted, non-whites came to comprise a larger component of the free population, and, ultimately, full emancipation was achieved with less violence.[6] Such areas present a better opportunity to study certain aspects of manumission than does the United States. Here the focus will be on the French colony, Guadeloupe. Guadeloupe's slave population never reached 100,000, less than 2.5 percent that of the United States; but even though the colony was not a major player in the slave market, the limited scale of the economy, the fact that the economy was based almost exclusively on sugar, and perhaps most importantly the excellent records that were kept of manumissions, help make Guadeloupe an ideal case study.[7]

The colony of Guadeloupe, two small islands in the eastern Caribbean, was first settled by the French in 1635.[8] At first, the colony was run by the Compagnie des Isles de l'Amerique; then, in 1674, it came under the direct control of the Crown. African slaves were introduced when the colony was established, but in the early years indentured servants (*engagés*) were the more important source of labor. By the nineteenth century, however, the population had become more than 75 percent slaves. Most slaves worked on plantations where sugar was the primary output, accounting, in 1840, for 80 percent of the value of cash crops.[9] There was, at that time, a significant – 20

---

[5] These blacks would have been free mainly as a result of the earlier abolitions, although included in this group were freed slaves who left the South. United States Bureau of the Census, *Historical Statistics of the United States, Colonial Times to 1970* (Washington, 1975), pp. 18, 24–37.

[6] With the exception of the slave revolt in St. Domingue, the transition to freedom in the Americas came about with minimal violence on the part of slaves; and, perhaps just as surprisingly, modest resistance on the part of slave owners for whom abolition meant the expropriation of property with little or no compensation.

[7] Annual population estimates are given in *Tableau de Relevés de Population: 1839–1860*, series geographique, Guadeloupe.

[8] Their combined area is under 1,500 km². Henri Bongou gives a good overview that covers the years prior to abolition in *La Guadeloupe, 1492–1848* (Aurillac, 1962).

[9] Coffee was the other major cash and export crop.

percent – urban population of whom half were slaves. France, especially after the restoration of the Monarchy in 1815, began exerting strong influence through the appointed governor. The governor received a steady stream of ordinances and ministerial dispatches from the center that affected nearly all aspects of colonial life including the process of manumission.

Following the Royal Ordinance of April 12, 1832, which modified the procedures by which slaves could secure their freedom and included the elimination of a substantial fee, there was a flood of manumissions (*affranchissements*).[10] During the years 1832 though 1835 alone, 6,591 *patents de liberté* were granted, representing 6.6 percent of the (1832) slave population. By December 1835, the number of free non-whites was one-fifth the number of slaves and non-whites comprised more than 60 percent of the free population. Over the next six years, an additional 4,520 slaves gained their freedom through manumission. Thus, even though full emancipation in Guadeloupe did not come until March 4, 1848, significant numbers were freed well before that date.

How slaves were manumitted in Guadeloupe and elsewhere varied, but the specific reasons given in the applications for *affranchissements* offer insights into the process. In a summary of patents issued up to October 1832, the most widely cited motivating factor by far was *bon service*.[11] Of the 292 manumissions granted to those 14 years of age and older, 50 percent were given for this reason. In 27 percent of the cases a relative applied for the patent, and 14 percent were a result of *mariage*. The proportions were similar for men and women. In some cases there appears to have been an implicit agreement whereby a slave would be freed upon the death of the owner. From 1838 to 1841, the applicants listed on 127 patents or 9 percent of the total were widows or other heirs of the owner.[12] Some slaves petitioned directly for a patent in which case the applicant was listed as the *procureur du roi*, but in the vast majority of cases it was the owner of the slave who was the specified applicant.

Given the legal process that was in place in Guadeloupe and other French colonies, manumission was, at least in principle, an option for those in bondage. Moreover, if we treat manumission strictly as a market transaction, all that was required of the slave was to pay the owner his or her market price. Given the restrictions on property ownership by slaves, such

---

[10] The various ordinances and ministerial dispatches affecting manumission are recorded in the *Bulletin Officiel de la Guadeloupe* (Basse-Terre, Guadeloupe, 1832–1842). For a discussion of manumission in Guadeloupe, see Josette Follope, "Les Affranchissements d'Esclaves à la Guadeloupe entre 1815 et 1848," *Annals de l'Université d'Abidjan 6, Histoire* (1978): 5–32.

[11] The information on manumissions has been drawn from the *Bulletin Officiel de la Guadeloupe*.

[12] These patents were for slaves aged 14 years or older.

Frank D. Lewis

payments were rarely explicit; but tacit agreements could be made whereby an owner offered freedom to a slave as a reward for past effort. Consistent with this arrangement, manumission, in this paper, will be treated as a contract between a slave and an owner, where the slave either makes an explicit payment, or provides extra labor to the owner over and above what normally would be expected, in return for his or her eventual freedom.

The economic literature on slavery has tended to view those affected, both slave owners and slaves, as economic agents; but agents facing very different constraints. Owners were contrained in terms of the amount of labor they could extract from their slaves and by the payments needed to induce slaves to provide that labor. Slaves, of course, were constrained in much more profound ways, although for the purpose of the analysis here, they will simply be constrained to work according to conditions stipulated by the owner. Given this interpretation, the relationship between slave and owner might be described as one of principal and agent. The owner, as principal, is trying to induce the slave, as agent, to act in the owner's interest. Ronald Findlay, who was the first to approach slavery in this way formally, argued that it was in the owner's interest to combine positive incentives with physical force or threats of force to increase his slaves' effort.[13] Findlay further argued that the reaction of slaves to these incentives would ultimately determine how much income both in cash and in kind they would receive, as well as the degree of coercion.[14]

The analysis here is in the Findlay tradition. Slave owners are assumed to offer incentives to slaves, which would normally be in the form of increased consumption, but may include a commitment to manumit at a future date. Thus, manumission is seen as one of an array of incentives that owners had available to induce greater effort from their slaves and thus increase their value.[15] The model in this principal–agent relationship, as is usual in models of this type, will be developed mainly from the perspective of the agent, in this case, the slave. Owners are viewed as offering a range of contracts to slaves, some of which include a promise to manumit; but it is the slave who chooses the contract. Manumission, if it occurs, is therefore treated primarily as the slave's decision, though crucial to that decision are the various terms the owner has specified.

---

[13] Ronald Findlay, "Slavery, Incentives, and Manumission: A Theoretical Model," *Journal of Political Economy* 83 (1975): 923–33.

[14] In Findlay's model the slaves' output share is the product of the elasticity of output with respect to labor, and the elasticity of the (slave) labor input with respect to the output they receive as positive incentives.

[15] In the formal model developed in Section 2, the productivity of slaves is treated as given and slaves are assumed to turn over more of their output to the owner. An alternative approach would be to allow for a productivity effect as well. This would complicate the analysis, but would not change the main message of the paper.

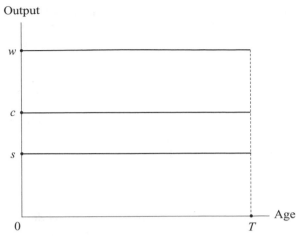

FIGURE I. Marginal Product (*w*), Consumption (*c*) and the Level of Expropriation (*s*) with Perfect Capital Markets

II

A slave is assumed to be manumitted once he acquires his purchase (market) price. The model is concerned with the conditions under which this amount will be accumulated. First, consider an agent, again to use the terminology of the principal–agent model, who, as a slave, must give up a portion of his marginal product to the owner. In Figure 1, the marginal product of the slave is denoted by *w* and the expropriated amounts by *s*. In the absence of saving or borrowing, the slave's consumption, *c*, is the difference between the two.[16] In this stylized framework, the owner cares only about the amount he expropriates, which is also the payment stream that determines the price of the slave each period.[17] It follows that if the slave can borrow an amount equal to that price, it will be in the interest of the owner to manumit the slave, and at the earliest possible time.[18]

---

[16] To simplify the figure, *w* and *s* have been treated as constant; and, because there is no saving or borrowing, *c* is constant as well. But in the empirical work to follow, all will be allowed to vary.

[17] The lifetime of the slave would also affect his price, but this is assumed not to depend on the actions of the owner, at least as they relate to manumission.

[18] This result depends on the marginal product of the freedman being at least as great as that of a slave. Fogel and Engerman argue that the high productivity associated with plantation slavery may have been one of the factors that discouraged manumission in the United States. Robert W. Fogel and Stanley L. Engerman, "Philanthropy at Bargain Prices: Notes on the Economics of Gradual Emancipation," in Fogel and Engerman (eds.), *Without Consent or Contract: The Rise and Fall of American Slavery, Technical Papers*, Vol. II (New York, 1992), pp. 379–83.

The intuition is immediate. If an owner is prepared to free a slave for his market value and if a slave can borrow this amount, then, as long as his productivity is not reduced, the slave's (or freedman's) consumption will be at least as great regardless of when or even whether he purchases his freedom.[19] Assuming the agent prefers freedom over slavery, both the owner and the slave receive the greatest total benefit if manumission occurs at the start of the slave's (working) life.[20] But this outcome requires borrowing on the part of slaves. The implication, then, is that slaves' inability to borrow may have been the key impediment to manumission. The importance of borrowing also suggests a potential role for government as a source of funds; and it suggests that a large population of free blacks, willing to provide loans to slaves, would tend to increase the rate of manumission.[21] Ruling out all borrowing in the model helps sharpen the analysis but, as will be discussed later, some of those manumitted likely made commitments to provide additional work to their former owners. This form of forward contracting of labor seems to have allowed some slaves to attain their freedom at younger ages than would otherwise have been possible.

Manumission with No Borrowing

In a model with borrowing and no productivity effect due to slavery, slaves are predicted to purchase their freedom at the start of their (working) life. In this section, such borrowing is ruled out. Instead, slaves who are manumitted must accumulate their full purchase price before they are freed.[22] This restriction delays manumission, and, depending on how severe the effect, may altogether prevent slaves from being manumitted, which in fact was the more common outcome.

The model, described formally in the Appendix, is illustrated in Figure 2. As before the agent's marginal product is constant as is the amount the owner

---

[19] In some regions, the U.S. South for example, freedmen typically had lower productivity than plantation slaves. Although the disamenities associated with slavery more than offset any productivity advantage, the lower productivity associated with freedom did mean the sacrifice of some consumption.

[20] Because the possibility of manumission might make the slave better off, a potential surplus is created. Not only does the slave benefit, but the owner may gain as well because it opens up the possibility that a greater amount can be expropriated. Note that even if freedom leads to lower productivity, manumission should still occur at the start of the slave's life as long as the disamenities associated with slavery more than offset the productivity advantage.

[21] Lawrence Kotlikoff and Anton Rupert, to cite an example from the United States, found that free blacks played a major role in manumitting slaves in New Orleans over the period 1827–46 (Lawrence J. Kotlikoff and Anton J. Rupert, "The Manumission of Slaves in New Orleans, 1827–1846," in Fogel and Engerman, *Without Consent or Contract: Technical Papers*, pp. 606–613).

[22] In the formal model, slaves are assumed to accumulate their purchase price through saving. In practice, saving in the form of money or financial assets would have been very rare; rather, slaves accumulated implicit credits from the owners that resulted in their eventual freedom.

Output

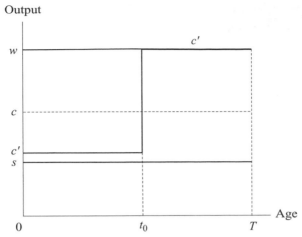

FIGURE 2. Marginal Product (w), Consumption (c), and the Level of Expropriation (s) with Borrowing

expropriates each period. But, because the slave must save to purchase his freedom, the pattern of consumption is different. Consumption is lower prior to manumission time, t_0, and then jumps to the worker's full marginal product, w. Note that in this framework $c - c'$ represents the amount the slave accumulates each period up to t_0, whether as explicit savings or as implicit commitments by the owner. At time t_0 the cumulated amount equals the slave's purchase price. Regardless of when the slave purchases his freedom, his aggregate lifetime consumption will be the same;[23] but the earlier manumission takes place the lower will be his consumption prior to t_0.

Given that slaves would have had to maintain at least a subsistence level of consumption, the earliest time manumission was possible depended on the ratio of a slave's marginal product to subsistence, as well as the expropriation rate of the owner. The relation is described in Figure 3 (p. 158) for a expropriation rate of 50 percent, discount rates of 4 and 8 percent, and a working lifetime of 40 years. Because the owner is assumed to expropriate half the slave's marginal product, that marginal product must be at least double subsistence to make manumission feasible. As the marginal product increases beyond that point, minimum age at manumission declines, although at a decreasing rate. At a ratio of marginal product to subsistence of 2.2, and a 4 percent discount rate, minimum time to manumission is 33 years; it is 23 years at a ratio of 3.0 and 17 years at a ratio of 5.0. Note

---

[23] More exactly, the present value of the agent's lifetime consumption will be independent of manumission time.

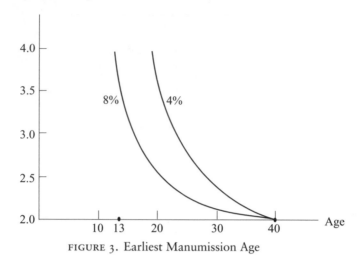

FIGURE 3. Earliest Manumission Age

that because the slave is saving toward the eventual purchase of his freedom, minimum age at manumission is lower if the discount rate is 8 percent.[24]

The relation in Figure 3 between marginal product and minimum age at manumission is based on a constant rate of expropriation. Findlay argued that the expropriation rate would depend largely on how elastic was the supply of effort of slaves with respect to their wage. If, as seems likely, more productive slaves were more responsive to positive incentives, they would receive a larger share of their marginal product, and Figure 3 would tend to understate the negative relation between manumission age and marginal product.[25]

Manumission and the Value of Freedom

The foregoing results illustrate that, for a given expropriation rate, manumission would have been possible at high enough levels of slave productivity. But slaves who purchased their freedom would have faced a cost additional to the amount they paid the owner. The nature of this cost is illustrated by Figure 2, where total lifetime consumption of the slave is the same regardless

---

[24] Minimum age at manumission, t_{min} is derived from

$$\int_0^{t_{min}} [(1 - k)w - c_m]e^{-rt}dt = \int_{t_{min}}^T kwe^{-rt}dt.$$

[25] A comparison of slave prices with the wages of equivalent workers in Guadeloupe suggests that, in fact, more productive slaves did receive a larger share of their marginal products.

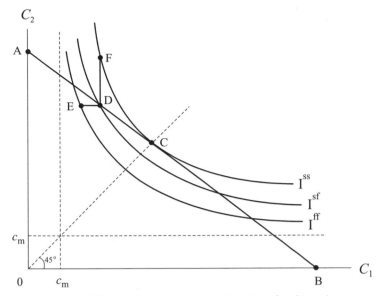

FIGURE 4. The Consumption-Equivalent Benefit of Freedom

of whether the slave purchases his freedom. What differs is the consumption path. In the absence of manumission, consumption c is constant; but if the slave is manumitted at time t_o, consumption c' is lower prior to t_o and higher thereafter. Given the usual preference for a roughly equal level of consumption over the lifetime, consumption path c would be preferred. Alternatively, an agent would choose c' over c only if there were an additional benefit. The implication is that a slave, who chose to be manumitted at time, t_o, would do so only if the freedom he would enjoy after t_o was sufficient compensation for the inferior consumption path.

The calculation of the benefit, presented in detail in the Appendix, is illustrated in Figure 4 for the case of two periods. The agent's consumption in each of the periods is given by C_1 and C_2; and along AB the value of total consumption is the same.[26] Three states are considered: the agent is a slave both periods, the agent is a slave the first period and free the second, and the agent is free both periods.[27] Corresponding to the three states are three indifference curves, I^{ss}, I^{sf}, and I^{ff}, drawn in such a way that the agent is assumed to regard all points on all the curves as equivalent. Thus, the lower

[26] In this stylized representation, both the discount rate and the pure rate of time preference (the rate at which utility is discounted) are set equal to zero.

[27] In principle, one could imagine a scenario where the agent, free in the first period, chooses to be a slave in the second for much higher consumption. Because the purpose here is to shed light on manumission, this case, although certainly possible and not unknown, is not addressed.

consumption represented along I^{sf} and, even more so, along I^{ff} is offset by the benefit of freedom. Included in the figure is subsistence consumption c_m, an amount below which consumption may not fall. As a slave both periods, the agent would choose point C, consuming the same amount each period; but, if he is to be free in the second period, the best he can do is choose point D, where consumption is lower in the first period and higher in the second. Because of the borrowing constraint, no point on I^{ff} is attainable by the agent.

The benefit of freedom is derived from the perspective of point D and involves two hypothetical exercises. In the first, the agent is asked how much consumption he would be willing to give up in the first period, as a slave, in order to be free both periods. ED represents that amount, and is one measure of the benefit of freedom, expressed in terms of consumption. The second measure involves asking the agent, again from the perspective of point D, how much his consumption in period 2 would have to be raised in order that he would agree to be a slave both periods rather than just the first. This measure assumes that the slave has accumulated enough to purchase his freedom. The amount, DF, is larger, indeed in the simulations it is found to be very much larger, than ED. The differential results from the fact that, in the case of ED, consumption is being reduced from what would already be a low level; whereas in the case of DF, consumption is being increased from a much higher level.

In the example illustrated by Figure 4, the agent is indifferent between purchasing his freedom after the first period and remaining a slave for both periods. The actual estimation will extend the comparison to any two consecutive periods. Thus, the consumption-equivalent benefit of freedom will be calculated for agents who are indifferent between purchasing their freedom at any two consecutive ages. The benefit will turn out to depend to a large degree on the age at which the indifference relation holds.

III

In this section, simulations are presented that illustrate the relationship between (optimal) manumission time and the implied benefit of freedom.[28] Although illustrative in nature, the calculations are based on conditions faced by slaves in the mid nineteenth century U.S. South. Following the earlier discussion, the benefit of freedom will be interpreted as the change in consumption that would make an agent indifferent between remaining a slave an additional period and becoming a freedman. The calculation is illustrated

---

[28] For an interpretation of the cost of freedom see Pieter C. Emmer, "The Price of Freedom: The Constraints of Change in Post-Emancipation America," in Frank McGlynn and Seymour Drescher (eds.), *The Meaning of Freedom: Economics, Politics, and Culture after Slavery* (Pittsburgh, 1992), pp. 23–48.

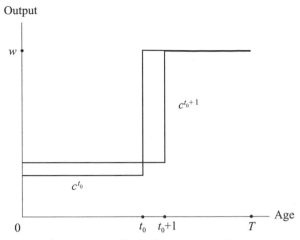

FIGURE 5. Consumption Paths for Manumission at t_0, $t_0 + 1$

by Figure 5, where c^t represents the consumption path of an agent who is manumitted at time t. Because the consumption path of an agent who is manumitted at time t_0 rather than $t_0 + 1$ includes an additional period of low consumption, manumission at the earlier time imposes an additional cost on the agent. If, despite this cost, the agent is indifferent between manumission at the two dates, it follows that the benefit of the additional year of freedom must equal that cost. Equation (1) describes the relationship formally:

$$f = \sum_{t=1}^{t_0} u\left[c_s^I(t)\right] + \sum_{t=t_0+1}^{T} u\left[c_f^I(t)\right] - \left\{ \sum_{t=1}^{t_0-1} u\left[c_s^O(t)\right] + \sum_{t=t_0}^{T} u\left[c_f^O(t)\right] \right\}, \quad (1)$$

where f is the benefit of (one year of) freedom, $u(c)$ represents the utility from consumption each period, $c_{s(f)}^O$ is the consumption, while a slave (while free), of an agent who is manumitted at time t_0, and $c_{s(f)}^I$ corresponds to an agent who is manumitted at time $t_0 + 1$. The benefit of freedom to a slave whose optimal manumission time is t_0 is the difference between the total utilities provided by the two consumption streams.

In the context of Equation (1), why freedom provides a benefit is not addressed, but one might imagine three classes of effects. First, slaves were constrained in terms of the type of work they were required to perform, the conditions of work especially as it involved supervision and physical coercion, and the organization of labor. Fogel and Engerman, for example, have valued the aversion of slaves to working on plantations with systems of gang labor.[29] Second, much of slave income was received in kind and thus was

---

[29] See, for example, Robert W. Fogel, Robert A. Galantine, and Richard L. Manning (eds.), *Without Consent or Contract: The Rise and Fall of American Slavery, Evidence and Methods* (New York, 1992), p. 379.

dictated to a large degree by owners. To the extent that the composition
of slaves' consumption differed from what they would have freely chosen
with the equivalent income, there would be a loss in utility. Finally, there
were the more intangible benefits of freedom that someone who has never
been a slave cannot appreciate. No attempt is made here to distinguish between these benefits; rather, the three effects are subsumed within the single
measure f.

To estimate the benefit of freedom using this approach, simulations have
been run based on values roughly consistent with the estimates in Fogel and
Engerman and Fogel, Galantine, and Manning[30] Central to the calculations
is the assumption that slaves are unable to borrow against income they will
receive once they are free.[31] Results are derived for marginal products of
labor of $100, $150, and $200.[32] Subsistence is put at $30, and 50 percent
of the marginal product of a slave is assumed to be expropriated by the
owner.[33] Time 0 is interpreted as age 18 and lifetime (i.e., additional years
of life) T is assumed to be 40 years.[34] Note that the expropriation rate of
50 percent is well above the 12 percent rate that has been widely cited and
disputed; but as Fogel, Galantine, and Manning point out, the lower estimate
is a lifetime value which includes the cost of rearing the slave and the cost of
those slaves whose early mortality prevented them from providing a return

[30] Robert W. Fogel and Stanley L. Engerman, *Time on the Cross: Evidence and Methods – A Supplement* (Boston, 1974); and Fogel et al., *Without Consent or Contract: Evidence and Methods.*

[31] As well, an agent's labor productivity as a slave and a freedman is assumed to be the same. The latter assumption is certainly implausible in light of Fogel and Engerman's productivity estimates. Fogel and Engerman, *Time on the Cross*, estimate a substantial total factor pro-ductivity advantage on slave farms, especially those with large numbers of slaves; moreover Fogel et al., *Without Consent or Contract: Evidence and Methods*, pp. 379–83, argue that because the capital input per worker on slave farms was higher, the differential in labor productivity was even greater. Fogel et al. put the ratio of the marginal product on free and slave farms at 1.98, which compares to the ratio of 1.44 assumed in Fogel and Engerman, *Time on the Cross*. Fogel and Engerman do not claim, however, that slavery, per se, led to higher productivity; rather they suggest that the sources of the productivity gain were the economies of scale and production methods used on mid- and large-scale plantations. By and large free labor refused to work on plantations, despite the higher wage they could have earned. One possible source of higher productivity implied by Findlay's work, was the level and types of coercion associated with slavery and not available to employers of free labor.

[32] The simulations assume marginal products are the same whether the worker is slave or free.

[33] In the figures of the previous section, the marginal product of a slave is constant, but in fact the labor productivity of slaves followed an inverted U pattern, not unlike current wage profiles. The estimates used in the analysis are from Fogel et al., *Without Consent or Contract: Evidence and Methods*, p. 206. The base marginal products apply to those aged 30–34.

[34] Ibid., p. 285. It would be possible to derive results for an uncertain lifetime. That is, rather than assuming that everyone lives 40 years, each agent could face yearly mortality rates consistent with a life expectancy of 40 years. It seems unlikely that this complication would affect the main results.

to the owner.[35] Subsistence consumption is taken to be two-thirds of the Fogel and Engerman estimate of basic income.[36] As described in Figure 4, the level of subsistence c_m can be especially important because, depending on its relation to the slave's net income, it may seriously limit the amount a slave can potentially save toward the purchase of his freedom.

Simulations of the consumption-equivalent benefit of freedom are presented in Table 1.[37] To obtain numerical results, assumptions must be made about an agent's preferences over consumption in different periods or, in terms of Figure 4, about the nature of the agent's indifference curves.[38] Preferences aside, the first result is that, in the absence of borrowing and assuming a base marginal product of $150, manumission cannot take place for at least 20 years or until age 38. This is essentially the result illustrated in Figure 3. Even if a slave were to consume no more than subsistence, it would take that time to accumulate his purchase price.[39] For ages 38 and higher, however, manumission would have been feasible, and for these ages the implied benefit of freedom can be computed. The benefit, described as the consumption "loss," represents the amount in period $t_0 - 1$ that the slave would be willing to give up to attain his freedom 1 year sooner. It corresponds to ED in Figure 4. At age 40, for example, the benefit of freedom using this interpretation is $10.30, not a large sum; but it would drive the agent close to subsistence. The consumption "gain," which corresponds to

---

[35] Ibid., pp. 383–87.

[36] The "basic income" of slaves is put at $34, adjusted to $48 for adult slaves (Fogel and Engerman, *Time on the Cross: Evidence and Methods*, p. 117). Subsistence is thus being treated as roughly 2/3 this basic income. One factor not considered in the simulations is the effect of increased consumption on slave productivity.

[37] The first column in Table 1 is consumption in the agent's last year of slavery; the second column is the most consumption the slave would be willing to give to be manumitted in that year; the third column is consumption during the first year of freedom; and the fourth column is the minimum additional consumption that would be required for the person to agree to remain a slave for that year.

[38] In the formal model the pure rate of time preference (the degree to which future utility is discounted) is assumed to be 2 percent, and the intertemporal rate of time preference (a measure of the curvature of the intertemporal indifference curves) is set equal to 2. Given the life-cycle pattern of marginal products and assuming the intermediate value of $150, the implied price of an 18-year-old slave is about $1,400. This estimate is not far off the $1,850 price reported by Fogel et al., *Without Consent or Contract: Evidence and Methods*, p. 263. But it should be noted that the discount rate is much less that the rate of return to capital on slave farms. Applying the higher productivity estimates of $200 gives rise to a price of $1,900 at the 4-percent discount rate.

[39] The delay is partly due to the inverted U-shaped pattern of marginal products (Fogel et al., *Without Consent or Contract: Evidence and Methods*, p. 206). Assuming that the rate of expropriation was proportional to the marginal product of slaves, the high marginal products, from ages 30 to 40 particularly, gave rise to high purchase prices early in the slave's life; and the comparatively low marginal products of slaves younger than age 30 meant that not enough output would have remained after the owner's share and subsistence to accumulate this amount prior to age 38.

Frank D. Lewis

TABLE I. *Age at Manumission and the Value of Freedom*

Age	Consumption $t_0 - 1$	Value of Freedom (loss)	Consumption t_0	Value of Freedom (gain)	f
$w = 100$					
42	31.5	1.5	78.4	>1,000	23.259
44	35.6	5.6	77.6	>1,000	6.655
46	39.4	8.9	76.3	880.00	2.996
48	42.3	10.6	75.6	275.40	1.951
50	45.1	11.2	74.3	128.30	1.361
52	47.4	9.0	73.0	46.10	0.729
54	49.4	8.3	72.1	31.20	0.555
56	51.3	4.3	68.8	9.70	0.223
$w = 150$					
38	34.0	4.0	117.2	>1,000	15.363
40	43.4	13.3	116.5	>1,000	4.640
42	51.3	19.1	115.6	756.90	2.286
44	58.1	21.4	114.7	271.70	1.437
46	64.1	18.9	112.9	102.90	0.807
48	69.1	17.3	112.1	64.90	0.583
50	73.7	15.1	110.3	42.30	0.423
52	77.8	9.2	108.7	18.80	0.214
54	81.3	7.5	107.6	13.30	0.158
56	84.8	2.5	103.0	3.5	0.047
$w = 200$					
36	32.4	2.4	155.0	>1,000	26.630
38	47.5	17.4	154.7	>1,000	5.023
40	60.3	27.7	153.8	>1,000	2.421
42	71.2	30.5	152.8	350.70	1.349
44	80.5	29.9	151.7	176.40	0.896
46	88.9	23.5	149.4	79.50	0.510
48	95.9	20.4	148.6	53.00	0.370
50	102.4	16.9	146.3	35.40	0.265
52	108.2	9.4	144.3	15.6	0.128
54	113.3	7.2	143.1	10.6	0.090
56	118.3	1.8	137.1	2.3	0.021

Note: $r = .04$, $\rho = .02$, $\delta = 1$, $T = 40$ years, $m = \$30$, $s = .5w$
Source: see text.

DF in Figure 4, is the minimum increase the agent would accept, in period t_0, in order to agree to remain a slave for that year (only). The amount declines dramatically with age, and perhaps better reflects the advantage to slaves of delaying the purchase of their freedom. At manumission ages of 40 or younger, the implied benefit of freedom is over \$1,000; and it is only at ages above 50 that the benefit declines to comparatively modest values.

As the marginal product of the agent rises from $100 to $200 the benefit of freedom required to induce manumission declines sharply. Consider a slave who chooses to purchase his freedom at age 50. The benefit, as reflected by the "gain," falls from $128 at a marginal product of $100 to $35 at a marginal product of $200. These simulation results suggest that rising slave productivity would have created strong incentives for slaves and owners to enter into agreements leading to eventual manumission. At the same time, even at a marginal product of $200, slaves would likely have waited until at least age 40 before purchasing their freedom. Finally, it is worth pointing out again that the simulations in Table 1 assume that the transition from slavery to freedom has no impact on the agent's productivity. Allowing for a drop in productivity of the order estimated by Fogel, Galantine, and Manning. would increase optimal age at manumission, although the extent is quite sensitive to the parameter assumptions.[40]

Manumission was less common in the U.S. South than in other slave regions of the Americas, yet the model suggests that the high productivity of U.S. slaves, particularly in the years just prior to the Civil War, should have led possibly to higher rates of manumission. Given the limited evidence, the reasons for the small number of manumissions in the United States must be somewhat speculative; but it appears that constraints against the freeing of slaves played an important role. Perhaps the most serious impediment was a combination of a lack of formal procedures and increasingly severe restrictions on manumission.[41] Another factor, emphasized by Fogel and Engerman, and alluded to previously, was the much lower productivity of freedmen. Certainly the effect on later consumption of the lower productivity reduced the incentive of slaves to save toward their eventual freedom; but simulations that allow for differential productivity suggest that the effect on the manumission decision was small.[42] The racial composition of the population in the U.S. South, in comparison with other slave regions, may have contributed to a lower rate of manumission. In areas where a larger proportion of the free population was of mixed blood, slaves appeared to

---

[40] Ibid., pp. 379–83. Suppose the productivity effect of manumission is assumed to be −30%. If $f = 1$, optimal manumission age increases from 45 to 48; but at $f = .5$, manumission would not be optimal at any age if lower productivity is assumed. With no productivity effect and $f = .5$, the optimal manumission age is 49. Note that if slaves did not anticipate a drop in their productivity then the original calculations would apply.

[41] Kotlikoff and Rupert's, "The Manumission of Slaves," summarizes the changing rules in Louisiana. In 1807 manumitting slaves under thirty years old was prohibited. In 1830, an act was passed requiring the owner to post a $1,000 bond to ensure that any slave manumitted would leave the state within thirty days, unless exempted. In 1852, owners were required to post $150 to be used to ship the manumitted slave to Africa; and in 1857, manumission of slaves was outlawed.

[42] More important was the ability of the slave to save, which was not affected by their productivity after manumission.

have better access to borrowing. Many of these slaves were freed with the help of friends or relatives, where it appears implicit commitments were made by the slave to repay these loans after their freedom was secured. Finally, many slaves were freed for reasons having more to do with family ties than economics.

Many factors not directly included in the model influenced the decision of owners to manumit some of their slaves; nevertheless, the life-cycle framework, suggested here, provides a useful way of framing the issues. Moreover, as we will see in the next section, the model yields important insights about Guadeloupe, a French colony where manumission became quite widespread, and where evidence on the *affranchis* is more complete.

IV

Because of the lack of formal procedures in the United States, we have very little data on the characteristics of those who secured their freedom through manumission.[43] By contrast, the formal process that was followed in the French colonies has left us excellent records. The Royal Ordinance of July 12, 1832 put in place policies that were the basis of manumissions until 1848, when slavery was abolished in the French colonies.[44] The process began with a declaration to the *état civil* that included the name, gender, and age of the slave, along with details on the owner or other person making the application. The details had to be published in three consecutive issues of the newspaper, and interested parties were given six months to present objections.[45] If none were raised, or if all objections were rejected by the tribunal, the *patent de liberté* was granted. In earlier years, the authorities had charged substantial fees for patents, but in March 1831 the last of these, a fee of 58F, was removed. The rescinding of this fee, equivalent to perhaps 15 percent of the earnings of workers in agriculture, and other changes in procedures, led to a flood of applications and eventual patents. In just the years 1833–35, 5,900 slaves, or 6 percent of the slave population, secured their freedom through manumission. But these numbers reflected, in part, a pent-up demand for *affranchissements*; from 1836 to 1842, the rate of manumission fell to much lower levels, averaging about 650 per year, or 0.7 percent of the slave population.[46]

---

[43] Kotlikoff and Rupert's, "The Manumission of Slaves," analyses some evidence from New Orleans, but a small number of slaves were involved and little information on them was provided.

[44] *Bulletin Officiel de la Guadeloupe* (1832); also Follope, "Les Affranchissements d'Esclaves."

[45] Included among those who might raise objections was the *ministère publique*, who was repsonsible for ensuring that the slave would be self-supporting, or that provision had been made by the applicant to support the slave in the cases of children and the elderly or infirm.

[46] *Bulletin Officiel de la Guadeloupe* (1835–1842); *Tableau de Relevés de Population: 1839–1860*, série geographique, Guadelopue; Follope, "Les Affranchissements d'Esclaves."

TABLE 2. *Manumissions in Guadeloupe: 1838–1841*

		Age		
	Number	Mean	Median	Standard Deviation
Males (14+ years)	509	34.2	29.8	15.1
Females (14+ years)	847	36.4	32.3	15.9
Children	809			

Source: Bulletin Officiel de la Guadeloupe (1838–1841).

As further regulations were introduced more information was collected, and from mid 1839 the report on each manumitted slave includes age, gender, number and ages of any children freed, and occupation. As well there is information on the applicant: gender, whether a widow or other inheritor of an estate, and whether the applicant was a relative of the slave. In some cases, the *procureur du roi* was listed, in which case it was really the slave making the application. Here I report on evidence for 1838–1841, a period when 2,165 slaves were manumitted (see Table 2). Of the total, 809 or 37 percent were children (under age 14); 847 were women, and 509 or 24 percent were men. On average, women were manumitted at somewhat older ages than men, the mean and median were 36.4 and 32.3 years, repectively, but the standard deviations reveal wide variation within both groups.

Figure 6 describes the frequency of manumission by age. In comparison with the overall age distribution of the slave population, male manumissions exhibit a roughly unimodal pattern. Manumission rates peaked in the mid twenties, and thereafter followed a path generally consistent with the slave

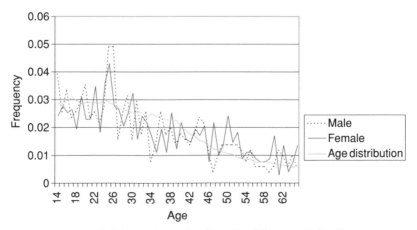

FIGURE 6. Manumission by Age: Guadeloupe, 1838–1841

TABLE 3. *Age and Occupation of Those Manumitted: Guadelopue, 1840 and 1841*

Occupation	Age			Number
	Mean	Median	Standard Dev.	
MALE				
charpentier	29.8	27	11.7	58
charp. (18+)[a]	30.5	27	11.5	50
cordonnier	24.3	25	2.4	4
cuisinier	31.9	28	12.1	10
cultivateur	43.1	41	14.7	56
domestique	28.7	23	13.8	18
dom. (18+)[a]	32.2	28	13.8	14
forgeron	38.5	38	7.5	4
maçon	32.6	29	14.1	21
maçon (18+)[a]	34.5	29	13.4	19
marin	28.4	26	9.7	17
marin (18+)[a]	31.1	29	8.4	15
pecheur	40.3	40	12.9	9
tonnelier	34.4	35	13.4	12
tonn. (18+)[a]	36.3	42	12.4	11
sans profession	38.7	38	16.7	46
sans (18+)[a]	41.6	41	15.5	41
TOTAL (14+)				266
TOTAL (18+)				242
All Males (14+)				292
FEMALE				
blanchisseuse	41.0	37	14.3	41
colporteuse	36.1	35	14.0	9
couturière	28.2	25	11.8	112
cultivatrice	43.4	43	15.8	51
domestique	35.6	33	14.6	32
journalière	41.2	34	18.4	5
lessive	44.1	42	15.1	21
menagère	41.8	29	22.3	13
marchand	35.6	33	12.3	13
repasseuse	31.8	27	10.2	4
servante	42.8	46	14.2	19
sans profession	40.2	38	19.3	125
TOTAL				445
All Females (14+)				477

[a] Only those aged 18 and over.

Note on occupations: MALE: charpentier (charpentier, menuisier) – carpenter, joiner; cordonnier – shoemaker; cuisinier – cook; forgeron – blacksmith; marin (marin, voilier, calfat) – seaman, sailor, caulker; pecheur – fisherman; tonnelier – tinsmith; sans profession – no occupation (there were also cases with no entry for occupation). FEMALE: blanchisseuse – laundress; colporteuse – hawker; couturière – seamstress; journalière – day worker; lessive and menagère – cleaner; marchand – seller; repasseuse – ironer.

Source: Bulletin Officiel de la Guadeloupe (1840, 1841).

population but with somewhat lower rates over ages 30 to 40. The pattern for women was closer to bimodal. There was a peak in the mid twenties, but, as well, rates were unusually high over the age range 47 to 53. In general, though, manumissions took place throughout the lifetime of slaves; and, with the exception of males in their mid twenties, there was no strong concentration of manumissions in any age group.

In order to get a better sense of the factors that influenced when and whether a slave would be manumitted, the overall distribution has been broken down by occupation as well as age (see Table 3). Perhaps most striking is the extent to which the occupations of those receiving *affranchissements* differed from their proportions in the labor force. In 1835, for example, the breakdown of male slaves was approximately as follows: 60 percent agricultural workers, 15 percent domestics, 8 percent fishermen or seamen, 5 percent day laborers, and 12 percent in the more highly skilled occupations.[47] Although numbers within the latter class are not given, it seems unlikely that carpenters and masons, who were the most highly paid workers, could have comprised more than half this group, or 6 percent of the total.[48] Yet carpenters and masons made up 36 percent of those manumitted. By contrast just 25 percent were classified as *cultivateur*. Thus, carpenters and masons secured their freedom at a rate more than ten times that of farm workers.[49] There is no report on the occupational distribution of women; but, even so, it is clear that what would have been the most skilled occupation, *couturière* (seamstress or dressmaker), was disproportionally represented among the female *affranchissements*. More than one-third of female manumissions were in this single occupation, whereas only 16 percent of those manumitted were reported as farm workers.

Applying the approach of Section III, optimal manumission ages are derived for a range of values drawn from scattered evidence on Guadeloupe and Martinique. According to plantation records and other sources, food consumption per slave was about 100F.[50] Subsistence, which includes an allowance for clothing and shelter, is put at 150F. There was considerable variation in the reported marginal products of field workers; 400F is a conservative estimate. The earnings of non-farm workers ranged from 700F to about 1,000F for blacksmiths and *ouvriers*, and earnings were

---

[47] *Bulletin Officiel de la Guadeloupe,* 1837–1840.

[48] A listing of wages in various occupations in the late 1830s is available for Martinique. See *Notices Statistique sur Les Colonies Français,* 4 vols., Martinique (Paris, 1837–1840), p. 106.

[49] Over the two years, 1840 and 1841, at least 4.25 percent of carpenters and masons were manumitted. The rate for farm workers was under 0.3 percent. It may be that those listed as *sans profession* were disproportionally farm workers, but even allowing for this possibility by treating most of them as farm workers would not change the basic result.

[50] See, for example, *Notices Statistique sur les Colonies Français,* Guadeloupe (1837–1840), pp. 92–96.

TABLE 4. *Optimal Age at Manumission*

	$k = .5$			$k = .4$		
f	∞	1	.5	∞	1	.5
Wage (F)						
400 A	45	–	–	38	45	51
400 B	45	–	–	38	50	–
700 A	37	46	51	33	38	42
700 B	37	49	–	33	41	51
1000 A	36	43	47	31	36	38
1000 B	36	45	57	31	38	46
1350 A	35	41	45	31	35	38
1350 B	35	43	53	31	37	44

Notes: See appendix; $c_m = 150F$, $r = .04$, $\delta = 1$, $\rho = .02$. A – no productivity effect; B – freedom reduces productivity by 25 percent.
Source: see text.

perhaps 1,350F or even higher for masons and carpenters.[51] The share expropriated by the owners was reported to be about 50 to 67 percent for farm workers, but it was likely less for the more highly skilled slaves.[52] Here results are derived for expropriation rates, k, of 40 and 50 percent.

These values and the preference parameters, assumed in Section III, allow us to the estimate the optimal age at manumission (see Table 4). Each optimum corresponds to a different "benefit" of freedom, f, where a value of .5 applies to an agent who is willing to give up 40 percent of his consumption above subsistence in exchange for freedom, and a value of 1 applies to an agent who is willing to give up 60 percent. If f is infinite, the agent is prepared to give up all his consumption (above subsistence). The results highlight the importance of slave productivity to age at manumission and, indirectly, to the likelihood of manumission. For an expropriation rate of 50 percent, the rate more appropriate for farm workers, no agent with a market wage of 400F and a value of f equal to 1 or less would find it optimal to be manumitted. To the extent, then, that 400F reflected the marginal productivity of farm workers, the model helps to explain the low rate of manumission among this group. Put simply, their low market wage relative to subsistence, combined with an expropriation rate of 50 percent or higher, meant that these workers were unable to accumulate their purchase price in a reasonable enough time to make manumission optimal. At higher wage

---

[51] Josette Follope, *Esclaves et Citoyens: Les Nois à la Guadelopue au 19 me Siècle dans les Processus de Résistance et d'Integration (1802–1910)* (Basse-Terre, 1992), pp.118–119; *Notices Statistique sur les Colonies Français*, Martinique (1837–1840), p. 106.
[52] Follope, *Esclaves et Citoyens*, pp. 118–119.

rates, however, the estimates suggest that manumission would have been more likely. At a wage of 700 and a freedom benefit f of .5 to 1, optimal manumission age is between 46 and 51; and at a wage of 1,350, the optimal age is 41 to 45. For the lower expropriation rate of .4, optimal manumission age for the highest productivity group is between 35 and 38.

The ages of those who were manumitted in Guadeloupe during the years 1840 and 1841 are roughly consistent with these simulation results. As noted previously, manumission rates were much greater for those in skilled occupations; but, in addition, there was a marked difference in the age at which they were freed. Those *cultivateurs* who were manumitted did not obtain their freedom until age 43 on average; whereas the average age at manumission for carpenters and masons was close to 30. There is also an age gap between fisherman, a low-skilled occupation, and seaman. Indeed the difference in age at manumission between the less and more highly skilled slaves may indicate that more than differential ability to save was at work. Perhaps better skilled workers had access to borrowing, even implicit borrowing, that would have allowed them to secure their freedom at ages younger than those implied by the model.

Another factor tending to reinforce the relation between slave productivity and manumission may have been the effect of the transition to freedom on the agent's productivity. Table 4 illustrates the relation by including a calculation where freedom is assumed to reduce productivity by 25 percent, perhaps a conservative value for farm workers on sugar plantations. Assuming the "benefit" f is .5, reducing the productivity of freedmen markedly increases optimal age at manumission particularly for lower skilled workers. In fact, for an expropriation rate of 50 percent, manumission at any age is non-optimal for those with marginal products as slaves of 700F or less, a level of productivity that would have included nearly all farm workers. Assuming the same productivity effect, 25 percent, raises the manumission age of skilled workers as well; but the carpenters, masons, blacksmiths, and other skilled workers could transfer more easily from the plantation to the free-labor market. Indeed, many were already living in the urban areas. For these workers a smaller productivity adjustment, or no adjustment at all, may be appropriate.

The occupational pattern of manumission rates and ages, so evident among males, is also exhibited by those females who were emancipated. The average and median age at manumission of female farm workers was 43; and other slaves in low-skilled occupations, *blanchisseuses* and *lessives* (laundresses), for example, were also emancipated at about that age, on average. The highest skilled female occupation would have been *couturière* (seamstress or dressmaker), and their age at manumission averaged 28. Indeed the low mean (and median) age at manumission of this group suggests not only that these workers could shift easily from the slave to the free-labor market, but also that, like the carpenters and masons, they may have had access to some borrowing to help them attain their freedom.

V

Despite the support of the authorities, the relaxing of the rules governing the process of manumission, the continuing ban on the slave trade, and the apparently large numbers of *affranchissements* in the mid 1830s, Guadeloupe continued to have a predominantly slave population. After peaking at 99,500 in 1832, the number of slaves declined by 4,000 during the 1833–35 wave of manumissions; but in 1842, a full 10 years after the new rules were introduced, the slave population stood at 92,600, just 7 percent below its peak. It seems unlikely, then, that manumission by itself would have led to full emancipation, at least not for a very long time. The Guadeloupe experience may have implications for the United States and other slave regions. If government encouragement and a reduced racial element were insufficient to promote widespread emancipation in Guadeloupe, perhaps in the United States as well, economic factors were decisive. On the other hand, the high rates of manumission among the highly skilled slaves of Guadeloupe suggest that, as capital markets improved and worker productivity increased, there would have been a progression toward freedom even in the absence of abolition.

With the exception of Findlay,[53] this paper has perhaps the only formal analysis of manumission, yet the approach and main results, especially for Guadeloupe, are fully in keeping with what researchers have found in other slave areas. Libby and Paiva, in their study of a slave parish in eighteenth century Brazil, point out that slave women who were active in street vending had the opportunity to accumulate savings, which could be used for self-purchase.[54] And, consistent with the notion that a period of saving was necessary, they conclude: "manumission rarely came early in life."[55] Moreover, they found that the age at manumission of Africans, who would have comprised the lower-skilled group, was "especially high."[56] Finally, they hypothesize that self-purchase represented the "most frequent form by which Brazilian slaves obtained their freedom during the colonial period."[57]

---

[53] Findlay, "Slavery, Incentives, and Manumission."
[54] Douglas C. Libby, and Clotilde A. Paiva, "Manumission Practices in a Late Eighteenth-Century Brazilian Slave Parish: Sao José d'El Rey in 1795," *Slavery and Abolition* 21 (2000): 96–127.
[55] Ibid., p. 113.
[56] Ibid., p. 114.
[57] Ibid., p. 122.

Brana-Shute also finds similar features of manumission in her study of Suriname.[58] In that colony, as well, manumission was largely an urban phenomenon with a higher rate for mulattos than blacks and a concentration, in terms of slave owners, among shopkeepers and craftsmen. And fully consistent with the principal–agent formulation that is the basis of the model presented here, she concludes: "slaves were active in pursuing their own manumissions," and "manumissions were negotiated settlements between slaves and free people."[59] Bergad et al.'s study of the Cuban slave market includes a discussion of the role of self-purchase, which was better defined in Spanish and Portugese America than in the British colonies.[60] Their work also makes reference to the importance of skills in encouraging manumission.[61] Indeed the consensus of these studies is that economic opportunities, rather than owner's compassion, was the key to most manumissions.

The analysis presented here, while apparently having wide application to manumission in the Americas, may also have implications for two other phenomena that have received attention in the slavery literature: the cost to slave owners of forced emancipation and the effect of urbanization on slavery. Measures of the cost of emancipation have been based on the market price of slaves.[62] But to the extent that manumission became important and slaves were accumulating implicit credits toward the purchase of their freedom, using market prices would overstate the cost to owners. In fact, by reducing the cost of full emancipation to slave owners, the practice of manumission may have contributed to abolition. A second implication relates to urbanization. In the United States as in Guadeloupe, slavery predominated in the rural areas. The analysis of manumission gives one interpretation of why this was so. Urban slaves with better skills, more flexibility in moving to the free labor market, and perhaps greater access to borrowing were better placed than plantation slaves to secure their freedom. According to this interpretation, then, slavery and urbanization were incompatible not because

---

[58] Brana-Shute, "Approaching Freedom."

[59] Ibid., pp. 52–53.

[60] Bergad et al., *Cuban Slave Market*.

[61] The lack of formal procedures in the British colonies did not completely prevent manumission from occurring. Michael Craton, *Searching for the Invisible Man: Slaves and Plantation Life in Jamaica* (Cambridge, MA, 1978), p. 222, reports that, on the Worthy Park plantation in Jamaica, "it was sure to be known that Sir Charles Price the elder was in the habit each year on his birthday of freeing the slave who had most distinguished himself by hard work and fidelity." At the same, it should be pointed out that there were over 300 slaves on this plantation.

[62] See, for example, Robert W. Fogel and Stanley L. Engerman, "Philanthropy at Bargain Prices: Notes on the Economics of Gradual Emancipation," in Fogel and Engerman (eds.), *Without Consent or Contract: Technical Papers*, pp. 587–605; Claudia Goldin, "The Economics of Emancipation," in Fogel and Engerman, *Without Consent or Contract*, pp. 614–28.

slaves were unable to adapt to urban life, but because they could adapt so well.

Appendix

A Model of Manumission

A slave, at the start of his (working) life, has the option of remaining in servitude, or at any time purchasing his freedom by compensating the owner with an amount equal to his market price. While a slave, the worker is assumed to give up a portion of his market wage (marginal product) to the owner. Thus the net earnings of the worker can be represented by

$$y(t) = \begin{cases} w(t) - s(t), & 0 \leq t < t_o \\ w(t), & t_o \leq t \leq T \end{cases} \tag{1a}$$

where w is the market wage, s is the transfer to the owner, t_o is the time the worker is manumitted, and T is the lifetime of the worker.[63] Manumission is assumed to be a life-cycle decision, where the worker's (instantaneous) utility is based on his consumption and whether he is free. Thus

$$u(t) = \begin{cases} u[c(t)], & 0 \leq t < t_o \\ u[c(t)] + f, & t_o \leq t \leq T, f > 0 \end{cases} \tag{2a}$$

where c is consumption and f represents the benefit of freedom.[64] In order to gain his freedom, the slave must pay the owner his market price, equivalent to what the owner would have expected to expropriate over the remainder of the slave's life:

$$P(t) = \int_t^T s(\tau) e^{-r(\tau - t)} d\tau, \tag{3a}$$

where P is the price of the slave at time t and r is the discount rate. The life-cycle problem of the worker involves two related decisions: the optimal amount to consume each period and the optimal time to purchase his freedom. Where there is no constraint against borrowing, this problem can be

---

[63] In this framework, lifetime is known, as indeed are all the parameters. Treating lifetime as uncertain would complicate the presentation without, in all likelihood, altering the main conclusions.

[64] One could, instead, treat slavery as imposing a utility cost. In this specification, the benefit of freedom is additively separable from consumption. A possibly more realistic alternative would be to assume that the benefit of freedom depends positively on the level of consumption.

described as

$$
\max_{t_o, c(t)} U = \int_0^{t_o} u[c(t)]e^{-\rho t}dt + \int_{t_o}^{T} \{u[c(t)] + f\}e^{-\rho t}dt +
$$

$$
\lambda \left\{ \int_0^{t_o} [w(t) - s(t)]e^{-rt}dt + \int_{t_o}^{T} w(t)e^{-rt}dt - P(t_o)e^{-rt_o} - \int_0^{T} c(t)e^{-rt}dt \right\},
$$

$$\tag{4a}$$

where ρ is the pure rate of time preference. The income constraint requires that the present value of the worker's lifetime consumption be equal to the present value of his lifetime output less the amount the owner expropriates. It follows from the definition of the market price of a slave, Equation (3a), that the income constraint of the optimization problem is formally equivalent to

$$
\int_0^{T} [w(t) - s(t)]e^{-rt}dt - \int_0^{T} c(t)e^{-rt}dt = 0. \tag{5a}
$$

Note that, because this constraint does not depend on the time of manumission, the consumption stream will also be independent of when the slave is manumitted. In fact the only effect of postponing freedom, in this framework, is the loss of utility f. It would be optimal, therefore, for slaves to purchase their freedom at time o.

Where borrowing is ruled out, slaves must accumulate their purchase price prior to manumission. Of course, in the event they do not accumulate enough, they never purchase their freedom. In such a case, their lifetime consumption stream will be determined by

$$
\max_{c(t)} U = \int_0^{T} u[c(t)]e^{-\rho t}, \tag{6a}
$$

subject to

$$
\int_0^{T} [w(t) - s(t)]e^{-rt}dt = \int_0^{T} c(t)e^{-rt}dt. \tag{7a}
$$

This constraint requires that the present value of the lifetime consumption of slaves be equal to the present value of their income.[65]

---

[65] Strictly speaking, the constraint requires that consumption be no greater than income; but, given the utility specification, the constraint will be satisfied with equality. This constraint allows for borrowing by slaves against future income. Given the usual parameter values (r is generally assumed greater than ρ), relaxing the capital market constraint has no effect. Alternatively, one might argue that because of the nature of slavery, owners could lend to slaves and be quite assured that the loan would be repaid.

Where slaves purchase their freedom at a time $t_0 < T$, the life-cycle problem is more complex:

$$\max_{c(t), t_0} U = \int_0^{t_0} u[c(t)]e^{-\rho t}dt + \int_{t_0}^T \{u[c(t)] + f\}e^{-\rho t}dt, \tag{8a}$$

subject to

$$\int_0^{t_0} [w(t) - s(t)]e^{-rt}dt - P(t_0) = \int_0^{t_0} c(t)e^{-rt}dt \tag{9a}$$

and

$$\int_{t_0}^T w(t)e^{-rt}dt = \int_{t_0}^T c(t)e^{-rt}dt. \tag{10a)^{66}}$$

Note that, from Eq. (3a), the constraint given by Eq. (9a) can be written as

$$\int_0^{t_0} w(t)\,e^{-rt}\,dt - P(0) = \int_0^{t_0} c(t)\,e^{-rt}\,dt. \tag{11a}$$

Equation (11a) has the perhaps surprising implication that the pattern of expropriation by owners plays no role in determining optimal manumission time; all that matters is the present value of all the amounts expropriated over the lifetime of the slave.

Given the nature of the utility function and constraints (10a) and (11a), the problem facing the slave can be decomposed into two periods, those prior to and following manumission. Within each period, the slave or freedman can be treated as facing a life-cycle problem with no borrowing constraint.[67] Let the solutions to the two problems be $c_s^*(t)$, $0 \le t \le t_0$ and $c_f^*(t)$, $t_0 \le t \le T$. Maximized total utility over each of the time periods is given by

$$U_s(t_0) = \int_0^{t_0} u[c_s^*(t)]e^{-\rho t}dt$$

and

$$U_f(t_0) = \int_{t_0}^T \{u[c_f^*(t) + f\}e^{-\rho t}dt, \tag{12a}$$

---

[66] Constraints (9) and (10) are in fact

$$\int_0^n [w(t) - s(t)]e^{-rt}dt \ge \int_0^n c(t)e^{-rt}dt, \quad 0 \le n < t_0$$

and

$$\int_{t_0}^n w(t)e^{-rt}dt \ge \int_{t_0}^n c(t)e^{-rt}dt, \quad t_0 < n \le T.$$

The constraints in the text simplify the analysis without changing the results for the parameter values assumed.

[67] Imposing borrowing constraints within each period would complicate the analysis without materially affecting the results.

where $U_{s,f}(t_o)$ are the aggregate utilities over each sub-period of someone who is manumitted at time t_o and follows an optimal consumption path before and after manumission. Finally, assuming optimal consumption, the problem facing the worker is to choose that manumission time which maximizes total lifetime utility:

$$\max_{t_o} U_L(t_o) = U_s(t_o) + U_f(t_o). \tag{13a}$$

In deriving results, a constant-elasticity, Stone–Geary utility function is specified:

$$u = \frac{(c - c_m)^{1-\delta}}{1 - \delta}, \tag{14a}$$

where δ is the inverse of the intertemporal rate of time preference and c_m represents subsistence consumption.[68] Substituting Eq. (14a) into Eq. (8a), explicit solutions can be obtained for consumption, and these in turn allow us to derive the value of f corresponding to different optimal manumission times.

---

[68] This funtional form is widely used in empirical life-cycle models. For $\delta = 1$, the utility function takes the form $u = \ln(c - c_m)$, which is in fact the specification used in the simulations.

PART III

PRODUCTIVITY CHANGE AND ITS IMPLICATIONS

6

Prices of African Slaves Newly Arrived in the Americas, 1673–1865: New Evidence on Long-Run Trends and Regional Differentials

David Eltis and David Richardson

I

Prices of slaves in the Atlantic slave trade are of central importance to understanding not only the slave trade, but also the larger Atlantic economy in the two centuries after 1660. In the last thirty years, a range of sources have yielded data from sales of slaves for the nineteenth century United States, Cuba, Brazil and Mauritius. Although the status of slaves from which these data are drawn has varied almost as much as the geographic location, the price patterns they have revealed have striking similarities.[1] Apart from Minas Gerais and perhaps Bahia in Brazil, the pre-1800 period is much less well represented. Moreover, even for the nineteenth century, the data have derived from sales of individuals who had lived in the Americas for some time. The one substantial body of data for newly arrived Africans, and, indeed, for the pre-1800 era is for the island of Barbados, between 1673 and 1723.[2] However, recent work on the shipping of slaves from Africa to the Americas, which has culminated in the publication of the Cambridge slave trade

The authors thank Stanley L. Engerman, Frank D. Lewis and Stephen D. Behrendt for comments on an earlier version of this essay.
[1] Laurence J. Kotlikoff, "Quantitative Description of the New Orleans Slave Market, 1804–1862," in Robert W. Fogel and Stanley L. Engerman (eds.), *Without Consent or Contract: Markets and Production: Technical Papers* 1: 31–53; Katia M. de Queirós Mattoso, *To Be a Slave in Brazil, 1550–1888*, trans. from the French by Arthur Goldhammer (New Brunswick, 1986), pp. 55–81; Laird W. Bergad, Fe Iglesias García and María del Carmen Barcia, *The Cuban Slave Market, 1790–1880* (Cambridge, 1995), 38–78; Laird W. Bergad, *Slavery and the Demographic and Economic History of Minas Gerais, Brazil, 1720–1888* (Cambridge, 1999), pp. 163–87, and Laird Bergad's essay that forms Chapter 7 of the present volume; Shirley Chenny, Pascal St-Amour and Désirée Vencatachellum, "Slave Prices from Succession and Bankruptcy Sales in Mauritius, 1825–1827" (2002), at http://www.cirano.qc.ca/fr/bref.php.
[2] David Galenson, *Traders, Planters and Slaves: Market Behavior in Early English America* (Cambridge, 1986).

TABLE 1. *The Volume of Transatlantic Slave Departures by African Region and Period of Years, 1519–1867 (thousands)*

	Senegambia	Sierra Leone	Windward Coast	Gold Coast	Bight of Benin	Bight of Biafra	West Central Africa	Southeast Africa	All Regions
1519–1600	10.7	2	0	10.7	10.7	10.7	221.2	0	266.1
1601–1650	6.4	0	0	5.2	2.4	25.5	461.9	2	503.5
1651–1675	17.7	0.4	0.1	35.4	21.9	58.6	104.3	1.2	239.8
1676–1700	36.5	3.5	0.7	50.3	223.5	51.5	132.6	10.9	509.5
1701–1725	39.9	7.1	4.2	181.7	408.3	45.8	257.2	14.4	958.6
1726–1750	69.9	10.5	14.3	186.3	306.5	166	552.8	5.4	1,311.3
1751–1775	130.4	96.9	105.1	263.9	250.5	340.1	714.9	3.3	1,905.2
1776–1800	72.4	106	19.5	240.7	264.6	360.4	816.2	41.2	1,921.1
1801–1825	91.7	69.7	24	69	263.3	260.3	700.8	131.8	1,610.6
1826–1850	22.8	100.4	14.4	0	257.3	191.5	770.6	247.5	1,604.5
1851–1867	0	16.1	0.6	0	25.9	7.3	155	26.8	231.7
All years	498.5	412.7	183	1,043.2	2,034.6	1,517.9	4,887.5	484.5	11,062
% of trade	4.5	3.7	1.7	9.4	18.4	13.7	44.2	4.4	100

Source: David Eltis, "The Volume and Structure of the Transatlantic Slave Trade: A Reassessment," *William and Mary Quarterly*, 60 (2001): 17–46.

CD-ROM,[3] has thrown up a substantial body of new data on prices that cover not only a wide range of regions in the Americas, but also the period when the slave trade rose from quite modest levels in the mid seventeenth century to its peak in the late eighteenth century and the beginning of its slow decline thereafter. As it is also possible to incorporate post-1808 slave price data into the analysis, we can now present a reasonably complete price picture for the rise and fall of the slave trade that considerably extends and offers clear advantages over Richard Bean's thirty-year-old compilation.[4] As Table 1 makes clear, it now seems likely that no fewer than 92 percent of all slaves carried across the Atlantic sailed during the period for which reasonably good price data are now available.

The rest of this paper falls into four sections. In Section II we briefly describe the nature of and adjustments made to the data used to construct our new price series for slaves. In Section III we outline changing levels and patterns of slave shipments from Africa to the Americas through time as a backdrop for the discussion of the long-term trends and cross-sectional analysis of slave prices in the Americas undertaken in Section IV. We conclude in Section V by examining the relative importance of demand and supply side factors in shaping patterns of slave prices through time.

II

The slave price series presented here is largely based on published and unpublished primary data relating to prices for some 242,274 enslaved Africans carried to the Americas on 1056 transatlantic voyages between 1673 and 1808. The data set contains some voyages to mainland Spanish America, but the great majority were to the West Indies (including Suriname and Demerara) and mainland British North America. The data derive from sources relating to the British, Dutch, French and mainland North American slave trades. About two-thirds of the voyages were British; most of the rest were French or Dutch. The name of the ship involved is known for about 91 percent of voyages; most of the unknown ships were almost certainly British. Because the names of ships are known, the price data underlying this series

---

[3] David Eltis, Stephen D. Behrendt, David Richardson and Herbert S. Klein, *The Transatlantic Slave Trade: A Database on CD-ROM* (Cambridge, 1999) (henceforth *TSTD*).

[4] "Prices of Slaves Newly Arrived in the Americas: A Data Base" (henceforth PSNA. It is expected that the new data will be incorporated into a second edition of Eltis et al., *The Transatlantic Slave Trade: A Database on CD-ROM*). Richard Nelson Bean, *The British Trans-Atlantic Slave Trade, 1650–1775* (New York, 1971). See also the new slave price series for South Carolina between 1722 and 1809 in Peter C. Mancall, Joshua L. Rosenbloom and Thomas Weiss, "Slave Prices and the South Carolina Economy, 1722–1809," *Journal of Economic History*, 61 (2001): 616–39. Based on probate records, this is not strictly comparable to our series for newly imported slaves, but some comparisons between the findings of this South Carolina series and our own are made later.

can be linked in most cases directly to the much larger data set for some 27,233 transatlantic slave voyages in the Cambridge CD-ROM. A supplementary set provides data on 40,000 African-born male slaves between the ages of 15 and 40 sold in Cuba between 1796 and 1867. After appropriate adjustment, these may be used to carry the price series down to the close of the transatlantic slave trade.[5]

In computing the price series, we use evidence of mean prices of slaves arising from actual sales of shiploads of slaves or contemporary reports of them. Where possible we used price data for complete shiploads of slaves, but this sometimes involved the breakup of "cargoes" into smaller groups sold in different markets. On average the number of slaves sold on each voyage in the sample was 229 (885 voyages); this was used to impute the number of slaves on board the remaining 171 voyages where we have an average price, but no record of quantity sold. We have not adopted an arbitrary shipload figure as a minimum requirement for including price data in the series, though we have consciously tried to avoid reliance on very small groups or partial shiploads of slaves. The largest group of slaves sold by a ship included in the data set is 764, the smallest 13. Only 25 shiploads or groups, however, numbered less than 50 slaves. The raw data underlying the price series, therefore, relate overwhelmingly to mean prices of shiploads totaling 50 or more enslaved Africans. Some complete shiploads – especially in the case of mainland North American ships – were very small. Numbers under 50 do not therefore necessarily mean part loads. Moreover, part shiploads that clearly involved groups of sick slaves sold at the end of a sale were not included.[6]

Accounts or reports of slave prices were sometimes made in European currencies, sometimes in colonial currencies, and sometimes in both, the last allowing the calculation of exchange rates between European and colonial currencies. We have tried to standardize all prices to pounds sterling using data on exchange rates internal to accounts in the historical record or supplied by other sources such as McCusker's compendium of exchange rates.[7] We cannot guarantee that we have always succeeded in unscrambling

---

[5] Collected by Bergad, Iglesías García and Barcia. We would like to thank these authors for making their data available to us.

[6] There are price data for slaves sold in Suriname by public auction in 1742–84, but these appear to be incomplete shiploads in some cases and have thus not be included in our database at this stage. See Cornelis Ch. Goslinga, *The Dutch in the Caribbean and in the Guianas 1680–1791* (Maastricht, 1985), pp. 615–19.

[7] Prices converted to pounds sterling according to John J. McCusker, *Money and Exchange Rates in Europe and America, 1600–1775: A Handbook* (Chapel Hill, NC, 1978) and for post-1790, the "BW" series in Appendix table 1 of Lawrence H. Officer, "Dollar-Sterling Mint Parity and Exchange Rates, 1791–1834," *Journal of Economic History*, 43 (1983): 610–12; and Edward J. Perkins, "Foreign Interest Rates in American Financial Markets: A Revised Series of Dollar-Sterling Exchange Rates, 1835–1900," *Journal of Economic History*, 38 (1978): 410–12.

European and colonial currencies in accounts, but we are confident we have identified the great majority of instances where accounts were reported in colonial currencies, and have thus made appropriate adjustments.

The price series presented here relates to prices in pounds sterling in cash of prime age male slaves in Jamaica, the single largest disembarkation point for enslaved Africans in British America in 1673–1808. Prices are presented first in current values, and then in terms of constant pounds.[8] Production of this series involves some adjustments to the original price data. Specifically, it requires (a) adjusting or discounting credit prices to allow for changing credit conditions on slave purchases; (b) converting mean cash prices for mixed groups of slaves into prime male equivalents; and (c) adjusting slave prices in different American markets to what they would have been in Jamaica (see the following discussion). In the case of (a), we discounted prices to allow for reported terms of credit, assuming an appropriate time period when this was not given in the source of the price data. For discounting purposes, we assumed interest rates were 10 percent per year before 1697, 7 percent in the peace years 1697–1701, 8 percent in the war years 1702 to 1713, and thereafter 5 percent in peacetime and 6 percent in wartime. To convert cash prices for mixed groups of slaves into prime age male equivalents we followed Galenson, using the mean price of adult males sold in the first third of a shipload of slaves relative to the mean price of whole shiploads of slaves.[9] Based on breakdowns of prices of 73 shiploads of slaves between the 1670s and 1800, the ratio of prime male prices to mean "cargo" prices was 1.31 (standard deviation = 0.16). Mean cash prices were thus raised by 31 percent to estimate prime age male equivalents. Finally, to convert slave prices at a range of markets to Jamaican equivalents, we used evidence on transport costs of slaves to distinguish three market zones for slaves. These are (1) Eastern Caribbean (including Barbados, the Windward and Leeward Islands, Suriname, Demerara, and Buenos Aires); (2) Western Caribbean (Cuba, Jamaica, and St. Domingue); and (3) the North American mainland. To standardize prices on Jamaica, prices of slaves sold in markets in Zone (1) were inflated by 6 percent (10 percent before 1691) and those in Zone (3) were reduced by 5 percent to accommodate differentials in transport costs between markets.[10] For the period before 1690 a further adjustment is made

---

[8] For price indexes, see B. R. Mitchell, *British Historical Statistics* (Cambridge, 1988), pp. 719–22.

[9] Galenson, *Traders, Planters and Slaves*, ch. 3. Curiously, the standard practice in Brazil was the opposite to what held in the British Caribbean. Merchants offered the least desirable slaves for sale first (Mattoso, *To Be a Slave in Brazil*, 55–59).

[10] Some information on inter-colonial transport costs is provided in Bean, *British Trans-Atlantic Slave Trade*, 175–80. Contemporaries were aware of inter-colonial transport costs, as the Liverpool merchant, Robert Bostock, revealed in 1789 when he noted that "I always take off 1/4 of the Gross Sales if sell at Jamaica, to Windward 1/5 but does not quite take 1/5"; Bostock papers, Liverpool Record Office.

to allow for the fact that piracy and general instability of the seventeenth century western Caribbean increased risk for vessels sailing to that region.[11] Accordingly, to derive Jamaican equivalents, we multiplied slave prices in Zone (1) by 1.10 before 1691 and 1.06 thereafter, while we multiplied prices in Zone (3) by 0.95. No adjustments were made to prices of slaves sold in markets outside Jamaica included in Zone (2).

For the post 1807 period (actually, post-1805), we have elected to use records of individual male slaves between the age of 15 and 40 who were sold in Cuba through to 1865 and were identified as African. Because the majority of individuals sold would have been in Cuba for some time prior to the sale, they would have passed through the period of increased mortality often associated with arriving in the Americas on a slave ship and would therefore have commanded a higher price than bozales, or newly arrived slaves, that make up the pre-1808 sample. Contemporaries called this "the seasoning period." To make the pre- and post-1808 observations compatible, prices of the Cuban slaves are therefore deflated by 10 percent.[12] Despite this adjustment, however, the two data sets cannot be easily combined. Before 1808, prices are essentially averages calculated from the total value of the complete shipment of slaves and adjusted to yield a prime male price – in other words the basic unit is the total number of slaves on board upon arrival in the Americas. After 1807, the unit of data is the individual slave. Nevertheless the two types of data may be combined for the derivation of a time profile, yet treated as separate data sets to derive useful cross-sectional comparisons.

III

An analysis of prices has to be set against the backdrop of what we now know of the structure of the slave trade. That structure is laid out in Figure 1 and Tables 1 and 2. While the first transatlantic slave voyage from Africa probably arrived in 1519, the first century and a half of the direct traffic probably saw less than a million slaves in total (or about eight percent of the aggregate traffic) leaving Africa. The great majority of these early victims of the slave trade were taken from West Central Africa to Brazil. Increasing levels of slave shipments in the second half of the seventeenth century were followed by major rises during the following century. Overall, nearly 85 percent of African slaves crossed the Atlantic between 1700 and 1850. Within this period of intense slave-trading activity, there were huge quinquennial

[11] The western Caribbean was the quintessential "beyond-the-line area." Although the great age of piracy lasted to the 1720s, an increased naval presence associated with war reduced its incidence in the 1690s and much of the activity thereafter occurred off Africa.
[12] For a justification of this procedure see David Eltis, "The Prices of Newly Arrived African Slaves in Cuba and Brazil, 1810–1867" (unpublished paper, 1987).

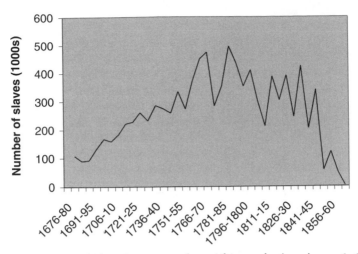

FIGURE 1. Quinquennial Slave Departures from Africa to the Americas, 1676–1867. *Source*: Eltis, Behrendt and Richardson, *The Transatlantic Slave Trade; A New Census.*

variations, entirely imposed by generalized war in the Atlantic, represented by the jagged trend line in Figure 1.[13] On the African side, for a century at the beginning, and a quarter century at the end of the trade, West Central Africa dispatched more slaves than all other regions combined, and between 1800 and 1850 it came close to doing the same. Every African region experienced a single marked rise in numbers of people sent into the trade followed by a plateau.[14] West Central Africa was the first to experience this large upswing, probably at the end of the sixteenth century when the slave trade to Brazil and the Spanish Americas became substantial. Use of African slaves spread slowly in the Americas initially and it was not until a century later that expansion of sugar output, mainly in the English Caribbean, pulled the Bight of Benin into the slave trade orbit. Further expansion, this time in both the Caribbean and Brazil, drew the Gold Coast into the maelstrom after 1700, followed by the Bight of Biafra after 1725, the three Upper Guinea regions together after 1750, and lastly, as the Brazilian coffee and sugar boom got under way, Southeast Africa at the end of the eighteenth century. After the

[13] It is probable that during the 12 years from 1763 and the decade after 1782, the mean annual number of people carried across the Atlantic was higher than at any point prior to the 1880s.

[14] West-Central Africa appears as an exception to this rule, but in reality it was very much part of the general pattern. First, the intervals in Table 2 prior to 1650 are for 50 years or longer, whereas those after 1650 are for only 25 years. Second, the present data are only for transatlantic trading. Slave vessels carried slaves to Old World ports in earlier years and though the numbers were far below what they were to become in the traffic to the Americas, a disproportionate share of these departures were from West-Central Africa.

TABLE 2. *Volume of Transatlantic Slave Arrivals by Region of Arrival in the Americas and Mainly Quarter Century, 1519–1867 (thousands)*

	British Mainland N. America	British Leewards	British Windwards + Trinidad/Tobago	Jamaica	Barbados	Guianas	French Windwards	St. Domingue
1519–1600	0	0	0	0	0	0	0	0
1601–1650	0.8	1	0.2	0	22.4	0	1	0
1651–1675	0.9	5.6	0	22.3	63.2	8.2	6.5	0
1676–1700	9.8	26.6	0	73.5	82.3	27.8	16.6	4.8
1701–1725	37.4	35.4	0.6	139.1	91.8	24.4	30.1	44.5
1726–1750	96.8	81.7	0.3	186.5	73.6	83.6	66.8	144.9
1751–1775	116.9	123.9	120	270.4	120.9	111.9	63.7	247.5
1776–1800	24.4	25.3	197.5	312.6	28.5	71.2	41.2	345.8
1801–1825	73.1	5.3	43	70.2	7.6	71.8	58.8	0
1826–1850	0	0	0.5	2.1	0.9	4.8	19.5	0
1851–1867	0.3	0	0	0.4	0	0	0	0
All years	360.4	304.2	362	1,077.1	491.2	403.7	304.2	787.4
% of trade	3.7	3.2	3.7	11.2	5.1	4.2	3.1	8.2

TABLE 2. *Volume of Transatlantic Slave Departures by Region of Arrivals in the Americas and Mainly Quarter Century, 1519–1867*

	Spanish American	Spanish Caribbean	Dutch Caribbean	N. E. Brazil	Bahia	S. E. Brazil	Other Americas	Africa	All Regions
1519–1600	151.6	0	0	35	15	0	0	0	201.6
1601–1650	187.7	0	1	86.3	60	30	0	0	390.4
1651–1675	0	0	38.8	15.6	15.6	15.6	0.6	0	192.8
1676–1700	6.9	0	26	56.1	104	54.5	11	0	500
1701–1725	30	2.1	30.5	24.3	199.6	122	14.2	0	825.8
1726–1750	12.7	1.6	10.2	51.4	104.6	213.9	8.3	0	1136.9
1751–1775	5	13	15.3	126.9	94.4	210.4	13.8	0	1653.9
1776–1800	10.2	56.9	6.9	210.8	112.5	247.2	44.1	0.4	1735.4
1801–1825	17.4	268.7	0	212.5	182	408.7	14.1	22.7	1455.9
1826–1850	5.8	297	0	78.5	146.5	736.4	3.9	91.3	1387.2
1851–1867	0	152.6	0	1.4	1.9	3.6	0.4	16.8	177.3
All years	427.2	791.9	128.7	898.8	1036.1	2042.3	110.4	131.2	9657.1
% of trade	4.4	8.2	1.3	9.3	10.7	21.1	1.1	1.4	100

Source: Same as Table 1

initial upsurge, most regions experienced high levels of departures for a century or more. Upper Guinea was an exception to this pattern. The Windward Coast remained at these higher levels for just two decades, Senegambia for somewhat longer, and Sierra Leone for half a century. Except for the third quarter of the eighteenth century, these three regions together were never able, before 1800 at least, to match the volume of slaves leaving any of the four major regions, and for most periods should be considered minor suppliers of slaves to the Americas.

In the Americas, the dominance of the Portuguese and British slave trades was such that it is hardly surprising that Brazil and British America garnered most Africans. Brazil accounted for 41 percent of the slaves arriving in the New World and the British Americas for 29 percent.[15] After making best guesses at the subsequent movement of slaves to other jurisdictions, about seven out of every ten slaves remained in Brazil or the English-speaking Americas (though with the mainland claiming a larger share than shown in Table 2). The French Americas absorbed half the number of slaves that the British Americas did, with St. Domingue taking in fewer slaves than Jamaica (even after adjusting Jamaican arrivals for Spanish buyers). The French Americas actually took in fewer slaves than any of the major European empires in the Americas. The explanation is that St. Domingue, which accounted for nearly 80 percent of all slaves coming to the French Americas, was a major plantation colony for a relatively short time. Insignificant at the beginning of the eighteenth century, in ruins at the end, and usually on the losing end of wars that disrupted the traffic in slaves, it nevertheless took in more slaves than Jamaica between 1750 and 1791.

The British Americas were more extensive geographically and began to take large numbers of slaves earlier than the French islands. The trade to the Spanish mainland began earlier than anywhere else and, through Cuba, grew explosively even as the slave trade to the rest of the Americas was shutting down. As Fogel has observed, slaves crossed the Atlantic to be put to work primarily in sugar production, or the economies that sugar exports made possible. Tobacco, rice, indigo and cacao were minor sectors overall though locally important. Gold and silver production in the early Spanish Americas and Minas Gerais in Brazil after 1695 was an important source of demand. But although Spanish America dominated the early slave trade, the flow of slaves to this area was quite small compared to what it would become; and, although gold discoveries in Minas Gerais are credited with the large expansion of the Brazilian trade in the early eighteenth century, far more slaves arrived after the gold boom subsided – both in total and per year. Moreover, in both Spanish America and Brazil, specie booms were associated with the arrival of more people from Europe than from Africa, whereas in the sugar colonies in the two centuries after 1650, increased sugar exports

---

[15] After distributing the Guianas total between French, Dutch and British.

almost invariably meant far greater new African arrivals than European. From the late sixteenth century to 1820, ninety percent of the slaves brought across the Atlantic came because of sugar, and the geographic and temporal distribution in Table 2 essentially reflects shifts in the sugar economy.[16]

IV

With this backdrop we can now turn to a time series and cross-sectional examination of the new data. A descriptive summary broken down by quinquennia and African region of origin is presented in Appendix Table A1. Appendix Table A2 provides a similar summary for the major regions of arrival in the Americas for which data have survived. As noted, the prices are for prime males standardized on Jamaica, or more broadly, western Caribbean markets. Whereas all the prices in the appendix tables are in current values, Figures 2(a) and (b) show the result of deflating these prices and fitting a long-run profile in constant pounds sterling. Figure 2(a) presents the results before 1808 for the Americas as a whole (no weighting by region), and Figure 2(b) does the same for Cuba after 1805. Two separate figures are shown because, as previously explained, the basic unit used for the two databases differs. Each coordinate in Figure 2(a) represents the average price of a group of prime males sold from a complete shipment, whereas in Figure 2(b) each coordinate is for a single male slave between the ages of 15 and 40. Moreover, different British price indexes are used to deflate current prices in the two periods.[17] The trend line shown in both scattergrams provides the best fit.[18] The increase over nearly two centuries of slave trading is readily apparent, but less obvious is the accelerating nature of this increase. Between the mid 1670s and 1805–7, prices increased steadily by an average of 0.75 percent a year with most of the major variations explained by war. In the post-1805 Cuban data, the variance is much greater than in the earlier period for the Americas as a whole. The trend line nevertheless suggests that the annual rate of increase more than doubled in the nineteenth century

---

[16] Robert W. Fogel, *Without Consent or Contract: The Rise and Fall of American Slavery* (New York, 1989), pp. 18–21.

[17] The Schumpeter-Gilboy series is used before 1808 (an average of the Consumers' and Producers' goods series A for 1673 to 1695 is spliced to the Consumers' goods other than Cereals for 1696–1807 from series B to provide a continuous series), and the Gayer, Rostow and Schwartz series is used for 1806 to 1850 and spliced to the Rousseau index for 1851 to 1865. See Mitchell, *British Historical Statistics*, 719–22. British slave voyages form the largest national component of the pre-1808 database and the British dominance of the nineteenth century international economy is well known. These two facts are the basis of our use of British price indexes to deflate prices set in an international market.

[18] A cubic function in both figures.
Fig. 2 (a) shows $P = 1497.5 - 1.41Y + 0.000019Y^3$ $r^2 = 0.66$ $F_{stat} = 1042$
Fig. 2 (b) shows $P = -485.9 + 0.00009Y^3$ $r^2 = 0.24$ $F_{stat} = 302.8$

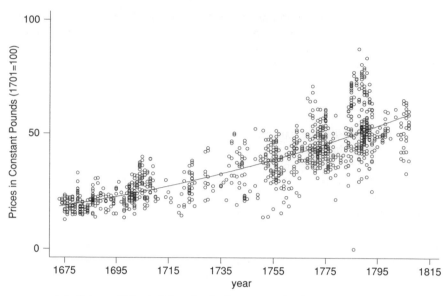

FIGURE 2(a). Prices of Newly Disembarked Prime Male Slaves in Western Caribbean Equivalences, 1673–1807, Constant Pounds. *Source*: PSNA and see text.

to 1.7 percent a year, but unlike the previous century, much of the increase was concentrated at the end of the period – after 1840.

A comparison of Figure 1 with Figures 2(a) and (b) shows that the time series of slave prices does not quite track the trend in the volume of slaves carried from Africa (or vice versa). Slave prices in real terms in the Americas and the volume of slave departures both grew steadily in the course of the last third of the seventeenth and throughout the eighteenth centuries, but while the numbers of slaves quadrupled, slave prices increased only two to threefold in this period.[19] After 1800, however, the direction of the two series diverges. Slave prices continue to increase – indeed after 1840 they increased more rapidly than at any point in the eighteenth century – but the volume of slave departures declined erratically from the late 1790s, with a sharp decline

[19] The trend in nominal prices shown by our series is similar to that of Mancall, Rosenbloom and Weiss for South Carolina ("Slave Prices," p. 623), where it is shown that slave prices tripled between 1722 and 1809. In real terms, however, the rise in prices in South Carolina in the same period was much shallower than that revealed by our series for the Americas. In part, this may reflect the use of different deflators to adjust the nominal series, but it also probably reflects differences through time in the market conditions for the crops produced by slaves. Whereas sugar production dominated the lives of newly imported slaves throughout most of the Americas, in South Carolina slaves were largely employed before 1775 in rice and indigo cultivation, the latter being heavily dependent on British subsidies. After 1783, market conditions for the two staples of South Carolina were much less favorable than earlier and especially in comparison with sugar.

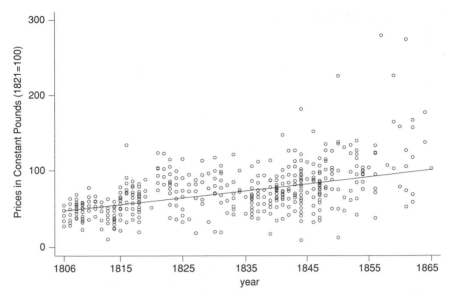

FIGURE 2(b). Prices of Newly Disembarked Prime Male Slaves in Western Caribbean Equivalences, 1806–1865, Constant Pounds. *Source*: Data collected by Laird Bergad, Fe Iglesias García and María del Carmen Barcía.

to zero coming after 1850, coinciding with the rise in the prices of slaves to what was likely their highest levels in the history of slavery anywhere, however measured. More formally, it is possible to get a good fit between 5-year averages of the volume of slaves on the one hand, and the price of slaves on the other, before 1800, with the sign of the prices coefficient being positive. After 1800, prices and volumes are negatively correlated, and the fit generally is less good. By contrast, no significant results whatsoever are possible if we ignore the 1800 dividing line and run the data for the whole period combined, 1673–1865.[20]

Slaves produced mainly sugar in the Americas during the slave trade era, as already noted. How did sugar production change over time? Early data on total sugar prices and output are scarce, but estimates for three benchmark

[20] A simple least-squares regression of the volume of slaves on price before 1800 yielded

$$Q = -129,801 + 12,649.3\,P$$
$$\text{SE} \quad (32,765) \quad (1,167.3)$$
$$t\text{-stat} \quad (10.8) \quad (4.0) \quad r^2 = 0.83$$

For the period after 1800, the estimating equation was

$$Q = 568.9 - 4.246P$$
$$\text{SE} \quad (173.6) \quad (2.179)$$
$$t\text{-stat} \quad (3.3) \quad (1.95) \quad r^2 = 0.19$$

years in the Caribbean alone, 1700, 1770 and 1850 suggest that the total value of all plantation crops increased four or fivefold between the first two of these years and then increased further by between two and three times in the 1770 to 1850 period. The Caribbean was flanked by the U.S. South, where plantation production probably grew more rapidly than in the Caribbean after 1800, and to the south, Brazil, where output growth was somewhat slower, at least until 1825. In other words if, as seems possible, the Caribbean represented the average experience of all the slave Americas, the value of slave output increased more strongly than either the volume of slave arrivals or slave prices for most of the eighteenth century and perhaps kept pace with slave prices in the early nineteenth century as the volume of slave arrivals fell.[21] An interpretation of these secular patterns is presented later.

The long-term rise in both real and nominal slave prices revealed by our data was shadowed by increasing costs of transporting slaves, at least during the eighteenth century. Evidence on such costs is limited, largely because shippers of slaves owned rather than hired the vessels they employed. The evidence that does survive, however, suggests that, notwithstanding falling levels of shipboard slave mortality, per capita transport costs of slaves more or less doubled in money terms between the beginning and end of the eighteenth century.[22] This reflected both changes in trading times of ships in Africa during the century and inflation in factor costs, notably wages, after 1750. Such increases in costs ensured that even though some decline in the

---

[21] From £1.7 million in 1700 to £7.5 in 1770, and £18.2 million in 1850. For the derivation of these estimates, see Eltis, "The Slave Economies of the Caribbean: Structure, Performance, Evolution and Significance," in UNESCO *General History of the Caribbean*, 5 vols. (Kingston, 1997–), vol. 3, Franklin W. Knight (ed.), *The Slave Societies of the Caribbean*, pp. 110–18. For sugar and coffee prices see Richard B. Sheridan, *Sugar and Slavery: An Economic History of the British West Indies, 1623–1776* (Barbados, 1974), pp. 496–98, for the eighteenth century; and David Eltis, *Economic Growth and the Ending of the Transatlantic Slave Trade* (New York, 1987), pp. 283–86, for the nineteenth century. Time series regressions were also run on the basis of a variety of voyage characteristics. For such analysis it was possible to use the voyage-based data from the slave ship data set, rather than the five-year averages necessary for examining links between slave prices and quantity, and produce characteristics. We asked, in effect, whether the price of slaves was dependent on length of voyage, the size of vessel – to the extent this was reflected in standardized tonnage data, the number of slaves on board, and voyage mortality. Only the time trend was highly significant in these runs. Shipboard mortality was weakly significant with a negative coefficient, with the most likely explanation being that survivors of high mortality voyages were in poor health and thus sold for less. However, inclusion of all these variables in an estimating equation generated multicolinearity problems.

[22] David Richardson, "The Costs of Survival: The Transport of Slaves in the Middle Passage and the Profitability of the 18th-Century British Slave Trade," *Explorations in Economic History*, 24 (1987): 183. On slave mortality trends, see Robin Haines and Ralph Shlomowitz, "Explaining the Mortality Decline in the Eighteenth-Century British Slave Trade," *Economic History Review*, 52 (2000): 263.

ratio of transport costs to American slave prices appears to have occurred through time, the transport cost "wedge" remained an important influence on American slave prices. This applied not only to the time trend in prices but also to inter-regional price variations.[23]

Variations in price across regions are of particular interest given the wide geographic reach of the trade and the highly uneven distribution of the slave trade across the sub-Saharan African coast. In Africa, information on inter-regional cost differentials is not easily available and is in any event complicated by complex wind and current systems. Voyage time provides one proxy. If we define voyage time broadly to take into account time elapsed between departure from the home port of the slave vessel to the point at which the slaves disembarked in the Americas, then the length of the voyage may be taken as a proxy for costs. In broad terms, voyages that targeted Senegambia were at least 50 percent shorter than those from the rest of West and West Central Africa. Voyages drawing slaves from Southeast Africa, on the other hand, were substantially longer than all others. Within the broad region from the western Gold Coast through to southern Angola from which some 85 percent of slaves were drawn, there were further differences between one African embarkation region and another in voyage times (and therefore costs). These were partly on account of prevailing winds and ocean currents. Thus it was generally quicker to sail from Angola to North America than it was from any point on the Gold Coast to the Bight of Biafra inclusive, despite the fact that Angola was further away geographically. Offsetting this in part, however, was the fact that vessels could obtain their slaves more quickly from the Bight of Biafra, especially the port of Bonny, than from any other African region, so that total voyage time from say Liverpool or Nantes to the Caribbean was often quicker via the Bight of Biafra than other regions.[24]

These differences are highlighted in Table 3, which presents average time in days spent sailing from the Americas or Europe to various African regions and then to the western Caribbean – defined here as Jamaica or St. Domingue. Most of the vessels in the sample are French and British. For reasons that will become apparent shortly, only data for selected periods are presented in the table. Table 3 incorporates the results of tests of statistical significance using a regression-based analysis of variance (anova) contained in Appendix Table A5. Two patterns are immediately apparent from the table. First, for most of the years shown, slave vessels obtaining their slaves in

---

[23] On the transport cost "wedge" see David Eltis, "The Relative Importance of Slaves and Commodities in the Atlantic Trade of Seventeenth-Century Africa," *Journal of African History*, 35 (1994): 237–49.

[24] On loading speeds at Bonny compared to other places in Atlantic Africa, see Paul E. Lovejoy and David Richardson, "'This horrid hole': Commerce and Credit at Bonny 1690–1840", unpublished paper.

TABLE 3. *Average Voyage Times (days) for Slave Vessels Leaving Ports in Europe and the Americas to St. Domingue or Jamaica by Major Slave Provenance Regions in Africa, Selected Quinquennia, 1676–1795 (Number of Voyages in Parentheses)*

	1676–1705	1751–1755	1771–1775	1786–1790	1791–1795
Upper Guinea	225.9*** (10)	314.4 (42)	312.0 (21)	259.5*** (85)	300.4*** (55)
Gold Coast	280.6 (20)	357.9*** (66)	303.6 (14)	300.4*** (64)	313.9*** (44)
Bight of Benin	335.3* (42)	366.6*** (54)	347.0 (46)	348.0*** (85)	324.1*** (20)
Bight of Biafra	305.9 (14)	302.6 (46)	339.9 (16)	249.2 (105)	252.7 (122)
West Central Africa	346.3* (29)	361.6*** (53)	359.2 (107)	370.9*** (179)	275.3* (105)
Southeast Africa				487.5*** (37)	444.3*** (9)
All regions#	315.4 (115)	343.7 (261)	346.8 (205)	327.3 (555)	283.2 (355)

For the equations on which this table is based see Appendix Table A5.
* Significantly different from the Bight of Biafra mean at the 20 percent level.
** Significantly different from the Bight of Biafra mean at the 5 percent level.
*** Significantly different from the Bight of Biafra mean at the 1 percent level.
# Includes some regions not listed in previous rows.

Sources: TSTD; Table A-5.

the Bight of Biafra completed much faster voyages to the major slave markets of the Caribbean than did vessels trading in other regions. On average,
in the second half of the eighteenth century, such voyages were nearly 15
percent faster than those from adjacent regions. Though not shown here, it
is possible to demonstrate that such an advantage derived from the length
of time needed to collect a full human cargo, rather than from differences
in time spent at sea. Second, the advantage of the Bight of Biafra increased
over time, peaked in the 1780s and then, though not shown in Table 3,
probably disappeared after 1800.[25] In addition, there is now considerable
evidence that shipboard mortality was not the same for all regions of departure, or, indeed, ports within those regions. Moreover, given the nature
of these deaths, morbidity and mortality were closely related so that those
slaves who survived the middle passage ordeal from high-mortality regions
were weaker, and therefore sold for less than those setting out from low-
mortality regions. Once more these differences center on the Bight of Biafra,
vessels from which during most of the slave trade era experienced on average
one-third greater mortality than vessels going to the same destinations in the
Americas that left from West Central Africa and the Bight of Benin. Interestingly, this differential disappeared after 1807 when shipboard mortality
increased everywhere in the illegal phase of the slave trade. The implication
of these patterns for prices derives from the fact that transportation costs (including losses from on-board mortality) accounted for more than 50 percent
of the selling price of the newly arrived slave. In short, we would not expect
prices for slaves arriving in the Americas from different African regions to
have been the same, nor would we expect any differences between African
regions to have remained constant over time.[26]

Table 4 focuses on the African regional groupings for which formal testing
is possible. It presents the cross-sectional price data for slaves in the Americas
from different African regions. Given the previous discussion of transport
costs and mortality, these prices, it should be stressed, do not necessarily reflect the price of slaves in Africa, but rather the prices of slaves in the Americas
from different African regions. The two quinquennia in Table 4 for which the
data are adequate before the peak of the slave trade – 1676–1680 and 1701–
1705 – show little indication of statistically significant differences between

[25] Although not shown in Table 3, an analysis of 123 voyages to Cuba after 1800 (there was
no slave trade to Jamaica and St. Domingue after 1807, and very little from the Gold Coast)
shows no significant differences in time between the Bight of Benin, the Bight of Biafra, and
West Central Africa.

[26] Our conclusion here is based solely on slave supply and shipping costs. It ignores the possible
influence of planters' views on the quality of newly imported slaves. Some historians have
followed contemporaries in drawing attention to the low esteem with which slaves from some
African regions (notably the Bight of Biafra) were held among planters. The price differentials
by African origin are consistent to some extent with perceived planter preferences, but we are
skeptical about attributing such differentials solely or even largely to demand side factors.

TABLE 4. *Average Nominal Prices in Pounds Sterling, Standardized on Jamaica, of Prime Male Slaves Newly Arrived in the Americas, by Regions of Departure from Africa, Selected Quinquennia, 1676–1795 (Number of Slaves Sold in Parentheses)*

	1676–80	1701–1705	1751–1755	1771–1775	1786–1790	1791–1795
Upper Guinea	15.7* (184)	26.2 (363)	34.3*** (1,277)	47.9** (2,472)	50.8 (4,045)	60.5* (2,490)
Gold Coast	19.8 (2,945)	28.9* (3,465)	34.9*** (4,129)	47.5** (4,350)	58.5*** (2,742)	65.7*** (2,627)
Bight of Benin	18.6 (2,482)	27.5 (5,115)	32.9 (391)	48.5** (2,568)	67.5*** (1,979)	58.0 (207)
Bight of Biafra	18.8 (2,401)	23.9 (468)	26.1 (2,171)	42.7 (5,296)	48.1 (7,515)	54.7 (8,193)
West Central Africa	18.1 (1,117)	21.0 (798)	34.7** (7,943)	49.4*** (4,403)	77.4*** (5,114)	63.7** (2,377)
Southeast Africa					65.1*** (1,244)	
All regions#	18.8 (9,129)	27.1 (10,209)	33.0 (10,013)	46.5 (19,089)	58.9 (22,639)	59.0 (15,894)

For the equations on which this table is based see Appendix Table A3.
* Significantly different from the Bight of Biafra mean at the 20 percent level.
** Significantly different from the Bight of Biafra mean at the 5 percent level.
*** Significantly different from the Bight of Biafra mean at the 1 percent level.
# Includes some regions not listed in previous rows.

Sources: PSNA; Table A-3.

African regions. The samples for the low- and high-cost regions – Upper Guinea and Southeast Africa, respectively, are small or non-existent, but the eight samples in the two quinquennia for West and West Central African regions throw up only one significant difference, and that at only the twenty percent level of significance. This suggests that at the beginning of the era of growth in the slave trade, price differentials for slaves from different African regions as they arrived in the Americas were small, and markets were likely well integrated. Although not shown in the tables, this situation may also have held for the close of the trade. For the period after 1790 there are very good data for Cuba differentiated by African nation. Identifications of nation in Spanish America must be handled with care. They are not always either fixed (ethnic identities might shift over time) or accurate, and assigning them to the eight stretches of the coastline defined in Table 1 presents an additional problem. Laird Bergad and his colleagues have pointed to differences between mean prices paid for African nations in nineteenth century Cuba, but tests on these data for five-year groupings of males between the ages of 15 and 40 reveal that the differences between African nations are, in fact, not statistically significant at any point in the nineteenth century.[27]

By contrast, at the height of the trade in the second half of the eighteenth century, slaves from different regions in what might be termed the slave provenance heartlands of West and West Central Africa sold for substantially different prices in the Americas (after adjusting for distances between different markets there). Table 4 shows large differences for the four quinquennia that center on the Bight of Biafra. Slaves from that region sold in the Americas for from one-fifth to one-third less than those from all other coastal areas during the period. These differences are statistically significant at the one or five percent levels for both the Gold Coast and Angola for every quinquennium, and for Upper Guinea and the adjacent Bight of Benin for two of the four five-year periods. The differences are largest in the early 1750s and late 1780s. Thus the expectation that slaves from different regions in Africa would sell for different prices is in fact borne out.

For the Americas, Table 5 shows the result of a similar analysis of the standardized Jamaica prices for seven major markets in the Caribbean and the North American mainland. The table provides the results of a regression-based analysis of variance for these major markets. The grouping of Antigua and Barbados in one market, and Dominica, St. Vincent, and Grenada in another, is made necessary by the sample size requirements for significance testing. These islands in any event had close trade relations with each other and comparisons within the group for those quinquennia for which data

---

[27] For a review of the literature on ethnicities in the Spanish and other parts of the Americas, see Russell Lohse, "Slave Trade Nomenclature and African Ethnicities in the Americas: Evidence from Early 18th-Century Costa Rica," *Slavery and Abolition*, 23 (2002): 73–92; For price data grouped by ethnicity see Bergad et al. *Cuban Slave Market*, 73–4.

TABLE 5. *Average Nominal Prices in Pounds Sterling, Standardized on Jamaica, of Prime Male Slaves Newly Arrived in the Americas, by Regions of Arrival in the Americas, and Selected Quinquennia, 1676–1795 (Number of Slaves Sold in Parentheses)*

	1671–1675	1676–1680	1681–1685	1686–1690	1691–1695	1696–1700	1701–1705	1706–1710	1741–1745
South Carolina									18.1*** (230)
Guianas									29.7** (1,653)
Jamaica	25.0 (1,249)		17.6 (3,480)	19.8 (4,770)	19.8 (2,383)	23.1 (1,163)	24.4 (2,724)	25.9 (1,727)	
St. Domingue									38.5* (1,980)
Dominica, St. Vincent, Grenada									
Barbados and Antigua	20.4*** (1,643)	18.0** (5,083)	17.0 (3,941)	18.7 (3,835)	21.5* (3,106)	25.4* (5,321)	26.0 (9,397)	24.8 (5,639)	35.1 (1,492)
All regions#	21.0 (2,892)	18.4 (9,334)	16.8 (7,421)	19.4 (9,397)	21.4 (5,798)	24.9 (7,640)	26.2 (13,242)	25.3 (7,969)	29.3 (8,718)

	1751–1755	1756–1760	1766–1770	1771–1775	1776–1780	1781–1785	1786–1790	1791–1795
South Carolina	35.1 (1,049)	31.0*** (1,923)	38.7 (514)	53.0** (2,428)		58.5* (790)		
Guianas	36.6* (1,618)	28.0*** (2,447)	48.0** (3,024)	43.0*** (2,525)	44.1 (1,175)	51.5 (145)	54.4 (669)	65.5 (939)
Jamaica	32.6 (4,040)	36.7 (4,014)	40.6 (1,390)	49.0 (6,171)	41.0 (5,536)	47.1 (1,168)	52.5 (6,917)	59.7 (11,959)
St. Domingue	35.4 (688)	45.6* (588)	51.9** (622)	53.4** (3,426)	50.2*** (1,448)	65.5*** (8,282)	73.9*** (11,016)	63.1 (2,280)
Dominica, St. Vincent, Grenada			39.1 (2,144)	41.9*** (3,574)	35.6** (1,279)	42.0 (1,493)	48.2** (5,565)	53.3* (1,725)
Barbados and Antigua	26.6** (1,422)	29.0** (681)	34.6* (750)	42.7*** (1,610)	37.5 (442)	43.2 (1,067)	48.3* (1,300)	51.6 (745)
All regions#	33.0 (10,652)	32.8 (12,494)	42.6 (9,353)	46.1 (22,860)	41.2 (11,533)	57.5 (14,770)	59.3 (25,803)	59.2 (18,044)

For the equations on which this table is based see Appendix Table A4.

* Significantly different from Jamaica at the 20 percent level (except for 1741–45 when the reference is Barbados and Antigua).

** Significantly different from Jamaica at the 5 percent level (except for 1741–45 when the reference region is Barbados and Antigua).

*** Significantly different from Jamaica at the 1 percent level (except for 1741–45 when the reference region is Barbados and Antigua).

Includes some regions not listed in previous rows.

Sources: PSNA; Table A-4

are adequate show no significant differences. The seven markets together accounted for nearly ninety percent of the total non-Brazilian slave trade prior to 1808, and Jamaica, Barbados, St. Vincent, Dominica and Grenada were at different times major entrepôts from which Spanish America and the smaller French and English colonies drew many of their slaves in an intra-American slave traffic.[28] It is hard to conceive of the general price pattern for slaves varying markedly from what held for these large markets.

Table 5 points to differences in slave prices that cannot be explained purely by the costs of transportation between the major markets. Between 1673 and 1690, and again in the third quarter of the eighteenth century, prices of slaves in Jamaica were higher than those in Barbados by more than the amount required to pay transportation costs between the two islands. Although there were no significant price differentials in the early part of the eighteenth century nor in the last quarter, there was a sudden and temporary reversal of the Jamaican premium during the decade of the 1690s, when general war brought both the threat and reality of a French invasion of the island and Jamaica temporarily lost its role of as a major entrepôt for Spanish American buyers of slaves. After 1740, the significance tests suggest a three-tier market, topped by St. Domingue with Jamaica in the second tier and most of the rest paying lower prices again and forming a third tier. Occasional exceptions to this pattern were the Dutch Guianas in the second half of the 1760s and South Carolina in the early 1770s, when slave prices moved temporarily into the St. Domingue tier. As we might expect, these were periods when the plantation sectors of both regions underwent strong expansion and high prosperity.[29] Perhaps, however, the most striking of the differences are those within the same broad region such as developed in the second half of the eighteenth century. Jamaica and St. Domingue are similar distances from the major African slave provenance zones, as well as the eastern Caribbean. They present identical problems of winds and currents for vessels sailing from the east. Yet between 1760 and 1790 slave

---

[28] For some indication of the scale of the inter-colonial movement of slaves, see David Richardson, "The British Empire and the Atlantic Slave Trade," in P. J. Marshall (ed.), *Oxford History of the British Empire: The Eighteenth Century* (Oxford, 1998).

[29] David Richardson, "The British Slave Trade to Colonial South Carolina," *Slavery and Abolition*, 12 (1991): 133–4; Goslinga, *Dutch in the Caribbean*, 315–16. Goslinga's data also suggest that slave imports into Suriname reached an all-time peak in 1771 (p. 423). A report from Suriname in 1768 complained about the high and rising price of slaves in the colony relative to those in other Dutch colonies such as St. Eustatius (Public Record Office, Colonial Office Papers, CO 116/36, f.128, report of 27 November 1768). Strong growth of course occurred in both areas in earlier periods, with, in the case of South Carolina at least, possibly similar consequences for slave prices there relative to other colonies (see Mancall, Rosenbloom and Weiss, "Slave Prices in South Carolina," 627, where they suggest that between the 1720s and late 1730s slave prices in South Carolina rose relative to prices in the West Indies and Chesapeake, but then fell back in the 1740s). Unfortunately, price data are as yet lacking for earlier years in the case of Surinam.

prices averaged 20 percent higher in St. Domingue than in Jamaica, and, indeed, anywhere else in the Americas that was buying slaves from Africa. Differences developed even within St. Domingue itself, with planters in the north of the colony paying substantially lower nominal prices than those in the west and south.[30] By contrast, slave prices in the French and Dutch South American mainland colonies, and the smaller British islands and North American mainland normally lagged behind those in the major Caribbean markets by more than it would have cost to move slaves from one market to another. When we consider the size of the slave market after 1660, the relative ease of entry in Africa as well as Europe and the Americas, and what has long been regarded as the ineffectiveness of governments to shape the market through mercantilist regulations, the persistence of these regional differences in the Americas, and to a lesser extent Africa, is worthy of attention.

V

The rise together of slave prices and quantities over one and a quarter centuries is strongly suggestive of a secular increase in the demand for slaves, based no doubt on the expansion of sugar output. If, indeed, the aggregate supply curve of slaves arriving from the West, West Central and Southeast African coasts held constant in this period, as demand expanded, then between 1676 and 1810 the price elasticity of supply of slaves would have been considerable. A fourfold increase in prices and a two and a half fold increase in the number of slaves sold suggests a supply elasticity of just over 0.5. The supply function for newly arrived slaves in the Americas through most of the eighteenth century comprised about 50 percent transatlantic transportation costs, 25 percent factoring costs on the African coast and 25 percent the costs of obtaining and delivering slaves to the factor on the coast. In the course of the century, there do not seem to have been major technological breakthroughs in the first two of these. Voyage times increased slightly and the proportion of the slave price in the Americas taken up by transportation declined somewhat as the ratio of African to American slave prices increased. Within Africa, less is known about the supply function, but we do know that in the third quarter of the eighteenth century the time taken to obtain a full

---

[30] David Geggus, "La Traite des esclaves aux Antilles françaises à la fin du 18me siècle: quelques aspects du marché local," in Silvia Marzagalli and Hubert Bonin (eds.), *Négoce, Ports, et Océans, XVIe–XXe Siècles: Mélanges offerts à Paul Butel* (Bordeaux, 2000), pp. 235–245; idem, "The French Slave Trade: An Overview," *William and Mary Quarterly*, 58 (2001): 129. There remains the possibility that the definition of prime slaves employed here – adult males sold in the first third of the period of the sale – does not sufficiently standardize the price of slaves. It is possible that more slaves from preferred African regions, or, say, taller African slaves, were sold in the prime market of St. Domingue than in the second and third tier markets as defined here. If this was the case – and further research on these issues is likely possible – then the price differentials indicated here are biased upward.

complement of slaves increased sharply, suggesting increased costs in the interior.[31] By the end of the century, the waiting time for slaves had reverted close to levels that held in the first half of the century, but for most of the half-century after 1750, such an increase in waiting times no doubt offset the small improvement in sailing times.

After 1810, a quite different demand and supply situation held. While demand continued to increase with rising incomes in Europe and the widening impact of industrialization, there were major shifts in the supply of slaves to the Americas brought about by abolition of the slave trade. Abolition as manifested in naval interference with the trade, and more especially massive bribes to government officials in Brazil and Cuba to permit illegal arrivals, introduced a major cost wedge that increased prices in the Americas and reduced prices of slaves on the African coast.[32] Voyage times shortened markedly in the nineteenth century, but the cost-reducing impact of this was more than offset by the measures to evade British cruisers, the expense of avoiding regular port facilities in the Americas, and the aforementioned bribes. Most of this impact came after 1840 when prices increased most strongly. It is particularly striking that this pattern held across those countries that continued to accept new slave arrivals – Cuba and Brazil – as well as those who did not – such as the United States and the British Caribbean. It is also striking that this was the period when the intra-American traffic in slaves came into its own as owners moved slaves around within each of the major slave jurisdictions. Although the British were able to hold the intra-Caribbean trade within their own jurisdiction to quite low levels, they could not prevent the emergence of huge differentials in the price of slaves on adjacent islands in British West Indies between the abolition of the transatlantic slave trade to British territory, and the abolition of slavery itself.[33] That slave owners could pay such relatively high prices in Brazil, Cuba, the United States, Trinidad and British Guiana indicates that the productivity of labor was also increasing strongly, an issue that has been widely explored in the literature in the last thirty years.

On the African side, given the pattern of regional involvement in the trade outlined at the beginning of this essay, it is likely that the major African

---

[31] This paragraph is based on David Eltis and David Richardson, "Productivity in the Transatlantic Slave Trade," *Explorations in Economic History*, 32 (1995): 465–84.

[32] The timing of the fall in prices in Africa varied across regions, reflecting, among other things, the geographical intensity of suppression activity (Paul E. Lovejoy and David Richardson, "British Abolition and Its Impact on Slave Prices Along the Atlantic Coast of Africa, 1783–1850," *Journal of Economic History*, 55 [1995]: 98–120).

[33] Barry Higman, *Slave Populations of the British Caribbean, 1807–1834* (Baltimore, 1984), pp. 80–85. For inter-island productivity and slave price differentials, see Stanley L. Engerman, "Economic Adjustments to Emancipation in the United States and the British West Indies," *Journal of Interdisciplinary History*, 13 (1982): 195–200.

provenance zones had different cost structures in the supply of slaves as well as different middle passage transportation costs. A given price for a slave in the Americas would elicit a different quantity supplied in each of the eight regions, and as prices rose after 1675 each region would respond differently, or more formally would exhibit different elasticities of supply. A threshold price, below which supply would be zero, would be necessary to pull a coastal (and indeed an interior) region into the trade after which the responsiveness of quantity of slaves offered to changes in price would be much more pronounced. Thus each region would be pulled into the traffic (as well as leave it during the suppression era) at different times in the step pattern described previously. There are analogies here in markets for skilled labor where lengthy training periods ensure strong upward pressure on remuneration in the short run as demand rises, but a much more moderate pattern in the long run as supply responds to the higher prices. Many capital-intensive primary products such as oil, or in the period under examination here, sugar, show the same large differentials in short- and long-term responsiveness to price changes. For slaves, wars could yield a surge of slaves that would fill many transatlantic vessels, but such conflict was not reliable or predictable enough to provide a foundation for a transatlantic trading network that hinged on coordinating a flow of goods and services from five or six continents and timing vessel departure and arrival times according to crops grown in both Africa and the Americas.[34]

For the slave trade within Africa, the key adjustments were probably as much social and cultural as economic in nature. An alternative and more dependable network for the supply of slaves could not appear overnight. Cultural adjustments, specifically value changes in perceptions of whom it was permissible to enslave, might be a prerequisite to such a network, and the social diversity of sub-Saharan Africa suggests large regional variations in the time that these adjustments would take. One crude measurement possible is the time lapse between the first slaves entering the transatlantic traffic in each region and the period when the large step-up in the volume of slaves occurred. This appears to have been shortest in West Central Africa (an area, however, that is so vast, that it is hard to describe it as a single region), where large-scale slave departures for the New World were taking place by the mid sixteenth century. In the Bight of Biafra, by contrast, slaves are recorded as leaving the Niger Delta and Cross River areas in the early seventeenth

---

[34] Stephen D. Behrendt, "Markets, Transaction Cycles, and Profits: Merchant Decision Making in the British Slave Trade," *William and Mary Quarterly*, 58 (2001): 171–204. For an excellent micro-examination of the relationship between the supply of slaves and war on the eighteenth century Gold Coast, see Stephanie Ellen Smallwood, "Salt-Water Slaves: African Enslavement, Forced Migration, and Settlement in the Anglo-Atlantic World, 1660–1700," Unpublished Ph.D. thesis, Duke University, 1999, especially, ch. 2.

century, but 80 percent of all slaves leaving the region entered the trade only after 1740 – many decades after severe demand pressures began to build according to Figure 1.

The Slave Coast and West Central Africa had relatively low threshold levels, and high price elasticities of supply thereafter, while the three Upper Guinea regions, but especially Sierra Leone and the Windward Coast, and then Southeast Africa (at least with respect to the Atlantic trade) had higher slave price entry levels. The Gold Coast, where entry of the region was likely related to the exhaustion of gold deposits, and the Bight of Biafra fall in between these two extremes. Moreover, within the Bight of Biafra, two major embarkation points, Old and New Calabar, became involved in the trade when prices were low in the seventeenth century, while the rise of the largest slave port, Bonny, may have hinged on the much higher threshold price that evolved in second half of the eighteenth century and was associated with the huge increase in slave departures sustained by the Bight of Biafra at that time. Thus, the full exploitation of the Bonny system required a higher price than was possible in the seventeenth century. It is worth noting in this context that the geographical area on which Bonny drew was probably much larger than that of Calabar, and that Bonny merchants perhaps relied more completely than those at Calabar on the culturally complex Aro network for their supply of slaves.[35] Both these features of the Bonny traffic would require higher prices for slaves initially.

The African price differentials are thus consistent with differences between long- and short-term elasticities of supply within regions (and ports) as much as inter-regional differentials in either long- or short-term elasticities. Something of this pattern is apparent in the Americas. Table 5 provides examples of temporary price differentials between regions during particular quinquennia, particularly when markets for slaves expanded rapidly, and the disappearance of these in the long run. Jamaica between 1673 and 1680 was not only beginning to enter the sugar market, it was becoming the major entrepôt for slaves to the Spanish Americas.[36] By the 1670s, in contrast, Barbados had already undergone its first sugar revolution. For a

---

[35] For the cultural and social changes associated with the rise of the Aro network and the emergence of Bonny, see the early chapters of G Ugo Nwokeji, "The Biafran Frontier: Trade, Slaves, and Aro Society, c. 1750–1905" (Unpublished Ph.D. thesis, University of Toronto, 1999). Nwokeji argues "A look at such social facts as marriage and the incest prohibition immediately reveals how hopelessly entangled these were with slaving. The people's belief system and deities were grounded in, and reinforced by, slaving-related processes. The value system celebrated the ownership and proliferation of people, and encouraged the sale of others into Atlantic slavery. The decision regarding who to send to Atlantic slavery and who to retain was central to Aro political economy. . . ."

[36] "Considerations about the Spaniards buying negro's of the English Ro'll Company and receiving 2/3 at Jamaica and 1/3 at Barbados," Jamaica, Feb 2, 1675, Egerton ms, British Library Add ms, 2395, f 501. Also in CO31/1, ff. 6–7 in PRO.

time, price differentials were in excess of what was required to pay the cost of transportation between the two islands, but an equilibrium hinging on transportation costs was apparently in place by the 1680s when the price differential disappeared. After 1690, prices in Jamaica fell behind those of Barbados for two quinquennia though these results are significant at only the 20 percent level. This was a time when war interfered with the flow of slaves from Jamaica to Spanish America and occasioned massive French raids on the north side of the island.[37] The equilibrium was disturbed once more in the third quarter of the eighteenth century, when Jamaica was expanding muscovado sugar production rapidly, at a time when Barbados was diversifying into less labor intensive sugar byproducts such as rum and molasses. For most quinquennia between 1751 and 1775, a prime male slave is estimated to have cost 20 percent more in Jamaica than in Barbados after adjusting for transportation costs. Some short-run differences also show up in South Carolina in the eighteenth century. We still lack price information for the period before and after the first spurt of heavy slave arrivals before the Stono Rebellion in 1739 – setting aside the quinquennia with small sample sizes – as well as the peak years of 1804–1807. In the two quinquennia before the Revolution, where numbers make testing feasible, slave prices in the colony lagged behind those in Jamaica in 1756–60, and then in the very prosperous five years just before the Revolution, planters in South Carolina were able to pay St. Domingue prices – unlike their Jamaican counterparts.

But the major differences in the prices of slaves in Table 5 have little to do with adjustments between long and short terms. Heavily segmented markets for slaves in the Americas, and indeed for produce, too, were the norm prior to the nineteenth century, when over two-thirds of all enslaved Africans made the journey to the Americas. There were five separate transatlantic systems for most of this era – British, French, Dutch, Spanish and Portuguese – and a sixth if we include the independent United States. The price of sugar in Amsterdam or North Germany, where the surplus sugar of all European systems was sold, acted perhaps as the ultimate arbiter of the price of slaves in the America. Yet markets for sugar were themselves sufficiently segmented with tariffs and subsidies to permit regional differences

---

[37] The Jamaica factors told the RAC in December, 1690 that the war had prevented them from meeting the terms of the Asiento contract of the previous year. (Penhallow and Ruding to RAC, Dec. 9, 1690, T70/57, f. 55). Just over a year later the factor wrote "the Asiento in the hands of Nicholas Porcio and Sr James Castell is confirmed for 5 yeares more and Greate Supplys of Negroes are brought them by the Dutch." (Walter Ruding to RAC, Feb 2, 1692, T70/17, f. 51). By 1694 the factor was writing "Cannot encourage the sending of negroes. Assentista dead ... without that they know not what to do with the Negroes" (idem, Feb 14, 1694, ibid). And the following year, "Unless the Assienta be Established little Plate or Gold to be Expected." (Chas Whittall, Aug 22, 1695, T70/12, p.151). For the effect of French raids, see Beeston, Barnard and Whittall to the RAC, July 28, 1693, T70/12, f. 94; idem, June 21, 1694, ibid, f. 96; idem. Dec. 12, 1694, ibid.

in what planters could pay for their labor. Each colonial power was able to enforce some mercantilist restrictions that preserved the domestic market for sugar and the colonial market for slaves for its own traders. Thus, for example, English ships could not trade freely in either the French Americas without first registering as French property (a hazardous and costly procedure) or in Brazil and the Spanish Americas without a licence. In addition, the French government subsidized the slave trade. The restrictions and preferences were, of course, porous. Smuggling was on a large scale and British firms did find ways to register their vessels as French. Nevertheless, if we measure the results against what would have happened in the absence of barriers – a standard that perhaps economists are more likely to use than historians – rather than what would have happened if the laws had been 100 percent effective, mercantilism clearly had an impact.

As a consequence, in the western Caribbean at the height of the slave trade, there were three major adjacent markets for slaves, St. Domingue, Jamaica and Cuba, that essentially had far less to do with each other than they would have done under free-trade conditions. Table 5 shows that before 1795 price differentials between the national slave systems of England, France and Cuba were far more significant than those between regions within each system, even after adjusting for transportation costs. Prices in St. Domingue were usually 25 to 30 percent greater than in Jamaica. Indeed, prices for newly arrived Africans were persistently greater in St. Domingue than anywhere else in the Americas between 1756 and the colony-destroying rebellion that began in August, 1791. Between 1786 and 1790 they achieved levels not to be surpassed until the mid 1840s in Cuba. Such a pattern is entirely consistent with the French colony's extraordinary rise to world dominance at this time not only in the sugar market, but also in coffee and indigo. As we might expect from the foregoing, the next peak in prices to surpass that of 1786–90 corresponded with Cuba's occupation of a similar dominance in world sugar markets in the early 1840s.[38] In the third quarter of the eighteenth century, however, Cuba was effectively unable to compete with St. Domingue and Jamaica, thanks to the severe strictures of Spanish colonial policy. Table 5 contains no Cuban data at this time because, except when the British occupied Havana in 1762–3, very few slaves direct from Africa were sold in Cuba before the late 1780s. The slaves that did sell, mainly Creoles, went for prices far above what held in Jamaica, a level high enough to help delay the development of the Cuban sugar industry for between one and two centuries if, as seems reasonable, this pattern existed in the early

[38] As previously noted, the sugar-dominated northern section of St. Domingue was where the highest prices of all were paid. It should also be noted that although prices of slaves in the U.S. South exceeded those of Cuba during the 1830s and 1840s, there was a protective barrier of sorts in place between these two markets also, in the form of a largely effective prohibition of the African slave trade to the United States.

seventeenth century as well.[39] Differences between the British and Dutch systems also show up in the third quarter of the eighteenth century as the slave trade approached its peak. All the observations for Guiana at this time are from the Dutch South Americas, mainly Suriname. The region appears to have operated with some independence from mainstream markets, with slave prices generally below those of the rest of the Americas, yet, during a period of strong expansion of sugar in Suriname, prices in 1766–70 temporarily approached those of St. Domingue. Thereafter, and especially after 1780, the differences disappear – though sample sizes for the Guianas diminish. It was at this time that the British destroyed the Dutch slave fleet and began to supply slaves themselves to Dutch colonies and also that British planters increasingly established themselves in Demerara, Berbice and Essequibo. It seems clear that after 1775 barriers between the English and Dutch systems eroded significantly and that as a consequence differentials in slave prices diminished significantly.

Overall, trends in the prices and quantities of slaves in 1673–1867 are consistent with a demand-driven explanation of the dynamics of the market down to the beginning of the nineteenth century. Thereafter, and from the perspective of slave markets in the Americas at least, supply (or more precisely, efforts to suppress the trade) came to play a much larger role. The central importance of sugar on the demand side is clear. As the slave trade did not die because of a collapse of demand, supply-side factors had the ultimate effect of shutting down the traffic in the sense that it became too expensive to pay the costs of avoiding proscription of the traffic. Throughout the era of the slave trade, markets on the African side of the Atlantic seem to have been more integrated than those on the American side. There were major differences between broad African regions that clearly determined the prices and quantities of slaves sold in response to an Atlantic demand at the coast, and that added to the domestic African demand for slaves. In addition, both European and African slave traders were at times able to extract rents at particular embarkation points.[40] But there was no contemporary counterpart in Africa to the segmented markets in the Americas that might be observed

---

[39] For a few decades in the mid sixteenth century a minor sugar export economy flourished in the Spanish Antilles. Thereafter, with the Portuguese concentrating on Brazil, and the Spanish on the mainlands of North and South America, the three Spanish strongholds of the Antilles – Cuba, Hispaniola and Puerto Rico – became strategic settlements protecting trade routes that also produced some non-plantation exports. For the large Jamaica–Cuba slave price differential in the first half of the eighteenth century, see Colin A. Palmer, *Human Cargoes: The British Slave Trade to Spanish America, 1700–1739* (Urbana, 1981), pp. 123–24. The Spanish colonial land tenure system was also clearly important in delaying development. See Manuel Moreno Fraginals, *The Sugarmill: Socioeconomic Complex of Sugar in Cuba* (New York, 1976), pp. 20–25.

[40] See E. W. Evans and David Richardson, "Hunting for Rents: The Economics of Slaving in Pre-Colonial Africa," *Economic History Review*, 48 (1995): 665–86.

for large parts of the eighteenth century, a feature that is not unrelated to the inability of Europeans to establish sovereignty in sub-Saharan Africa prior to the mid nineteenth century. Only in Angola, the one region in Africa where a European sovereign presence was established, were there markets exclusively and successfully reserved for one national group of slave traders – in Luanda and Benguela. Ironically, at the very point in the nineteenth century when Europeans began to seem capable of imposing segmented markets on the African coast through Americas-type direct occupation, the slave trade became the subject of suppressive action. From the late eighteenth century in the case of Sierra Leone, the late 1820s in the case of Senegal and the late 1830s in the main ports of Angola, European colonialism became associated with suppression of the transatlantic slave trade rather than its promotion.[41] As a consequence, supply pressures on the price of slaves newly arrived in the Americas came to be of much greater importance than hitherto.

[41] Eltis, *Economic Growth*. For the Senegal case see Michael Kielstra, *The Politics of Slave Trade Suppression in Britain and France, 1814–48: Diplomacy, Morality and Economics* (Basingstoke, 2000), pp. 93–148.

APPENDIX TABLE A1. *Average Nominal Prices in Pounds Sterling of Slaves Newly Arrived in the Americas Distributed by African Region of Slave Embarkation, Five Year Intervals, 1671–1810 (Number of Slaves in Parentheses)*

	Senegambia	Sierra Leone	Wind Coast	Gold Coast	B. of Benin	B. of Biafra	WC Africa	SE Africa
1671–75					22.7 (645)	19.1 (536)		
1676–80	14.9 (184)			19.3 (2,945)	17.8 (2,482)	18.4 (2,401)	17.5 (1,117)	
1681–85	16.4 (908)	18.11 (137)		16.2 (129)	17.1 (2,865)	16.8 (1,268)	16.3 (2,114)	
1686–90	21.1 (725)	21.7 (354)		18.7 (361)	19 (5,897)	20.6 (226)	18.5 (1,834)	
1691–95	19.6 (1,235)	27.8 (131)		24.7 (767)	21.47 (3,056)	25.5 (108)	16 (277)	
1696–1700	18.3 (112)	16 (151)		25.3 (2,406)	25.8 (2,775)	22.6 (188)	23.3 (232)	
1701–5	27.6 (183)			28.9 (3,465)	27.5 (5,115)	23.9 (468)	21 (798)	
1706–10	22.2 (576)	24.4 (139)	23.5 (180)	27 (4,963)	24.1 (1,219)	21.3 (164)		
1711–15				26.1 (315)	24.7 (496)			
1716–20	13.7 (211)			20.5 (471)	17.3 (332)			
1721–25	24.5 (1,484)	23 (63)		25.6 (1,922)	25.9 (2,318)	27.3 (274)	24 (1,086)	
1726–30				37 (909)		25.3 (665)	26.9 (500)	
1731–35	22.7 (382)				23 (230)	27.1 (230)	23.5 (909)	
1736–40				33 (543)	34.4 (1,311)	27 (230)	26 (169)	

Period								
1741–45	35.1 (1,153)		42.3 (367)	33.1 (2,155)	22.7 (958)		25.4 (1,285)	
1746–50				36.7 (1,050)	36.5 (438)	21.9 (230)	20.5 (196)	
1751–55	35.2 (522)	33 (185)	33.9 (570)	35 (4,129)	33 (391)	26.1 (2,171)	34.7 (2,045)	
1756–60	33.2 (798)	32 (1,069)	38 (840)	39.6 (1,537)	35.8 (357)	30.1 (1,724)	28.8 (3,685)	
1761–65	44.3 (200)	44.4 (500)	42.5 (1,118)	39.3 (1,511)	33.8 (496)	35.6 (327)	31 (3,030)	
1766–70	37.8 (138)		37.8 (296)	45.9 (899)	36.7 (745)	37.6 (2,752)	44.5 (2,230)	
1771–75	50.8 (878)	45.3 (1,220)	48.2 (374)	47.5 (4,350)	49.5 (2,568)	42.7 (5,296)	49.4 (4,403)	
1776–80	45.3 (280)	41.8 (1,201)	43.5 (560)	40 (1,267)	45.4 (1,809)	38 (3,579)	53.8 (429)	
1781–85		54.1 (1,263)	45.4 (392)	55.4 (792)	55.6 (1,336)	43 (3,034)	66.2 (5,616)	58.1 (203)
1786–90		50 (1,586)	51.8 (2,459)	58.5 (2,742)	67.5 (1,979)	48 (7,515)	77.4 (5,114)	65.1 (1,244)
1791–95	57.9 (358)	59.7 (1,695)	66.3 (437)	65.7 (2,627)	58 (207)	54.7 (8,193)	63.7 (2,377)	
1796–1800						71.6 (3,843)	72.5 (697)	
1801–05				75.3 (230)		83 (1,707)	67.5 (1,658)	
1806–10				77.9 (1,482)	85.2 (238)	92.6 (1,052)	75.6 (508)	

Source: PSNA.

212

APPENDIX TABLE A2. *Average Nominal Prices in Pounds Sterling, Standardized on Jamaica, of Prime Male Slaves Newly Arrived in the Americas in Selected Major Slave Markets, Five-Year Intervals, 1671–1810 (Number of Slaves in Parentheses)*

	South Carolina	Guianas	St. Domingue/Jamaica	Dominca/Grenada/St. Vincent	Barbados/Antigua
1671–75			25.0 (1,249)		19.3 (1,643)
1676–80			19.9 (4,225)		17.1 (5,083)
1681–85			17.6 (3,480)		16.1 (3,941)
1686–90			19.8 (4,770)		17.8 (3,835)
1691–95			19.8 (2,383)		21.5 (3,106)
1696–1700			23 (1,163)		25.4 (5,321)
1701–5			24 (2,724)		26 (9,377)
1706–10			25.9 (1,727)		24.8 (5,639)
1711–15					26.1 (315)
1716–20			22.7 (239)		18.3 (232)
1721–25	21 (150)		24 (2,290)		27.6 (908)
1726–30			30.3 (1,554)		27.8 (924)
1731–35					23 (230)

Period					
1736–40					
1741–45	18.1 (230)				
1746–50		29.7 (1,653)	37.1 (230)		24.5 (1,198)
1751–55	35.1 (1,049)	23.3 (777)	32.6 (4,040)		35.1 (1,492)
1756–60	31 (1,923)	36.6 (1,618)	36.7 (4,014)		35.7 (730)
1761–65	43.1 (2,772)	28 (2,447)	40.3 (835)		26.6 (1,422)
1766–70	38.7 (750)	38.5 (1,279)	40.6 (1,154)	39.1 (2,144)	29 (681)
1771–75	53 (2,428)	48 (3,024)	49 (6,171)	41.9 (3,574)	30.8 (98)
1776–80		43 (2,525)	41 (5,536)	35.6 (1,279)	34.6 (750)
1781–85	58.5 (790)	44.1 (1,175)	47 (1,168)	42 (1,493)	43 (1,610)
1786–90		51.5 (145)	52.5 (6,917)	48.2 (5,565)	37.5 (442)
1791–95		54.4 (669)	59.7 (959)	53.2 (1,725)	43.2 (1,067)
1796–1800		65.5 (939)	73 (5,596)	66.5 (460)	48.3 (1,300)
1801–05		63.6 (230)	78.7 (2,423)	90.4 (230)	51.6 (745)
1806–10	67.1 (230)	84.6 (705)	82.9 (1,865)	90 (460)	64.3 (418)

Source: PSNA.

214

APPENDIX TABLE A3. *Regression-Based Anova of Prices of Prime Male Slaves Newly Arrived in the Americas, in Pounds Sterling, Standardized on Jamaica, by Regions of Departure from Africa, Selected Quinquennia, 1676–1795 (First Number in Cell is Beta Coefficient, with t-Statistic in Parentheses)*

	1676–1680	1701–1705	1751–1755	1771–1775	1786–1790	1791–1795
Upper Guinea	−3.107 (−1.748)	2.25 (0.6)	8.17 (2.8)	5.22 (2.3)	2.71 (1.0)	5.8 (1.6)
Gold Coast	.941 (1.07)	4.92 (1.8)	8.78 (3.3)	4.89 (2.5)	10.35 (2.9)	11.05 (2.8)
Bight of Benin	−.278 (−0.302)	3.54 (1.3)	6.84 (1.0)	6.85 (2.6)	19.36 (4.7)	3.31 (0.8)
West Central Africa	−.745 (−0.616)	−2.92 (0.4)	8.62 (2.6)	6.7 (3.1)	29.28 (9.9)	8.99 (2.3)
Southeast Africa					16.97 (3.4)	
Intercept	18.83 (32.65)	23.94 (9.91)	26.1 (11.9)	42.66 (33.4)	48.14 (24.7)	54.67 (28.1)
r^2	0.121	0.18	0.22	0.15	0.58	0.16

Note: Reference variable (intercept) for each equation is the Bight of Biafra
Source: Calculated from PSNA.

APPENDIX TABLE A4. *Regression-Based Anova of Prices of Prime Male Slaves Newly Arrived in the Americas, in Pound Sterling, Standardized on Jamaica, by Regions of Arrival in the Americas, Selected Quinquennia, 1671–1795 (First Number in Cell is Beta Coefficient, with t-Statistic in Parentheses)*

	1671–1675	1676–1680	1681–1685	1686–1690	1691–1695	1696–1700	1701–1705	1706–1710	1741–1745
South Carolina									−16.97 (−4.2)
Guianas									−2.56 (−2.6)
St. Domingue									3.36 (1.5)
Dominica, St. Vincent, Grenada									
Barbados and Antigua	−4.53 (−3.1)	−1.8 (−2.7)	−0.56 (−0.95)	−1.10 (−1.16)	1.75 (1.4)	2.34 (1.5)	1.67 (0.9)	−1.1 (−0.5)	
Intercept	25.0 (20.1)	19.83 (41.2)	17.57 (41.7)	19.81 (29.7)	19.79 (19.9)	23.08 (16.8)	24.35 (14.6)	25.94 (12.2)	35.1 (22.8)
r^2	0.44	0.14	0.02	0.04	0.08	0.08	0.02	0.01	0.69

	1751–1755	1756–1760	1766–1770	1771–1775	1776–1780	1781–1785	1786–1790	1791–1795
South Carolina	2.47 (1.0)	−5.74 (−2.8)	−1.88 (−0.4)	3.93 (2.1)		11.39 (1.6)		
Guianas	3.98 (1.46)	−8.74 (−4.2)	7.41 (2.34)	−6.06 (−3.2)	3.13 (1.2)	4.38 (0.4)	1.85 (0.4)	5.76 (1.0)
St. Domingue	2.77 (0.6)	8.9 (1.8)	11.36 (2.4)	4.4 (2.3)	9.23 (3.4)	18.4 (3.7)	21.35 (11.4)	3.38 (0.9)
Dominica, St. Vincent, Grenada			−1.45 (−0.4)	−7.14 (−4.4)	−5.36 (−2.1)	−5.1 (−0.8)	−4.34 (−2.0)	−6.44 (−1.7)
Barbados and Antigua	6.01 (−2.2)	−7.7 (−2.5)	−5.94 (−1.5)	−6.67 (−3.1)	−3.46 (−0.9)	−3.9 (−0.5)	−4.26 (−1.4)	−8.1 (−1.2)
Intercept	32.63 (23.0)	36.73 (30.9)	40.58 (15.0)	49.0 (45.9)	40.98 (36.5)	47.09 (10.1)	52.55 (36.0)	59.69 (36.5)
r^2	0.22	0.22	0.43	0.44	0.41	0.55	0.70	0.10

Source: Calculated from PSNA.

APPENDIX TABLE A5. *Regression-Based Anova of Voyage Times in Days of Vessels Arriving in Jamaica and St. Domingue from Regions of Departure in Africa, Selected Quinquennia, 1676–1795 (First Number in Cell is Beta Coefficient, with t-Statistic in Parentheses)*

	1676–1705	1751–1755	1771–1775	1786–1790	1791–1795
Upper Guinea	−80.0 (−3.1)	11.75 (0.6)	−27.98 (−1.0)	10.37 (0.6)	47.62 (3.0)
Gold Coast	−25.26 (−1.6)	55.3 (3.2)	−36.29 (−1.1)	54.45 (2.8)	61.15 (3.5)
Bight of Benin	29.41 (−1.5)	63.92 (3.5)	7.04 (0.3)	98.82 (5.6)	71.31 (3.0)
West Central Africa	40.42 (1.98)	−2.92 (3.2)	19.25 (0.8)	121.74 (8.2)	22.53 (1.7)
Southeast Africa			116.06 (1.2)	238.36 (10.3)	191.60 (5.6)
Intercept	305.86 (18.2)	302.63 (22.6)	339.9 (15.3)	249.15 (21.0)	252.74 (28.3)
r^2	0.26	0.08	0.05	0.23	0.12

Reference variable (intercept) for each equation is the Bight of Biafra

Source: TSTD.

7

American Slave Markets During the 1850s: Slave Price Rises in the United States, Cuba, and Brazil in Comparative Perspective

Laird W. Bergad

I

For well over fifty years, historians studying slavery in the Western Hemisphere have been drawn to comparative aspects of slave systems in the Americas. The publication of Frank Tannenbaum's *Slave and Citizen* in 1947 established the broad parameters of consideration by dividing slavery into two fundamentally different systems.[1] Slavery in the United States and in another entity referred to uniformly as Latin America was deemed to be not one but two distinct institutions despite the obvious legalistic similarities in the consideration of slaves as property.[2] Furthermore, race relations and the dynamics of racism after slavery was abolished were also framed in a dichotomous fashion. Tannenbaum's arguments and conceptualizations of U.S. and Latin American variants in New World slave systems were reinforced by Stanley Elkins over a decade later, and together the "Tannenbaum–Elkins thesis" served as an important reference point in the development of slave studies, particularly in the United States.[3] The parameters of their arguments, and the many scholarly responses which followed, are well known and hardly need repeating.

Despite the repudiation of many of Tannenbaum's and Elkins' ideas in the historiography of slavery and race relations in the Americas over the past half century, especially the notion of a more benign institution in Latin America, it is generally accepted that indeed there were great differences in

---

[1] Frank Tannenbaum, *Slave and Citizen, the Negro in the Americas* (New York, 1947).
[2] Tannenbaum made little attempt to differentiate slavery in Latin America and the Caribbean by region, specific colony or nation, time period, or any other variable such as gender, national origins, occupation, and so forth, which have been the focus of sustained research from the 1950s on.
[3] Stanley M. Elkins, *Slavery, a Problem in American Institutional and Intellectual Life* (Chicago, 1959).

the way slavery developed in the United States and in Latin America and the Caribbean. Whether considering demographic patterns, the evolution of slave culture and family structures, emancipation profiles, or the long-term impact of slavery on economic development, most historians have concluded that there were significant distinctions through time between slavery in the United States and in Latin America and the Caribbean.

Historians today still pay much attention to the structural similarities found especially with respect to economic aspects of slave labor. This essay will focus on the striking parallels exhibited in the dynamics of slave-based economic expansion in the southern United States, Cuba, and Brazil during the decade of the 1850s with particular attention to the rise in slave prices found in all three regions.

II

Our collective knowledge of economic growth patterns in the United States is extraordinary in relation to what we know about economic organization in both Cuba and Brazil. This is in part due to the nature and volume of historical documentation found in the libraries and archival collections within the three countries. Statistical data on U.S. economic and demographic history are abundant and have been plumbed effectively by those working on slave economics. One only needs to note the detailed decennial population and agricultural censuses dating from 1790 and available on-line in the United States and compare this documentary situation with Cuba and Brazil.

In Brazil no national census was undertaken until 1872 and the data collected were exclusively on demographic variables. There was no census on property in Brazil prior to the twentieth century, with the exception of an effort in the late 1850s to gather data on land ownership that has never been brought together or analyzed. No historical information on income or any other economic variables other than export data exists at the national level prior to the twentieth century. Thus, even the most basic data on land tenure structures are largely unknown, and to attempt to reconstruct wealth distribution patterns during the epoch of slavery is all but impossible. Additionally, there are no reliable price indexes for Brazil for the eighteenth or nineteenth centuries that may be used to convert nominal prices into real prices adjusted for inflation. To make matters more difficult, Brazilian archival collections have not yet yielded any detailed account ledgers for estates or firms, with the exception of English mining companies, that could be analyzed to determine the economic dynamics of rural or urban economic endeavors prior to abolition. And finally, few systematic notarial records exist in time series, and local-level economic censuses, so often found in the documentation in Spanish America, are rarely located. It should be evident that the documentary situation cannot generate materials available for reconstructing

U.S. economic history. There are, however, many tools for research and the situation is not as grim as the foregoing would suggest if we set aside comparisons. There are abundant manuscript population censuses at the local level, and these have been painstakingly digitized and analyzed in various regions and time periods by a number of historians. In addition, probate records have been preserved in nearly every municipal district throughout the country, although often these are unorganized and sometimes are nearly impossible to work with.

Cuban sources for the economic history of slavery are better in many ways than the Brazilian collections. First there were occasional, though not regular, island-wide censuses undertaken: in 1792, 1817, 1827, 1841, 1846, and in 1862. These contain varying types of data, although they focus on population. These censuses, all published volumes, also contain significant general economic information, but there are no farm-by-farm or income data that would permit the distribution of landed wealth or changing income profiles to be measured, and in general they are simply not comparable to the U.S. census materials in the quality of data. Second, local-level Cuban archival sources have proven to be rich in materials on slave economy and demography. Especially useful have been municipal property censuses that recorded data from which ownership patterns over land and slaves may be calculated and on occasion, about production. However, there is no consistency in these sources in that materials found for one region are rarely replicated in others. There is not even much uniformity over time for any region and most documentation is concentrated in the period after 1860. This makes time-series observations difficult at best. Yet, the existence of well-preserved notarial records in nearly every district throughout the island dating from the sixteenth century has proved invaluable in reconstructing slave-market conditions as well as in gleaning characteristics of the slave-owning class. As in Brazil, few account books for plantations or business enterprises of any sort are found that could be used to better understand slave economics.

Although the Cuban data on the economic aspects of slavery are richer than the Brazilian materials, it should be stressed that it is impossible to produce the kinds of detailed calculations on slave economies that have been so central to the historiography of slavery in the United States. Proxies and circumstantial evidence must thus be used to deductively arrive at conclusions on the economics of slave labor. This is where the comparative price history of slave markets may prove useful in evaluating the economic dynamics of slavery in the three nations. I have chosen to focus on the 1850s because of the significant rises in slave prices found in all three of the major remaining slave markets of the Americas and to ask what these price increases may imply about slave economies for Brazilian and Cuban slave history. The U.S. patterns are well known and do not need elaborating here.

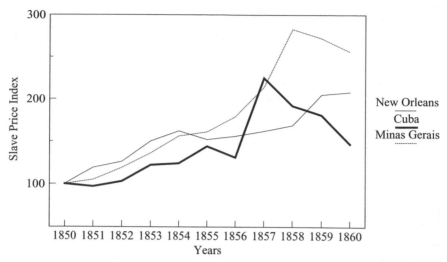

FIGURE 1. Indexed Slave Price Movements in New Orleans, Cuba, and Minas, in nominal prices (1850 = 100)

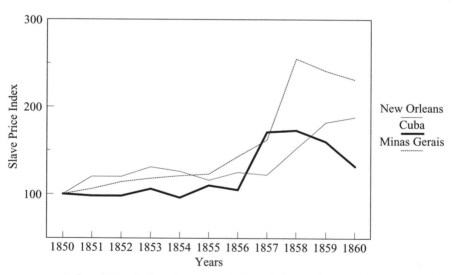

FIGURE 2. Indexed Slave Price Movements in New Orleans, Cuba, and Minas, in real prices using U.S. deflators (1850 = 100)

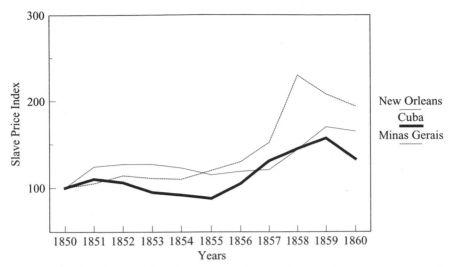

FIGURE 3. Indexed Slave Price Movements in New Orleans, Cuba, and Minas in real prices using British deflators (1850 = 100)

III

Figures 1 through 4 depict the trends in prices during the 1850s for healthy male slaves between 21 and 38 years of age from the New Orleans sample of slaves derived by Kotlikoff, the Cuban slave price series derived by Bergad et al., and the Minas Gerais slave price series from Bergad.[4] Figure 1 indicates trends in nominal prices; Figure 2 in prices deflated using U.S. price indices; Figure 3 in prices deflated using British price indices; and finally Figure 4 indicates trend lines in all three slave markets. All graphs are derived from data that are indexed with 1850 equal to 100.[5]

Although the curves for each nation differ in the timing of their peaks, whether examined in nominal or deflated prices using U.S. or British price indexes, the upward trend lines during the course of the decade are quite clear. The fundamental questions to be raised revolve around the comparative aspects of the impressive economic expansion taking place in each country

---

[4] Laurence J. Kotlikoff, "Quantitative Description of the New Orleans Slave Market, 1804 to 1862," in Robert William Fogel and Stanley L. Engerman (eds.), *Without Consent or Contract: Markets and Production, Technical Papers, Vol. 1* (New York, 1992), pp. 31–53; Laird W. Bergad et al., *The Cuban Slave Market, 1790–1880* (New York, 1995); and Laird W. Bergad, *Slavery and the Demographic and Economic History of Minas Gerais, Brazil 1720–1888* (New York, 1999).

[5] Indexes were derived by converting nominal prices to indexes with 1850 = 100. Then U.S. and British price indexes were also converted to 1850 = 100 separately. "Real" price indexes were then created by dividing the nominal price indexes by the U.S. and British price indexes.

Slave Price Index

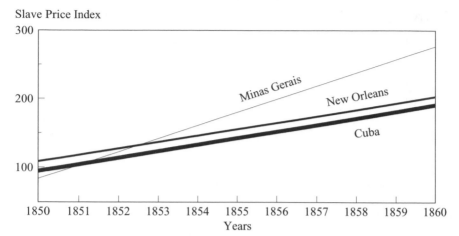

FIGURE 4. Trend Lines for Indexed Slave Price Movements in New Orleans, Cuba, and Minas, in current prices (1850 = 100)

and the relation of slave markets to these processes of economic growth. The relative efficiency of the southern U.S. slave-based agriculture during the cotton boom of the 1850s, especially during the rapid growth in production after 1857, led to the rising profitability of slave labor on the eve of the U.S. Civil War, the higher prices of the southern U.S. slave market notwithstanding.[6] The Cuban and Brazilian cases have not been thoroughly studied, but it is striking that there were five marked similarities in the processes of economic growth that should be emphasized when compared with the southern United States.

1) First, in all three nations the agricultural expansion of principal crops – cotton in the United States, sugar in Cuba, and coffee in southern Brazil – were based on the spatial movement of production into high-yielding soils in previously under-populated frontier regions during the 1850s. The westward movement of cotton and slaves in the United States is depicted in Map 1. In the case of Cuba, sugar moved rapidly into the extraordinarily fertile central plains of the island to the east of the province of Havana in the 1840s and 1850s, an expansion which was facilitated by the construction of the most sophisticated railway system developed in Latin America prior to the 1860s. This expansion is depicted in Map 2. Brazilian coffee production expanded westward and northwest, first moving from the older areas of production in the Paraíba Valley in Rio de Janeiro province west along the same valley system but in the province of São Paulo. Then coffee moved

---

[6] For a concise summary of these processes in the United States see Robert William Fogel, *Without Consent or Contract: The Rise and Fall of American Slavery* (New York, 1989), chs. 3 and 4, pp. 60–113.

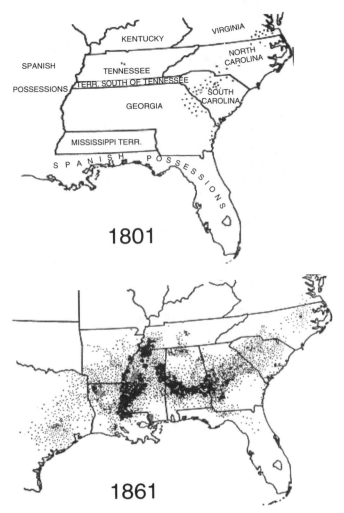

MAP 1. The Spread of Cotton Production Westward in the United States 1801–1860.
Source: Robert William Fogel, *Without Consent or Contract: The Rise and Fall of American Slavery* (New York, 1989), p. 66.
 Note: Each dot represents 1,000 bales.

northwest toward the forested interior frontier of the western São Paulo.[7]
This process is depicted in Map 3.

[7] For these processes in Cuba and Brazil see Laird W. Bergad, *Cuban Rural Society during the Nineteenth Century: The Social and Economic History of Monoculture in Matanzas* (Princeton, 1990); Stanley Stein, *Vassouras: A Brazilian Coffee County, 1850–1890* (Cambridge, MA, 1957); Warren Dean, *Rio Claro: A Brazilian Plantation System, 1820–1920* (Stanford, 1976); and Emília Viotti da Costa, *Da Senzala à Colônia* (São Paulo, 3a ed., 1989) pp. 57–98. For a discussion of the debates of slave profitability in Brazil see Viotti da Costa, *Da Senzala à Colônia* ns. 12–13, pp. 49–50.

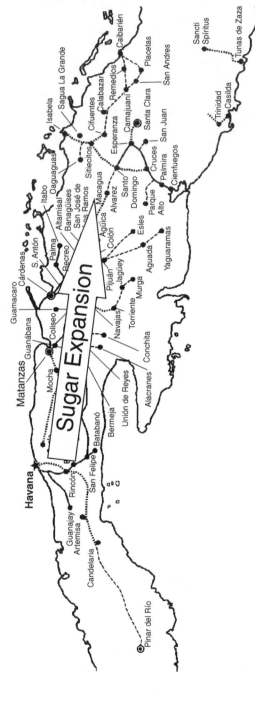

MAP 2. Cuban Sugar and Railroad Expansion Eastward, 1837–98. *Source:* Oscar Zanetti and Alejandro García, *Sugar and Railroads, A Cuban History, 1837–1959* (Chapel Hill, 1998), p. 46.

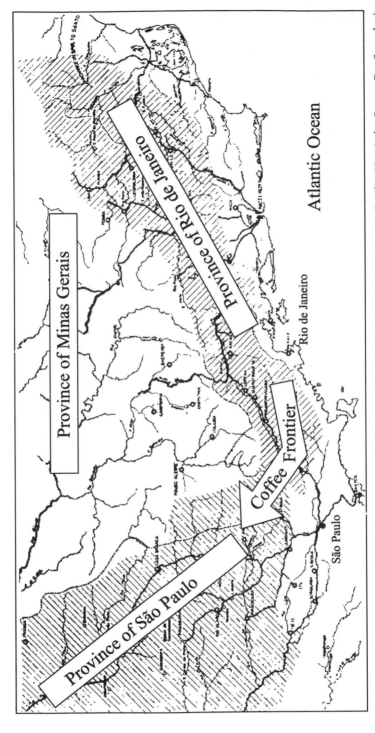

MAP 3. The Spread of Coffee Cultivation Westward in Southern Brazil, 1800–1884. *Source:* Emília Viotti da Costa, *Da Senzala à Colônia* (São Paulo, 1989, 3a edição), p. 58.

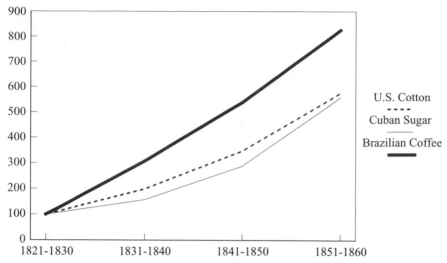

FIGURE 5. U.S. Cotton Production, Cuban Sugar Production, and Brazilian Coffee Exports in Volume, 1821–1860 (Indexed, 1821–30 = 100). *Sources:* B.R. Mitchell, *International Historical Statistics, The Americas 1750–1988* (New York, 1993), pp. 205, 281, 294–5; Manuel Moreno Fraginals, *El Ingenio* (Havana, 1978), vol. III, pp. 35–6.

2) Second, absolute increases in production in the principal crop linked to slave labor in each of the three nations – cotton, sugar, and coffee – demonstrate similar trends and are depicted by decade from the 1820s through the 1850s in Figure 5.

The annual rates of production growth, and in the case of Brazil the export trade, are comparable, although Cuban sugar increases lagged behind somewhat. These are shown in two ways in Table 1: yearly rates of growth between 1821 and 1860; and between 1850 and 1860.

3) Third, productive expansion was paralleled by, and related to, important technological transformations in the U.S. and Cuban cases, although these were less critical in the growth of the Brazilian coffee economy during the 1850s. Railroad construction and the intense utilization of steamboats along the major southern river systems lowered transportation costs dramatically in the U.S. South, while the arrival of telegraph lines which communicated a wide variety of market conditions to merchants and planters was a factor in making resource allocation decisions more efficient.[8] The resulting rising productivity of southern agriculture was more than sufficient to offset the secular decline in raw cotton prices that dated from the early nineteenth century, although cotton supply lagged behind demand during the

[8] Fogel, *Without Consent or Contract*, 67–8.

TABLE 1. *Yearly Rates of Growth in U.S. Cotton Production, Cuban Sugar Production, and Brazilian Coffee Exports, 1821–1860*

	U.S. Cotton	Cuban Sugar	Brazilian Coffee
1821–1860	3.6%	3.4%	5.6%
1850–1860	6.0%	3.8%	5.2%

Source: Same as Figure 5.

1850s and prices rose after 1855. Increasing productivity and profitability, then, increased the value and prices for slaves.[9]

The parallels in technological innovation between the U.S. southern cotton economy and the Cuban sugar economy should be stressed. The fertile black-dirt central plains of Cuba encompassing the provinces of Matanzas and Santa Clara (east of Havana) were opened by the railroad during the 1840s and 1850s. Like cotton in the southern United States, sugar thrived on high-yielding virgin soils, and indeed the Cuban sugar economy constantly shifted its matrix toward frontier regions. The railroad heralded two major transformations. First was the utilization of internal railroad systems within estates that resulted in the more efficient movement of cane from field to mill for processing. This alone resulted in an enormous rise is productivity because often, depending on weather conditions, cut cane was not ground because of the internal transportation difficulties related to the utilization of inefficient oxen-drawn carts. If it rained heavily during the harvest season, a huge amount of cane was simply lost, remaining in the fields to rot. Additionally, the faster cane was transported from fields to be milled, the higher the yield of sugar extracted. Thus, internal railroad systems alone led to generalized increases in productivity in the sugar sector irrespective of the labor system.

Second, the ports of Matanzas, Cárdenas, Cienfuegos, and Havana were connected to the cane-growing/sugar-producing regions and this dramatically reduced transportation costs and increased communication efficiency. Along all of the railroad lines which penetrated the sugar frontier telegraph lines were strung, and this had the same kind of impact on Cuban planters in terms of communication with market conditions and general economic information, as was found in the southern United States.[10]

Cuban sugar production also benefited from the application of new technologies in the processing of cane into sugar. The first was the complete mechanization of Cuban sugar mills in frontier regions during the 1850s through utilization of the steam engine for milling.[11] New mills installed vacuum

[9] Fogel, *Without Consent or Contract*, 95 indicates that the 1850s was a decade of enormous profits for cotton planters.

[10] Oscár Zanetti and Alejandro García, *Caminos para el azúcar* (Havana, 1987).

[11] In 1846 only 18.1% of the mills in Matanzas province and 9.5% in Havana were mechanized. By 1862 92.3% were mechanized in Matanzas and the corresponding number was 86.3% in

pan evaporators, rather than the older Jamaican trains, and centrifuges for the final extraction of sugar. Cane-grinding capacity was increased not only because of the utilization of internal railroad lines but also because of mill mechanization and indeed the two processes were complimentary. Higher cane/sugar yields resulted because of steam power and these other technological innovations in the manufacture of sugar. If southern U.S. agriculture was more efficient and profitable during the 1850s because of rapid technological innovation, the same may be concluded about the Cuban sugar economy.

The Brazilian case is somewhat different in terms of technological innovation, especially with respect to transportation in the coffee regions. The first Brazilian railroad lines were not initiated until the 1850s and indeed the São Paulo coffee frontier was not penetrated by railways until the 1870s. Traditional mule trains continued to move coffee from the interior to the ports of Santos or Rio de Janeiro. Thus, the kinds of cost-saving innovations in transportation and communications found in the southern United States and in Cuba were not a major part of the southern Brazilian coffee economy. There were, however, significant transformations in the processing of coffee that had the effect of freeing labor for agricultural tasks, increasing efficiency, and decreasing costs of production. These came in the form of drying machines which were widely applied during the 1850s on *fazendas* in Rio de Janeiro and São Paulo.[12] Additionally pulping and hulling machines, which separated the bean from the pulp and, when dry, from the thin flaky white hull – the final stage before roasting – were also widely applied during the 1850s and after.[13] These were significant cost-saving measures that resulted in the more efficient use of labor.

4) A fourth similarity was found in the upward trend in prices for coffee, sugar, and cotton during the second half of the 1850s which followed a long period of downward pressures on prices for these commodities. Although the general trend in cotton prices over the course of the decade was still downward, the bounce in prices after 1856 probably stimulated, in part, the impressive expansion of production in the U.S. South after 1857. Coffee and sugar prices moved significantly upward in the second half of the decade,

---

Havana. See Levi Marrero, *Cuba: Economía y Sociedad, Azúcar, Ilustración, y Conciencia (1763–1868) (II)* (Madrid, 1984), p. 189.

[12] The coffee bean must be separated from the pulp and then dried before it may be hulled and readied for market. Before mechanization, pulping was a labor-intensive task using mortars and pestles. Drying was accomplished by spreading the coffee beans by hand on drying patios and constantly moving them around. If it rained, the beans had to be quickly covered, or moved. Both were labor-intensive tasks. The application of pulping and drying machines meant that a significant portion of laborers could be utilized in other tasks, thus raising productivity. See Viotti da Costa, *Da Senzala à Colônia*, 204–5.

[13] See Dean, *Rio Claro*, 38 for a discussion of the utilization of pulping and hulling machines during the 1850s in Rio Claro, São Paulo.

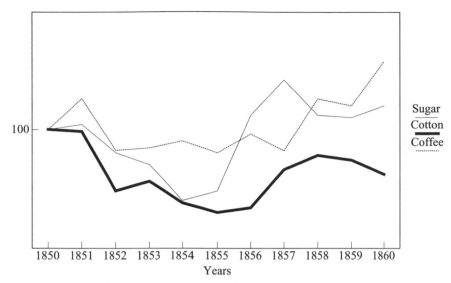

FIGURE 6. Indexed Sugar, Cotton, and Coffee Prices in the United States 1850–1860 in "real" prices using U.S. "deflators" (1850 = 100). *Source:* U.S. Department of Commerce, Bureau of the Census, *Historical Statistics of the United States, Colonial Times to 1970* (Washington, 1975), Part 1, p. 209; Part 2, p. 902.

and although the timing of the curves was different, there is no question that labor cost increases in the form of higher real slave prices were made more tolerable because of increased income linked to higher product prices. These price movements are depicted in Figure 6.[14]

5) A fifth similarity was with respect to the efficient reallocation of slave labor toward the dynamic activities of cotton, sugar, and coffee production as market demand, profitability, and prices increased. The reallocation of slave labor westward in the U.S. South is well known and has been considered to be a major indicator of the flexibility, efficiency, and profitability of the southern U.S. slave-based economy.[15] The same processes of slave labor reallocation were found in Cuba and in the coffee-producing zones of southern Brazil.

The Cuban case is quite graphic. During the 1850s, as sugar cultivation was transformed technologically and spatially, there was a significant reallocation of slave labor toward sugar estates in regions where the most technologically advanced mills were located. The Cuban census of 1846 indicated that approximately 33% of all slaves resided on *ingenios*, an increase from about 25% in 1827. But by the next population count in 1862, nearly

[14] The data on which the lines were based in Figure 6 were derived from the source indicated and reduced to "real" prices by using the U.S. price indexes with 1850 = 100. Coffee prices are indicated as the prices per pound paid for imports to the United States.

[15] See Fogel, *Without Consent or Contract*, 90–1.

50% of all Cuban slaves lived and worked on sugar plantations and nearly two-thirds of all male Cuban slaves were found in the sugar sector.[16] This is only part of the labor reallocation process in Cuba, for these labor transfers also must be seen in the context of an escalating African slave trade during the decade and the large scale importation of Chinese contract laborers who were mainly destined for the sugar zones. Between 1850 and 1860 some 124,000 African slaves were imported to Cuba as were over 58,000 Chinese laborers.[17] It may be assumed that a significant portion of imported slaves and nearly all of the Chinese were destined for the sugar sector, given the 1862 census data previously indicated. If the United States reallocated re-sources in part because of the internal inter-regional slave trade, Cuba did so through the shifting of extant slaves and channeling newly imported slaves and Chinese workers to sugar plantation zones.

The gradual reallocation of resources toward southern coffee zones during the 1850s was also a fundamental aspect of mid nineteenth century Brazilian economic history, although it should be kept in mind that cotton and sugar exports in other geographical regions were still important components of the Brazilian export trade.[18] With the closing of the Brazilian slave trade during the early 1850s, slave-based coffee plantations depended on extant populations or the transfer of slaves from other economic sectors or regions in Brazil if they were to expand their work forces.[19] It ought to be stressed that data for the inter-regional and intra-regional Brazilian slave trade are scarce due to the absence of regional, provincial, or national population counts until the census of 1872.[20] Yet Robert Slenes, in the most detailed study of internal Brazilian slave movements during the 1850s, has concluded

[16] See the discussion in Bergad et al., *The Cuban Slave Market*, 29–32. Many slaves also worked on cattle ranches and food-producing farms in the sugar zones, which supported the *ingenios*.

[17] For data on Cuban slave imports see David Eltis, *Economic Growth and the Ending of the Transatlantic Slave Trade* (New York, 1987), p. 245. Data on the Chinese are found in Bergad, *Cuban Rural Society in the Nineteenth Century*, p. 250 and were derived from documentation in the Public Records Office (London), ZHC1/3831, p. 6, "Report of the British Consulate General, Havana, September 1, 1873." I thank David Eltis for pointing out to me that although slave imports rose during the 1850s to Cuba, yearly average imports (including Chinese) were lower than in any earlier five-year periods during the nineteenth century. At the same time the growth of sugar output during the 1850s was greater than at any period before mid century. These points buttress arguments concerning the increased efficiency of slave labor in the Cuban sugar sector.

[18] Between 1851 and 1860, coffee accounted for about two-thirds of Brazilian exports by value; sugar for one-quarter; and cotton for about 8%.

[19] As in the southern United States, a large number of slaves were transferred to dynamic regions of growth because they were brought by their owners, rather than being imported through purchase.

[20] Klein has discounted the importance of the inter-regional slave trade during the early 1850s. See Herbert S. Klein, "The Internal Slave Trade in Nineteenth-Century Brazil: A Study of Slave Importations into Rio de Janeiro in 1852," *Hispanic American Historical Review*, 51 (1971): 567–85.

that indeed there were clear indications of slave imports to the Paulista coffee frontier during the 1850s although these were not nearly as voluminous as during the 1870s when more accurate data are available.[21] Slenes has carefully examined slave prices and their relation to coffee exports from São Paulo during the decade and has found that rising real prices for slaves did not act as inhibiting factors to either output increases or slave purchases. This, of course, is a clear indicator of the coffee economy's ability to grow profitably regardless of increased slave prices.

IV

To conclude, the essay highlights the striking similarities in the development of slave-based export agricultural activities in the three countries under consideration. The abundance of economic data for the United States that has led historians to nearly uncontestable conclusions on the rising profitability and efficiency of slave labor in the southern cotton-producing zones prior to the Civil War are simply not mirrored in Cuban or Brazilian documentary collections, at least for the 1850s. However, that similar slave price curves were found in all three nations suggests that the Cuban and Brazilian slave systems were as rational and profitable as the southern U.S. economy. The strong positive correlation between increased real slave prices in all three nations during the 1850s and the rising output of major slave-based export crops is one indicator that the economics of slavery were extraordinarily similar. There is suggestive empirical evidence as well.

In my study of the sugar industry in Cuba during the mid nineteenth century, I found a pattern of increasing productivity per slave laborer during the 1860s and 1870s.[22] Not only did the income generated per slave rise substantially, but it was greatest on the largest capital-intensive estates which had adapted the most sophisticated transportation and sugar-processing technologies and toward which the slave population was increasingly concentrated.[23] Additionally, even with escalating slave prices, the payback time to

---

[21] Slenes has established a close statistical correlation between São Paulo coffee exports, for which data are available, and its slave population which expanded gradually during the decade. See Robert Slenes, "The Demography and Economics of Brazilian Slavery: 1850–1888," Ph.D. thesis, Stanford University, 1976, ch. III, "The Volume and Organization of the Interregional Slave Trade: 1850–1888," pp. 120–178.

[22] See Bergad, *Cuban Rural Society in the Nineteenth Century*, pp. 217–28; and Laird W. Bergad, "The Economic Viability of Sugar Production Based on Slave Labor in Cuba: 1859–1878," *Latin American Research Review*, 24 (1989): 95–113.

[23] Income per worker on the largest estates grew from 363 Spanish pesos per worker in 1859 to 416 Spanish pesos per worker in 1876 in the jurisdiction of Colón, one of Cuba's largest sugar-producing districts. In contiguous Cárdenas, over the same period income per worker grew from 430 to 590 Spanish pesos per worker. See Bergad, *Cuban Rural Society in the Nineteenth Century*, 227.

recover the cost of the most expensive male slaves in their early twenties fell constantly. Finally, when comparing the cost of free labor to slave labor by considering hire rates in relation to slave prices I found that after about 2.5 years slaves purchased even at peak prices would begin to be more economically advantageous than free salaried labor. Although the economic data for the 1850s are less voluminous, it is probable that the economic dynamics of slave-based sugar production found in the 1860s and 1870s may be projected backwards to the 1850s which was a period of rapid technological innovation in the Cuban sugar industry. Cuban slave-based sugar production was probably as efficient and rational as the U.S. cotton economy during the 1850s, even with the upturn in slave prices.

Further, the economics of Brazilian slavery during the 1850s has not been closely examined by scholars for want of documentary materials. Studies on the 1870s and after, however, when abundant documentation has been located, have reached the same conclusions concerning the continued high profitability and efficiency of slave labor right up to abolition.[24] Coffee cultivation expanded regardless of price rises in real terms for slaves who constituted nearly all of the laborers in the coffee economy until the late 1880s when large-scale migration and abolition shifted the labor foundations of coffee plantations.

In my study of slavery in Minas Gerais I found that gross rates of return on newly purchased prime-age slaves during the late 1850s, when slave prices peaked during the decade, were as high as 20% yearly.[25] This was comparable to the rates of return found by Carvalho de Mello during the 1870s in Brazil and with those found in the U.S. South.

It is evident then that the slave price rises found in the three major American slave markets during the 1850s reflected the increased productivity and profitability of the economic endeavors in which slave labor was concentrated. Although this conclusion was initially contentious in U.S. slave studies, it has been generally accepted. In the Brazilian and Cuban cases, economic studies of slavery during the decade have been few and far between and often older generalizations still hold sway. These include the notion that the

---

[24] See the works of Pedro Carvalho de Mello, "Expectation of Abolition and Sanguinity of Coffee Planters in Brazil, 1871–1881," in Robert William Fogel and Stanley L. Engerman (eds.), *Without Consent or Contract: Conditions of Slave Life and the Transition to Freedom, Technical Papers*, vol. 2 (New York, 1992), pp. 629–46; and "Rates of Return on Slave Capital in Brazilian Coffee Plantations, 1871–1881" in Fogel and Engerman, *Without Consent or Contract*, vol. 1, pp. 63–79. Also see his "The Economics of Labor in Brazilian Coffee Plantations, 1850–1888," Ph.D. thesis, University of Chicago, 1977. Slenes has reached similar conclusions. See Slenes, "The Demography and Economics of Brazilian Slavery: 1850–1888," ch. v, "The Rational Planter and the Threat of Abolition: Changes in the Sanguinity of Slaveholders Over Time," pp. 234–69.

[25] See Bergad, *Slavery and the Demographic and Economic History of Minas Gerais, Brazil, 1720–1888*, 204.

slave price rises of the 1850s were linked to rampant inflation, or in the Brazilian case, as a reaction to the closing of the slave trade because of British intervention early in the decade.

With respect to the economic aspects of slave labor, the striking similarities in American slave systems must be stressed. The notion of U.S. and Latin American variants of slavery, first popularized by Tannenbaum, may hold true for a wide variety of other variables including the evolution of slave culture, family structures, reproductive patterns, access to freedom through self-purchase or manumission, and so forth. However, when the economics of slave labor is examined using comparative perspectives, the connections between technological innovation, increased production, and the economic viability of slavery, even during the price increases of the 1850s, were prevalent in all three nations and indicate marked economic parallels between the U.S., Brazilian, and Cuban slave systems.

8

The Relative Efficiency of Free and Slave Agriculture in the Antebellum United States: A Stochastic Production Frontier Approach

Elizabeth B. Field-Hendrey and Lee A. Craig

The relative efficiency of slave agriculture in the American South has stimulated comment and speculation since the mid-nineteenth century.[1] In their path-breaking work on the economics of slavery, Robert Fogel and Stanley Engerman offered the seminal empirical investigation of the relative efficiency of slave agriculture. More recently economists have applied increasingly sophisticated statistical techniques to the investigation.[2]

The authors thank Michael Edelstein, Frank Lewis, Ray Palmquist, V. Kerry Smith, David Weiman, and two anonymous readers for helpful comments on an earlier draft.

[1] See Jonathan Elliot Carnes, *The Slave Power: Its Character, Career, and Probable Designs* (New York, 1862); Lewis Cecil Gray, *History of Agriculture in the Southern United States to 1860* (New York, 1941); and Frederick Law Olmsted, *The Cotton Kingdom: A Traveller's Observations on Cotton and Slavery in the American Slave States* (New York, 1861).

[2] The evolution of the debate and techniques employed can be followed chronologically in Robert Fogel and Stanley Engerman, *Time on the Cross: The Economics of American Negro Slavery* (Boston, 1974); Paul David and Peter Temin, "Slavery: The Progressive Institution?" *Journal of Economic History*, 34 (1974): 739–783; Robert Fogel and Stanley Engerman, "Explaining the Relative Efficiency of Slave Agriculture in the Antebellum South," *American Economic Review* 67 (1977): 275–96; Paul David and Peter Temin, "Explaining the Relative Efficiency of Slave Agriculture in the Antebellum South: A Comment," ibid., 69 (1979): 213–218; Gavin Wright, "The Efficiency of Slavery: Another Interpretation," ibid.: 219–26; Robert Fogel and Stanley Engerman, "Explaining the Relative Efficiency of Slave Agriculture in the Antebellum South: Reply," ibid., 70 (1980): 672–90; Elizabeth Field, "The Relative Efficiency of Slavery Revisited: A Translog Production Function Approach," ibid., 78 (1988): 543–549; Richard Grabowski and Carl Pasurka, "The Relative Efficiency of Slave Agriculture: An Application of a Stochastic Production Frontier," *Applied Economics*, 21 (1989): 587–595; Richard Grabowski and Carl Pasurka, "The Relative Technical Efficiency of Slave and Non-Slave Farms in Southern Agriculture," *Eastern Economic Journal* 15 (1989): 245–258; Richard Hofler and Sherman Folland, "The Relative Efficiency of Slave Agriculture: A Comment," *Applied Economics*, 23 (1991): 861–868; Richard Grabowski and Carl Pasurka, "The Relative Efficiency of Slave Agriculture: A Reply," ibid., 23 (1991): 869–870; and Elizabeth Field-Hendrey, "Application of a Stochastic Production Frontier to Slave Agriculture: An Extension," ibid., 27 (1995): 363–368.

Despite these contributions, many questions remain unanswered. Among the most important of these is the role that crop mix played in the organization of antebellum agriculture. Large slave plantations grew relatively more cotton than any other Southern farm type, and, obviously, the vast majority of Northern farms grew no cotton at all. In addition, it remains to be determined whether Northern and Southern farms were on different production possibility frontiers (with the higher frontier representing technical superiority), which is a separate question from how close in practice those farms were to their respective frontiers (technical inefficiency).[3] To carry out a comprehensive investigation, such as that suggested by these questions, one must compare the efficiency of North v. South, Old South v. New South, and free v. slave farms, employing econometric techniques designed for such a task. For these comparisons to be meaningful, the analysis must control for variations in crop mix, with cotton production being the key factor.

Unlike previous contributions, this paper controls for the effect of cotton's share of output, treating that variable as endogenous. In addition, we employ a stochastic production frontier to compare the technical superiority and the technical inefficiency of all of the previously mentioned farm types and regions. This approach differs from many of the earlier studies, which largely confined themselves to Southern farms. We also utilize a standardized measure of farm output. Earlier studies of Northern and Southern agriculture used various measures of output, which often made interpreting the results difficult. In the next section we discuss in detail the issues involved in the debate over the relative efficiency of Southern agriculture. Section II contains a description of the methodology and data. Section III describes the empirical tests and results, and the final section examines implications for the historiography and economic interpretation of American slavery.

I

The nineteenth century British economist John Elliot Cairnes commented on American slavery on the eve of its demise. His basic argument was that the production of Southern staples "requires for its efficient conduct that labour should be combined and organized on an extensive scale." That is to say, the production of cotton, tobacco, rice, and sugar "favour(s) the employment of slaves in the competition with peasant proprietors."[4] Similarly, in this century the historian Lewis Cecil Gray reasoned that because planters could "produce at price levels that left little more than the expense of maintaining the slave, white labor could bid no lower."[5] Further, the geographical

---

[3] For a detailed explanation of the underlying issues, see Jeremy Atack and Peter Passell, *A New Economic View of American History*, 2nd ed. (New York, 1994), pp. 310–316.
[4] Cairnes, *Slave Power*, 41–42.
[5] Gray, *History of Agriculture*, 474–475.

concentration of slaves in the most fertile areas, and the areas most conducive to marketing farm output, was a manifestation of the planters' ability to pay a premium above that of free farmers for the acquisition of land. This outcome put free Southern farms at a productive disadvantage. Early commentators seemed convinced that Southern slave owners could produce at lower average costs than free farmers, but they were not always clear about whether these lower costs were achieved by economies of scale, efficiency, or both.

In *Time on the Cross*, Fogel and Engerman (FE) explicitly present the arguments concerning both potential scale economies and efficiencies associated with slave agriculture. They conclude that slave farms were substantially more efficient than free agriculture in either the North or the South. They defined "efficiency" as higher total factor productivity (TFP).[6] The key to their argument was that the division of labor afforded by the sowing and cultivation of cotton was realized on neither Southern non-slave farms nor the primarily grain- and livestock-producing farms of the North. This argument in fact revolves around the use of slave labor in gangs on large (greater than 15 slaves) farms and therefore implies that these large farms would have been more efficient than either small slave farms or free farms. In addition, FE argue that free farms, both in the North and the South, were less efficient than small slave farms. FE reach these conclusions based on a comparison of TFP indices for slave farms of various sizes (measured by numbers of slaves owned) and for free Southern farms, in the New and Old South, as well as for Northern farms.

David and Temin (DT) strongly question FE's methodology and main conclusions.[7] DT's primary contention is that because FE used farm revenue as their measure of output, and because FE used national prices to construct their output index, they are measuring only the efficiency with which a farm produced revenue. Furthermore, DT argue that it is not possible to infer technical efficiency from a comparison of revenue under these circumstances, because the North was largely prohibited by climate from growing cotton. The point is that because prices are generated by the interaction of supply and demand forces, what appear to be efficiencies in FE's results merely reflect the robust demand for cotton, which Northern farmers, for the most part, could not grow. FE respond to this criticism by demonstrating, through the use of a series of production possibilities diagrams, that although DT's scenario is theoretically possible, it does not appear to be consistent with the production frontiers (or relative prices) actually faced by Northern or Southern farmers, even if one compares, as FE do, the physical units of output rather than

---

[6] Fogel and Engerman, *Time on the Cross*. Total factor productivity is defined as the difference between outputs and (variously measured) inputs and thus represents an indicator of the efficient use of those inputs.

[7] David and Temin, "Slavery: The Progressive Institution?" and David and Temin, "Comment."

revenue.[8] Although this graphical evidence is suggestive, it does not, in the view of some scholars, firmly refute DT's fundamental objection, because FE's key conclusions are still based on the use of revenue as the measure of output.

In addition, FE's approach has been criticized for its overly aggregate level of analysis, and for the use of a common production function for all farm types and regions. This aggregate approach is called into question in a paper by Schaefer and Schmitz, which concludes that "a single production function is not adequate to describe the entire cotton South"; rather, Schaefer and Schmitz (SS) find differences in production functions both regionally and by scale of slaveholding.[9] In other words, free farms and large and small slave farms need to be considered separately, because they essentially employed different production technologies.

Among the main areas to be reconsidered was the functional form used to represent the technology of antebellum agriculture. Elizabeth Field investigates FE's choice of functional form (the Cobb–Douglas) by estimating a flexible form production function (the translog) from the micro-level data available from the manuscript censuses.[10] Thus, her approach avoids the problems raised by the highly aggregate nature of FE's work. She limits herself to consideration of slave farms, which tended to grow cotton, in order to avoid the problem of variation in crop mix raised by DT, but she does consider small and large slave farms separately, as SS suggest. Various threshold values were tested, and Field demonstrated that a threshold of approximately fifteen slaves was most probable, which corresponds to FE's historical evidence. Chow tests demonstrate that gang (large) and non-gang (small) slave farms had different production functions.[11]

---

[8] Fogel and Engerman, "Reply."

[9] Donald F. Schaefer and Mark D. Schmitz, "Efficiency in Antebellum Southern Agriculture: A Covariance Approach," *Southern Economic Journal*, 49 (1982): 88–98.

[10] Elizabeth Field, "Elasticities of Complementarity and Returns to Scale in Antebellum Cotton Agriculture," Ph.D. dissertation, Duke University, 1985; Field, "The Relative Efficiency of Slavery Revisited"; and Elizabeth Field, "Free and Slave Labor on Large and Small Farms: Perfect Substitutes or Different Inputs?" *The Review of Economics and Statistics*, 70 (1988): 654–659.

[11] Field, "Elasticities of Complementarity," 74. Field also investigates the substitutability of free and slave labor on both gang and non-gang farms, testing for functional separability determine the possibility of substitution of inputs. Weak separability between inputs is necessary for the existence of some consistent aggregate labor index, and it cannot be rejected for either size farm (p. 91). However, examination of the Hicks elasticities of complementarity reveals that free and slave labor were complements rather than substitutes on gang farms (p. 87), meaning that simply adding free and slave labor to form a single labor input is not acceptable for larger slave farms. Tests for separability can also establish whether certain functional forms of the production function are appropriate. Specifically, CES and Cobb–Douglas are both special cases of the translog, which assume complete strong separability. However, complete strong separability is rejected for both gang and non-gang farms (p. 92), indicating that the Cobb–Douglas production function underlying FE's approach is not appropriate.

Other scholars have analyzed the relative efficiency of slave agriculture by employing stochastic production frontiers. A stochastic frontier specifies a one-sided error term, which more accurately reflects production technology than the usual deterministic production frontier. This result follows from the fact that farms could not achieve more output than that which would be possible with best practice techniques, but they could certainly achieve less. It allows one to distinguish between technological superiority (a higher production frontier) and inefficiency (the extent to which a farm falls below that frontier.); Grabowski and Pasurka (GP) use a nonparametric approach which allows them to employ a multi-product analysis, rather than using farm revenue as a single measure of output.[12] However, the computational requirements of this method leave them with a very small sample, and they treat all Southern farms as having a common production technology. GP also consider slave and non-slave production functions separately, but they employ Cobb–Douglas production functions, which, as previously stated, were rejected by Field.[13] Richard Hofler and Sherman Folland (HF) refine Field's approach by combining her use of a translog production function and separation of large and small slave farms with a stochastic production frontier approach.[14] They find that large slave farms, which employed the gang system of labor organization, were technologically superior to small slave farms, but they also find that large slave farms displayed greater inefficiency, which was, however, outweighed by the technological advantage of the gang system.

Although the use of stochastic production frontiers represents a significant methodological improvement in the analysis of the efficiency of slavery, all of the studies cited have shortcomings. Although GP's nonparametric approach is intriguing because it offers a possible solution to the problem of crop mix, it limits them to a very small sample size. In addition, they never apply this analysis to large and small slave farms separately, and they employ the Cobb–Douglas production function. HF's analysis suffers from the same limitation as Field's, because it considers only slave farms, and does not control for cotton's share of output. Field-Hendrey broadens HF's approach by considering free as well as slave farms, and by including cotton share as an independent variable in the production function, but she treats cotton production as exogenous, which may not be a valid assumption, because a farmer would have chosen desired output and cotton share simultaneously.[15]

All of these comparisons, however, are limited to Southern farms and therefore cannot answer the question originally posed by Fogel and

---

[12] Richard Grabowski and Carl Pasurka, "The Relative Technical Efficiency of Northern and Southern U.S. Farms in 1860," *Southern Economic Journal*, 54 (1988): 598–614; and Grabowski and Pasurka, "The Relative Efficiency of Slave Agriculture."

[13] Grabowski and Pasurka, "Reply."

[14] Hofler and Folland, "Comment."

[15] Field-Hendrey, "Application of a Stochastic Production Frontier."

Engerman, which we previously restated. Specifically, did Northern and Southern farms face the same production possibility frontier? Furthermore, regardless of what frontier they faced, how close to the frontier was each type of farm? In addition, because free Southern farmers were profoundly affected by the presence of slavery, in order to draw conclusions about the efficiency of slave agriculture and free agriculture in the absence of slavery, a better comparison is of Northern free farmers to Southern slave owners.[16] There are two reasons for this comparison. First, as pointed out, more than half a century ago by Gray, free Southern farmers farmed less well-located, less productive lands. Second, free Southern farmers may well have been on the bottom rung of an agricultural ladder. Farmers with managerial skills, and without a moral aversion to slave ownership, might have aspired to climb that ladder, the top rung of which was plantation ownership. This process would have left the lower rungs of the Southern ladder occupied by those who maintained qualms about slavery or who lacked some combination of experience, wealth, initiative, or ability.

In order to make this comparison, it is necessary to consider data from the North as well as the South, which we do later. Few attempts have been made since Fogel and Engerman's *Time on the Cross* to compare Northern and Southern farms directly. We argue that our comparison is a significant improvement over earlier work. Like Field, HF, and GP, we use micro-level data and employ a stochastic production frontier. Unlike those earlier papers, we control for crop mix by making the cotton share of output endogenous, in order to address the problem of comparison of large slave farms with Northern farms, which did not grow cotton, or with small slave farms or free farms in the South, which grew less cotton than the large slave farms.

As in the studies previously cited, our measure of output is really revenue, not physical output, because we aggregate the crops and products reported in the Census, weighted by prices. Thus any measurement of efficiency shows efficiency in producing revenue, not truly technical efficiency, as first noted by David and Temin.[17] The crux of the problem is that the cotton share of output increased with the number of slaves held (see Table 1). In addition, 1859 may have been an exceptionally good year for cotton, both in terms of yield and price.[18] Schaefer suggests that the high yields occurred primarily in the New South; whereas the Old South had a relatively poor cotton crop in 1859.[19] Using a total factor productivity approach similar to FE's, Schaefer concludes

[16] Of course, in a general equilibrium sense, the existence of slavery affected Northern as well as Southern farms, although not as directly, but Northern farmers may be as close as we can get to examining antebellum agriculture in the absence of slavery.

[17] David and Temin, "Slavery: The Progressive Institution?" and David and Temin, "Comment."

[18] Wright, "The Efficiency of Slavery."

[19] Donald Schaefer, "The Effect of the 1859 Crop Year upon Relative Productivity in the Antebellum Cotton South," *Journal of Economic History*, 43 (1983): 851–865.

TABLE 1. *Sample Means and Variable Definitions*

Variable Name	Variable Definition	North	Free Farms Old South	Free Farms New South	Small Slave Farms Old South	Small Slave Farms New South	Large Slave Farms Old South	Large Slave Farms New South
Q	Output ($)	1,124	503	568	1,224	1,612	4,254	6,694
F	Free labor (adult male equivalents)	3.31	1.94	1.99	1.88	1.97	1.58	1.80
S	Slave labor (adult male equivalents)	0	0	0	2.23	2.37	10.87	12.26
K	Capital ($)	1,477	504	661	1,279	1,850	3,863	6,196
I	Improved acreage (#acres)	72	54	42	136	110	467	378
U	Unimproved acreage (#acres)	61	140	154	296	357	717	684
COTSHARE	Cotton share of output (%)	0	18	24	28	37	41	57
SLAVES	Number of slaves held (#)	0	0	0	6.35	6.30	34.24	34.26
N		8,010	643	1,613	616	861	251	402

Notes: Small slave farms are those with 1–15 slaves. Large slave farms have 16 or more slaves.

Sources: Bateman–Foust and Parker–Gallman samples.

that much of the "efficiency" advantage enjoyed by slave agriculture is a result of the atypical crop year. Thus large slave farms, especially in the New South, might have had higher revenue based on the high price of cotton and the high cotton share; thus, the apparent advantages of slavery were not based on any technical superiority, but merely on the fact that Southern planters grew a valuable crop that yeoman farmers of the North could not produce. Controlling for cotton's share of output should address this issue to some extent.

II

The key to actually addressing – which is to say controlling for – the impact of cotton production on farm revenue is to treat cotton production as an endogenous variable, which we do. By including (predicted) cotton share of output as an independent variable in the farm's production function, we can predict what output would have been *if the farm grew no cotton*. Although the choice of crop mix was largely endogenous, the key determinants of climate and soil were associated with location.[20] Hence conditions in the cotton market could yield locational quasi-rents, which would be reflected in the revenue figures. By using the predicted cotton share as an independent variable we avoid this problem. We also separate Old and New South farms to allow for the possibility that desired cotton share had different effects on output by region, as suggested by Schaefer, and also by Schaefer and Schmitz. Although our measure of output is still revenue, the main difficulty in inferring technical efficiency differences from revenue differences stems largely from the increase in the percentage of revenue derived from cotton as the number of slaves increased. Controlling for this effect allows us to compare the efficiency of North v. South, Old South v. New South, and free v. slave farms, and to draw conclusions about the technical efficiency of slave agriculture relative to free agriculture, both in the presence and in the absence of slavery.

Thus our work addresses many concerns about earlier investigations of the relative efficiency of slave agriculture. We use micro-level (that is farm-level) data; a flexible form production function – specifically, the translog production function; and a stochastic production frontier (see the Appendix). We consider possible differences in production functions by region and slave-holding within the South. We make North–South as well as intra-South comparisons, and we address the problem of crop mix not only by controlling its influence, but also by recognizing its endogeneity. Many earlier

---

[20] For example, the strains of short-staple cotton grown before the Civil War required 200 consecutive frost-free days to reach maturity; thus during the 1859 crop year there were less than 10,000 bales produced above latitude 36°30′, and the vast majority of this output came from southern Virginia.

studies have overcome one or more of the objections raised to FE's analysis of the efficiency of slave agriculture, but we think that this is the first study that confronts all of them.

We compare farm groups in two ways. First, we estimate the parameters of a production function for each farm type in each region. We then compare the average predicted frontier output for each group to the output that would have been produced if the farmer employed an alternative technology – that is, the technology from another farm type and/or region. For example, we compare the output of free farms in the Old South with slave farms in the Old South if slaves had been treated as free workers – that is, if the free farm technology had been employed. So, for a given set of inputs, say those of large slave farms in the New South, this comparison tells us which technologies were superior. Of course, the farmer would also have to consider how close to this frontier he was likely to get – that is, his technical inefficiency. So we also compare the average values of our inefficiency measure for each group. The final question we address is, if some methods of production were technologically superior but had higher inefficiency, did the technology advantage outweigh the disadvantage of higher inefficiency? We combine our estimates of frontier (or best possible) output with our measures of inefficiency in order to answer this question.

We draw our sample of Northern farms from the Bateman–Foust sample of rural households drawn from the manuscript censuses for 1860.[21] For the South, we used the Parker–Gallman sample, which is described in Gallman.[22] We exclude all farms with non-positive values of output or any of the inputs. We have made input and output definitions comparable for the North and South, which entailed modifications of the measures used in previous studies of the regions such as Craig, FE, and Field.[23] Our measure of output is the market value of all crops reported by quantity in the Census, evaluated at regional prices, and the value of meat output. For the North, this is taken to be the reported value of animals slaughtered, but for the South we compute meat output according to the formulas given in Field.[24] Unlike FE and Field, we also include estimates of output not recorded in the Census, such as lumber, poultry and eggs.[25] Thus this study broadens the types of outputs

---

[21] For a description of the sample, see Jeremy Atack and Fred Bateman, *To Their Own Soil: Agriculture in the Antebellum North* (Ames, Iowa, 1987), Appendices to chs. 2 and 7.

[22] Robert Gallman, "Self-Sufficiency in the Cotton Economy of the Antebellum South," *Agricultural History* 44 (1970): 5–23.

[23] Lee A. Craig, "The Value of Household Labor in Antebellum Northern Agriculture," *Journal of Economic History*, 51 (1991): 67–82; idem., *To Sow One Acre More: Childbearing and Farm Productivity in the Antebellum North* (Baltimore, 1993); Fogel and Engerman, *Time on the Cross*; and Field, "Elasticities of Complementarity."

[24] Field, "Elasticities of Complementarity."

[25] This is the measure of output used in Craig, *To Sow*; and Lee A. Craig and Elizabeth Field-Hendrey, "Industrialization and the Earnings Gap," *Explorations in Economic History*, 30

considered for Southern farms compared to previous studies of Southern agriculture, which might well affect comparisons within the South as well as between regions.

Our labor inputs are free and slave prime age male equivalent labor. The productivity weights used in the computation of the Northern labor force are described in Craig; for the South we apply weights derived from FE to each of these groups.[26] Therefore, the difference between the number of slaves and the slave labor input reflects both labor force participation and the relative productivity between males and females over the life cycle.[27] We exclude farms with very high or low output-to-labor ratios, in order to avoid including farms which had substantial hired labor which is not captured in our free labor measure, as well as farms where residents actually worked on other farms, and would be incorrectly included in the labor force of their home farm. Our capital input is the sum of the value of farm machinery and equipment reported in the Census, the imputed value of farm buildings, and the value of livestock. Our land inputs are improved and unimproved acreage.[28]

Table 1 contains the means and definitions of the variables, for all farm types (free, small slave, and large slave) and regions (Old and New South, and North). Northern farms were larger than free farms in either region, but smaller than slave farms, large or small. Compared to the North, Southern farms had a smaller percentage of improved acreage. Farms in the New South were larger and grew more cotton than farms in the Old South.

(1992): 60–80, except that we do not include capital gains on land. Because the Parker–Gallman sample does not include the value of real estate, we cannot distinguish tenants from owners. Because slave owners were probably more likely than average to be farm owners (especially large slaveowners), there is a bias against finding any advantage for slave farms, and would strengthen such a finding. We regress this new definition of output on Field's earlier measure, which is based much more closely on FE's, and exclude any farms with a Studentized residual above 1.5 or below −1.5 in order to exclude farms with unreasonable values of imputed output. We do not include the value of home manufactures because FE suggest that these were undercounted in the South.

[26] Craig, *To Sow*; and Fogel and Engerman, *Time on the Cross*.

[27] The Bateman–Foust and Parker–Gallman samples were drawn differently. Bateman–Foust is a cluster sample that contains all of the households in a township, including farm laborers not resident on farms; however, Parker–Gallman includes only those workers residing on a sampled farm. Because of this difference and in an attempt to make the samples as comparable as possible, we have not adjusted Northern farm labor for off-farm labor.

[28] Acreage is used, rather than a land input adjusted by a soil quality index, such as that described in Field, "The Relative Efficiency," for the South, because it is not possible to construct a comparable index for the Northern sample. We did not use farm value because it includes structures, which would have been less directly related to output than acreage, and, perhaps more important, farm value reflects locational rents that would make slave farms appear more efficient than other farms. See the discussion at the beginning of this section above.

III

Discussion of the results is grouped under the headings technological superiority, technical efficiency, and technological advantage versus inefficiency.

A. Technological Advantage

We first consider the possible technical advantage of large slave farms, because the use of the gang system on these farms is at the heart of FE's contention that slave agriculture was more efficient than free farming. In order to determine whether gang-system farms were indeed technologically superior to other types of farms, as FE contend, we compute average predicted frontier output for large slave farms, and compare it to average predicted output on those same farms using the Northern farm frontier, the small slave farm frontiers, and free Southern farm frontiers.[29] We do this comparison both for Old and New South farms. In addition, for large slave farms in each region, we compute the predicted frontier output (revenue) had those farms been located in the other region of the South. The average predicted values are reported in Table 2.[30] We provide predicted means using the mean value of PCOT, as well as predicted means if the cotton share were set equal to zero, in order to remove the possible revenue advantage of growing cotton.

Comparing predicted outputs after controlling for the cotton share of output allows us to compare true technological superiority – not superiority in producing revenue. We first test the hypotheses that predicted output on the large slave farm frontier in each region (Old v. New South) was less than or equal to predicted output using the frontier for different groups, with and without removing the cotton effect.[31] In essence, what we are doing is combining the productive inputs of one farm type with the technology (e.g., the production function) of another farm type. We then compare the output (revenue) that would have been generated by a farmer using one technology or the other.

In both regions, we reject the hypothesis for most comparisons, but there were a few exceptions. Starting with the Old South in the first panel of Table 2, we cannot reject the hypothesis that large slave farm frontier revenue ($3,348) was significantly less than Northern farm revenue ($4,251) if cotton share was set to zero. We also conclude that these farms would have enjoyed

---

[29] As HF did, we evaluate each of the production frontier functions at the means of the log values of the inputs, yielding the mean of the logarithm of predicted frontier output.

[30] Note that we do not compare large farms in one region to small or free farms in the other region, because this would confound the effects of region and size. In addition, for the Northern farms, we only present predicted output when the percent cotton is set to zero, because Northern farms grew virtually no cotton. Consequently, there are a number of blank cells in Table 2. These cells represent comparisons that, although possible, would not be easily or meaningfully interpreted.

[31] The *t* statistics are available from the authors on request.

TABLE 2. *Mean Predicted Frontier Revenues*

		Farm Function Used					
	North	Free Old South	Free New South	Small Slave Old South	Small Slave New South	Large Slave Old South	Large Slave New South
Evaluated at means for Large Slave Farms Old South							
PCOT set at mean	–	3,885	–	4,180	–	4,727	6,192
PCOT set at zero	4,251	3,156	–	2,838	–	3,348	5,029
Evaluated at means for Large Slave Farms New South							
PCOT set at mean	–	–	7,518	–	6,884	6,021	8,544
PCOT set at zero	4,670	–	8,201	–	5,250	3,718	6,380
Evaluated at means for Small Slave Farms Old South							
PCOT set at mean	–	1,360	–	1,368	1,758	–	–
PCOT set at zero	1,569	1,181	–	1,052	1,541	–	–
Evaluated at means for Small Slave Farms New South							
PCOT set at mean	–	–	1,763	1,570	1,963	–	–
PCOT set at zero	1,699	–	1,872	1,105	1,647	–	–

Notes: PCOT is the predicted cotton share of output.

Sources: Bateman–Foust and Parker–Gallman samples. Figures are calculated from stochastic frontier regression results available from the authors on request.

greater output had they been located in the New South, regardless of whether we removed the cotton effect. This finding suggests that both Northern farms and large slave farms in the New South had a higher production frontier than large slave farms in the Old South.

In the New South, large slave farms had significantly higher frontier output ($8,544) than all groups. However, this advantage disappears relative to New South free farms, when cotton shares were controlled ($6,380 v. $8,201 in the second panel of Table 2). Free farms in the New South were the only Southern farm group for which the coefficient on the predicted cotton share was negative and insignificant, which meant that removing the cotton effect actually raised frontier output. In short, this finding suggests that using inputs from large slave farms in the New South with the technology of free farms in the same region would have generated the greatest output ($8,201) in the absence of any gains associated with cotton production. Other than these exceptions, we conclude that large slave farms enjoyed a technological advantage over other farm types, free and slave, Northern and Southern, in both regions, even if the possible advantage of growing cotton was removed.

Next, we consider small slave farms, in order to determine whether there was an efficiency gain associated with slavery per se, even when the farm was too small to make employment of the gang system practical. We compare predicted average frontier revenue in both regions of the South to each other, and to free farm output in the North and the relevant region of the South.[32] Small slave farms in the Old South had no advantage over other farm types (the third panel of Table 2). In this region, small slave farms are predicted to have slightly higher frontier output than if they operated as free farms with cotton share set at its mean value ($1,368 v. $1,360), but the difference is not significant. Even including the cotton advantage, small slave farms in the Old South had lower predicted output than they would have enjoyed in the North, or in the New South. In addition, once the cotton effect is removed, small slave farms in the Old South could have had higher frontier output had they been free farms ($1,181 v. $1,052). The picture in the New South is slightly different (the fourth panel of Table 2). Small slave farms did enjoy a significant advantage over free farms in the New South and in the North, when cotton share is set at its mean value ($1,963 v. $1,763 and $1,699, respectively). However, it cannot be concluded that this is a true technological advantage, for once the cotton effect is removed, the advantage disappears, with free farms in both the North ($1,699) and the New South ($1,872) dominating the small slave farms ($1,647).

We conclude that Fogel and Engerman were generally correct in identifying the gang system as a key to the technological superiority of antebellum

---

[32] We do not evaluate small farms using the large farm frontier, because these farms were not large enough to operate with the gang system. As with large farms, we do not make the comparison to smaller farms in the other region of the South, and we present Northern farm output only on the "zero cotton" line of the panels.

TABLE 3. *Average Inefficiency by Farm Group and Region*

		Old South			New South		
	Northern Farms	Free Farms	Small Slave Farms	Large Slave Farms	Free Farms	Small Slave Farms	Large Slave Farms
Inefficiency as a percent of Frontier Revenue	25.6%	31.8%	26.1%	30.4%	37.4%	33.4%	37.6%

Sources: Bateman–Foust and Parker–Gallman samples. Figures are calculated from stochastic frontier regression results available from the authors on request.

southern agriculture – though the positive impact of the gang system seems to have been particularly effective in the New South. Indeed, controlling for cotton's role in the measurement of output, Northern agriculture was technologically superior to large slave farms in the Old South, a finding which contrasts with that of Fogel and Engerman.

B. Technical Inefficiency

The question of technological superiority at the frontier is only part of the story, however. Large slave farms could have enjoyed a technological advantage but in practice still fallen so far below their frontiers as to negate the advantage. Southern free farms could potentially have produced as much output as a Northern farm of equal size and labor force but in practice could have produced much less due to inefficiency. Therefore, we now consider how close to these frontier outputs a farmer in each group was likely to come. Average technical inefficiency for each farm group is presented in Table 3.[33]

The group with the smallest inefficiency – that is, the one that achieved the highest percentage of possible output – was the North. In the South, all groups in the Old South had smaller inefficiency than in the New South, which would tend to negate the technological advantage we found in the New South. Within each of the Southern regions, as we consider slave farms by size, mean inefficiency declines as one moves from free to small slave farms, and then increases as one moves to the larger slave farms. This finding suggests that at low levels, slaveholding conferred an efficiency advantage,

---

[33] We show inefficiency as a percent of mean frontier revenue. It is calculated by $1 - 1/\exp(\bar{u}_{ij})$ where

$\bar{u}_{ij}$, the mean residual from the frontier production function,

$$= \ln(Q_{ij,frontier}) - \ln(Q_{ij,actual}).$$

Thus, although small slave farms in the Old South could potentially produce revenues of \$1,368 with no inefficiency (Table 2), in reality, on average they would only have achieved 73.9% of that due to inefficiency.

but that at higher levels of slave holding, that advantage declined, perhaps because of increased shirking by slaves, and increased monitoring costs, or both. Both of these findings are consistent with Fogel and Engerman's observations on the use of slaves as managers, particularly on larger plantations.[34] In addition, Southern free farmers were more inefficient than Northern free farmers, and more inefficient than small slave farms, although less inefficient than large slave farms, at least in the New South.

This comparison of means across major farms groups may be misleading, however, because it reflects, at least partly, farm size. Within the North, for example, inefficiency was inversely related to farm size and output. Because free farms in the South were smaller than Northern farms, perhaps they appear more inefficient merely due to their small size. A more interesting comparison would be of free farms in the South to comparably sized farms in the North. The same problem affects comparison of free Southern farms to slave farms, because slave farms were, on average, much larger.

In order to control for these differences, we estimate the impact of output, number of slaves held, and the cotton share of output on our measure of inefficiency. We expect the coefficient on output to be negative, indicating that, holding other things constant, larger farms were more efficient (lower inefficiency).[35] We include the number of slaves in order to test the hypothesis that increases in slaveholding would have also increased inefficiency due to shirking and monitoring costs, resulting in a positive coefficient on the slaveholding variable. We also include two regional dummy variables, NEWSOUTH and NORTH, to ascertain whether differences in inefficiency remained even after output was held constant. If so, the coefficient on NEW-SOUTH should be positive, and that on NORTH, negative. In addition, we include a dummy variable, DSLAVE, which took the value one, if there were any slaves on the farms, and a dummy variable, DGANG, with the value one for farms with sixteen or more slaves, Fogel and Engerman's cutoff for use of the gang system.[36]

---

[34] Fogel and Engerman, *Time on the Cross*, pp. 149–150.

[35] That is to say, we regress the residuals from the various frontier equations (see the Appendix) for all groups and regions on the key variables listed in the text.

[36] We also include several regional variables interacted with the cotton share in order to account for the fact that 1859 was an unusually good year for cotton in certain areas of the New South, although not for the South as a whole. For example, Schaefer finds that cotton yield was about 25 percent higher than normal for the New South as a whole, and was especially good in Louisiana, Mississippi, and Alabama, but only 13 percent above normal for Arkansas, and actually lower than normal in Texas; see Schaefer, "The Effect," 859–862. Higher than normal cotton yields should manifest themselves as lower residuals from the best practice frontier. We interact a dummy variable for Alabama, Mississippi, and Louisiana, one for Arkansas, one for Texas, and one for the rest of the New South with the cotton share, to see if farms with higher cotton shares in the New South showed lower inefficiency, in keeping with Schaefer's observations.

TABLE 4. *Estimated Regression Coefficients
(Dependent Variable is Inefficiency)*[a]

Variable	Coefficient
Constant	0.429 (59.588)**
Q	−0.205E−05 (−1.493)
SLAVES	0.856E−02 (22.867)**
COTSHARE	−0.401 (−18.881)**
NEWSOUTH	0.181 (20.855)**
NORTH	−0.130 (−16.508)**
NSCOT1	−0.125 (−5.066)**
NSCOT2	−0.216 (−6.110)**
COTAR	−0.211 (−6.261)**
COTTX	−0.025 (−0.817)
DSLAVE	−0.062 (−10.210)**
DGANG	−0.068 (−6.162)**
Adjusted r^2	0.248
n	12,397

[a] Calculated from frontier regression results available
from the authors on request.

Notes:
NSCOT1 = COTSHARE * a dummy variable which
equals one if the farm was in MS, LA, or AL.
NSCOT2 = COTSHARE * a dummy variable which
equals one if the farm was in FL or TN.
COTAR = COTSHARE * AR
COTTX = COTSHARE * TX
DSLAVE = 1 if slaves > 0
DGANG = 1 if slaves ≥ 16
Sources: Bateman–Foust and Parker–Gallman samples.

The regression coefficients are presented in Table 4.[37] The results are
generally as expected. The coefficient on output is negative, but is not
significantly different from zero, indicating that there was no relationship
between size and efficiency. Farms in the New South show greater inefficiency, *ceteris paribus*, but farms growing more cotton in the various sub-
regions of the New South come closer to their frontiers, although the coefficient for Texas is not significantly different from zero.[38] The findings
for the slaveholding variables indicate that owning slaves allowed farmers to reach a higher percentage of best practice output, that operating a

[37] Because Northern and Southern observations come from different samples, we weight each
observation by the ratio of the number of sampled farms in a region divided by the total
number of farms reported in the Census for that region.
[38] This result is consistent with Schaefer's finding that Texas did not experience a good cotton
year in 1859, although the rest of the New South did.

gang-system plantation conferred a further efficiency advantage, but that when we consider plantations significantly above the gang-system threshold, this advantage was offset by increased inefficiency associated with the numbers of slaves held. Interestingly, a farm located in the North achieved a higher percentage of potential output, even when output is held constant. Of course, the main issue remains not whether a farm possessed a theoretical advantage, but whether a typical farmer experienced an advantage in practice once both technological superiority and inefficiency are considered together.

C. *Technological Advantage v. Inefficiency*

Finally, we combine our findings on predicted frontier output and on inefficiency (the degree to which farms fell below that frontier) in order to see which farms enjoyed an advantage in practice, and to what extent any advantage was explained by the ability to grow cotton. To predict actual output (as opposed to frontier, or potential output), we take the predicted mean frontier revenues for each group using the results from Table 4. (We use predicted inefficiency from Table 4 instead of the actual figures from Table 3 in order to predict inefficiency for the counterfactual as well.) We also compute a counterfactual output for each farm in group A, if it had fallen into group B, to see whether, in practice, a group A farm would have been better off in group B. This is the question that would have been relevant to the farmer; that is, a farmer would not care if he had an efficiency advantage if that did not result in higher output in practice. In order to make this comparison, we take the predicted frontier output for group A using the group B frontier, from Table 2, and subtract from that the predicted inefficiency for a farm with group A characteristics, but which fell in group B. We predict inefficiency from the results in Table 4, which is preferable to simply assigning the mean inefficiency for group B to group A, because groups A and B presumably differed on average, by farm size and crop mix, so that even if group A farms all behaved as if they were in group B, they still would not have the same inefficiency, on average, as group B farms, unless they had identical characteristics. Thus if we predict how group A farms would have done using the group B production function, we must also predict what their average inefficiency would have been. Because we take a computed measure (inefficiency) and regress it on the same explanatory variables that were used to predict farm revenue, and then use it in computing predicted revenue, we cannot make any statistical inferences about the predicted revenues in Table 5. However, it is instructive to compare the point estimates, because they provide a way of combining the comparisons of frontier production with inefficiency.

We look first at large slave farms (the first panel of Table 5). In the Old South, gang farms are predicted to have higher output ($3,109) than small slave farms ($2,568) or free farms in the region ($3,008) when differences

TABLE 5. *Mean Predicted Revenues*

	North	Free Old South	Free New South	Small Slave Old South	Small Slave New South	Large Slave Old South	Large Slave New South
				Farm Function Used			
Evaluated at means for Large Slave Farms Old South							
PCOT set at mean	–	3,008	–	2,568	–	3,109	3,398
PCOT set at zero	3,181	2,074	–	1,480	–	1,871	2,343
Evaluated at means for Large Slave Farms New South							
PCOT set at mean	–	–	5,608	–	4,052	5,059	5,383
PCOT set at zero	3,516	–	5,162	–	2,455	2,411	3,194
Evaluated at means for Small Slave Farms Old South							
PCOT set at mean	–	992	–	1,006	1,079	–	–
PCOT set at zero	1,167	771	–	692	846	–	–
Evaluated at means for Small Slave Farms New South							
PCOT set at mean	–	–	1,763	1,570	1,963	–	–
PCOT set at zero	1,265	–	1,021	608	950	–	–

Sources: Bateman–Foust and Parker–Gallman samples. Figures are calculated from results reported in Tables 2–4.

in inefficiency were accounted for. When the cotton effect is removed, that advantage remains relative to small slave farms, but it disappears relative to free Southern farms. Gang farms in the Old South are predicted to have higher output using the Northern farm function when cotton share is set to zero for the Southern farms ($3,181 v. $1,871). Note that we obtain the same result even if we compare the predicted output from the Northern farm function to Southern farm output with the *actual* cotton share. In other words, once we take inefficiency into account, the theoretical advantage of Old South gang farms over Northern farm technology (based on output resulting from "best practice") disappears.

In the New South (the second panel of Table 5), gang plantations are predicted to have higher output in practice than small slave farms, when cotton share is evaluated at its mean value ($5,383 v. $4,052), but lower output than free farms in the region ($5,383 v. $5,608). When the possible advantage of growing cotton is removed, plantations still have an advantage over small slave farms ($3,194 v. $2,455, respectively), but not over free farms in the region ($5,162) or Northern farms ($3,516).

In the Old South (panel 3), small slave farm output was less than that of Northern farms even when cotton is included in Southern farm output ($1,006 v. $1,167, respectively). Small slave farms did produce more than a free farm with otherwise identical characteristics, if the cotton effect was included ($1,006 v. $992), but the advantage was based on cotton production and disappears when cotton output is set at zero ($692 v. $771).

In the New South (panel 4), small slave farms are predicted to have higher output in practice than Northern farms ($1,963 v. $1,265), but that advantage disappears when the cotton effect is removed, with slave farms' output falling to $950. Also, small slave farms in that region are predicted to have higher output than if they had acted as free farmers in the South ($1,963 v. $1,763), but again that benefit vanishes when the cotton effect was removed ($950 v. $1,021).

Although Fogel and Engerman did not pose their comparison of free and slave agriculture in exactly the same terms as we have, at least some our key results confirm their conclusions. Specifically, gang farm output exceeded output from other slave farms using the same level of inputs in both the Old and New South, and gang farms in the New South had greater output then Northern farms. However, the comparison with free Southern farms yields decidedly mixed results, as do the comparisons with Northern farms. The results that support Fogel and Engerman tend to be driven by the inclusion of the cotton effect. In the absence of that effect, in practice Northern agricultural technology was superior to slave agriculture on large and small farms in both the Old and New South. In short, Fogel and Engerman were correct in identifying the potential gains from plantation agriculture; however, those gains were inextricably tied to the production of cotton.

IV

This study compares Northern and Southern farms in 1860 in order to revisit the question of the relative efficiency of slave agriculture, an important historical question, which heretofore has been addressed extensively though not necessarily satisfactorily. Our approach overcomes at least some of the shortcomings of previous work on this subject. We use a micro-level approach rather than the aggregate approach employed by Fogel and Engerman. We consider a wider range of outputs on farms than did Fogel and Engerman or subsequent studies of Southern agriculture. We control for cotton's share of output, because it has been widely suggested that ability or willingness to grow cotton had significant revenue advantages. We recognize that cotton share was in fact determined simultaneously with the overall decision about what factors to employ and what level of total output to produce, and therefore treat cotton share as an endogenous variable. We employ a stochastic production frontier approach that allows us to model agricultural production in a more realistic way and also permits us to distinguish between technical superiority and technical efficiency.

Generally speaking, we find that large plantations in the antebellum South did have a technological advantage over smaller slave farms, and over free farms both in the North and the South. This finding supports Fogel and Engerman's original hypothesis that use of the gang system represented a superior technology attainable only through the employment of slave labor, and practical only when sixteen or more slaves were present. Gang-system farms enjoyed this technical superiority even when we controlled for the possible advantages offered by cotton production. In addition, we found that farms above the sixteen-slave threshold for use of the gang system had lower inefficiency, *ceteris paribus*. Not only did gang-system farms have a higher frontier, but they achieved a higher percentage of frontier output. Our inefficiency measure was positively correlated with the number of slaves held, however, perhaps due to organizational issues associated with shirking by slaves, and higher monitoring costs. This finding is consistent with the fact that large slave plantations had higher inefficiency on average than smaller slave farms, than Northern farms, and, in the New South, than free Southern farms.

Still, even when this greater inefficiency is taken into account, large slave farms produced greater output in practice than they could have had they operated as small slave farms, or as free farms in the Old South or in the North. Once the benefit of being able to grow cotton is removed, however, Southern plantations would have had higher output had they operated using the Northern farm technology. As critics of Fogel and Engerman suggested, the effect of crop mix explains much, though not all, of the edge possessed by plantation owners.

We found no technical advantage for small slave owners. Although small slave owners were able to reach a higher frontier than free farmers, the benefit is explained by the greater cotton share of output on such farms. Because Fogel and Engerman's hypothesis revolves around the use of the gang system, this is perhaps not surprising. We did find, however, that being a slave owner resulted in a threshold reduction in inefficiency, although that decrease was offset by the effect of additional slaves for plantations significantly above that threshold. In practice, small slave farms were able to produce greater output than free farms with otherwise identical characteristics, but that ability was linked to their greater ability or willingness to grow cotton. Again, cotton production was the key to the resulting advantage.

Overall, then, we paint a mixed picture of the advantages of slave agriculture. We support earlier findings that large slave plantations did have a technical edge due to use of the gang system, but slavery, per se, did not allow farms to reach a higher frontier, although it did allow them to produce a higher fraction of frontier output. When we combine the technical advantage of using the gang system, the effects of slavery and the gang system on inefficiency, and the revenue effects of growing cotton we find that gang-system farms had an advantage over other Southern farms that could not be explained by their different cotton shares. However, although we do find that gang system had an advantage over Northern farms, that advantage is explained by the cotton effect. Our findings seem to reconcile earlier, apparently contradictory, findings. Controlling for cotton share, and treating it as an endogenous variable, we still find that use of the gang system represented a superior technology. However, we also support the contentions made by researchers such as David and Temin that crop mix explains a large part of the apparent efficiency advantage of slavery, particularly when a comparison is made to the North.

Appendix

We use the stochastic production frontier developed in Aigner, Lovell, and Schmidt and outlined in HF, whose notation we follow:[39]

For slave farms:

$$\ln Q_{ij} = g_i(\ln F_j, \ln S_j, \ln K_j, \ln I_j, \ln U_j, \mathrm{PCOT}_j) + v_{ij} - u_{ij}$$

$\quad i =$ Old South small slave (sso), Old South large slave (lso),
$\quad\quad\quad$ New South small slave (ssn), New South large slave (lsn),
$\quad j = 1, \ldots, n_i$

---

[39] See D. Aigner, C. A. Knox Lovell, and P. Schmidt, "Formulation and Estimation of Stochastic Frontier Production Function Models," *Journal of Econometrics*, 6 (1977): 21–38; J. Jondrow, C. A. Knox Lovell, I. S. Materov, and P. Schmidt, "On Estimation of Technical Efficiency in the Stochastic Frontier Production Function Model," *Journal of Econometrics*, 19 (1982): 233–8; J. A. Olson, P. Schmidt, and D. M. Waldman, "A Monte Carlo Study of Estimators of Stochastic Frontier Production Functions," *Journal of Econometrics*, 13 (1980): 67–82; and Hofler and Folland, "The Relative Efficiency."

For free farms:

$$\ln Q_{ij} = g_i(\ln F_j, \ln K_j, \ln I_j, \ln U_j, \text{PCOT}_j) + v_{ij} - u_{ij}$$
$$i = \text{free Old South (fo), free New South (fn)},$$
$$j = 1, \ldots, n_i$$

For Northern farms:

$$\ln Q_{ij} = g_i(\ln F_j, \ln K_j, \ln I_j, \ln U_j) + v_{ij} - u_{ij}$$
$$i = \text{North},$$
$$j = 1, \ldots, n_i$$

We employ a translog production function in which Q is output, as measured by revenue; F is free labor; S is slave labor; K is capital; I is improved acreage; and U is unimproved acreage. PCOT is predicted cotton share, which is obtained by regressing cotton share for each group on F, S, K, I, and U, as well as state dummies included to capture intra-regional differences in cotton share. Because cotton share is bounded by 0 and 1, we obtain our estimates by TOBIT regressions. (For reasons of space, parameter estimates for the cotton share equations and production frontiers are not reported here, but are available on request from the authors.) Also, u is a one-sided error term, measuring the extent to which actual revenue falls short of maximum potential (frontier) revenue, and v is assumed to have a normal distribution, whereas u is assumed to have a half-normal distribution.

PART IV

IMPLICATIONS FOR DISTRIBUTION AND GROWTH

9

Wealth Accumulation in Virginia in the Century before the Civil War

James R. Irwin

The basic facts of American economic growth and economic structure before circa 1840 have yet to be documented.[1] This shortcoming represents a major obstacle to our understanding because by 1840 two defining features of U.S. economic history were already in place. First, by 1840 economic growth was already underway in the United States (and in its distinctive regions – what we call the Northeast, the Midwest, and the South). Second, by 1840 the South and the North had generated profoundly different economic and social structures. The Northeast, a free-labor economy and society, was emerging as one of the world's first urban–industrial economies. The South, a slave-labor economy and society, was emerging as the richest and most powerful slave society the world would ever see. Documenting the quantitative record before 1840 promises to advance our understanding of the origins and meanings of both American economic growth and of North/South cleavage.

This paper offers a modest addition to our historical knowledge, presenting one perspective on the American economy and society in the period of

Thanks to Stanley Engerman, Frank Lewis, Catherine McDevitt, and Lorena Walsh for helpful comments and suggestions. Thanks also to the many research assistants who helped me collect the Virginia inventory data. In recent years the efforts of Cagdas Agirdas, Erin Barkow, Eric Beckman, Dan Kreuger, Steve Marshall, and Sergei Rahmail were especially valuable. Thanks to Margaret Dodd and Norah Horning of Park Library Interlibrary Loan for their patient efforts over many years. Collection of much of the inventory data from the years 1830–1860 was supported by NSF research grant SBR 9309494.

[1] Gallman's estimate of GNP for 1840 is the generally accepted start of the record of U.S. national product. For the period before, substantially more empirical work is required to move beyond various "conjectural estimates" which extrapolate back from that value. See Paul David, "The Growth of Real Product in the United States Before 1840: New Evidence, Controlled Conjectures," *The Journal of Economic History*, 27 (1967): 151–97; and Thomas Weiss, "Economic Growth Before 1860: Revised Conjectures," in Thomas Weiss and Donald Schaefer (eds.), *American Economic Development in Comparative Perspective* (Stanford, 1994), pp. 11–27, and references there.

1755–1860. Adopting a narrow geographic focus, I document a century-long record of wealth accumulation in Virginia. Arguably the pre-eminent colony and state in the first two centuries of American economic history, Virginia receded from national importance in the wake of westward expansion and free immigration. Nonetheless, as the most populous of the founding states, any account of the history of economic growth (or not) in the early national period should include developments in Virginia. Similarly, any account of the comparative economic performance of the Northern free-labor and Southern slave-labor economies also will need to consider Virginia. Although on the periphery of the burgeoning cotton economy that was the center of the southern slave economy in the antebellum period, Virginia remained the largest and most powerful of the slave states on the eve of the Civil War.

I

This paper presents a view of Virginia's economy in the century before the Civil War using inventories of deceased men's estates as recorded by Virginia's County Courts.[2] The County Courts supervised and documented the routines of inheritance, compiling a hodgepodge of handwritten wills, inventories, and accounts in "Will Books" that survive and offer a rich but challenging source of historical evidence. The inventories are the "inventory and appraisal" of the personal estates of decedents. Generically such inventories are now commonly referred to as "probate records" (after the probate courts responsible for administering the law of inheritance). As a rule, the inventories list and value the wide range of personal property held by decedents but they do not include real estate. The lack of data on real estate is an obvious and important gap in the view we get of the Virginia economy. But that shortcoming has to be weighed against the gains from looking over more than one hundred years using a consistent source of data.[3]

---

[2] Women were about 13.5% of the decedents identified in the Will Books. In this paper I exclude the estates of female decedents because women had very limited rights to own and control property. An unmarried woman (*femme sole*) had full legal standing to own and dispose of her real and personal property, but if married a woman's property rights were subordinated to those of her husband. See Elizabeth Bowles Warbasse, *The Changing Legal Rights of Married Women, 1800–1861* (New York, 1987 [reprint of 1960 dissertation]), pp. 5–48. My understanding of these issues relies on Catherine L. McDevitt, "Women in a Virginia Real Estate Market: 1782–1858" (unpublished manuscript, 2001), and sources there on the legal status of women in Virginia in this period.

[3] There is no source of data for Virginia decedents' real estate that is comparable to the probate records on personal estate. It is possible to use tax, deed, and other sources to develop estimates of real estate wealth linked to probate data; probably the best known example is the work of Alice Hanson Jones, *American Colonial Wealth, Documents and Methods* (New York, 1978), and *Wealth of a Nation to Be: The American Colonies on the Eve of the Revolution* (New York, 1980).

To organize the analysis and discussion, I use three categories to describe decedents' personal property: slaves, financial assets, and capital. Slaves were the single largest component of personal wealth throughout the period. (In this category I also include the occasional indentured servant scattered among a few of the eighteenth century inventories.)[4] Financial assets were mostly personal obligations (bonds, notes, open accounts), but they also include cash, bank deposits, and other nonpersonal assets.[5] Finally, capital (physical capital) embraces the wide range of other personal property that people owned in the Old Dominion and contributed to domestic or market production. It includes livestock; farm tools, equipment, and supplies; furniture, furnishings, and household supplies; as well as various items, personal (e.g. apparel or jewelry) or otherwise (e.g., blacksmith or carpenter tools). In practice, capital is the residual category, calculated as the difference between a decedent's total personal estate and the value of his slaves and financial assets.

For the current paper, I use summary data on more than five thousand inventories from the Will Books of six counties drawn from the two main regions of the slave economy of Virginia: Tidewater and Piedmont. The Tidewater extends from the Atlantic coast west to the "fall line," where river rapids mark the eastern edge of the Piedmont. The Piedmont, the broad central plateau of the Old Dominion, extends to the Blue Ridge Mountains. Taken together, these regions comprised over three-quarters of the economy and society of Virginia on the eve of the American Revolution. As late as the eve of the Civil War, the Tidewater and Piedmont still included over 85 percent of Virginia's slaves and slave holders, as well as the majority of the state's free population (with the Shenandoah Valley and what would become West Virginia accounting for the rest of the state).[6] As early as the time of the American Revolution the frontier had long ago passed through Tidewater, Virginia and through to the western edge of the Piedmont.[7]

A sampling approach within counties was not used; rather, these wealth data represent an exhaustive listing of all inventories located in the microfilm

---

[4] There are a total of 28 servants included with more than 3200 slaves in the Virginia inventories from the Colonial period. All but three of the servants were found in 18 different inventories from Richmond, the oldest Tidewater county in the study.

[5] Other nonpersonal financial assets included state bonds, and "shares" or "stocks" or "bonds" of banks, canal companies, and railways.

[6] For the regions of Virginia see Joseph Clarke Robert, *The Tobacco Kingdom* (Gloucester, MA, 1965 [reprint, originally 1938]), p. 17.

[7] Lewis Cecil Gray, *History of Agriculture in the Southern United States to 1860*, 2 vols. (Gloucester, MA, 1958 [reprint, originally 1933]); Vol. 1, pp. 117–118; and Allan Kulikoff, *Tobacco and Slaves, The Development of Southern Cultures in the Chesapeake, 1680–1800* (Chapel Hill and London, 1986), pp. 92–97, 141–48. See also Richard R. Beeman, *The Evolution of the Southern Backcountry. A Case Study of Lunenburg County, Virginia 1746–1832* (Philadelphia, 1984); and Philip D. Morgan and Michael L. Nichols, "Slaves in Piedmont Virginia, 1720–1790," *William and Mary Quarterly*, 46 (1989): 211–51.

records of the Will Books of the County Courts of the selected counties.[8] The inventory data set began as a listing of inventories which I compiled in order to identify estates of the planter elite of Virginia in twelve counties in the period of 1820–1860 (for a larger study of the slave economy of Virginia). For the current project, I extended the list of inventories for five counties back to before the American Revolution. Unfortunately, the relevant records for Henrico County in the 1760s and 1770s were destroyed, apparently by fire during the War of 1812. I collected inventories from nearby Surry County to fill the resulting gap in the data for the eighteenth century.[9] Summary data were collected for each inventory, including the decedent's name, total inventory value, number and value of slaves, cash, other financial assets (bonds, etc.), real estate (mentioned in fewer than five percent of estates), and dates of appraisal and/or recording. Occasionally I also gathered information from wills and other documents, for example to identify the sex of a decedent or the date of an inventory.[10]

To put the Virginia wealth data into perspective, it helps to note that they are drawn from the same sort of sources that Alice Hanson Jones used for her oft-cited research on *American Colonial Wealth*. Using a sampling approach, Jones assembled a sample of 919 estate inventories to represent wealth-holdings in the thirteen colonies in the year 1774. Jones went to heroic lengths to extend her estate data in two ways, adding evidence on the personal characteristics of decedents (e.g., age and occupation), and on real estate holdings. My more modest data do not cover decedents' real estate, and sex is the only personal characteristic enumerated. Jones offers a much fuller picture of wealth and wealth-holders than I can compose. That said, the Virginia data do have two advantages over Jones's data; first they offer a view of wealth over time, and second, with their much larger number of observations sampling, error is less of a concern.[11]

---

[8] Inventories were recorded along with a jumble of wills, estate accounts, and other documents, so it would not be surprising if some were missed. However, each microfilm Will Book was scanned at least twice.

[9] We collected Surry County inventories for the period 1755–1790. As a result of the gap in the Henrico data, I have two different consistent series on Virginia wealthholdings: one for the period 1780–1860, covering the counties of Henrico, Richmond, Prince Edward, Albemarle, and Bedford; the second for the period 1755–1790, with Surry County in place of Henrico.

[10] It is worth noting that over 2% of the decedents in the data set had multiple estates, with inventories recorded in different parts of the Will Books of one county (even if the estates were located in different counties). Multiple estates were located by identifying duplicated names in a given county's Will Books after the first pass of locating and recording inventories. Jones's Virginia data do not include any decedents with multiple estates. Her sampling approach to gathering inventories would have been unlikely to identify decedents with multiple estates because such estates were rarely listed together in the Will Books (see *Colonial Wealth, Documents and Methods*, pp. 1813–38, 1844–45, 1852, on Jones's sampling methods).

[11] On this point see Lee Soltow, *Distribution of Wealth and Income in the United States in 1798* (Pittsburgh, 1989), p. 315, n.37, who expresses concern about the possible magnitude of sampling error in Jones's estimates.

II

There are a number of issues that can be important for understanding what probate records can tell us about the wealth of the living. Of primary concern is the fact that probated estates are not representative of the estates of the population of living wealth-holders. There is a probate bias: probated decedents tended to be wealthier than non-probated decedents, if only because those with negligible wealth-holdings were not subject to probate. Also, there is an age bias: life-cycle effects made decedents relatively older and relatively richer than the living. On both counts, a representative cross section of estate inventories tends to overstate wealth levels and to understate inequality at a given time. Studies with a cross-sectional focus seek to correct these selection biases, using demographic evidence in combination with assumptions on the characteristics of potential wealth-holders whose estates were not recorded in the probate records.[12] In this paper I focus on patterns over time in Virginia wealth-holdings, and I do not attempt to correct for the age bias or the probate bias inherent in the data. It seems reasonable to abstract from the issue of age bias, and to expect pronounced trends in wealth-holdings over time to show up among the wealth-holdings of decedents, notwithstanding the fact that they were older than average. The issue of probate bias requires more attention, however.

Table 1 presents summary evidence on the extent to which decedents' estates were probated in the five Virginia counties.[13] I use the number of White males aged 45 or older as a proxy for the pool of potential decedents at census benchmarks. To correct for yearly fluctuations and potential dating errors, I look at the average number of probated decedents in the five years centered on the census year. The "inventory rate" for each county expresses the number of inventories as a proportion of the population of White males age 45 or more. Abstracting from deaths of younger men, we can think of the

---

[12] For a useful summary statement of the issues see Clayne Pope, "Inequality in the Nineteenth Century," in S. L. Engerman and R. E. Gallman (eds.), *The Cambridge Economic History of the United States*, 3 vols., 2: *The Long Nineteenth Century* (Cambridge, 2000), p. 133, as well as Jones, *Wealth of a Nation to Be*, pp. 44, 347–51. As Jones's work on colonial wealth demonstrates, given the relevant demographic data it is a simple matter to re-weight estate data to correct for age bias. More problematic is correcting for probate bias, which requires answers to a number of questions. For example: What fraction of decedent estates was probated?. What was the average level of wealth of non-probated estates? To estimate the level of Southern wealth in 1774, Jones estimated that the estates of 68% of decedent wealth-holders were probated, and she assumed that non-probate estates averaged one-quarter the wealth of probated estates. The implication is that the average level of decedent wealth was 76% of the average level of probated decedent wealth (given age). To estimate the size distribution of wealth for the living requires further assumptions, as Jones describes.

[13] Table 1 presents evidence for the five counties used to describe the period after the Revolution. Surry County replaces Henrico to describe the period 1755–1790. Looking circa 1790, I estimate Surry County had 136 "older white men" and 6.4 inventories on average per year, for an "inventory rate" of 4.7%, very close to that estimated for Richmond County. See Table 1 for definitions and sources.

TABLE 1. *The Extent of Probate among Likely Decedents*

	1790	1800	1810	1820	1830	1840	1850	1860
Albemarle								
Older white men	418	547	589	605	667	745	931	998
Inventories	6.0	8.8	11.2	17.6	20.8	17.8	18.8	17.0
Inventory rate	1.4%	1.6%	1.9%	2.9%	3.1%	2.4%	2.0%	1.7%
Bedford								
Older white men	466	611	599	680	700	755	1,000	1,096
Inventories	6.0	8.2	9.6	21.2	16.8	17.2	23.0	21.8
Inventory rate	1.3%	1.3%	1.6%	3.1%	2.4%	2.3%	2.3%	2.0%
Prince Edward								
Older white men	222	274	310	317	335	334	316	358
Inventories	6.0	9.0	11.4	12.8	6.8	12.2	9.2	10.3
Inventory rate	2.7%	3.3%	3.7%	4.0%	2.0%	3.7%	2.9%	2.9%
Henrico								
Older white men	342	392	540	639	655	899	1,491	2,486
Inventories	9.0	15.2	12.4	8.8	12.6	9.8	11.2	16.0
Inventory rate	2.6%	3.9%	2.3%	1.4%	1.9%	1.1%	0.8%	0.6%

Richmond

Older white men	165[a]	161[a]	158	139	163	183	191	231
Inventories	8.0	9.2	6.6	4.8	5.0[b]	7.0	11.0	10.5
Inventory rate	4.9%	5.7%	4.2%	3.5%	3.1%	3.8%	5.8%	4.5%

Notes: Older white men: the number of white men aged 45 or more. For 1800, 1810, 1820, this is the sum of relevant age-groupings in the published census volumes; for the other years it is estimated from numbers in related age categories. Inventories: the average annual number of estates (of men) inventoried by the County Court, including those with incomplete data (e.g., illegible inventories, and those not appraised or partially appraised) which are not used for wealth estimates. I use the 5-year average centered on the census year except for 1856–60, which is the 5-year average for 1860. Inventory Rate: inventories relative to the population of older white men.

[a] The 1790 and 1800 estimates of older white men in Richmond do not use 1800 census data, which appear to be in error. The census reports population for Richmond and Westmoreland Counties together in 1800, but a comparison with adjacent years indicates there was a substantial undercount.

[b] The inventory count for Richmond in 1830 is the average for the years 1827 to 1830 and 1833; the years 1831 and 1832 are missing due to a gap in the Will Books.

Source: Virginia Inventories data; see notes.

observed inventory rate as the product of a rate of death and a rate of probate for the decedents. In part, the table's value is to illustrate the challenging nature of probate data, for there are rather substantial variations in the observed inventory rates, both across counties and over time. Those variations reflect an unknown combination of variations in rates of mortality and probate.[14] But supposing that mortality variations show up randomly among the observed inventory rates, there are a couple of noteworthy patterns in the table.

Richmond County stands out with a relatively high inventory rate (see Table 1). Perhaps the county had relatively few propertyless or poor decedents whose estates were too small to warrant probate. Certainly it would not be surprising if propertyless men avoided this long-settled Tidewater county and sought opportunity in frontier areas.[15] On this reading, Richmond's average levels of probated wealth are less subject to probate bias than is the case in the other counties, and comparing probated wealth levels will tend to understate Richmond's relative wealth. This could be an important and troublesome effect to consider for the purposes of cross-sectional estimates of wealth, but it is less important for this study.[16] Changes in inventory rates

[14] Moreover, even if we observed them, differences in probate rates would be difficult to interpret. For example, probate rates would be inversely related to the proportion of decedents with very little wealth, and to transportation costs. Growing population density and transportation improvements both served to lower transportation costs in the nineteenth century, so the tendency for inventory rates to drift downward from 1820 to 1860 may indicate a growth in the proportion of decedents with too little wealth to warrant probate.

[15] The count of tithables gives one indication that the settlement process was complete in Richmond County well before mid century. Between 1724 and 1749 Richmond's tithable population grew just 0.7% per year (from 1,551 to 1,811), compared to 2.7% per year for the colony as a whole; Evarts B. Greene and Virginia D. Harrington, *American Population before the Federal Census of 1790* (Gloucester, MA, 1966 [reprint, originally 1932]), pp. 150–51. Comparisons of the various counties' white population counts in the 1790 Census and the 1755 list of tithables for Virginia also illustrate Richmond's stagnant population, in contrast to the other counties I examine. See Greene and Harrington, pp. 150–51, 154–55.

[16] It is difficult to be precise about the magnitude of the effects of differential probate bias, but with simplifying assumptions we can illustrate the logic. One extreme case arises when non-probated decedents have zero wealth; then true mean wealth (of decedents) equals probated wealth times the rate of probate. Assuming equal mortality rates across counties, we could correct for relative probate bias by multiplying counties' mean probated wealth by their inventory rates. The correction would not change much if, as Jones assumed, the non-probate mean was 25% of the probate mean. Random variation of mortality across counties would also change the correction factor, but not by much (e.g., for Richmond in 1790, if the probate rate was 100%, then one more wealth-holder death would raise the inventory rate from 4.85% to 5.45%, or by a factor of 1.12). For her estimates of colonial wealth Jones assumed a constant rate of probate within each region of the country (*Wealth of a Nation to Be*, p. 45). That may not be a problem; for example, the effects of differential probate rates across counties could cancel out in her random sample. More generally, in the face

over time do affect the interpretation of observed trends in probated wealth, but except for Henrico County, they are not a major consideration.

Henrico County stands out for the large decline in the inventory rate in the years from 1800 to 1860, starting at over 4% and falling to below one-sixth of that value (0.6%) by 1860. The decline is particularly noteworthy from 1830 to 1860, when the county's population growth accelerated with the expansion of the city of Richmond.[17] In the late antebellum period, Henrico's very low inventory rate stands out in sharp contrast to those of the other counties. There is no reason to suppose that mortality dropped in this period; rather, it seems clear that a shrinking fraction of decedents entered probate. That in turn was presumably because a shrinking proportion of decedents had enough personal property to require the probate process.[18] The magnitude of the change in Henrico's probate rate was substantial enough to affect the interpretation of trends in probated wealth there. However, Henrico was probably small enough that long-term trends in eastern Virginia as a whole are not substantially affected (see below).

III

Jones's well-known work offers one of the few empirical perspectives available for exploring the reliability of the Virginia inventory data. Jones's sample includes 78 estates from Virginia, drawn from three "clusters" (groups) of counties in the years 1773–1775. None of Jones's estates is from the counties I work with. For comparison, I focus on the estates in my data set from the years 1772–1775 (using the four-year period to increase sample size and reduce sampling error). A summary view of the data is presented in Table 2. The point that jumps out is that Jones's decedents were distinctly wealthier than those from my data set, with average personal estate 42% greater than in my data (386 Virginia pounds as compared to 271). That pattern is evident across all three categories of personal wealth that I measure: capital, slaves, and financial assets (see Table 2). However, the greater average wealth in Jones's sample is in large measure a reflection of a greater extent of slaveholding: 67% of Jones' decedents held slaves, compared to

---

of variation of probate rates across counties, the number of counties sampled would be an important consideration in sample design for cross-sectional wealth estimates.

[17] The free population of the city of Richmond grew 3.3% per year in the period 1830 to 1860, compared to 2.5% per year in the county of Henrico as a whole, and 1.3% per year in the state as a whole (see Table 1 for sources of population data).

[18] Apparently the rapid urbanization of Henrico saw a swelling of the free propertyless working class, an intriguing development in one of the slave South's largest cities. It is worth noting that there was no shift in the age structure of Henrico's free population to help explain the decline in Henrico's measured inventory rate (e.g., a shift toward younger ages would have resulted in fewer deaths and a lower inventory rate).

TABLE 2. *Two Views of Decedent Wealth-Holdings in Virginia circa 1774*

	Personal Estate	Capital	Slaves	Financial Assets	Number of Slaves (Average)	Estates w/Slaves	Number of Estates
		(Virginia Pounds)					
Jones Sample	386.4	126.9	252.3	7.2	5.6	67%	72
Irwin Sample	271.3	95.8	174.7	0.8	4.4	53%	150
Jones sample							
slaveholders	552.6	163.5	378.3	10.8	8.2	100%	48
nonslaveholders	53.4	53.4	0	0	0	0%	24
Irwin sample							
slaveholders	473.7	141.3	331.7	0.6	8.4	100%	79
nonslaveholders	46.0	45.1	0	0.9	0	0%	71

Notes: Jones's Virginia data include 78 estates but 6 of the decedents were females; I consider male decedents only. "Slaves" includes the very few indentured servants in the inventories (the Jones sample has 1 estate with 4 servants; the Irwin sample 5 estates with 6 servants).

Source: Alice Hanson Jones, "American Colonial Wealth Estimates, 1774" [Computer file], ICPSR Study 7389 (Ann Arbor, 2001), corrected for discrepancies with *American Colonial Wealth, Documents and Methods* (New York, 1978), pp. 1295–1403. The Irwin sample is comprised of the estates from the years 1772 to 1775 in the Virginia Inventory data set.

53% in my data.[19] Controlling for slaveholding status, average levels of wealth are much closer in the two sets of estates. Jones's slaveholders had 17% greater average wealth than those in my sample; her nonslaveholders had 16% greater wealth than mine. Jones's decedents still appear somewhat wealthier, but the differences are small relative to the underlying variation in the data.[20]

If our goal was to document cross-sectional patterns of wealthholding in Virginia on the eve of the American Revolution, then it would be important to explain the differing extents of slaveholding in the two sets of estates. However my interest is in changes over time, so I prefer to sidestep the issue by noting that the two data sets represent different populations.[21] Jones's Virginia estates were collected as part of a sampling strategy designed to produce a representative view of wealthholdings in the South as whole, and not Virginia *per se*. Even if Jones's Virginia estates over-represent Virginia slaveholders, her data could be representative of the South as a whole because there could be offsetting biases in her samples from southern counties outside of Virginia.[22]

A second empirical perspective on the reliability of the Virginia inventory data is afforded by published data from the 1860 census, which includes reports of personal wealthholdings and slaveholdings at the county level. Table 3 reports summary comparative evidence from the inventory data and the 1860 census for the five counties represented in the estate sample.[23] I

[19] Calculations use the data from the ICPSR computer file (see notes to Table 2), with corrections of observed discrepancies between the computer file and the published text of the inventories (accepting the latter as valid). For example, the computer file is missing one of the slaves of the estate of Samuel Johnson of Fairfax County that is listed in Jones' text (1978, p. 1383).

[20] For example, pooling Jones's inventories with mine from the same period, an ordinary least squares regression that controls for slaveholding status yields a point estimate that Jones's decedents had 14.2% more personal wealth than those in my sample, with an estimated standard error of 11.5%.

[21] I suspect that Jones's sample over-represents slaveholders in her sampled counties. In Jones's sample of county cluster 81, 79% (19 of 24) of male decedents held slaves; in county cluster 83, 69% (20 of 29) of male decedents did. Those rates of slave ownership are simply much higher than I found in similarly located counties that also were similar in terms of the proportion of population slave and the average number of slaves per estate.

[22] See Jones, *American Colonial Wealth*, p. 1859, on this point. Jones notes that her "sample design" is not expected to yield estimates representative of the "wealth of the particular colony" in which the sampled counties lay, and that across the southern colonies the "sampled counties complement each other." For example, a lack of "older Virginia coastal counties" is compensated for by the presence of "older coastal counties in Maryland and in South Carolina."

[23] I use the average over the entire decade in order to get large enough sample sizes to look at for each county individually. I express census values relative to an estimate of the number of free families, calculated from the reported free population using an assumption on free family size (see table). In my discussion I ignore possible problems with the census data on wealth; on such problems, see Richard H. Steckel and Carolyn M. Moehling, "Rising Inequality:

TABLE 3. *1860 Census and Probates*

	Personal Property		Slaveholdings		Slaveholding Size	
	Probates (per Estate)	Census (per Family)	Probates (per Estate)	Census (per Family)	Probates (per Estate)	Census (per Holding)
Prince Edward	$11,411	$8,369	84.1%	68.9%	16.3	12.6
Albemarle	$9,837	$6,762	66.0%	54.8%	18.1	10.7
Bedford	$5,373	$4,299	54.1%	40.4%	12.1	9.0
Henrico	$6,876	$3,786	57.7%	30.0%	12.3	8.6
Richmond	$3,102	$2,312	30.6%	31.4%	13.6	9.5

Notes: To get reasonable sample sizes for the individual counties, the probate values are averages for the period 1851–1860. The census reports total free population, I assume an average of 5.33 free persons per family.

Sources: Virginia Inventory data; and calculations from published census data: U.S. Bureau of the Census, *Population of the United States in 1860* (Washington, 1864), for personal property and population; *Agriculture of the United States in 1860* (Washington, 1864), for slaves and slaveholdings.

compare the two sources using three indicators: average level of personal property, rates of slaveholdings, and average size of slaveholdings. Before delving into the details of the data, it is worth noting that the expected bias in the probate data is evident with each of the three indicators. With only one exception, in each of the counties the levels of personal wealth, rates of slaveholding, and slaveholding sizes were greater for the sample decedents than for all free families. The only exception to the general pattern is Richmond County, where the estimated rate of slaveholding from the census is a shade above the rate among the probated decedents.

Although there are many possible ways to read the data, for current purposes the key point is that with the exception of Henrico County, the census data and the inventory data offer very similar pictures of comparative wealth across the counties. Leaving aside Henrico, both sources indicate the same ranking of personal property levels: Prince Edward levels of personal wealth were greatest, with Albemarle a close second; at substantially lower levels of wealth came Bedford and then Richmond County.[24] For Henrico, the probate data overstate the county's relative standing: it had the second lowest level of census wealth per family but the third lowest level of probated wealth. A similar pattern is evident in the data on rates of slaveholding: Henrico aside, the ranking of counties is the same in both sources. Slaveholding was most prevalent in Prince Edward, followed by Albemarle then Bedford then Richmond. According to the census data, Henrico had the fewest slaveholders relative to free population (30 slaveholdings per 100 free families), but in the estate data Henrico had the third highest rate of slaveholding (58% of estates). Finally, the two sources suggest different rankings of counties in terms of average slaveholding size, but the differences strike me as small. Both sources suggest the same grouping: Prince Edward and Albemarle had larger average slaveholding size, Bedford, Henrico and Richmond had smaller average holdings.

The distinctive position of Henrico County in Table 3 is not surprising if we recall that a relatively small proportion of Henrico's decedents were covered by the probate process in 1860 (refer to Table 1). It seems likely that as the free urban population of the city of Richmond swelled, average wealth levels fell, and that decedents with enough property to warrant processing by the probate systems became increasingly unrepresentative of the free population. On this reading, the relatively low "inventory rate" of Henrico serves to explain why the county appears relatively more wealthy in the probate data than in the census data. In my view, it is clear that Henrico

Trends in the Distribution of Wealth in Industrializing New England," *Journal of Economic History*, 61 (2001): 163–64 and references there.

[24] It may be worth noting that across these four counties the ratio of census wealth to probated wealth fell in a fairly narrow range, from 69% (Albemarle) to 80% (Bedford). That is one way of gauging the consistency of the two sources.

was distinctive because it had a substantial poor urban population whose existence is reflected in the census data but not in the probate data.[25] Subject to that caveat, the comparison of census and probate evidence for 1860 does provide some assurance that the Virginia inventory data set captures key patterns of wealthholding in the late antebellum period.[26]

IV

The Virginia Inventories data offer two overlapping views of wealth accumulation in Virginia. The larger part of the data set covers the period from the end of the Revolutionary War until the eve of the Civil War (1783–1860) and is comprised of the surviving inventories from five counties, Albemarle, Bedford, Prince Edward, Richmond, and Henrico. Because the Will Books for Henrico in the decades before 1783 do not survive, Surry County replaces Henrico in the smaller part of the data set, covering the period of 1755–1792. I focus on two dimensions of the evolution of Virginia wealth-holdings for each of the periods under consideration. I start with an overview of wealth accumulation over time to identify patterns in the levels and composition of personal wealth. Then I narrow my focus to the evolution of "capital" holdings over time, with an eye toward implications for the course of economic growth. Capital (personal wealth exclusive of slaves and financial assets) embraces the wide range of household and farm items that people owned in the Old Dominion. I treat the broad patterns of change in capital per estate as an indicator of the broad trends in the capacity of the Virginia economy to provide for the material welfare of its people. Implicitly, I treat the wide array of physical non-human property in the estates as non-human capital used to produce goods and services, whether for market or household use.[27]

The period from 1755 to 1792 is considered first. Table 4 presents an overview of the Virginia inventory data for these years, using five-year averages in order to reduce random variability and reveal key patterns. Two of the half-decades stand out. First, before the American Revolution, the early

[25] Henrico had a relatively large free black population, but that is not why Henrico's census wealth values are so much lower than the probated values. If we assume zero wealth for free blacks and calculate average wealth per free white family, it remains that Henrico has the fourth highest census wealth but third highest probated wealth. Presumably Henrico's urban white population included relatively more families with little or no wealth.

[26] Similar patterns are evident when comparing evidence on slaveholding and slaves in the three counties. In both the census and the probate data, Bedford had fewer slaves and slaveholdings; and Prince Edward appears wealthier than Albemarle in the census data but not in the probates.

[27] Looking at capital holdings offers a broader than usual perspective because conventional measures of economic growth omit most household production. The capital holdings in the Virginia inventories include the wide array of household equipment, furnishings, supplies, and other tangible items that would have been direct inputs into household production.

TABLE 4. *Personal Wealth-Holdings in the Eighteenth Century*

Period	1755–59	1760–64	1765–69	1770–74	1783–87	1788–92
			(Average values, Virginia £)			
Personal estate	248	323	250	254	274	507
Capital	103	98	91	91	93	151
Financial assets	10	9	4	1	4	22
Slaves	136	216	156	162	177	334
Number of estates	132	173	132	158	175	145
with slaves	53%	59%	57%	53%	57%	58%
slaveholding size	8.8	9.2	7.7	7.5	6.5	12.9
slave price	29	40	36	41	48	45

Notes: The years 1775–1782 are excluded in order to avoid dealing with currency depreciation over the course of the American Revolution (e.g., in 1781 the average appraised price per slave was over £13,000 Va., and the average price per slave in individual estates ranged from £49 to £60,000, reflecting inconsistencies across appraisers).

Source: Virginia Inventory data (Albemarle, Bedford, Prince Edward, Richmond, and Surry Counties).

1760s had a very high level of average wealth, almost 325 pounds per estate, compared to about 250 pounds in each of the other colonial half decades. That distinctively high average wealth was almost entirely due to a relatively high level of slave wealth in the period. That in turn reflected relatively high levels of the three factors determining average slave wealth: the proportion of estates that held slaves, the average number of slaves per holding, and the average price of slaves (see Table 4). I expect that the "spike" in slave wealth in the early 1760s will prove to be a reflection of random sampling error, and not a reflection of some distinctive historical episode, but more research is required to pin down the point.[28]

The last set of years in Table 4 (1788–92) also stands out for relatively high levels of wealth, and sampling error is probably not at work. The average level of wealth per estate in this half-decade was roughly twice as large as in the earlier half-decades shown in Table 4. This higher level of wealth was not a temporary peak, as wealth levels stayed up in the years following (see Table 6). Greater slave wealth was part of the story, as average slaveholding size and average slave price were near their peak values for the period shown in the table. However, capital holdings and financial assets also were much greater than in the earlier years. It is clear that the value of personal estates increased sharply in the period after the end of the Revolution.

More research is required to understand the late eighteenth century increase in wealth, but at this stage we can rule out one possible answer – inflation. Available estimates indicate that the average level of prices in the United States as a whole in the years 1788–92 was perhaps 10% above the level in 1770–74.[29] Moreover, the average price of slaves in the estate data was about 10% greater in the later than in the earlier years (see Table 4). Given these two points of evidence, inflation can account for only a small part of the almost doubling of average wealth per estate from 1770–74 to 1782–92. Decedent wealthholders in the early 1790s were distinctly richer than their counterparts in the late colonial period. That result is somewhat surprising in light of prevailing perspectives on U.S. economic growth in the late eighteenth century.

For a long time now, the period of the American Revolution and the Confederation has been seen as one of economic difficulties for the United

[28] Table 4's slave price series is remarkably consistent with data for slaves newly arrived in South Carolina shown in Appendix Table 2 of the Eltis and Richardson essay (Chapter 6) in this volume, though not with the series developed by Mancall, Rosenbloom, and Weiss (both nominal and deflated slave prices) from South Carolina probate records (Peter C. Mancall, Joshua L. Rosenbloom, and Thomas Weiss, "Slave Prices and the South Carolina Economy, 1722–1809," *Journal of Economic History*, 61 [2001]: Table 1).

[29] Based on either the Warren and Pearson wholesale price index (U.S. Bureau of the Census, *Historical Statistics of the U.S.*, Series E52) or the cost of living index of Paul A. David and Peter Solar, "A Bicentenary Contribution to the History of the Cost of Living in America," *Research in Economic History*, 2 (1977): 16–17.

States as a whole, and especially for the South. The consensus view is that per capita output fell sharply during the Revolution and did not recover until sometime in the 1790s.[30] Whether implicitly or explicitly, current views rely on a simple export-led growth model, with a decline in per capita exports pulling down per capita output.[31] Given the relatively larger role of exports in the Southern economy, the implication is that the decline in Southern per capita output would have been particularly pronounced.[32] However, the evidence from the Virginia inventory data indicates that any decline in Southern per capita output in the War and its aftermath was not of a magnitude and duration to affect measured patterns of wealth accumulation.

Table 5 zeroes in on the evidence on capital holdings in eighteenth century Virginia. In addition to the simple arithmetic average of capital holdings in each period, I also present the geometric average and the median capital holding. Looking at all three provides some check on the reliability of the data; any patterns over time will be more compelling if evident in all three measures. On a practical level, the occasional appearance of extremely wealthy decedents has much less effect on the median and the geometric average than

[30] Stanley L. Engerman and Robert E. Gallman describe the consensus view with some skepticism, pointing out theoretical and empirical weaknesses ("U.S. Economic Growth, 1783–1860," *Research in Economic History*, 8 [1983]: 17–19). Recent examples that reflect the consensus view include Robert E. Gallman, "Economic Growth and Structural Change in the Long Nineteenth Century," in Engerman and Gallman (eds.), *The Cambridge Economic History*, 2: 9, 21–22; Peter C. Mancall and Thomas Weiss, "Was Economic Growth Likely in Colonial British North America?" *Journal of Economic History*, 59 (1999): 26–27; Russell R. Menard, "Economic and Social Development of the South," in S. L. Engerman and R. E. Gallman (eds.), *Cambridge Economic History of the United States*, 3 vols., 1: *The Colonial Era* (Cambridge, 1996), pp. 293–94; and John J. McCusker and Russell R. Menard, *The Economy of British America, 1607–1789, with supplementary bibliography* (Chapel Hill, 1991), pp. 369–76. Claudia D. Goldin and Frank D. Lewis also contributed to the consensus view when they indicated that U.S. per capita income declined somewhat from 1774 to 1793 ("The Role of Exports in American Economic Growth during the Napoleonic Wars, 1793–1807," *Explorations in Economic History*, 17 [1980]: 22–23). However, the bulk of their analysis demonstrates that exports played only a minor role in late eighteenth century U.S. economic growth, which is inconsistent with the consensus view.

[31] McCusker and Menard, *The Economy of British America*, p. 376. The consensus relies heavily on James F. Shepherd and Gary M. Walton's finding that U.S. per capita exports were lower in the early 1790s than before the Revolution ("Economic Change after the American Revolution: Pre- and Post-War Comparisons of Maritime Shipping and Trade," *Explorations in Economic History*, 13 [1976]: 397–422). See also Engerman and Gallman, "U.S. Economic Growth," pp. 19–20; implicit criticism of export growth models is in their comment that because exports accounted for less than "ten percent of national income" they were not large enough "to dominate income movements." Goldin and Lewis, "The Role of Exports," p. 18 make a similar point.

[32] Menard, "Economic and Social Development of the South," pp. 293–94; McCusker and Menard, *Economy of British America*, p. 375; Stanley L. Engerman, "A Reconsideration of Southern Economic Growth, 1770–1860," *Agricultural History*, 49 (1975): 348–350.

TABLE 5. *Capital Holdings in the Eighteenth Century*

Years	Geometric Average	Median	Arithmetic Average	Number
	(Appraised values, Virginia £)			
	County set 1			
1755/59	46	51	103	132
1760/64	59	59	98	173
1765/69	56	67	91	132
1770/74	57	61	91	158
1783/87	62	65	93	175
1788/92	84	93	151	145
	County set 2			
1783/87	72	71	137	178
1788/92	86	93	156	159
1793/97	97	102	165	204
1798/02	131	150	255	228

Note: County set 1 is comprised of Albemarle, Bedford, Prince Edward, Richmond, and Surry Counties. In County set 2 Henrico replaces Surry.
Source: Virginia Inventory data.

on the simple arithmetic average.[33] The table uses two different but overlapping sets of wealth data. The first set is the same as in Table 4 and runs from 1755 to 1792. The second set has Henrico County in place of Surry in order to look further past the Revolutionary War; these data cover the period 1783 to 1812.

All three measures of the level of capital holdings provide a similar picture, with two key features. First there is no sign of economic decline across the watershed of the American Revolution, as levels of capital per estate in the 1780s were at (1783–87) or above (1788–92) colonial levels. Second, after the Revolution capital holdings increased fairly steadily from half-decade to half-decade, with only minor variations in the timing and magnitude of the growth depending on which measure is used. At this stage, the Virginia inventory data certainly remind us of the need for more research to document the record of economic growth. But they also point to the possibility that a mercantilist emphasis on trade and exports has misled scholars about the economic consequences of the American Revolution and the adjustments to independence. Perhaps there was a downturn along the lines of a business cycle fluctuation, rather than a persistent shock to economy's productive

[33] More formally, I expect the geometric average to be a more accurate estimator of mean wealth when wealth is distributed log-normally; certainly this was the case in various simple Monte Carlo simulations that I have tried. Wealth distributions often are approximately log-normal; see Soltow, *Distribution of Wealth and Income*, pp. 22–24, 122–23.

capacity. If so, the results in Table 5 are consistent with Engerman's view that "the southern economy had recovered by the early 1780s" and not with accounts that place the nadir of U.S. economic fortunes in the 1790s.[34] It may be that closer attention to fluctuations in the general level of prices will change the picture provided by the Virginia inventories. However at this stage it seems more likely that prevailing views exaggerate the impact of the Revolutionary War and its aftermath on the southern economy.[35]

For the second period – between the Revolutionary War and the Civil War – the patterns of wealth accumulation in Virginia revealed here do not offer any particular challenges to current knowledge. Fogel and Engerman showed that the antebellum Southern economy was neither poor nor slow-growing, except perhaps in comparison to the Northeastern region in the half-century before the Civil War. Consistent with that result, Virginia wealth-holdings grew substantially over the period as a whole, even as the State's relative importance in the Southern and national economy shrank over the period. The first panel of Table 6 presents a summary overview of personal wealth-holdings in the Virginia inventory data in the decades between the Revolutionary War and the Civil War. By the end of the period, wealth levels had risen substantially – by more than a factor of four. That reflected growth in the real value of wealth, not inflation, for the general level of prices was about the same at the beginning and end of the period.[36]

Throughout the period (as in the later Colonial period), slaveholdings constituted the largest category of wealth, hovering around some two-thirds of the personal wealth appraised. The growth of slave wealth reflected a modest increase in the average number of slaves and a sharp increase in the appraised price of slaves. Those increases were partly counteracted by a small decrease in the extent of slave holding among decedents (62% at the

---

[34] Stanley L. Engerman, "A Reconsideration of Southern Economic Growth," p. 349. The results also provide some support for Merrill Jensen's sanguine view of post-Revolutionary America (*The New Nation, A History of the United States During the Confederation, 1781–1789* [New York, 1950], see e.g. pp. 177–78, 191–92, 246–47, 422–23).

[35] If the trade data are reasonably accurate, then perhaps prevailing views overstate the role of exports in Southern economic performance. However it might be worthwhile to explore whether pre- and post-Revolutionary trade statistics are comparable.

[36] Three different general price level measures are available for the period; each indicates that prices were about the same in the late 1850s as in the late 1780s. Robert A. Margo, *Wages and Labor Markets in the United States, 1820–1860* (Chicago, 2000), Table 3A.8, for the years 1821–1860; David and Solar, "A Bicentenary Contribution," p. 16; and *Historical Statistics*, Series E52 (the Warren and Pearson wholesale price index). See also Gallman, "Economic Growth and Structural Change," p. 7, and "American Economic Growth Before the Civil War: The Testimony of the Capital Stock Estimates" in R. E. Gallman and J. J. Wallis (eds.), *American Economic Growth and Standards of Living Before the Civil War* (Chicago, 1992), p. 88.

TABLE 6. *Personal Wealth-Holdings in the Long Antebellum Period*

Years	1783–90	1791–00	1801–10	1811–20	1821–30	1831–40	1841–50	1851–60
	(Average appraised value, U.S. $)							
Total estate	1,663	1,822	2,589	3,331	2,912	4,312	4,036	7,393
Capital	446	628	843	846	765	963	877	1,306
Financial assets	31	113	69	180	179	429	596	1,370
Slaves (value)	1,186	1,080	1,677	2,306	1,968	2,921	2,562	4,716
Number	265	410	486	652	626	545	651	706
with slaves	62%	65%	63%	65%	70%	68%	60%	58%
slaveholding size	11.5	11.6	13.2	12.8	13	12.8	14.1	14.8
avg. slave price	166	143	201	278	216	336	301	551
Deflated value of	(U.S. $ of 1860)							
Total estate	1,759	1,554	2,001	2,319	3,093	4,155	5,502	7,744
Capital	467	536	651	583	808	942	1,205	1,358
Financial assets	33	97	52	130	200	395	809	1,440
Slaves	1,259	921	1,298	1,605	2,084	2,817	3,488	4,946
Avg. slave price	176	122	156	194	229	324	410	578
Implied price level	94.5	117	129	144	94.2	104	73.4	95.5

Notes: Before 1810 estates were often appraised in Virginia pounds rather than U.S. dollars; these were converted at the rate of $10 per £3, the rate consistently used in the wide variety of estates which included values denominated in both currencies. Deflated values: calculated using Margo's price deflator for the South Atlantic region, which covers the years 1821–1860; for the years 1783–1821 I extrapolated on Margo's series using the Warren and Pearson wholesale price index. The "implied price level" value is the ratio of the average appraised value to the average deflated value in each period.

Sources: Virginia Inventory data (Albemarle, Bedford, Henrico, Prince Edward, Richmond Counties). Margo, *Wages and Labor Markets*, Table 3A.8, for the years 1821–1860; U.S. Bureau of the Census, *Historical Statistics*, Series E52.

start, 58% at the end of the period).[37] The value of financial assets rose the most dramatically across the period, increasing by a factor of 40 from the 1780s to the 1850s. At the start of the period, paper wealth was a distinctly minor category, but by the end it had eclipsed capital holdings in value. In part, that reflected a spread in the rate of ownership of financial assets. Only 6% of estates had paper wealth in the 1780s, some 11 to 13% did in the five decades following. Then the incidence of financial assets increased sharply, to about 25% in the 1840s and 33% in the 1850s. Of course, the growth of the average value of financial holdings was even more pronounced, rising from about $500 in the 1780s to over $4000 in the 1850s.[38]

From decade to decade, the average level of personal wealth generally increased. The 1820s and 1840s stand out as exceptions because, in each, average wealth was less than in the decade before. However those exceptions reflect surges in the general level of prices in the 1810s and 1830s. Deflating appraised values by available price indexes yields a simpler pattern of increasing average wealth over time. The final row of Table 6 shows average wealth expressed in terms of the dollars of the year 1860. Using the deflated values, every decade except the 1790s had greater average wealth than the decade before. The dip in (deflated) wealth in the 1790s reflected a sharp drop in the relative price of slaves which more than offset increases in the deflated values of capital and financial assets. In sum, we can discern a general pattern of increasing personal wealth among Virginia decedents in the eight decades before the Civil War, but details of timing and magnitude vary depending on the treatment of price-level changes.

The general pattern of growing personal wealth reflected diversity in the movements of the different components of wealth, a diversity that belies easy generalizations. The decades of the 1830s and 1850s stand out as all three components of wealth (capital, financial assets, and slaves) hit historically high levels. We could add the decade of the 1800s to the list except that there was a decline in the smallest component, financial assets. The decades of the

---

[37] Note that the rate of slave holding among decedents reached relatively high levels in the 1820s and 1830s before dropping down to relatively low levels in the 1840s and 1850s (see Table 6).

[38] The incidence and value of financial assets is a feature of wealth-holdings that is rather difficult to determine with accuracy. First, many inventories of bonds etc. were made and recorded separately from inventories of physical property, requiring the researcher to find and match the holdings. Second, based on my experience with the Will Books, it seems clear that for many decedents bonds etc. were not inventoried, but were recorded in accounts related to the settlement of the estate. However in such cases it is often impossible to discern whether a bond payment received was to settle a debt that the decedent was due at the time of his death, or rather payment for a bond accepted as payment for sales of the decedent's physical property. Recalling also that financial assets are gross of debts owed by the decedent (such debts generally do not appear in the inventories), the category is probably the most unreliable in terms of levels of wealth. Nonetheless, the evidence of an increasing value and extent of financial assets is very strong (even if imprecise).

1820s and 1840s stand out because both capital and slave wealth fell pretty sharply from the levels of the decade prior. However, most of those peaks and valleys can be attributed to movements in the general level of prices, rather than movements in the real values of wealth. Looking at deflated measures of the various components of wealth eliminates almost all of the peaks and valleys evident in the nominal appraised values.

The second panel of Table 6 presents deflated values of the summary data on wealthholdings. Deflating by available price indexes, each of the components of wealth-holdings exhibits a general pattern of decade-to-decade increase. Capital values grew steadily from decade to decade with one exception, as deflated capital values in the 1810s averaged 10% less than in the 1800s. The value of financial assets also climbed steadily with one exceptional decade – the 1800s saw nominal and deflated capital values much lower than in the 1790s. Finally, the value of slave holdings also grew decade by decade with one exception; as previously noted, the 1790s featured a sharp drop in the relative price of slaves that pulled down the average value of slave holdings and of personal wealth more generally.

The Virginia inventory data may prove to be of particular interest for the perspective it offers us on the course of U.S. economic growth before the Civil War. As before, I use the evolution of decedents' capital holdings as a potential signal of economic growth and present three summary measures, the simple and geometric averages, and the median value (of capital holdings, see Table 7). Looking at the period of 1783–1860 as a whole, capital per estate clearly grew. Depending on the measure used, capital holdings per estate at the end of the period were some two to three times their value at the start. As previously noted, inflation was not a factor over the period as a whole, so it is clear that the real value of capital per estate grew. Using the arithmetic mean, capital holdings grew at an average annual rate of more then 1.5%; using the geometric mean, the rate was just under 1% per year. By either measure, capital per estate grew enough to suggest that economic growth was occurring in Virginia in the decades between the Revolutionary and Civil Wars.[39]

Looking at the appraised values of capital per estate from decade to decade, what stands out is the essentially flat profile of capital holdings over the first five decades of the nineteenth century. Each of the summary measures

---

[39] The growth is robust to corrections for the declining rate of probate in Henrico (see Table 1, above). For example, an extreme correction would scale down Henrico wealth in 1860 by a factor of three. That assumes probated estates represented just one-third of Henrico decedents, the other two-thirds being urban poor with zero capital. The implied capital per decedent in Henrico is $541, compared to $1237 in the other counties taken together. Supposing that Henrico County was typical of the 10% of Virginia's free population who were urban in 1860 population, we can average together those two values using a 10% weight for Henrico and a 90% weight for the rest; we get an average capital per decedent $1167 – still double the value of capital per estate circa 1790.

TABLE 7. *Capital Holdings in the Long Antebellum Period*

Years	1783–90	1791–00	1801–10	1811–20	1821–30	1831–40	1841–50	1851–60
Nominal values				(current U.S. $)				
Simple Average	446	628	843	846	765	963	877	1,306
Geometric Avg.	259	336	445	411	375	444	365	502
Median	253	381	492	478	408	478	413	536
Deflated values				(U.S. $ of 1860)				
Simple Average	467	536	651	583	808	942	1,205	1,358
Geometric Avg.	259	284	344	276	395	439	502	528
Median	260	325	373	311	421	472	560	560
Implied price level	94.5	117	129	144	94	104	73.4	95.5

Source: See Table 6.

of capital holdings shows the same basic pattern. Capital holdings increased over the first three decades (1780s, 1790s, 1800s), and then fluctuated irregularly in something of a rough plateau until the 1850s, when capital holdings climbed to peak values. However, a different picture emerges if we control for changes in the general level of prices. Looking at the deflated values of capital holdings, the period from nationhood to the Civil War featured two phases of growth.

The second panel of Table 7 presents the simple average, geometric average, and median values of deflated capital holdings. Each of these measures of the real value of capital holdings shows the same basic pattern. Capital values increased from decade to decade until they dropped sharply in the 1810s, after which they again grew from decade to decade. The apparent timing of nineteenth century growth differs depending on the measure used. The simple average of deflated capital holdings grew fairly steadily across the decades from 1810 to 1860; the geometric average and median values flattened out over the last two decades.

Taking the deflated values of capital per estate as indicators of the physical quantities of capital in different decades, the period as a whole saw growth of capital per estate at an average of 1.1% per year. Supposing that the growth of physical capital per estate can be used to proxy for economic growth, the suggestion is that Virginia experienced a fairly continuous economic growth in the eight decades before the Civil War, with the wartime decade of 1811–20 being the one major setback. Judged in the context of world economic history, such a growth experience is perhaps surprising. It is especially surprising because this was a period of substantial out-migration and presumably it was some of Virginia's most productive people, slave or free, who departed to help build the cotton kingdom.[40]

V

It would be premature to offer definitive conclusions from the rough patterns sketched out above, but it is worth noting some potential implications. Notwithstanding expected biases, the comparative evidence marshaled above gives some confidence that the Virginia inventory data offer a reliable perspective on wealth accumulation in one major Southern state. The results include both corroborations of and challenges to prevailing views of American economic history.

Physical capital holdings were roughly constant in the decades before the Revolution, which tends to corroborate Mancall and Weiss's conjectures that economic growth was not "likely" to have occurred during the colonial

---

[40] Whether slaves were sold South or migrated with their masters, we would expect the relatively more productive to have departed.

period.[41] However, capital holdings increased quite clearly across the Revolutionary War period, and then increased more sharply through the end of the eighteenth century. These results stand in opposition to the consensus view that the period from the Revolution until the early 1790s was one of economic decline and stagnation for the emerging nation, especially for the South.[42] If wartime inflation and a longer period of disrupted trade caused a downturn in economic activity, it was not severe enough to retard wealth accumulation in Virginia. The growth of physical capital holdings challenges the view that the transition from colony to nation was an economic calamity. However, it does make it easier to understand why slave imports rose to peak levels in the two decades before the 1808 ending of legal U.S. involvement in the Atlantic slave trade.[43]

The Virginia evidence may also offer some insight on one of the key puzzles of American economic history: how the South lost its initial economic advantage over the North. It is apparent that labor productivity and per capita income were greater in the Southern than Northern colonies well into the eighteenth century, given the timing and magnitude of transatlantic migrations to the two regions.[44] But a century later the pattern was clearly

---

[41] Mancall and Weiss, "Was Economic Growth Likely?" Their estimates of per capita GDP are "conjectural" in the sense introduced by Paul David, "The Growth of Real Product."

[42] The consensus posits a roughly U-shaped course of per capita income from circa 1774 to circa 1800, with various specific time-paths suggested. For example, Thomas Weiss suggested that "the economy suffered a setback during the Revolution and in the years immediately thereafter, but it was apparently quite mild." Weiss has per capita GDP about recovered by 1793, and rising 10% over the period 1774–1800 as a whole ("U.S. Labor Force Estimates and Economic Growth, 1800–1860," in Gallman and Wallis, *American Economic Growth*, p. 32). Mancall and Weiss have per capita GDP falling 1.5% from 1770 to 1800 ("Was Economic Growth Likely?," p. 26), but do not discuss its time path. McCusker and Menard argue for a "severe contraction" between 1774 and 1790, indicating that per capita GDP probably fell by more than 14% between those years (*Economy of British America*, pp. 374–75).

[43] Stanley L. Engerman, "Slavery and Its Consequences for the South in the Nineteenth Century," in Engerman and Gallman (eds.), *Cambridge Economic History*, I: 336–37; Robert W. Fogel and Stanley L. Engerman, *Time on the Cross*, 2 vols., (Boston, 1974), 1: 88.

[44] On this point, see Stanley L. Engerman, "Slavery and Emancipation in Comparative Perspective: A Look at Some Recent Debates," *Journal of Economic History*, 46 (1986): 319–321. For a useful summary view of regional net migration estimates, see Stanley L. Engerman and Kenneth L. Sokoloff, "Factor Endowments, Institutions, and Differential Paths of Growth Among New World Economies: A View from Economic Historians of the United States," in Stephen Haber (ed.), *How Latin America Fell Behind, Essays on the Economic Histories of Brazil and Mexico* (Stanford, 1997), p. 266. The period 1680–1730 saw net migration to the Southern colonies 3.5 times as large as that to the middle Atlantic colonies (by this time there was net out-migration from New England); in the period 1730–1780 the Southern net migration stream was over 2.8 times as large as the middle Atlantic's. Engerman and Sokoloff's summary view is based on the more detailed estimates of David W. Galenson, "The Settlement and Growth of the Colonies: Population, Labor, and Economic Development," in Engerman and Gallman (eds.), *Cambridge Economic History*, 1: 178, 180.

reversed: Engerman's oft-cited estimates of regional per capita incomes in 1840 and 1860 show that the South Atlantic (formerly the colonial South) had only one-half the per capita income of the Northeast (formerly the colonial North).[45]

Some explanation for the reversal of regional economic fortunes was available in the consensus view of economic calamity in the late eighteenth century. After all, if the disruption of export markets in the Revolutionary War and its aftermath was such an economic disaster for the South that it caused an "export-led" decline in per capita income for the nation as a whole, then it could also have caused the South to fall back of the North.[46] Potentially, the North/South income gap of 1840 could be traced directly back to the 1780s or 1790s. However, the Virginia wealth data suggest otherwise. The evidence of growing physical capital in decades following the Revolution suggests that the question of regional reversal is better posed as why the Northeast pulled ahead, rather than why the Southeast fell behind.[47] Looking over the longer period from the 1780s to the Civil War points further to that conclusion. The fairly steady pattern of growing physical capital holdings in Virginia suggests a continuing process of gradual economic growth in the nation's largest slave state until the Civil War. Again, the point that emerges is the likelihood that the emerging urban–industrial economy of the Northeast overtook a growing Southern economy.

For current purposes, the key point is the evidence of a long process of accumulation of physical capital in Virginia in the eight decades leading up to the Civil War. Although that evidence is not a basis for even conjectural estimates of U.S. economic growth before 1840, it is suggestive. The Virginia evidence fits into a picture of a national growth process that was broadly based, both geographically and sectorally (even if the industrializing Northeast experienced exceptionally rapid growth). It also is more consistent with a

---

[45] Stanley L. Engerman, "The Effects of Slavery on the Southern Economy," *Explorations in Entrepreneurial History*, 4 (1967): 87. Note that the overall North/South gap in 1840 was much smaller; the South's per capita income was two-thirds of the North's. Per capita income in the Midwest (the North Central census region) was just below the South Atlantic's, pulling down the northern average; per capita income in the West South Central region was the highest of any region, pulling up the southern average (the West South Central embracing Louisiana, Arkansas, Texas, and the Oklahoma territory). Engerman's estimates also appear in Robert W. Fogel and Stanley L. Engerman, "The Economics of Slavery," in Fogel and Engerman (eds.), *The Reinterpretation of American Economic History* (New York, 1971), p. 325; and Fogel and Engerman, *Time on the Cross*, 1: 248. They have been often reprinted and widely cited.

[46] McCusker and Menard, *Economy of British America*, p. 374 (on export-led decline). See above (notes 30, 31) for other references to the consensus view.

[47] Indeed, the inventory evidence serves to remind of a point that Engerman raised when teaching economic history: that characterizing the nineteenth century South as poor or stagnant is ahistorical, posing the historically extraordinary cases of England and the Northeastern United States as the norm.

gradual acceleration of economic growth coming out of the colonial period, than with some abrupt "take-off" into economic growth.[48]

The indications of a prolonged period of gradual economic growth in Virginia also have implications for competing perspectives on Southern economic growth in the late antebellum years. Engerman's estimates showed that the South (and each of its regions) was experiencing economic growth in the period 1840 to 1860. Given the longer period of growing physical capital among Virginia decedents, the observed per capita income growth looks more like the continuation of a longer term process, rather than some fortuitous export-led boom.[49] Recalling that the "Cotton Kingdom" rose in this period, as the slave economy expanded south and then west, a continuing process of economic growth in Virginia (largest of the slave states throughout the period) serves to reinforce Engerman's point that slavery was a flexible and adaptable economic institution that was not going to fade away.[50]

Finally, regardless of whether the particular patterns discerned here are borne out by subsequent research, there is one simple point by way of conclusion. The Virginia wealth data remind us that slavery in the United States was a very successful institution from the owners' point of view. That basic point is now perhaps obvious; if so, it is a testimony to the powerful effect of Stanley Engerman's scholarship on our knowledge of the economics of slavery and freedom.

---

[48] W. W. Rostow, *Stages of Economic Growth* (Cambridge, 1960).

[49] For an emphasis on the role of favorable export demand conditions in Southern growth in the late antebellum period see Gavin Wright, *Political Economy of the Cotton South* (New York, 1978), pp. 89–106; or Elizabeth Fox-Genovese and Eugene D. Genovese, *Fruits of Merchant Capital* (New York, 1983), pp. 42–49.

[50] See for example, "Slavery and Emancipation in Comparative Perspective," p. 329.

10

The Poor: Slaves in Early America

Philip D. Morgan

In most early American societies slaves *were* the poor. This claim would
not be true if the poor are defined as only those meriting charity, those unable to sustain themselves, "the impotent poor" or "dependent poor," to
use early modern terminology. But if living from hand to mouth, toiling
manually for survival, and leading a precarious and tenuous existence define
the able-bodied, the "labouring poor" (a term apparently coined by Daniel
Defoe in 1701), then slaves pre-eminently qualify. They worked without remuneration, legally owned no property, suffered often arbitrary and exces-
sive punishment, and lived at minimal subsistence levels. They were as poor
as it is possible to be, a truly impoverished people, suffering in Orlando
Patterson's phrase "social death." As Edmund Morgan noted of Virginia,
but by implication of much of early America, "Slavery, more effectively than
the Elizabethan Statute of Artificers, made the master responsible for the
workman and relieved society at large of most of its restive poor." Slaves
composed the majority of the able-bodied poor in a colony such as Virginia.
Virginia's metamorphosis into a slave society also transferred the responsi-
bility for the aged, the disabled, and the young – the dependent poor – from
the parish to the individual plantation owner. In a sense, then, slavery
"solved" the problem of the poor, whether dependent or able-bodied, by
privatizing it.[1]

Distinguishing between the dependent (deserving) and the able-bodied
(undeserving) is one useful historical way to think about the poor, but conceptions of poverty are not straightforward. Poverty, it might be thought, is
a state of near- or actual starvation, a denial of the basic requirements of
survival, but malnutrition is not always easily gauged, nor are all the poor

---

[1] Paul Slack, *The English Poor Law 1531–1782* (London, 1990), p. 12 (terminology); Orlando
Patterson, *Slavery and Social Death: A Comparative Study* (Cambridge, MA, 1982); Edmund
S. Morgan, *American Slavery, American Freedom: The Ordeal of Colonial Virginia* (New
York, 1975), pp. 340–341, 385–386.

necessarily malnourished. Poverty is low income or relative deprivation, it also might be thought, but again specifying precisely the relationship, distinguishing, for example, between feelings of inadequacy and conditions of deprivation, or drawing the line between absolute dispossession and some minimum standard of necessities is not easily achieved. For the most capacious definition of poverty, Amartya Sen simply describes the condition as "the lack of freedom to have or to do basic things that you value." It is, as he puts it, "the deprivation of elementary capabilities." By this broad definition, slaves supremely qualify as the poorest of the poor, denied the most basic of freedoms.[2]

Thus exploring the white poor in early America seems a somewhat misplaced activity, if the far more sizeable group of black poor is ignored. All discussions of poverty in early America should begin with slaves, not free whites. To be sure, the numbers of white poor in British America were not negligible, and in many places they increased over time. But, in relation to the Old World where poverty was far more extensive, white poverty in early America was small-scale. Peter Lindert and Jeffrey Williamson, for example, argue that *"in the aggregate* colonial inequality [by which is meant among free householders] was stable at low levels." It is all very well to say, as Gary Nash does, that "poverty [by which is meant largely white poverty] was a growing problem in the eighteenth century," but by how much had it grown by the end of the period? Was it growing everywhere? How extensive was it? How did it compare to Europe? Colonial America was undoubtedly "the best poor man's country," as Nash concedes, but it emphatically was *not* "a poor man's country nonetheless," as he also claims – unless slaves are encompassed. Alice Hanson Jones's conclusion that the standard of living in British America on the eve of the American Revolution was "probably the highest achieved for the great bulk of the population in any country up to that time" seems accurate. Or, as John McCusker and Russell Menard put it, "The colonies experienced little if any of the abject [white] poverty found in contemporary Europe or in the United States in the early nineteenth century." They continue, "Among the white colonists it seems that while the rich got richer the poor prospered as well, but at a slower rate." For white folk, colonial America was a middling person's country, where the majority enjoyed a modest competency, far more so than for their European counterparts.[3]

---

[2] Amartya Sen, *Poverty and Famines: An Essay on Entitlement and Deprivation* (Oxford, 1981), pp. 9–23; Sen, *Development As Freedom* (New York, 1999), pp. 20 (quote), 87–110; "How to Define Poverty? Let us Count the Ways," *New York Times*, May 26, 2001, A15, A17 (quote).

[3] Peter Lindert and Jeffrey Williamson, *American Inequality: A Macroeconomic History* (New York, 1980), pp. 10–11, and, for an update, see Peter H. Lindert, "Three Centuries of Inequality in Britain and America," in Anthony B. Atkinson and Francois Bourguignon, (eds.), *Handbook of Income Distribution* (Amsterdam, 2000), pp. 167–216; Gary B. Nash, "Poverty and Politics in Early American History," in Billy G. Smith (ed.), *Down and Out in Early*

What the New World had in abundance that the Old World lacked was not just land, which of course provided the basis for the modest competency of many whites, but rather a large group of people – slaves – who were exploited in unprecedented ways. Even Europe, with all the barbarities suffered by its poor, had no group as immiserated as slaves. It is thus misguided to exaggerate the dimensions of white poverty in early America, real though the distress suffered by a minority of whites undoubtedly was, when a much larger group of truly impoverished people should garner the most attention.

While slaves were the true poor in colonial America, they were far from being a homogeneous group and, in some respects, were materially better off than some white people. Their life expectancy, for example, was quite high for an early modern population, as was their stature. Some slaves had greater access to property, better levels of subsistence, and even more opportunities to earn cash than other slaves – and some poor whites. In some places and at certain times, many slaves experienced a material status superior to that enjoyed by poor folk. This essay will therefore attempt to accomplish two aims. First, it will compare the lot of slaves to that of other poor people. It will do so, first, by identifying various groups – from urban dwellers to Indians – that supplied many poor and then by contrasting their living conditions and quality of life with that of slaves. Second, it will try to disaggregate the monolith, slaves, and consider some key variations, particularly over time, across space, and by occupation among them. As J. H. Plumb noted many years ago in a comment still true today, "Yet in all this wonderful range of work on slavery, as exciting, as deeply original, as any going forward on any aspect of American social history, there is one singular omission. There is no comparative study of slavery and poverty."[4]

America (University Park, PA, forthcoming). For the best summary of wealth estimates, drawing on Jones' and others' work, as well as a good summary of the debate between those who argue for increasing inequality over time, such as Nash, and those, most notably Lindert and Williamson, who see stability at low levels, see John J. McCusker and Russell R. Menard, *The Economy of British America, 1607–1789* (Chapel Hill, NC, 1985), pp. 55–61 (quote from Jones on p. 55, and their own assessment on p. 59) and 258–276. For two superb articles that show the importance of including blacks in poverty estimates, see Carole Shammas, "A New Look at Long-Term Trends in Wealth Inequality in the United States," *American Historical Review*, 98 (1993), 412–431 and Daniel Scott Smith, "Female Householding in Late Eighteenth-Century America and the Problem of Poverty," *Journal of Social History*, 28 (1994), 83–107.

[4] For comparisons of material conditions between slaves and the poor, largely in the nineteenth century, see, most important, Robert William Fogel and Stanley L. Engerman, *Time on the Cross: The Economics of American Negro Slavery* (Boston, 1974). See also Eric Vaughn Snow, "Who was Better Off? The Standard of Living of American Slaves and English Farmworkers Compared, 1750–1875" (M.A. thesis, Michigan State University, 1997); J. H. Plumb, "Slavery, Race and the Poor" in *In the Light of History* (1972), reprinted in *The American Experience: The Collected Essays of J. H. Plumb*, vol. 2 (Athens, GA, 1989), p. 135. For an altogether different context but with interesting parallels, see Dharma Kumar, *Land and Caste in South India: Agricultural Labour in the Madras Presidency During the Nineteenth Century* (Cambridge, 1956), esp. 48 (I owe this reference to Stanley L. Engerman).

This exercise in comparison should not mask a major contrast between the conventional poor and slaves. Poverty is a relative condition, and varies according to the prevailing standards of time and space. Furthermore it is rarely a static state: a core of permanently poor usually exist and the condition of poverty often passed from generation to generation, but more typically a person moved in and out of poverty over a lifetime – when times were bad, for instance, or as they grew old – or through a family life-cycle, because the poor are often children and the typical beggar, as Olwen Hufton notes, was the child. The poor were, in Paul Slack's words, "a jumble of social groups and individuals with little in common besides their poverty." Or, as Stuart Woolf puts it, "The very fluidity and relativity of the condition of being poor denies the fixity of all categorizations." Although slavery was not uniform, an undeniable permanence or fixity attached to its status. An individual slave's status certainly varied along a broad spectrum of rights, powers, and protections, but a New World slave did not generally move in and out of the condition. True, some slaves – a tiny fraction in British America – moved from slavery to freedom through manumission, but most New World slaves remained slaves all their lives, as did their children and children's children. Slavery is a legal institution; poverty a material state. Slavery was an absolute, poverty a relative, condition.[5]

I

The non-slave poor can be organized into two main groups. One comprised the free poor, those who were tenuously integrated into the economy. They included some urban dwellers, tenants, rural laborers, Native Americans, and the traditional dependents. The other were bound laborers – primarily servants, convicts, and redemptioners – who were temporarily poor due to their status and because their owners regulated and restricted their consumption.

Much focus on the white poor is targeted at urban centers. Without a doubt, poverty increased markedly over the course of the eighteenth century in the major cities and towns of British America. But by the Revolution no more than about 10 percent of any city's residents received some form of public assistance, although the proportion of urban dwellers who lived at or below subsistence was perhaps three or even four times the size of those receiving charity. Urban poverty in America was on a much smaller scale than

---

5 Paul Slack, *Poverty and Policy in Tudor and Stuart England* (London, 1988), p. 7; Stuart Woolf, *The Poor in Western Europe in the Eighteenth and Nineteenth Centuries* (London, 1986), pp. 2, 4–5 (quote), 50. See also Tom Arkell, "The Incidence of Poverty in England in the Later Seventeenth Century," *Social History*, 12 (1987), 23–47; Steven King, *Poverty and Welfare in England, 1700–1850: A Regional Perspective* (Manchester, 2000), pp. 78–87; Olwen Hufton, *The Poor of Eighteenth-Century France, 1750–1789* (Oxford, 1974), pp. 2, 7. Poverty can be considered an absolute condition – as the minimum necessary to maintain a person's survival – but how to measure that minimum varies from society to society and over time. See John Iliffe, *The African Poor: A History* (Cambridge, 1987), pp. 1–2.

in Europe, where in some cities perhaps two-thirds or more of the population lived below or close to the poverty line, often in stinking slums, half-starving to death. Furthermore, urban life itself was far more exceptional in America than in Europe; indeed, relative to the total population, fewer Americans lived in cities at the end of the eighteenth century than at the beginning. On the eve of the American Revolution only five percent of the British North American population were urban residents. The urban poor in America was therefore a tiny fraction of the overall poor population.[6]

Tenancy, often associated with grinding poverty and oppressive landlords, increased markedly in eighteenth century British America. In some older set-tled areas, particularly in Maryland, Virginia, Pennsylvania, Massachusetts, and New York, as much as a half or more of the free population were tenants by the time of the American Revolution. In one Maryland county – Prince George's – the proportion of landless householders reached sixtynine percent by 1800. Not only was tenancy widespread, for many it was a permanent condition. Yet, although a significant number of tenants were near the bot-tom rung of the social ladder, many were far from impoverished. Indeed, most tenants in America were in a far better position than their European counterparts; the most important privilege that American tenants generally enjoyed was the ownership of their improvements. In colonial Virginia, some tenants were frequently behind in their rents and owned few possessions, yet others were "bold" enough to sell their lots and do "as they please[d] with the land." Poverty was endemic, Gregory Stiverson argues, among tenants on proprietory manors in Maryland, and yet most had secure long-term leases, were able to develop tracts with almost no interference from landlords, and paid rents that were only slightly higher than quitrents. In most respects, Stiverson concedes, proprietary tenants were "barely distinguishable from small freeholders." Stiverson assumed that proprietory tenants were better off than private tenants because the former paid a lower rent and held long-term leases, but two subsequent studies of tenants on private estates have found surprising levels of prosperity. Life leases on a Jesuit-owned estate in Charles County, Maryland gave tenants long-term security, a saleable asset, an inheritance for at least one child, the same political privileges as freehold-ers, and the same living standards as small freeholders in the area. Similarly, many tenants on Carrolton Manor in the Monocacy Valley, Maryland were, by contemporary standards, well off. Many owned slaves and either owned or could afford to purchase land off the manor; they achieved wealth lev-els equal to or in excess of many landowners. Finally, most tenants in both New York and Pennsylvania were fairly independent and prosperous. Two

[6] Billy G. Smith, "Poverty and Economic Marginality in Eighteenth-Century America," *Pro-ceedings of the American Philosophical Society*, 132 no. 1 (1988), 85–118, esp. 91, 96, 99–100 and his "Poverty," in Jacob E. Cooke (ed.), *Encyclopedia of the North American Colonies* (New York, 1993), I: pp. 483–493, esp. 489–491; Woolf, *The Poor in Western Europe*, p. 6.

conclusions about tenants seem warranted: they were not a homogenous group, and many, perhaps a majority, were far from being poor.[7]

Other landless workers existed in early America. The number of workers who called themselves "labourers" grew over the course of the eighteenth century. By the mid eighteenth century in parts of New England, as many as a third of men were landless laborers. Transients began tramping the roads in search of work, and communities began expelling or "warning out" an increasing number of newcomers who had no visible property. Even in a slave society such as the Chesapeake, free white laborers rapidly increased in number. By the end of the eighteenth century, many of the landless, perhaps a majority, were laborers, either overseers or those who worked for wages. Young single men and women in particular often worked for pay. The growth of slavery particularly expanded the work available to hired white women. Laborers were not always destitute; some employed capital equipment, most obtained a basic education, and a few even employed other workers. Typically, too, laborers were young men who were either waiting to inherit land from fathers or preparing to enter a craft. According to Christine Daniels, "they often achieved at least a meager competency," even if they also "lived close to disaster."[8]

---

[7] Willard Bliss, "The Rise of Tenancy in Virginia," *Virginia Magazine of History and Biography*, 58 (1950), pp. 427–441 (quote on p. 437); Gregory A. Stiverson, *Poverty in a Land of Plenty: Tenancy in Eighteenth-Century Maryland* (Baltimore, 1977), pp. 13, 48, 57, 137 et passim; Lorena S. Walsh, "Land, Landlord, and Leaseholder: Estate Management and Tenant Fortunes in Southern Maryland, 1642–1820," *Agricultural History*, 59 (1985), 373–396; Mary C. Jeske, "Autonomy and Opportunity: Carrollton Manor Tenants, 1734–1790" (Ph.D. diss., University of Maryland, 1999), and her "Prosperous Landholders: Carrollton Manor Tenants during the Era of the American Revolution," (unpublished paper, 2000); Steven Sarson, "Landlessness and Tenancy in Early National Prince George's County, Maryland," *William and Mary Quarterly*, 3rd Ser., LVII (1999), 569–598; Lucy Simler, "Tenancy in Colonial Pennsylvania: The Case of Chester County," ibid., 3rd Ser., XLIII (1986), 542–569; Sung Bok Kim, *Landlord and Tenant in Colonial New York: Manorial Society, 1664–1775* (Chapel Hill, NC, 1978). See also Bernard Bailyn, *The Peopling of British North America: An Introduction* (New York, 1986), pp. 83–85, 157–159.

[8] Douglas Lamar Jones, *Village and Seaport: Migration and Society in Eighteenth-Century Massachusetts* (Hanover, NH, 1981); Esther L. Friend, "Notifications and Warnings Out: Strangers Taken into Wrentham, Massachusetts, between 1732 and 1812," *New England Historical and Genealogical Register*, 141 (1987), 179–202, 330–357, and 142 (1988), 56–84; Steven Sarson, "Landlessness and Tenancy in Early National Prince George's County, Maryland," *WMQ*, 3rd Ser., LVII (1999), 569–598; Zachary Ryan Calo, "From Poor Relief to the Poorhouse: The Response to Poverty in Prince George's County, Maryland, 1710–1770," *Maryland Historical Magazine*, 93 (1998), 393–427; Paul Clemens and Lucy Simler, "Rural Labor and the Farm Household in Chester County, Pennsylvania, 1750–1820," in Stephen Innes (ed.), *Work and Labor in Early America* (Chapel Hill, NC, 1988), pp. 106–143; Lucy Simler, "The Landless Worker: An Index of Economic and Social Change in Chester County, Pennsylvania, 1750–1820," *Pennsylvania Magazine of History and Biography*, 114 (1990), 163–199; Christine Daniels, "Gresham's Laws: Labor Management on an Early-Eighteenth-Century Chesapeake Plantation," *Journal of Southern History*, LXII (1996),

Native Americans too can be included among the poor, although, with wants scarce and means fairly plentiful, they might be said to be remarkably free of material pressures, even if they experienced a low standard of living. Able to satisfy most of their people's needs quite readily, Indian communities can merit Marshall Sahlins' term, "the original affluent society." To be sure, many Indians remained apart from the conventional colonial economy before 1800; they relied on a mixed economy of hunting, gathering, and farming, and, as Claudio Saunt notes, they "measured worth in battle feats and spiritual power" rather than in material possessions. Chiefs gained renown for what they gave away, not what they owned. Indians often valued European goods primarily for their aesthetic properties and ceremonial uses. When fur traders described Hudson Bay Indians (who were subject to more constraints than most other Indian groups) as "starving," they might indeed be referring to their literal lack of food – walking skeletons "scarcely possessed of a necessary article to enable them to procure a living," as one trader put it – but equally they might speaking of their priorities, their avoidance of actual starvation, by hunting for food rather than obtaining furs. So when an Indian said "I am starving," he could be excusing his failure to supply furs or even engaging in a form of self-deprecatory etiquette.[9]

Increasingly, however, Native Americans were drawn into the colonial economy – whether by farming the land intensively, engaging in animal husbandry, peddling baskets and pots, going to sea, working for wages, toiling as bound laborers and as domestics, or consuming English goods. Over the course of the seventeenth and eighteenth centuries, Indians experienced a sharpened social stratification, not only in comparison to white colonists, but also among themselves. A few quite wealthy and a large number of poor native Americans became the norm. Indeed, so integrated were Indians into the colonial economy that two scholars have recently argued that the transfer of resources from Indians to colonists and the resulting lower incomes Indians experienced may well account for the real output per capita gains, estimated at about 0.6 percent per year as a maximum, generated by the eighteenth century British North American economy. Perhaps the best glimpse into the marked inequality among native groups are the claims for

205–238; Christine Daniels, "'Getting his [or her] Livelihood': Free Workers in Slave Anglo-America, 1675–1810," *Agricultural History*, 71 (1997), 125–161 (quotes on pp. 143–144); Laurel Thatcher Ulrich, *A Midwife's Tale: The Life of Martha Ballard, Based on her Diary, 1785–1812* (New York, 1992), pp. 80–82, 160–162; Daniel Vickers, *Farmers and Fishermen: Two Centuries of Work in Essex County, Massachusetts, 1630–1850* (Chapel Hill, NC, 1994), pp. 52–53, 241–242, 249–250, 302–303.

[9] Claudio Saunt, "Taking Account of Property: Stratification among the Creek Indians in the Early Nineteenth Century," *WMQ*, 3rd Ser., LVII (2000), 733–760 (quote on p. 747); Marshall Sahlins, *Stone Age Economics* (Chicago, 1972), pp. 1–39; Mary Black-Rogers, "Varieties of 'Starving': Semantics and Survival in the Subarctic Fur Trade, 1750–1850," *Ethnohistory*, 33 (1986), 353–383.

property lost by the Mohawks during the American Revolution and for property damaged or destroyed that belonged to Creeks during the Redstick War of 1813 and 1814. Among the fiftyeight Mohawk claimants, the top four claimants owned about a third of all lost property; among the Creeks the top decile of 589 claimants owned two-thirds of all destroyed property. That the vast majority of both Mohawks and Creeks seemingly owned little property (80 percent of Creeks, for example, held just a fifth of the claimed property) indicates the pervasiveness of the near-propertyless and the deep split between rich and poor in Indian society.[10]

Some of the poorest segments among free Americans were no doubt the so-called traditional or deserving poor – the infirm, disabled, widowed, and orphaned – but their overall numbers were smaller in North America than Europe. Women certainly endured poverty more often than men in early

---

[10] On the integration of Indians into the colonial economy, a huge literature now exists. Selective examples include Arthur J. Ray, *Indians in the Fur Trade: Their Role as Trappers, Hunters, and Middlemen in the Lands Southwest of Hudson Bay, 1660–1870* (Toronto, 1974); John A. Sainsbury, "Indian Labor in Early Rhode Island," *New England Quarterly*, 48 (1975), 378–393; Ray and Donald B. Freeman, *"Give Us Good Measure": An Economic Analysis of Relations between the Indians and the Hudson's Bay Company before 1763* (Toronto, 1978); Ray, "Indians as Consumers in the Eighteenth Century," in Carol M. Judd and Ray (eds.), *Old Trails and New Directions: Papers of the Third North American Fur Trade Conference* (Toronto, 1980), pp. 255–271; Christopher L. Miller and George R. Hammell, "A New Perspective on Indian–White Contact: Cultural Symbols and Colonial Trade," *Journal of American History*, 73 (1986), 311–328; James Merrell, *The Indians' New World: Catawbas and Their Neighbors from European Contact through the Era of Removal* (Chapel Hill, NC, 1989), pp. 49–91; Daniel Richter, *Ordeal of the Longhouse: The Peoples of the Iroquois League in the Era of European Colonization* (Chapel Hill, NC, 1992), pp. 75–104; Ann M. Carlos and Frank D. Lewis, "Indians, the Beaver, and the Bay: The Economics of Depletion in the Lands of the Hudson's Bay Company, 1700–1763," *Journal of Economic History*, 53 (1993), 465–494; Donna Keith Baron, J. Edward Hood, and Holly V. Izard, "They Were Here All Along: The Native American Presence in Lower Central New England in the Eighteenth and Nineteenth Centuries," *WMQ*, 3rd Ser., LIII (1996), 561–586; Daniel R. Mandell, *Behind the Frontier: Indians in Eighteenth-Century Eastern Massachusetts* (Lincoln, 1996); Jean M. O'Brien, *Dispossession by Degrees: Indian Land and Identity in Natick, Massachusetts, 1650–1790* (Cambridge, 1997), pp. 133–8, 156–7, 189–213; Ruth Wallis Herndon and Ella Wilcox Sekatura, "The Right to a Name: The Narragansett People and Rhode Island Officials in the Revolutionary Era," *Ethnohistory*, 44 (1997), 433–462; Peter C. Mancall and Thomas Weiss, "Was Economic Growth Likely in Colonial British North America?" *Journal of Economic History*, 59 (1999), 17–40; Mancall, Joshua Rosenbloom, and Weiss, "Measuring Indigenous Economies: Quantitative Estimates for the Carolinas and Georgia during the Eighteenth Century" (paper presented at AHA meeting, 2001); Jean R. Soderlund, "How the Indians Became 'Poor' in Colonial New Jersey," (unpublished essay); on property claims, see David B. Guldenzopf, "The Colonial Transformation of Mohawk Iroquois Society" (Ph.D. diss., State University of New York at Albany, 1986); and Saunt, "Taking Account of Property," *WMQ*, 3rd Ser., LVII (2000), 733–760. For stratification of another Indian nation a little later in time, see William G. McLoughlin and Walter H. Conser, Jr., "The Cherokees in Transition: A Statistical Analysis of the Federal Cherokee Census of 1835," *Journal of American History*, 64 (1977), 678–703.

America. Widowed, separated, or abandoned women, many with children, comprised a large part of the transients warned out of New England towns. The young and the elderly, especially those lacking a support network, were most at risk. Yet far more women were married in America than Europe. "Families in early modern England," Daniel Scott Smith notes, "were more than twice as likely to be headed by a woman as were white households in late eighteenth-century America"; and these women-headed households were "disproportionately prone to be impoverished." In the Chesapeake and Caribbean, the incidence of orphanhood may well have been higher than in Europe, but the proportion of elderly was smaller. Many young people were poor for only part of their lives, and escaped poverty as they matured. In fact, the proportion of younger adults (aged 25–44) among the poor declined quite markedly in New England – from thirtynine percent in the mid seventeenth century to twentyfour percent in the third quarter of the eighteenth century – as their proportion among the general population also declined. Apparently, the rural New England economy benefited poorer people.[11]

Those whites who were temporarily poor because of bound labor probably outnumbered the free white poor, particularly at certain periods of time. Throughout the seventeenth century, for example, servants were far more numerous than the urban poor. Between 1580 and 1775, colonial British America imported about 500,000 white bound laborers, approximately two-thirds of all white immigrants to the colonies. A majority of these bound laborers were indentured servants, who faced a harsher lot in the New World than did servants in England. Typical servants spent from three to five years paying off the costs of their transportation. Because they were under contract (or indenture) for a number of years, a master might buy and sell the remainder of that contract – in effect, sell the servant – "like a damnd slave," as one Virginia servant put it. By contrast, servants in husbandry in England generally worked for a master for only one year and their contracts were not negotiable currency. Corporal punishment was probably more common in the colonies than in England, because masters had fewer institutional checks on their behavior in the New World than the Old. In seventeenth century Virginia, John and Alice Proctor beat two servants to death, on one occasion administering 500 lashes to one of them. Yet New World masters probably did not engage in widespread physical abuse, because harming their servants reduced profits, although the tendency for a master to extract as much work as possible from a servant whose term would expire was undoubtedly real.[12]

---

[11] Daniel Scott Smith, "Female Householding in Late Eighteenth-Century America," *Journal of Social History*, 28 (1994), 83–107; Gloria L. Main and Jackson T. Main, "The Red Queen in New England?" *WMQ*, 3rd Ser., LVI (1999), 135.

[12] Philip D. Morgan, "Bound Labor: The British and Dutch Colonies," in Cooke (ed.), *Encyclopedia of North American Colonies*, II: pp. 17–32; Morgan, *American Slavery, American Freedom*, pp. 106–107, 126–129, 216–218, 281–282, 311; Darrett B. Rutman and Anita

The experiences of indentured servants varied greatly. Many, particularly in the seventeenth century Chesapeake and West Indies, never survived their terms – largely because they succumbed to a new disease environment. On the other hand, some servants had their terms extended because they ran away or, in the case of women, had a child. By contrast, other masters provided their servants with more than the legally required minimum levels of food and clothing, and some even paid wages to their servants or made bargains with them to release them early from their terms. Servants could choose their destinations, and thus the least favored destinations had to offer incentives to attract them. Most important perhaps, servants had basic legal rights: they could petition courts for redress of grievances. In one study of 260 complaints submitted to Maryland courts between 1652 and 1797, indentured servants won eightythree percent of the time. Servants, unlike slaves, had precious legal protections. Furthermore, through at least the first half of the seventeenth century, those servants who managed to survive their terms in the Chesapeake generally did well, often getting access to land and even modest political offices, although toward the end of the seventeenth and into the eighteenth centuries, ex-servants' opportunities for upward mobility declined markedly. Thus, in the eighteenth century, immigrants and pamphleteers usually advised against coming to America as an indentured servant, although one recent immigrant in 1772 still thought the prospects were good, especially for the "younger Class" whose "Servitude for a few years, is in my opinion of service to them & may be looked on only as an apprenticeship." For those of "advanced years," however, "the change of Climate, hardships they often undergo, during their Servitude, under tyrannical masters, with the pressure upon their minds on being rank'd & deemed as Slaves, are such, that they seldom surmount."[13]

H. Rutman, *A Place in Time: Middlesex County, Virginia 1650–1750* (New York, 1984), pp. 51–52, 72–75, 129–138, 175–176. See also Abbot Emerson Smith, *Colonists in Bondage: White Servitude and Convict Labor in America, 1607–1776* (Chapel Hill, NC, 1947); David W. Galenson, *White Servitude in Colonial America: An Economic Analysis* (Cambridge, 1981); Margaret M. R. Kellow, "Indentured Servitude in Eighteenth-Century Maryland," *Histoire Sociale – Social History*, XVII (1984), 229–255; Sharon V. Salinger, *"To Serve Well and Faithfully": Labour and Indentured Servants in Pennsylvania, 1682–1800* (New York, 1987); Hilary McD. Beckles, *White Servitude and Black Slavery in Barbados, 1627–1715* (Knoxville, TN, 1989), who exaggerates the similarities between indentured servitude and slavery; for more accurate analyses, see David Eltis, *The Rise of African Slavery in the Americas* (Cambridge, 2000), esp. chs. 2–3; and M. L. Bush, *Servitude in Modern Times* (Oxford, 2000), pp. 28–38, 57–68.

[13] In addition to n.11, see Christine Daniels, "'Liberty to Complaine': Servant Petitions in Maryland, 1652–1797," in Christopher L. Tomlins and Bruce H. Mann (eds.), *The Many Legalities of Early America* (Chapel Hill, NC, 2001), pp. 219–249; Russell R. Menard, "From Servant to Freeholder: Status Mobility and Property Accumulation in Seventeenth-Century Maryland," *WMQ*, 3rd Ser., 30 (1973), 37–64; Lois Green Carr and Russell Menard, "Immigration and Opportunity: The Freedman in Early Colonial Maryland," in Thad Tate and David

Not all servants were indentured. Perhaps about a half of all the seventeenth century white immigrants came without a contract and thus served according to "the custom of the country," which usually meant longer terms than experienced by indentured servants. Customary servants generally were younger and probably possessed fewer skills than indentured servants. They also were less likely to win in the courts than indentured servants, although in Maryland even they prevailed seventy percent of the time. Yet another group of servants arrived without an indenture, but they typically fared better than the customary servants. They were redemptioners, allowed a specific length of time upon their arrival in America to raise the unpaid portion of the costs of their transportation. Only if they failed did they or members of their family become indentees whose length of service was determined in part by the amount owed. Because redemptioners negotiated their own labor agreements or those of their children, their contracts could not be sold without their assent. One final form of servitude was debt peonage. A person who had been imprisoned for debt, for example, might bind himself, without time restriction, to a master until the obligation had been repaid. Although debt servants generally served shorter terms than indentured servants, their situation was susceptible to exploitation because masters could extend the terms through exorbitant subsistence charges and interest on the debt. Indian whalemen on Nantucket often served two- or three-year stints to pay off their debts to an individual merchant, but the cycle of dependence might often be nigh unending.[14]

Ammerman (eds.), *The Chesapeake in the Seventeenth Century: Essays on Anglo-American Society and Politics* (Chapel Hill, NC, 1979), pp. 206–242; Lorena Walsh, "Staying Put or Getting Out: Findings for Charles County, Maryland, pp. 1650–1720," *WMQ*, 3rd. Ser., 44 (1987), 89–103; Bernard Bailyn, *Voyagers to the West: A Passage in the Peopling of America on the Eve of the Revolution* (New York, 1986), pp. 172–173; Barbara DeWolfe (ed.), *Discoveries of America: Personal Accounts of British Emigrants to North America during the Revolutionary Era* (Cambridge, 1997), pp. 149–158; and for a recent summary of the literature, see Sharon V. Salinger, "Labor, Markets, and Opportunity: Indentured Servitude in Early America," *Labor History*, 38 (1997), 311–338; cf. Farley Grubb, "Labor, Markets, and Opportunity: Indentured Servitude in Early America, a Rejoinder to Salinger," ibid., 39 (1998), 235–241.

[14] Farley Grubb, "Redemptioner Immigration to Pennsylvania: Evidence on Contract Service and Profitability," *Journal of Economic History*, 46 (1986), 407–418 and his "The Auction of Redemptioner Servants, Philadelphia, 1771–1804: An Economic Analysis," ibid., 48 (1988), 583–603; Richard Morris, *Government and Labor in Early America* (New York, 1946), pp. 310–323, 345–363; Christine Daniels, "'Without any Limitation of Time': Debt Servitude in Colonial America," *Labor History*, 36 (1995), 232–250; Daniel Vickers, "The First Whalemen of Nantucket," *WMQ*, 3rd Ser., XL (1983), 560–583 and his "Nantucket Whalemen in the Deep-Sea Fishery: The Changing Anatomy of an Early American Labor Force," *Journal of American History*, 62 (1985), 277–296. See also Arnold Bauer, "Rural Workers in Spanish America: Problems of Peonage and Oppression," *Hispanic American Historical Review*, 59 (1979), 34–63.

Convicts were far less numerous than indentured and other types of servants, and their lot was probably the harshest of all bound white laborers. Between 1718 and 1775, Britain banished about 50,000 convicts – about a quarter of all British immigrants – to its American colonies. They served longer terms than servants: about three-quarters were sentenced to seven years, most of the remainder as long as fourteen, with a few servitude for life. Confined in prisons for about two months before boarding, shackled in chains, crowded onto ships, sold almost naked and half-starved at wharf-side, or driven in coffles from town to town by "soul drivers" – "Going to Hell in a Cradle" was how one prisoner described the process – convicts experienced conditions close to slavery. Indeed, convicts sometimes compared their condition to slavery and one female felon believed "Many Negroes are better used." Yet technically convicts chose their fate; some in fact elected not to be transported and suffered death, as did one convict who "had rather die than live under Bondage for so many Years" or another who "had rather bear strangling for a minute than to make sugar all his life-time" alongside slaves. Convicts apparently knew the rigors that awaited them: Benjamin Franklin said convicts "must be ruled with a Rod of Iron" and in general masters were said to be "cruel, barbarous, and unmerciful" toward convicts. Convicts were probably the one white group to receive floggings about as frequently as slaves. But the convicts' recourse, as with other servants, was their ability to petition courts for relief – an option limited in practice and in its chances of success. And over time colonial legislatures stripped away the rights of convicts, so that by the last third of the eighteenth century, in both Virginia and Maryland, convicts could not testify in court and, in Virginia, they were also denied freedom dues. Once freed, convicts probably enjoyed better opportunities in America than they would have experienced at home; nevertheless, Roger Ekirch concludes, "very few felons enjoyed even modest success."[15]

In conclusion, then, despite pockets of serious poverty, particularly among the temporarily unfree, a general sense of well-being was pervasive for most free colonists in early America. As Jackson Turner Main says of one New England colony, "the great majority of Connecticut's people fared as well in 1774 as in 1700 or 1670, and ... this majority included virtually all of the married men and their families. Indeed, by contrast with most other pre-industrial societies, these men did not simply escape poverty but enjoyed real plenty." If this was true of most white families in Connecticut, how much more must it have been true of most white families in the Mid-Atlantic and

---

[15] A. Roger Ekirch, *Bound for America: The Transportation of British Convicts to the Colonies 1718–1775* (Oxford, 1987), pp. 27, 59–60, 63, 86, 87, 92, 99–100, 120, 122–123, 125, 129, 147–156, 177–185; Bailyn, *Voyagers to the West*, 261–264, 292–295, 314–325, 334, 346; Farley Grubb, "The Transatlantic Market for British Convict Labor," *Journal of Economic History*, 60 (2000), 94–122; Eltis, *Rise of African Slavery*, 73–74.

Southern colonies where prosperity was even more evident than in New England. In fact, Crevecoeur, an astute observer of early America, thought a "pleasing uniformity of decent competence appears throughout our habitations." Even Allan Kulikoff, who has a keen nose for inequality, observes that an "astonishingly high percentage – two-thirds of colonial families – owned land."[16]

II

If most white Americans shared a "decent competence," more precise measurements of well-being need to be analyzed. This section explores six main indicators of well-being: demographic performance; diet; stature and general state of health; clothing; shelter; and work demands. These are not the only measures of the gap between competence and poverty, of course. Educational levels and basic literacy are another useful yardstick. Unfortunately, little concrete information on education is available, although the contrast was surely extreme – the vast majority of slaves were illiterate, and although many white poor shared the condition, they were not deprived of an elementary education. These six measurements are some of the most basic, and a fair amount of information is available, allowing some comparisons between the experiences of black and white populations.[17]

Perhaps the best guide to general well-being is the remarkable demographic performance of the early North American population. By the late eighteenth century, Robert Fogel notes, white Americans had "a twenty-year advantage in life expectancy at birth over the English" and had "reached levels of life expectancy that the general population of England and even the British peerage did not attain until the first quarter of the twentieth century." Overall, the mainland white population grew by an average of about three percent per annum in the eighteenth century – with the Mid-Atlantic and Lower South regions registering the fastest growth rates. During the same period, the black population increased in size at an even faster rate than its white counterpart. The black population grew just over 3 percent per year in the northern colonies, about 4.5 percent in the South. The Caribbean was a

[16] Jackson Turner Main, *Society and Economy in Colonial Connecticut* (Princeton, NJ, 1985), p. 151; Hector St. John de Crevecoeur, *Letters from an American Farmer and Sketches of Eighteenth-Century America*, Albert J. Stone (ed.), (New York, 1981), p. 67; Allan Kulikoff, *From British Peasants to Colonial American Farmers* (Chapel Hill, NC, 2000), pp. 3, 127–163.

[17] The generally accepted proportion of slaves who were literate is about 5 percent, although this estimate is pure guesswork. For a recent estimate of literacy among one region's poor, showing marked differences along gender, wealth, and particularly racial lines, see Ruth Wallis Herndon, "Research Note: Literacy Among New England's Transient Poor, 1750–1800," *Journal of Social History*, 29 (1996), 963–965.

much less rosy story; there, the white population was largely static, and the black population grew only about 1.5 percent a year, despite heavy forced migration.[18]

As the Caribbean experience especially indicates, immigration accounts for much of the population growth, and how immigrants arrived in the New World reveals a major difference in the experiences of the enslaved and the free. Mortality was always three or four times higher for slaves and crews of slavers than for white migrants and their crews. The slave trade on average recorded about sixty deaths per month per 1000 people shipped. This rate was four times greater than that among German emigrants to Philadelphia in the eighteenth century and about five times higher than that among British convicts to Australia in the late eighteenth and early nineteenth centuries. The only group to approximate mortality rates on slavers were British convicts to North America in the early eighteenth century (fiftysix deaths per month per 1000 during 1719–1736), and their mortality levels soon improved significantly (dropping to twelve per month per 1000 between 1768 and 1775). No recorded voyage in the North Atlantic appears to have generated the appalling conditions typical for a slave vessel and almost no ship carrying servants or convicts crowded its passengers on anything approaching slave ships, which generally included far more individuals per unit of space than did other vessels.[19]

Important as immigration was, by the eighteenth century at least, the North American population grew primarily from natural increase. A starving population, generally speaking, cannot reproduce itself; to that extent,

---

[18] Henry A. Gemery, "The White Population of The Colonial United States, 1607–1790," in Michael R. Haines and Richard H. Steckel (eds.), *A Population History of North America* (Cambridge, 2000), pp. 143–190, esp. 149; Lorena S. Walsh, "The African American Population of the Colonial United States," in ibid., 191–240; Robert William Fogel, *The Fourth Great Awakening and The Future of Egalitarianism* (Chicago, 2000), p. 141; E. A. Wrigley and R. S. Schofield, *The Population History of England 1541–1871* (Cambridge, 1981), pp. 208–209.

[19] Raymond L. Cohn, "Maritime Mortality in the Eighteenth and Nineteenth Centuries: A Survey," *International Journal of Maritime History*, 1 (1989), 159–191; Robin Haines, Ralph Shlomowitz, and Lance Brennan, "Maritime Mortality Revisited," ibid., 8 (1996), 133–172; Ralph Shlomowitz, Lance Brennan, and John McDonald, *Mortality and Migration in the Modern World* (Aldershot, 1996); Herbert S. Klein and Stanley L. Engerman, "Long-Term Trends in African Mortality in the Transatlantic Slave Trade," *Slavery and Abolition*, 18, no. 1 (1997), 36–48; Stephen D. Behrendt, "Crew Mortality in the Transatlantic Slave Trade in the Eighteenth Century," ibid, 49–71; Stanley L. Engerman, Robin Haines, Herbert S. Klein, and Ralph Shlomowitz, "Transoceanic Mortality: The Slave Trade in Comparative Perspective," *WMQ*, 3rd Ser., LVIII (2001), 93–117; Eltis, *Rise of African Slavery*, 78, 116–128, 156–158. The one exception regarding crowding is, for a brief period, in the German redemptioner trade: see Marianne S. Wokeck, *Trade in Strangers: The Beginnings of Mass Migration to North America* (University Park, PA, 1999), p. 79. Roger Ekirch found that slave ships entering Maryland were three times as crowded as convict ships (180 slaves versus 60 convicts per 100 tons): *Bound for America*, 100.

natural increase is a minimal indicator of well-being. What is impressive about the North American population, both white and black, is the speed at which it increased naturally. From 1730 to 1800, the natural rate of increase of Virginia's black population was about two or more percent a year. Even South Carolina's slave population grew through reproduction by over 1 percent a year from 1760 onward, except for the Revolutionary War years and their immediate aftermath. The one exception to this remarkable success story – unprecedented for slave populations in the New World to this point – concerned cities (where, of course, proportionately few North American slaves lived) such as Philadelphia, where fertility among slave women was sufficiently low and mortality in general so high that births failed to exceed deaths. Overall, from the early eighteenth century onward the mainland slave population grew faster, from natural increase, than contemporary European populations. Apart from the dislocations of the very first years of settlement, almost no North American, white or black, starved. Virtually all North Americans benefited from living in an environment where a few days' labor could produce a maize crop that would feed a person for a year, and where two sources of protein – fish from the ocean and meat (either game or livestock) – were widely available. In addition, extensive forests provided timber for housing and firewood, and low population density reduced the spread of communicable diseases.[20]

By contrast, throughout most of the British Caribbean, slave populations registered high rates of natural decrease. By 1750 the West Indies had imported almost 800,000 Africans, but deaths had so far exceeded births that the slave population then stood at less than 300,000. Only slave populations in marginal colonies such as the Bahamas were able to increase naturally during the eighteenth century, although the Barbadian slave population was beginning to do the same by the end of the century. Perhaps the single most important reason why the Caribbean was a graveyard for slaves and the mainland a breeding ground can be summed up in one word: sugar. Sugar cultivation was so onerous that it was literally a killing work regime. In addition, because the Caribbean islands generally had more hostile disease environments and more fragile ecologies than the mainland, seasonal and episodic cases of nutritional stress occurred. The "hungry times" in Caribbean islands, which lasted from June to September, occurred after the end of the

---

[20] Philip D. Morgan, *Slave Counterpoint: Black Culture in the Eighteenth-Century Chesapeake and Lowcountry* (Chapel Hill, NC, 1998), pp. 81, 84; Susan E. Klepp, "Seasoning and Society: Racial Differences in Mortality in Eighteenth-Century Philadelphia," *WMQ*, 3rd Ser., LI (1994), 473–506; Richard H. Steckel, "Nutritional Status in the Colonial American Economy," ibid., 3rd. Ser., LVI (1999), 44; Lois Green Carr and Lorena S. Walsh, "Changing Lifestyles and Consumer Behavior in the Colonial Chesapeake," in Cary Carson, Ronald Hoffman, and Peter J. Albert (eds.), *Of Consuming Interests: The Style of Life in the Eighteenth Century* (Charlottesville, VA, 1994), p. 60.

sugar harvest, when the access to cane juice declined and food crops were not yet available. Drought-induced famines occurred fairly frequently, hurricanes caused frequent devastation, and naval blockades during wartime – most notably, the American Revolutionary War – led to many thousands of slaves dying from starvation because of insufficient imported foods. The demographic performance of Caribbean slaves points to significant material deprivation.[21]

For the poor, whether white or black, how they lived was primarily how they ate. The diet for both poor whites and slaves was predominantly composed of cereals. Whites generally ate a range of grains, but for most slaves, certainly those in the Chesapeake, corn was the staff of life. The maize ration for slaves was not generous but was roughly the same as that which white indentured servants and convicts received – about thirteen to fifteen bushels a year. Although maize was a primary staple in the Lower South and Caribbean, it did not dominate either diet to the extent it did in the Chesapeake. In the lowcountry, rice and chickpeas were major components of the slave diet; and in the Caribbean, Guinea corn (sorghum or millet), plantains, and yams were important food crops. Contemporaries praised the nutritional content of maize; perhaps, therefore, the reduced corn intake of Caribbean and lowcountry slaves was to their nutritional detriment. Wherever plantations were not present – as in the Bahamas, Anguilla, and Barbuda in the Caribbean – or in towns, or on farms throughout North America, slaves experienced a better than average diet.[22]

Slaves undoubtedly ate less protein than servants or poor whites in America, though probably more protein than many European poor folk. A little

[21] Stanley Engerman and B. W. Higman, "The Demographic Structure of the Caribbean Slave Societies," UNESCO *General History of the Caribbean* Vol. III (London, 1997), pp. 45–104; J. R. Ward, *British West Indian Slavery, 1750–1834: The Process of Amelioration* (Oxford, 1988), pp. 23–24, 119–189; B. W. Higman, *Slave Populations of the British Caribbean, 1807–1834* (Baltimore, 1984), pp. 303–378; Richard B. Sheridan, "The Crisis of Slave Subsistence in the British West Indies during and after the American Revolution," *WMQ*, 3rd Ser., XXXIII (1976), 615–641.

[22] Hufton, *The Poor of Eighteenth-Century France*, 46; Morgan, *Slave Counterpoint*, 134–135; Ward, *British West Indian Slavery*, 18–29, 105–118; Higman, *Slave Populations*, 205–210. For a good summary of nutrition among the European poor, see Robert Jutte, *Poverty and Deviance in Early Modern Europe* (Cambridge, 1994), pp. 72–78; for the diet of the urban laborer in North America, see Billy Smith, *The "Lower Sort": Philadelphia's Laboring People, 1750–1800* (Ithaca, NY, 1990), pp. 95–103; for the late eighteenth and early nineteenth centuries, see Lorena S. Walsh, "Consumer Behavior, Diet, and the Standard of Living in Late Colonial and Early Antebellum America, 1770–1840," in Robert E. Gallman and John Joseph Wallis (eds.), *American Economic Growth and Standards of Living before the Civil War* (Chicago, 1992), pp. 217–261. See also Carole Shammas, "The Eighteenth-Century English Diet and Economic Change," *Explorations in Economic History*, 21 (1984), 254–269 and *The Pre-Industrial Consumer in England and America* (Oxford, 1990), pp. 121–156. In eighteenth century rural France, ninetyfive percent or more of the poor's diet was cereal – perhaps a larger proportion than the diet of some slaves.

salt pork or salt fish was the typical allotment for slaves. The distribution of meat to slaves seems to have been more common in the Chesapeake than in the lowcountry, and more common on the mainland than in the islands. In the Chesapeake, wildlife and pork were more important in poor white and slave diets than in that of the wealthy, though in all groups domestic mammals constituted the most common meat protein. Slaves supplemented their rations by hunting, trapping, fishing, gardening, and raising fowl – but the more the slaves provided their own food, particularly through provision grounds, as was particularly common on some Caribbean islands, the more likely it was that they suffered nutritional stress. One indicator in the colonial Jamaican slave population, for instance, is the presence of rats as rare items of protein in their diet. Even when slaves did not go hungry, their intake of proteins and vitamins was often inadequate; rickets, scurvy, and allied deficiency diseases were common. Analysis of slave skeletons at some sites has revealed health levels comparable to Native American populations threatened with extinction, although at other slave sites the levels were little different from that of whites. Dietary deficiencies help account for a description of a dozen slave men and women on one lowcountry estate as "all misshapen or disfigured." Similarly, an inadequate diet probably explains why a traveler thought that Carolina slaves were "shrivelled and diminutive in size, compared with those in Virginia." But, in fact, few travelers described slaves in the way some observers described entire villages in parts of Europe where, in Hufton's words, "the inhabitants were crippled or physically distorted."[23]

The daily caloric intake of slaves is almost impossible to measure, in part because rations varied from region to region, even from master to master, and in part because the slaves' independent activities may well have provided roughly as many calories as the masters' allocations. Nevertheless, historians have not refrained from offering such estimates: for example, the average estate ration in the late eighteenth century Caribbean was supposedly between 1,500 and 2,000 calories a day, whereas in eighteenth century Philadelphia

---

[23] Morgan, *Slave Counterpoint*, 136–140, 143; Henry Miller, "An Archaeological Perspective on the Evolution of Diet in the Colonial Chesapeake, 1620–1745," in Lois Carr, Philip D. Morgan, and Jean Russo (eds.), *Colonial Chesapeake Society* (Chapel Hill, NC, 1988), pp. 176–199; Joanne Bowen, "Foodways in the 18th-Century Chesapeake," in Theodore R. Reinhart (ed.), *The Archaeology of 18th-Century Virginia* (Richmond, Va., 1996), pp. 87–130; Higman, *Slave Populations*, 217–218; B. W. Higman, *Montpelier Jamaica: A Plantation Community in Slavery and Freedom 1739–1912* (Kingston, Jamaica, 1998), p. 208; Kenneth F. Kiple, *The Caribbean Slave: A Biological History* (Cambridge, 1984), pp. 89–103; Richard H. Steckel, Paul W. Sciulli, and Jerome C. Rose, "Skeletal Remains, Health, and History: A Project on Long Term Trends in the Western Hemisphere" in John Komlos and Joerg Baten (eds.), *The Biological Standard of Living in Comparative Perspective*: Conference, Munich, January 18–22, 1997, XIIth Congress of the International Economic History Association (Stuttgart, 1998), 139–154, esp. 150; Hufton, *The Poor of Eighteenth-Century France*, 46.

slaves apparently received about 1,800 to 2,400 calories a day at a time when the city Workhouse routinely provided 2,600. Such intakes, even if they are reliable estimates, do not seem to have been enough to meet the energy demands of a field hand or laborer, which have been put at about 3,000 calories per day, but then again some healthy modern West Indian populations subsist on less than 2,000 calories daily. Overall, few slaves (mostly confined to the Caribbean and during particular years or seasons) starved, even if some were malnourished.[24]

Somewhat more precise than estimates of caloric intake are measurements of height, which are fairly good indicators of net nutritional status. In the eighteenth century, the average height of white American men was about 68″, or approximately two inches taller than their European counterparts. In fact, native-born white Americans seem to have been the tallest people in the world, and their average height was close to that attained in modern times. Heights did increase slightly over the course of the eighteenth century. Occupational differences in stature were modest; farmers were not appreciably taller than artisans, for example. The most important variation was regional: native-born white American men from the Southern colonies were taller than their Northern counterparts. Nutritionally, then, white men in America seem to have been exceptionally well off.[25]

By the time of the Revolution, native-born North American blacks were almost the same height as whites – on average less than an inch shorter, although more so relative to Southern whites. In the late eighteenth century, the mean height of adult male slaves was about 67.2 inches. Creole

[24] Robert Dirks, "Resource Fluctuations and Competitive Transformations in West Indian Slave Societies," in Charles D. Laughlin and Ivan A. Brady (eds.), *Extinction and Survival in Human Populations* (New York, 1978), pp. 114–147 or 122–180; Kiple, *Caribbean Slave*, 76–88; Klepp, "Seasoning and Society," *WMQ*, 3rd. Ser., LI (1994), 481–485. In the nineteenth century, the daily energy intake of adult slaves is said to be "probably in the neighborhood of 2,500 to 3,000 calories": Robert William Fogel, *Without Consent or Contract: The Rise and Fall of American Slavery* (New York, 1989), pp. 132. See also Jutte, *Poverty and Deviance*, 77, and Hans-Joachim Voth, *Time and Work in England 1750–1830* (Oxford, 2000), pp. 162–171.

[25] Steckel, "Nutritional Status in the Colonial American Economy," *WMQ*, 3rd Ser., 56 (1999), 31–52; Kenneth L. Sokoloff and Georgia C. Villaflor, "The Early Achievement of Modern Stature in America," *Social Science History*, 6 (1982), 453–481; Steckel, "Stature and Living Standards in the United States," in Gallman and Wallis (eds.), *American Economic Growth and Standards of Living*, pp. 265–308; Fogel, *The Fourth Great Awakening*, 140–141. See also John Komlos, "A Malthusian Episode Revisited: The Height of British and Irish Servants in Colonial America," *Economic History Review*, XLVI (1993), 768–782; Farley Grubb, "Withering Heights: Did Indentured Servants Shrink from an Encounter with Malthus? A Comment on Komlos," ibid., LII (1999), 714–729; John Komlos, "On the Nature of the Malthusian Threat in the Eighteenth Century," ibid., LII (1999), 730–748; and Farley Grubb, "Lilliputians and Brobdingnagians, Stature in British Colonial America: Evidence from Servants, Convicts, and Apprentices," *Research in Economic History*, 19 (1999), 139–203.

slaves were thus about an inch taller than most Europeans; indeed, their physical stature was closer to that of European aristocrats than to that of peasants. By all accounts, then, most North American slaves avoided permanent undernourishment, the lot of many poor people in Europe. Slaves born in North America were taller than those born in the Caribbean, who in turn were generally taller than those born in Africa. The one exception was early nineteenth century Berbice where adult male creoles were somewhat shorter than male Africans – presumably a sign of that colony's extreme nutritional inadequacy, unfavorable environmental conditions, and harsh work regime. Sugar colonies produced consistently shorter creole slaves than non–sugar-producing colonies. In the early nineteenth century, American-born slaves were, on average 1.6 inches taller than even Africans from the Bight of Benin, the coastal region with the tallest slaves. The same regional variation was true of blacks as whites: American-born slaves were taller in the Upper South than in the Lower South. Slave children, particularly below the age of five, seem to have been staggeringly small (in the Caribbean they were considerably shorter than the factory children in the satanic mills of industrializing Britain – contrary to the arguments of pro-slavery advocates); but their catch-up as teenagers was remarkably rapid and seems to have been largely attributable to the distribution of meat when they began working. During the second half of the eighteenth century, a decline in stature seems to have occurred among North American slaves, but whether due to wartime disruptions of the American Revolution or to a southward shift of the slave trade catchment areas, which brought shorter slaves from West-Central Africa in greater numbers than before, is not clear.[26]

---

[26] David Eltis, "Nutritional Standards in Africa and the Americas: Heights of Africans, 1819–1839," *Journal of Interdisciplinary History*, 12 (1982), 453–475; Robert A. Margo and Richard H. Steckel, "The Heights of American Slaves: New Evidence on Slave Nutrition and Health," *Social Science History*, 6 (1982), 516–538, esp. 521; Gerald C. Friedman, "The Heights of Slaves in Trinidad," ibid., 6 (1982), 482–515; Higman, *Slave Populations*, 280–293; Richard H. Steckel, "A Peculiar Population: The Nutrition, Health, and Mortality of American Slaves from Childhood to Maturity," *Journal of Economic History*, 46 (1986), 721–742; Fogel, *Without Consent or Contract*, 138–147; Steckel, "Work, Disease, and Diet in the Health and Mortality of American Slaves," in Robert W. Fogel and Stanley L. Engerman (eds.), *Without Consent or Contract: Technical Papers vol. II*, vol. 4 (New York, 1992), 489–507; David Eltis, "Welfare Trends among the Yoruba in the Early Nineteenth Century: The Anthropometric Evidence," *Journal of Economic History*, 50 (1990), 521–540; John Komlos, "The Height of Runaway Slaves in Colonial America, 1720–1770," in Komlos (ed.), *Stature, Living Standards, and Economic Development: Essays in Anthropometric History* (Chicago, 1994), pp. 93–116, also included in his *The Biological Standard of Living in Europe and America, 1700–1900* (Aldershot, Eng., 1995), in which also see his "Toward an Anthropometric History of African-Americans: The Case of the Free Blacks in Antebellum Maryland"; Philip R. P. Coelho and Robert A. McGuire, "Diets Versus Diseases: The Anthropometrics of Slave Children," *Journal of Economic History*, 60 (2000), 232–246 and Richard H. Steckel, "Diets Versus Diseases in the Anthropometrics of Slave Children: A Reply," ibid., 247–259. See also more generally, Roderick Floud, "Anthropometric Measures

During the eighteenth century, masters began paying greater medical attention to their slaves than in the previous century – and slaves might well have had more access to doctors than poor whites – but it is doubtful that the slaves' health improved much, if at all. Some medical measures probably did more harm than good. The natural increase of a slave population cannot be correlated, for example, with the number of available European-trained doctors. Smallpox innoculation and vaccination, which was practiced toward the end of the century, was helpful, but it did not reduce mortality rates drastically. As Barry Higman notes, "The most direct intervention of the slaveowner aimed at reducing mortality levels, the provision of European medical attention, probably had a negative effect." There were probably more doctors and certainly more hospitals proportional to the population in the lowcountry than in the Chesapeake, but neither were sufficient to overcome the significant fertility and mortality differentials between the two regions. Similarly, those slaves who were most isolated from European medical practitioners, those living in the nonplantation colonies of the Caribbean (where environmental conditions were already conducive to longevity, it must be conceded), survived longest.[27]

Slaves and poor whites seem to have worn much the same kinds of clothing, although if possible masters clothed their slaves more cheaply than they did white servants. In 1691 substandard military clothing was deemed sufficient for slaves. Unbleached linens such as crocus, rolls, and "osnaburg" (which got its name from the German town of Osnabruck where it was originally made) and inexpensive woolens such as Welsh plains, Yorkshire kersey, and Kendal cotton constituted the most common materials. Homespun was rare before the American Revolution, but in 1711 Virginia's governor noted that some colonists mixed cotton with their wool "to supply the want of coarse Cloathing and Linnen, not only for their Negros, but for many of the poorer sort of house keepers" – another indication that the same type of cloth was destined for blacks and the white poor. Laboring folk of both races generally wore durable, coarse, uncomfortable, ill-fitting clothes. Textiles with trade names that touted their sturdiness – whether Foul Weather, Fearnothing, or Everlasting – were widely distributed. Men from all ranks wore leather breeches, dubbed the "blue jeans of the eighteenth century." An extant hunting shirt worn by a white soldier seems much the same as the description of a light blue hunting shirt, "plaited in the sleeves" worn by a slave. Working men, whether slave or free, usually wore a jacket or waistcoat,

---

of Nutritional Status in Industrialized Societies: Europe and North America Since 1750," in S. R. Osmani (ed.), *Nutrition and Poverty* (Oxford, 1992), pp. 219–241, espec. 231, 237.

[27] Higman, *Slave Populations*, 261–302, 376; Ward, *British West Indian Slavery*, 160–165, 184–185, 207; Richard B. Sheridan, *Doctors and Slaves: A Medical and Demographic History of Slavery in the British West Indies, 1680–1834* (New York, 1985); Morgan, *Slave Counterpoint*, 321–325.

shirt, breeches, and hat or cap; women typically wore a jacket and a petticoat. Some occupations had distinctive garbs: Some slaves were identifiable by the "Dress such as Sailors wear" or "such Clothes as Watermen generally wear"; slave blacksmiths donned the emblem of their trade, the leather apron; and male house slaves, like domestic servant men more generally, might wear livery. Convicts reported that they rarely had shoes; many slaves, particularly field hands, went barefoot. Manual workers, whether white or black, usually appeared in their own hair; few sported wigs. Poor children, both white and black, but particularly slaves, seem to have had few clothes, sometimes nothing at all.[28]

Despite similarities, there were differences in the appearance of slaves and poor whites. Because of shortcomings in the provision and distribution of clothing, many adult slaves – far more than poor whites, it would seem – were scantily clad. Field hands frequently wore only a mere rag around their loins, a "Breech Clout" or "Arse-Cloth," in contemporary parlance. Breechcloths or waist ties for men and wraparound skirts for women were a distinctive feature of African-American dress; and nakedness or semi-nakedness was a condition associated primarily with slaves. In addition, as Linda Baumgarten notes, "the absence of stays among the clothing assigned to female field slaves is another example of discrimination through clothing." Even English women living in the poor house were expected to have stays (made of bone or leather and designed to shape the female figure into a cone from waist to bust) and only American women in the backwoods left off their stays in the hottest summer months. Moreover, slaves probably preferred to wear scanty, loose-fitting clothing as a matter of choice, although masters shortchanged them too. As another possible matter of choice, slaves apparently believed heads should generally be covered; certainly they wore headcloths far more widely than whites, although white women in the Caribbean followed the practice fairly extensively (the headwrap had African origins, but headgear in general signified submissiveness and subjection). In part because their sartorial resources were so limited, slave clothing was probably distinctive for the extent to which it was patched and edged, often with bright

---

[28] Beverly Lemire, *Dress, Culture and Commerce: The English Clothing Trade before the Factory, 1660–1800* (Basingstoke, 1997), p. 34; Morgan, *Slave Counterpoint*, 125–133; Linda Baumgarten, "Plains, Plaid and Cotton: Woolens for Slave Clothing," *Ars Textrina*, 15 (1991), 203–221; Robert A. Brock (ed.), *The Official Letters of Alexander Spotswood* (Richmond, 1882), I, 72 (I am grateful to Linda Baumgarten for this reference); Ward, *British West Indian Slavery*, 151–153; Higman, *Montpelier*, 229–237; Linda Baugmarten, *What Clothes Reveal: The Language of Clothing in Colonial and Federal America* (New Haven, 2002); Linda R. Baumgarten, "Leather Stockings and Hunting Shirts," in Ann Smart Martin and J. Ritchie Garrison (eds.), *American Material Culture: The Shape of the Field* (Winterthur, DE, 1997), pp. 251–276, esp. 266; Ekirch, *Bound for America*, 149. For clothing among the European poor, see Jutte, *Poverty and Deviance*, 78–82 and John Styles, "Clothing the North: The Supply of Non-Elite Clothing in the Eighteenth-Century North of England," *Textile History*, XXV (1994), 139–166.

colors. Slaves often used natural dyes to add a welcome touch of color to their drab uniforms. Yet over time, it would seem, slaves especially on large plantations came to be associated with a standardized form of clothing, even if the range of imported cloths grew more varied and slaves gained greater access to variety in their leisure-time dress. Masters referred to their slaves as "clothed in the usual manner of laboring Negroes," "clothed in the common dress of field slaves," or wearing "the usual winter clothing of corn field negroes."[29]

Poor people, even slaves, could wear clothes above their supposed station. A Jamestown cowkeeper wore scarlet silk on Sundays; a lowly collier's wife, also in Jamestown, flaunted a beaver hat and a silk suit; two Mohawk Indians on horseback were "dressed a la mode Francois with laced hats, full trimmed coats, and ruffled shirts"; a maroon captain in Jamaica wore "a ruffled shirt, blue broad cloth coat, scarlet cuff to his sleeves, gold buttons, & he had with [that ensemble a] white cap, and black hat, white linen breeches puffed at the rims, no stockings or shoes on." Whites regularly complained of extravagantly dressed slaves, particularly on Sundays and holidays. In 1672 the justices of the peace of Surry County Virginia observed that the "apparrell commonly worne by negroes" heightened their "foolish pride," so banned white linen and ordered only "blew shirts and shifts" for slaves. One visitor to South Carolina noted that "there is scarce a new mode" of fashion "which *favourite black and mulatto women slaves* are not immediately *enabled* to adopt." A correspondent in the Chesapeake spoke of "the great Liberties" allowed slaves "particularly in their Dress." According to this observer, slaves stole "purely to raise Money to buy fine Cloaths, and when dressed in them, make them so bold and impudent that they insult every poor white Person they meet with." Wearing "Sunday or Holyday Cloaths" made slaves, he thought, as "bold as a Lion."[30]

Colonists in general experienced poorer housing than Europeans. Lavishing most of their time and resources on farm development, the earliest settlers scrimped on their accommodations. They generally huddled together

[29] Morgan, *Slave Counterpoint*, 128–129, 130, 132–133, 598–601; Baugmarten, *What Clothes Reveal*; Helen Bradley Griebel, "The West African Origin of the African-American Headwrap," in Joanne B. Eicher (ed.), *Dress and Ethnicity: Change Across Space and Time* (Oxford, 1995), pp. 207–226; Ward, *British West Indian Slavery*, 152, 210; Higman, *Slave Populations*, 223–225, 257.

[30] Karin Calvert, "The Function of Fashion in Eighteenth-Century America," in Carson et al. (eds.), *Of Consuming Interests*, 257, and Cary Carson, "The Consumer Revolution in Colonial British America: Why Demand?" ibid., 551; Timothy J. Shannon, "Dressing for Success on the Mohawk Frontier: Hendrick, William Johnson, and the Indian Fashion," *WMQ*, 3rd Ser., LIII (1996), 14; Douglas Hall, *In Miserable Slavery: Thomas Thistlewood in Jamaica, 1750–86* (London, 1989), p. 17; "Management of Slaves, 1672," *Virginia Magazine of History and Biography*, 7 (1899–1900), 314; Morgan, *Slave Counterpoint*, 601–602. See also Shane White and Graham White, "Slave Clothing and African-American Culture in the Eighteenth and Nineteenth Centuries," *Past and Present*, 148 (Aug. 1995), 149–186.

in cramped, drafty, dark, impermanent structures–nothing more than rams-hackle and temporary huts. Most dwellings had no foundations, but were constructed on posts placed directly into the ground, with clapboard sid-ing, earthen floors, and wooden chimneys. In material terms, the first couple of generations in America tended to lead a crude, spartan existence, often associated with poverty in Europe. Although middling farmers gradually in-vested in better housing over time, a broad cross section of the eighteenth century American population continued to live in crude, earthfast, one-, or at best, two-room houses without plaster walls, a lick of paint, wood floors, or glass windows. Houses were tiny. In late eighteenth century Maryland the most common size for a house was 16 × 20 feet; in Worcester County, Massachusetts one-sixth of the houses were less than 500 square feet; and urban tenements were even smaller. If being poor meant living in one room, many Americans in the colonial period were poor. Frontier settlers even as late as the American Revolution were often said to be living in primitive conditions.[31]

Although slaves and poor whites suffered similar housing conditions, slaves tended to be the worst off. For one thing, many slaves lacked sep-arate quarters, but rather lived in outbuildings, kitchens, or out-of-the-way spaces of principal dwellings – in attics, cupboards, or under the stairs. Only the poorest domestic white servant had to experience this lack of privacy. For another, many slave spaces were extremely small: cabins of between 150 and 250 square feet were commonplace (although poor tenant housing in the Chesapeake, for example, was not much bigger and the median house size for free whites in Spotsylvania County, Virginia in 1798 was just 280 square feet). The average living space for Caribbean slaves has been put at between 30 and 60 square feet each (in more than half of the dwellings of the poor in early nineteenth century Amsterdam, less than 60 square feet was available per person). Doors were small, windows rare, making for smoke-filled, dark, and unventilated spaces. Third, whereas whites increasingly lived privately, slaves increasingly lived communally in cramped, unsanitary villages, which were breeding grounds for communicable diseases. Finally, masters generally invested little in the flimsy and dilapidated huts that dotted their plantations; often the only items they bought for the construction of these huts were nails. Wattle-and-daub dwellings, thatched with canes or grasses, were the most common form of slave housing in the Caribbean. They cost almost nothing

---

[31] Edward A. Chappell, "Housing a Nation: The Transformation of Living Standards in Early America," in Carson et al. (eds.), *Of Consuming Interests*, pp. 167–232. esp. 169, 175–6, 181, 206–7, 210; Kulikoff, *British Peasants to Colonial American Farmers*, 121–2; James Horn, *Adapting to a New World: English Society in the Seventeenth-Century Chesapeake* (Chapel Hill, 1994), pp. 296–333; Lee Soltow, *Distribution of Wealth and Income in the United States in 1798* (Pittsburgh, 1989), 49–93. For the best European information, see Robert Jutte, *Poverty and Deviance in Early Modern Europe* (Cambridge, 1994), pp. 62–71, and Shammas, *Pre-Industrial Consumer*, 157–193.

but labor to construct. In 1800 the per capita value of shelter in the United States has been estimated at $6 for free persons and $3.00 for slaves.[32]

Poor folk, both white and black, not only inhabited squalid hovels but generally lacked basic household amenities. A few cooking utensils, bedding, and clothes often constituted the total assets of a poor person. Laborers furnished their houses with little more than a mattress or two, a cooking pot, and some chests. Slaves usually had less than this minimum: their "beds" were often collections of straw, old rags, a rush mat, or some animal skins. Tables, chairs, and bedsteads were usually out of reach of the white poor and almost certainly to the vast majority of slaves. Many of the poor ate from coarse earthenwares or woodenware, and rarely saw a mirror. Sleeping on a dirt floor, eating a pot-boiled stew, using fingers or a spoon, sitting on a box, or just squatting for lack of a stool were typical household experiences for the poor, not just slaves. Perhaps the only housing advantage the rural American poor had over their European counterpart was that they did not need to share their hovels with livestock – for heating purposes. In tropical climes, of course, slaves generally did not need heat; in temperate regions, "a good fire," as one master put it, was "the life of a negro," and enough firewood was usually available to keep warm. But even this advantage narrowed over time. Firewood became increasingly scarce and expensive by the end of the end of the eighteenth century. Even in rural areas landowners began restricting tenants to using only fallen wood, and some planters did the same to slaves. Firewood was a major item in outdoor poor relief budgets in northern towns and cities.[33]

Over the course of the eighteenth century, the poor's amenities benefited from a prospering economy. Dr. Alexander Hamilton once stayed in a poor

[32] Bernard L. Herman, "Slave and Servant Housing in Charleston, 1770–1820," *Historical Archaeology*, 33 (1999), 88–101; Morgan, *Slave Counterpoint*, 107–108, 110–112; Chappell, "Housing a Nation," in Carson et al. (eds.), *Of Consuming Interests*, 191–2; Stiverson, *Poverty in a Land of Plenty*, 56–84; Higman, *Montpelier*, 152, 176; Higman, *Slave Populations*, 218–223; Douglas V. Armstrong and Kenneth G. Kelly, "Settlement Patterns and the Origins of African Jamaican Society: Seville Plantation, St. Ann's Bay, Jamaica," *Ethnohistory*, 47 (2000), 369–397; Mancall and Weiss, "Was Economic Growth Likely in Colonial British North America?" *Journal of Economic History*, 59 (1999), 23. Thomas Jefferson expected that free workers would demand both more space and more independent access to it than slaves: Fraser Neiman, "Modeling Social Dynamics in Colonial and Antebellum Slave Architecture: Monticello in Historical Perspective" (unpublished paper, 1998), which also reports the Spotsylvania County data. Of the European poor, Jutte notes that "The cottages in which the day-labourers, cottagers and paupers lived were usually single-roomed, with an earth floor, mud walls, a thatched roof, a hole in the wall for a window and another for smoke to escape from the central hearth" – not all that dissimilar from the accommodation of slaves (Jutte, *Poverty and Deviance*, 68).

[33] Carr and Walsh, "Changing Lifestyles and Consumer Behavior," in Carson et al. (eds.), *Of Consuming Interests*, 63; Carson, "The Consumer Revolution in Colonial British America," ibid., 498, 598; Morgan, *Slave Counterpoint*, 121–122; cf. Hufton, *The Poor in Eighteenth-Century France*, 50.

family's home and observed "a looking glass with a painted frame, half a dozen pewter spoons and as many plates, old and wore out but bright and clean, a set of stone tea dishes, and a tea pot." Of the family's meagre possessions, the "tea equipage," a symbol of luxury, gave the gentleman the greatest offense. Even the inmates of the public hospital of Philadelphia, the city poorhouse, insisted on having bohea, a form of tea. By the late colonial era, tea and teaware appeared in about a quarter of poor estates in some Chesapeake counties. Some poor folk came to own chairs, bedsteads, coarse ceramics, linens, perhaps a book or two, table knives, and forks. By the late eighteenth century, some poor folk began to acquire some of the amenities previously beyond their reach.[34]

Even some slaves shared in these improvements in both household amenities and housing. Some acquired flatware, even an occasional piece of porcelain, as well as the odd remnants of tea services. An occasional slave cabin exhibited a few more comforts than normal, as in one Virginia slave dwelling that contained chairs, a bed, an iron and brass kettle, an iron pot, a pair of pot racks, a pothook, a frying pan, and a beer barrel. On another Virginia estate, those slaves who possessed large numbers of chickens traded them for stools. Slave housing too became more substantial and orderly over time. Single cabins and duplexes gradually supplanted dormitories; houses with sills, brick foundations, and plank floors little by little replaced earthfast dwellings; wooden chimneys were gradually replaced by brick. In the Caribbean, stone or boarded dwellings, with shingle roofs, sometimes took the place of wattle-and-daub structures. On the more established plantations, slaves began constructing two- and even three- or more room structures.[35]

Diet, shelter, and clothing all affected the ability to perform work – the prime activity of slaves and the laboring poor. Because of the chronic labor shortages in early America, labor participation was higher in the New World than the Old – as was the range of servitude. This effectiveness in extracting labor was most apparent for slaves, who began to enter the labor force as early as age 3 or 4 but more widely at age 8–10, and toiled until virtually

---

[34] Carl Bridenbaugh (ed.), *Gentleman's Progress: The Itinerarium of Dr. Alexander Hamilton, 1744* (Chapel Hill, NC, 1948), pp. 54–55, as cited in Ronald Hoffman, "Preface," in Carson et al. (eds.), *Of Consuming Interests*, p. viii; Carr and Walsh, "Changing Lifestyles and Consumer Behavior," ibid., pp. 67, 80–81, 145; T. H. Breen, "'Baubles of Britain: The American and Consumer Revolutions of the Eighteenth Century," ibid., p. 457; Carson, "The Consumer Revolution in Colonial British America," ibid., p. 617. See also Lorna Weatherill, *Consumer Behaviour and Material Culture in Britain, 1660–1760* (London, 1988); Shammas, *The Pre-Industrial Consumer* (Oxford, 1990); John Brewer and Roy Porter (eds.), *Consumption and the World of Goods* (London, 1993); Peter King, "Pauper Inventories and the Material Lives of the Poor in the Eighteenth and Early Nineteenth Centuries," in Tim Hitchcock, Peter King, and Pamela Sharpe (eds.), *Chronicling Poverty: The Voices and Strategies of the English Poor, 1640–1840* (Basingstoke, Eng., 1997), 155–191.

[35] Morgan, *Slave Counterpoint*, 104–124; Higman, *Montpelier*, 146–190, 238–240.

in the grave. Among the free American population (both in the North and South), about one-third was in the labor force; among slaves, the proportion was two-thirds. As David Eltis (building on Edmund Morgan) notes, "Europeans put African women to work in whip-driven field gangs in the Americas but were not prepared to see European women work under like conditions." Under-employment, such a feature of early modern European labor, was also less widespread in America. About a fifth of the early modern English population was too malnourished for regular work. Because of unemployment due to weather, illness, season, the interval between jobs, and simple lack of work, the typical working man in eighteenth century Europe worked about 200 to 210 days a year, and the poor worked even fewer days. In America, free laborers worked about 280 to 290 days, and slaves between 280 and 310 days, depending mostly on the crop. A more precise measure of the general conditions of labor is the number of hours involved. Slaves cultivating sugar had the most onerous schedule, with first-gang field laborers toiling on average about 3,500 hours a year (in Barbados the average was 3,200 but in Jamaica a staggering 4,000 hours). In North America, slaves averaged about 2,800 hours annually, although there were variations by crop. By comparison, free Northern farmers averaged about 3,200 hours per year, factory workers in early nineteenth century Britain 2,900, and the modern U.S. worker about 1,700 (1,600 in Germany and 1,400 in Sweden).[36]

The heightened intensity of labor per hour associated with gang-driven slave labor, as Robert Fogel has pointed out, was more important than the actual number of hours worked. In this regard, no other crop had such an extreme pace of labor as that of sugar. Not just the extreme hours of heavy labor, but the demands of night work during crop season, which lasted at least six months of the year, and the brutality of the gang-driving system made its regime extraordinarily onerous. In sugar's earliest phases in Barbados, white servants worked at the crop, but they soon learned of its rigors and avoided it at all costs; the crop became the preserve of slaves. Rice was another arduous crop, because of its long production cycle, the heavy pounding by hand, and the harsh environment in which it was grown – even though it was subject to a task, rather than gang, system. Like sugar, rice became associated solely with slave labor in the Lower South. Tobacco was the least physically demanding crop to grow. It was initially grown largely by servant labor, and well into the eighteenth century many a servant and convict worked

---

[36] Fogel, *The Fourth Great Awakening*, 11, 42, 75–77, 185–186; Hans-Joachim Voth, *Time and Work in England, 1750–1830* (Oxford, 2000), p. 121–130; Edmund S. Morgan, "Slavery and Freedom: The American Paradox," *Journal of American History*, 59 (1972), 26–27; Eltis, *Rise of African Slavery*, 85–113; Robert M. Schwartz, *Policing the Poor in Eighteenth-Century France* (Chapel Hill, 1988), 109; Higman, *Slave Populations*, 188; Fogel, *Without Consent or Contract*, 28, 52–54, 77–78; cf. Hugh Cunningham, "The Employment and Unemployment of Children in England, c. 1680–1851," *Past and Present*, 126 (1990), 115–150.

as a common fieldhand in the Chesapeake. "Among the Negroes to work at the Hoe" was how a Virginia convict described his fate. White servants complained about the drudgery, the sheer back-breaking toil, that such work entailed, although their lot was almost certainly better than slaves, who had no claim to the customary rights (such as a rest in the heat of the day or the many traditional holidays) that English servants brought with them from the Old World. Even in an activity, such as ironworking, that often employed slave and free labor together, the owners supervised slaves more closely and punished them more harshly than their white counterparts, whether free or indentured, and frequently relegated slaves to the dirtiest and most arduous tasks – mining, charcoal-making, and woodcutting.[37]

Although coercion was fundamental, the intense labor of slaves was not extracted solely by force; positive incentives also played a role, just as they did for free labor. The most important rewards masters offered slaves were holidays or rest days, special allowances of material goods, various tasking or piece-rate arrangements, and cash payments. Apart from the Christian holidays of Christmas, Easter, and Whitsuntide, planters generally kept Sundays free from estate labor and then gave occasional other days as indulgences, usually for good work. On eighteenth century Caribbean islands, where the provision ground system operated, slaves were usually allowed every other Saturday out of crop to tend their provisions. Such slaves typically had about about fifteen free days as well as Sundays. Masters were usually willing to trade with their slaves, thereby displaying their benevolence, rendering slavery a little more humane, while also buying the products at below market price, thereby serving their own self-interest. The slaves preferred to exchange their provisions – fish, poultry, small livestock, craft products – for cash. Tasking, which gave slaves some latitude in apportioning their time, was common in many slave work settings – especially rice, coffee, timber and naval stores production, and increasingly in some sugar and cotton operations. So-called "overwork" – production that exceeded a quota – was common in ironworking. Also, masters sometimes paid cash to get slaves to do extra work, perhaps on a Sunday, or long into the night.[38]

---

[37] Fogel, *Without Consent or Contract*, 78–79; Beckles, *White Servitude and Black Slavery*, 115–167; Morgan, *Slave Counterpoint*, 147–159, 164–170, 175–178; Ekirch, *Bound for America*, 152, 156; Wayne K. Durrill, "Routine of Seasons: Labour Regimes and Social Ritual in an Antebellum Plantation Community," *Slavery and Abolition*, 16 (1995), 161–187; Lorena Walsh, "Slave Life, Slave Society, and Tobacco Production in the Tidewater Chesapeake, 1620–1820," in Berlin and Morgans (eds.), *Cultivation and Culture*, 176–177; John Bezi-Selfa, "Slavery and the Disciplining of Free Labor in the Colonial Mid-Atlantic Iron Industry," *Pennsylvania History*, 64, Sp. Supp. (Summer, 1997), 270–286; idem., "A Tale of Two Ironworks: Slavery, Free Labor, Work, and Resistance in the Early Republic," *WMQ*, 3rd. Ser., LVI (1999), 677–700; idem., "American Crucible: Adventurers, Ironworkers, and the Struggle to Forge an Industrious Revolution, 1640–1830," ch. 3 (MS). I am grateful to Mr. Bezi-Selfa for sharing this chapter with me.

[38] Higman, *Slave Populations*, 202–204; Ward, *British West Indian Slavery*, 112, 200–202; Morgan, *Slave Counterpoint*, 195, 359–366, 373–376; Betty Wood, "'Never on a Sunday?'

In sum, there are two ways of assessing the material standards of early American slaves. First, they experienced a thoroughly spartan material existence. They worked extraordinarily hard and in many cases for more hours than free laborers. Harsh taskmasters drove them onward, the whip being the ubiquitous instrument. Just as Africans experienced worse mortality and more crowded conditions than any other transatlantic traveler, so once in America they lived in the flimsiest, most cramped quarters. Their everyday attire was as mean as their shelter. Masters forced slaves to wear cheap, drab, uncomfortable clothes. Many adults and most children went naked and barefoot. Slaves were as poorly fed as they were clothed. Their diet was high in starch, low in protein, and extremely monotonous in content. Richard Parkinson, a perceptive observer, noted that slaves were "both clothed and fed at less expence" than free men; the livelihood of the Southern planter, he continued, was "pinched and screwed out of the negro."

At the same time, poor whites experienced material conditions not all that dissimilar to slaves. In some respects, many slaves were better off than poor whites in strictly material terms. Certainly the stature of slaves suggests that their diet was no worse, perhaps even better, than that of many poor whites. Slaves rarely starved, even if they were malnourished. As J. R. Ward notes, "by emancipation [and probably well before] an adult British West Indian slave's material state, measured by quantity of food eaten and yards of cloth worn, at least matched that of many British workers." Some slaves, particularly on the mainland, worked fewer hours than free workers in the Northern colonies. And, of course, slaves were far from experiencing the same conditions; marked variations existed among them – and these need now to be explored.[39]

III

The slaves' bedrock material conditions were not uniform, even though social differentiation among slaves was always much less than among free people. Opportunity for individual advancement was obviously much more restricted for the unfree than for the free. Slaves rarely could change masters or move voluntarily. Their *peculium*, the small items of movable property

Slavery and the Sabbath in Lowcountry Georgia 1750–1830," in Mary Turner (ed.), *From Chattel Slaves to Wage Slaves: The Dynamics of Labour Bargaining in the Americas* (Bloomington, IN, 1995), pp. 79–96; Fogel, *Without Consent or Contract*, 191–194, 392; Philip D. Morgan, "Task and Gang Systems: The Organization of Labor on New World Plantations," in Innes (ed.), *Work and Labor*, pp. 189–220; for ironworks, see n.33 and Charles Dew, *Bond of Iron: Master and Slave at Buffalo Forge* (New York, 1994), pp. 108–121, 155–156, 162–163; O. Nigel Bolland, "Proto-Proletarians? Slave Wages in the Americas: Between Slave Labour and Free Labour," in Turner (ed.), *From Chattel Slaves to Wage Slaves*, pp. 123–147.
39 Parkinson, *A Tour in America, in 1798, 1799, and 1800...*, 2 vols. (London, 1805), I, p. 27; Ward, *British West Indian Slavery*, 263, 286–288.

that they might acquire – such as produce from gardens or provision grounds; small livestock, occasionally horses and cattle; extra clothing; or their own craft products – were always by their master's leave. Possession was always tenuous for slaves; legal ownership was never possible. Collective action to remedy grievances was also difficult; slaves tended to act individually rather than in groups. Nevertheless, although slavery always allowed much less room for maneuver than freedom, the institution was not homogenous or monolithic. The slave experience varied, most significantly in five major ways: over time, across space, according to the status of masters, through a hierarchy among slaves, and finally by the differential struggles of the enslaved.[40]

The material conditions of slaves, much like those of whites, changed over the course of the colonial period. As frontier societies became more settled, planters built more secure housing, displayed their wealth through their plantation establishment, and in general regularized the material conditions of their laborers. Housing evolved from barracks or quarters to family cabins and duplexes. Domestic life moved from public to private, perhaps symbolized best by the growing appearance of padlocks on slave cabin doors and the presence of personal sub-floor storage pits inside many cabins. Earthfast structures slowly gave way to more permanent architectural forms, and slave settlements grew more autonomous over time. Although eighteenth century slaves never wore a uniform, their dress grew more standardized. Similarly, cereals, vegetables, and some fish or meat protein became the core of the slave diet. In some cases, innovations such as pounding machines and the use of tidal flows in rice cultivation or more plowing and ratooning to reduce hand manuring and cane holing in sugar cultivation eased the labor of slaves at particular points of the year. As plantations grew larger and more slaves escaped field labor, the material lives of an increasing minority of slaves improved.[41]

But not all slaves, or the poor, experienced material progress. The regularization of conditions created a diminution of material standards in some cases. Some planters more precisely measured the yardage of cloth or food rations in order to cut costs; some imposed a more geometric, ordered layout to housing that slaves might not have preferred; some increased labor requirements, perhaps by undertaking elementary time and motion studies to accelerate workpace; some tried to monitor pilfering and night-time activities. The late eighteenth century trend toward the regularization of the

[40] On slaves' propensity to act individually, see Peter Kolchin, *Unfree Labor: American Slavery and Russian Serfdom* (Cambridge, MA, 1987), esp. 257–301.

[41] Morgan, *Slave Counterpoint*, 102–254; Barbara J. Heath, *Hidden Lives: The Archaeology of Slave Life at Thomas Jefferson's Poplar Forest* (Charlottesville, VA, 1999), 63–64; Fraser Neiman, "Sub-Floor Pits and Slavery in 18th and early 19th-Century Virginia" (unpublished paper, 1997); Ward, *British West Indian Slavery*, 72, 82, 88.

material and work conditions of slaves parallels attempts to do much the same with respect to the free poor – curtailing outdoor relief and forcing them into hospitals and workhouses. The same urge ostensibly to "improve," "standardize," and "ameliorate" material conditions by reducing autonomy seems to be at work.

Another way in which slavery changed over time was according to the lifecycle of the individual slave. Newly enslaved Africans, typically in their teens or early adult years, were at their most destitute when they landed in America. Literally stripped of almost everything – possessions, kin, their health, even memories – they arrived on New World soil virtually naked, physically debilitated, perhaps still smarting from a shipboard brand, soon to be separated from even shipmates, and sold most commonly as individuals. Disoriented and alienated, many would sicken and die within the first year. Often placed in the hut of another slave, perhaps even to be exploited by that host slave, it would be many years before the newcomer ever acquired anything. But, if the slave survived, job allocations depended above all on age. On sugar estates, for example, children usually worked in the first gang between the ages of 5 and 12, progressed to the second gang between 12 and 18, and then to the first gang between 18 and 45, before returning to the second gang when past their prime, usually over forty years of age. Typically, drivers had to wait for their appointment until they were in their mid-to-late thirties. Those slaves who entered trades usually did so much later than free persons. Most masters could not afford to apprentice slaves at the usual age (early teens), but rather had to single out a likely field slave, usually a mature adult, for on-the-job training. Watchmen were almost always old and weak. Lifecycle changes, then, clearly determined different jobs.[42]

Native-born slaves or creoles experienced slavery very differently from Africans. For one thing, creoles had more resistance to the local disease environment, and were almost always taller, better nourished, than Africans. For another, creoles almost completely abandoned the bodily aesthetic so important to Africans – cicatrization and teeth filing – in part because those practices had lost their function in the New World and in part because masters placed their own marks on the slaves' bodies. In place of permanent forms of bodily adornment, creoles channeled their interest in fashion and their commitment to personal style in varied and changing hairstyles, inventive headgear, occasional jewelry, and brightly colored clothes. Often described as brisk, lively, sharp, and sensible, or conversely as bold, saucy, sly, and cunning, native-born slaves inspired admiration and provoked consternation from masters in almost equal amounts. Planters generally thought that creoles made better tradesmen than Africans, and almost everywhere

[42] Morgan, *Slave Counterpoint*, 443–459; Ward, *British West Indian Slavery*, 18, 110–111; Higman, *Slave Populations*, 189–199.

native-born men dominated the artisanal ranks. In late eighteenth century St. Domingue, for instance, one in four creole men, compared to only one in ten African men, held positions outside the field. Native-born slaves of mixed racial ancestry were the most likely to avoid field labor. Mulatto or colored women were particularly over-represented among domestics. Considered physically weak and yet superior because of their light skin, and indeed often related to the slaveowner or his white employees, mulattoes were highly favored in occupational allocations. The light-skinned Hemings family's monopoly of household positions at Monticello was not unusual. Visitors to Jefferson's home who stayed close to the house would have encountered only Hemingses.[43]

Slavery varied not only over time but also across space. Three spatial distinctions are conspicuous. First were the obvious regional differences – between island and mainland, between large island and small island, between lowcountry and Chesapeake, between Tidewater and Piedmont, between highlands and lowlands, and between yeoman and plantation worlds. Slaves on large islands, for example, usually had access to mountain provision grounds; slaves on small islands relied mostly on imported foods. Also, slaves tended to be much healthier and fertile in interior rather than in coastal locations, in hilly or mountainous territory rather than in lowland ecosystems. Second, crops shaped slave life in fundamental ways. In Jamaica, for instance, the death rate on sugar plantations was fifty percent higher than on coffee plantations; in Trinidad it was nearly three times as high on sugar as on cotton plantations; and in South Carolina a slave child on a rice plantation was almost half as likely to survive to maturity as a child elsewhere in the South. Finally, slavery was markedly different in urban, as opposed to, rural environments. In the Caribbean, somewhat counterintuitively, living in a town generally increased the chances of survival. The superior housing and clothing of urban slaves probably helped ward off diarrhea and dysentry, the great killers in the cramped plantation quarters. In North America, on the other hand, living in a city generally reduced a slave's chance of survival. The difference is largely explained by the far more thinly dispersed rural populations of the mainland as compared to the densely settled sugar plantations of most islands. Also, urban living in North America reduced a

[43] Higman, *Montpelier*, 249–257; Morgan, *Slave Counterpoint*, 463–464, 594–609; Barbara J. Heath, "Buttons, Beads, and Buckles: Contextualizing Adornment within the Bounds of Slavery," in Maria Franklin and Garrett Fesler (eds.), *Historical Archaeology, Identity Formation, and the Interpretation of Ethnicity* (Williamsburg, VA, 1999), 47–69; Fogel, *Without Consent or Contract*, 48; David P. Geggus, "Sugar and Coffee Cultivation in Saint Domingue and the Shaping of the Slave Labor Force," in Ira Berlin and Philip D. Morgan (eds.), *Cultivation and Culture: Labor and the Shaping of Slave Life in the Americas* (Charlottesville, VA, 1993), pp. 73–98; Higman, *Slave Populations*, 194–197; Lucia Stanton, "'Those Who Labor for My Happiness': Thomas Jefferson and His Slaves," in Peter S. Onuf (ed.), *Jeffersonian Legacies* (Charlottesville, VA, 1993), p. 151.

slave's chances of survival because of a limited diet due to a lack of access to garden plots and because working for wages reduced time for self-sufficient activities. Craft opportunities were much greater in towns than in the countryside, not only in number but also in range. Also, the ability of a slave to hire his or her own time (and thereby earn money) was greater in towns than in the countryside.[44]

The status of the master had enormous ramifications for slave life. In the same way that the use of the term "servant class" to describe London's domestic servants gives a misleading impression of homogeneity, when in fact, as Tim Meldrum notes, "there were vast differences in the experience and remuneration between the smallest tradesman's household and a West End mansion house," so slavery and the "slave class" were similarly differentiated. Perhaps the greatest distinction was between slaves living in the household of a small farmer and that of a large planter. Small planters generally provided their slaves less clothing and flimsier accommodations, although not necessarily less food, than most large planters. In fact, the subsistence priorities of many small planters often guaranteed more food to their slaves than those owned by commercially oriented large planters. The size of plantation, as Robert Fogel has noted, was far more important than occupation in determining slave household structure. Mother-headed slave households were common on small plantations; two parent-headed slave households and extended slave households were common on large plantations. Slave families were more stable, less subject to disruption, on large than on small plantations. To be poor in Africa was usually to be without relatives, to have no kin connections, to be solitary; for many slaves, particularly of course the African newcomer, the same condition applied, but for creoles in particular, especially those on large plantations, kinfolk were often present and families acted as a haven in a cruel world.[45]

Just as the status of the master varied, so did that of the slave, although within a much narrower range. Skilled slaves and domestics usually enjoyed more comforts than fieldhands, even than many poor whites. Slave artisans might wear collars and cuffs made from lace or other expensive materials, gold-laced hats, shoes with metal buckles, beaver hats, and superfine cloth coats. One carpenter was only somewhat more ostentatious than usual in flourishing a silver watch, silver shoe buckles, and a brown wig. Personal

---

[44] Fogel, *Without Consent or Contract*, 127; William Dusinberre, *Them Dark Days: Slavery in the American Rice Swamps* (New York, 1996), pp. 80, 412; Higman, *Slave Populations* 376; Klepp, "Seasoning and Society," *WMQ*, 3rd. Ser., LI (1994), 473–506; Morgan, *Slave Counterpoint*, 229.

[45] Tim Meldrum, "London Domestic Servants from Depositional Evidence, 1660–1750: Servant-Employer Sexuality in the Patriarchal Household," in Hitchcock (ed.), *Chronicling Poverty*, 49; Fogel, *Without Consent or Contract*, 178–179, 182; Iliffe, *The African Poor*, 7, 33–35, 54, 57, 59, 63, 72, 76, 85–87; Morgan, *Slave Counterpoint*, 498–558.

manservants were the best-dressed slaves. One such waiting man cut a fine figure in his "blue Plush Breeches," "fine Cloth Pompadour Waistcoat," white shirt, neat shoes with silver buckles, and "fine Hat cut and cocked in the Macaroni Figure." Tradesmen generally experienced better nutrition and health than domestics and, to an even greater extent, field laborers. The death rate of field hands in the Caribbean was more than double those of privileged slaves. Slave ironworkers, in part because of the "overwork" system which allowed them to acquire cash or goods for surpassing daily or weekly production quotas, were able to purchase extra linen, clothing, bedding, and food to improve their quality of life. At one Chesapeake iron-works, the ration was six pounds of meat a week; when a slave foreman at a nearby plantation heard the news he said he would flee his plantation unless sent to the foundry. An investigation of sixteen adult skeletons dating to the late eighteenth century from Catoctin Furnance in Maryland found not only that the men outlived the women but also that male ironworkers outlived nineteenth century plantation workers. The opportunity to travel was another benefit that came to privileged slaves. Boatmen and sailors, manservants, and tradesmen who hired their own time were the most widely traveled slaves. Probably the most common privilege of skilled slaves – a regular supply of alcohol – owed to the customary right enjoyed by English artisans. Finally, privileged slaves could often bequeath an inheritance, some-thing not usually associated with slaves: They regularly transmitted their skills to their children. On some plantations a few slave families came to monopolize privileged positions.[46]

Nevertheless, occupational distinctions should not be exaggerated. On one Jamaican plantation studied in great detail, privileged slaves – drivers, carpenters, coopers, masons, blacksmiths, and domestics – were more likely to be sheltered under shingled than thatched roofs, but that was the extent of the improvement in housing that their status brought. Houses on this plantation were no bigger or better for slaves of mixed racial ancestry or for high-status workers than they were for fieldhands. Furthermore, the typical domestic and many skilled slaves (e.g., sawyers) often engaged in drudge labor, sometimes in the fields. The work of a washerwoman was no more glamorous than that of a fieldhand. Indeed, for women in general, occupa-tional differentiation was seriously limited. Skilled labor was generally con-sidered to be men's work. Removing men from the field meant that women composed the greater portion of those remaining. By the early nineteenth century, Richard Dunn found that a young man's chances of remaining a

---

[46] Morgan, *Slave Counterpoint*, 131, 136, 246, 347, 545–546; Higman, *Slave Populations*, 245–246, 288–289, 333–335, 345–347; S. Max Edelson, "Affiliation without Affinity: Skilled Slaves in Eighteenth-Century South Carolina," in Jack P. Greene, Rosemary Brana-Shute, and Randy J. Sparks (eds.), *Money, Trade, and Power: The Evolution of South Carolina's Plantation Society* (Columbia, SC, 2001), 221–259.

prime fieldhand on Mesopotamia plantation, Jamaica, was one in two; for a young woman, it was five in six. Occupational distinctions meant little to slave women.[47]

Finally, slavery varied in large part because slaves, like the white poor, actively strove for the means of their own survival. Individual slaves worked on their own time: hunted and gathered; fished; tended private gardens and, in some cases, provision grounds; raised livestock; and hawked the products of their labors. Some slaves were gifted healers, others renowned conjurors; some were noted preachers, others celebrated musicians; some were jockeys, others goldsmiths. Some traded in town markets, others stole from masters. Slaves were not defenseless, mere victims of their impoverishment. Some slaves acquired considerable cash and property. In late eighteenth century Jamaica, slaves held perhaps about a fifth of the coins circulating on the island, although the average slave probably owned little more than a shilling. A few slaves earned large sums for selling livestock or hiring their time. In the 1790s slaves typically carried goods worth ten to twelve shillings sterling when they went to market. A small minority of slaves earned enough to buy their freedom. Some slaves managed to accumulate substantial estates, at times equivalent to those of moderately successful free artisans or farmers, and some were able to bequeath those estates to their loved ones at death.[48]

Most of all, slaves, like the poor in both Europe and Africa, learned to survive; they engaged in strategies, "a whole series of ploys and subterfuges," akin to Olwen Hufton's classic portrayal of an "economy of makeshifts." For slaves, just like the English poor, "Reciprocity and neighbourliness were crucial. Although they lacked the real capital which enabled the better-off to weather difficult times without outside help, the poor could and did accumulate "social capital." By lending tools and possessions, and by offering physical and psychological assistance to neighbors and kin in times of need, they invested in the future, being able to draw on the resources of others." Families and kinfolk were just as important for slaves as for the white poor. Just as the mother in a conventionally poor household taught her children how and where to beg, so the slave mother who often brought up her children alone was the dominant figure in their lives. For slaves too, just like the African poor, "by hawking or begging or stealing, by endurance or industry or guile, by the resourcefulness of the blind or the courage of the cripple, by

[47] Higman, *Montpelier*, 180–181; Morgan, *Slave Counterpoint*, 244–253; Richard S. Dunn, "Sugar Production and Slave Women in Jamaica," in Berlin and Morgan (eds.), *Cultivation and Culture*, pp. 49–72.

[48] Higman, *Montpelier*, 243; Morgan, *Slave Counterpoint*, 358–376, 469–470, 537–538; Berlin and Morgan (eds.), *Cultivation and Culture*, 31, 35, 37; Larry E. Hudson (ed.), *Working toward Freedom: Slave Society and Domestic Economy in the American South* (Rochester, N.Y., 1994); Betty Wood, *Women's Work, Men's Work: The Informal Slave Economies of Lowcountry Georgia* (Athens, GA, 1995).

the ambition of the young or the patience of the old – by all these means the African poor survived in their harsh world."[49]

It is easy to dismiss these variations in the experiences of slaves as trivial. The material conditions of slaves were so impoverished, it can be argued, that it is futile to draw distinctions among them. Moreover, the material conditions of slaves rested heavily on the fortunes, decisions, and whims of individual masters; and, in that sense, distinctions between the slaves may seem merely idiosyncratic and arbitrary. But significant variations in slave life did occur, and they were patterned, not random. Some improvements occurred over time; age, birthplace, and color determined occupational allocations; territorial distinctions mattered; crops profoundly shaped slave experiences; size of plantation counted; status in the slave hierarchy was consequential; and slaves, like poor whites, always strove both individually and collectively to shape their material state.

IV

A major, perhaps the defining, experience of the conventional poor is their risk of dependency. Vulnerability, as Olwen Hufton notes, "was the main characteristic of the *pauvre*." The poor "lived under the constant threat" of "hunger, cold, pain, or physical deprivation." Life-cycle poverty was premised on insecurity. Thus a recently married couple with two or three young children could easily experience temporary poverty. Perhaps the wife was unable to work, the children too young to earn, the father ill-equipped to bring in enough money to meet the increased expenses. Another period of life – advancing years – was often a stage to fear. Earnings could dry up, and familial support might be unavailable. Ordinary everyday happenings like sickness or an increase in the price of basic foodstuffs could throw people on the margins of survival into poverty.[50]

Slaves faced all sorts of insecurities – about whether they might be sold, whipped, or have to endure some fresh humiliation. Slaves were dependents par excellence; the whim of a master determined a slave's fate. But the one compensation for such dependence was that a slave generally could expect a minimal subsistence. The master had an obvious and real incentive to see that the slave survived. The birth of a slave child would not strain a family budget – because the slave family had no budget. The conventional poor lived, as Hufton notes, "in a perpetual state of debt," but no slave suffered this fate. If a master had too many children among his slaves he might sell

---

[49] Hufton, *The Poor of Eighteenth-Century France*, 7, 69–127; Hitchcock, *Chronicling Poverty*, 12; Iliffe, *The African Poor*, 8. See also Jutte, *Poverty and Deviance*, 83–99, 143–157 and Marco H. D. van Leeuwen, *Journal of Interdisciplinary History*, XXIV (1994), 589–613.

[50] Hufton, *The Poor of Eighteenth-Century France*, 20. See also Mary E. Fissell, *Patients, Power, and the Poor in Eighteenth-Century Bristol* (Cambridge, 1991), p. 3.

some of them – thereby making it tragically clear that no slave family could ever feel secure – but he would have every inducement to keep them alive. Some masters did try to evade the expense of feeding aging slaves by freeing them, but such an action was rare; growing old was not a stage of life slaves had especially to fear. Nor did sickness or debility, say following childbirth, generally mean a reduction in rations. The insecurity of staying alive – of having no food, no clothing, no roof over one's head – was the one vulnerability the condition of slavery minimized. In some cases, then, the material conditions of slaves were not always inferior to other temporarily unfree or even free laborers. Almost all slaves were *pauvre*, struggling continuously to keep body and soul together, but few of them were *indigent*, always hungry and in chronic need of the means of survival. Such a comparison may seem to come dangerously close to the racism of George Fitzhhugh, but I prefer to see it as closer to the clear-eyed vision of say, J. H. Plumb, who wrote, "Slavery and poverty [in the early modern period] are not different in kind but different in degree, and the disadvantage was not always the slave's for, as property, he might be treated with greater consideration in sickness or in old age than the wage slave."[51]

To say that slaves had some material benefits, that few were absolutely destitute, is not to say that their lot was somehow better than the white poor. In the nineteenth century, Irish famine deaths proved to some people that wage slavery caused greater horrors than chattel slavery. Frederick Douglass would have none of it: "The Irishman is poor," he noted, "but he is not a slave. He is still the master of his own body." The Irish could at least organize, remonstrate, and emigrate. American slavery, that "grand aggregation of human horrors," rendered its victims as mute as the "silent dead," echoing Orlando Patterson's depiction of slavery as social death. The escaped slave Harriet Jacobs added, "I would ten thousand times rather that my children should be the half-starved paupers of Ireland than to be the most pampered among the slaves of America." Slaves strove to throw off the chains of slavery even if freedom brought starvation and economic deprivation. Conversely, Frederick Douglass found no takers among white workers when he advertised the job vacancy, with all its alleged material comforts, created by his having fled slavery.[52]

[51] Iliffe, *The African Poor*, 2; Hufton, *The Poor of Eighteenth-Century France*, 20; Plumb, "Slavery, Race and the Poor" in *The American Experience*, vol. 2, 139.

[52] David Roediger, "Race, Labor, and Gender in the Languages of Antebellum Social Protest," in Stanley Engerman (ed.), *Terms of Labor: Slavery, Serfdom, and Free Labor* (Stanford, CA, 1999), pp. 175, 177.

11

The North–South Wage Gap
before and after the Civil War

Robert A. Margo

I

In the several decades preceding the Civil War the Southern economy grew at about the same pace as did the economy of the rest of the United States. In the immediate aftermath of the Civil War, per capita incomes fell sharply in the South, absolutely and relative to per capita incomes in the North. Although there was some recovery after the initial decline, Southern incomes remained persistently low relative to Northern incomes for the remainder of the nineteenth century – indeed, until well into the twentieth century. Measured in terms of per capita incomes, the impact of the Civil War on the Southern economy was both severe initially and protracted.[1]

This chapter offers further assessment of the impact of the War on the Southern economy but in a way that has received relatively limited attention previously from economic historians. Specifically, I examine the evolution

I thank Mark Bils, William Collins, Stanley Engerman, David Feldman, Joseph Ferrie, Ronald Findlay, Claudia Goldin, Chris Hanes, James Irwin, Ronald Jones, Frank Lewis, Winnie Rothenberg, Gavin Wright, two referees, and workshop participants at the Conference in Honor of Stanley Engerman, the National Bureau of Economic Research, the University of Mississippi, and the University of Rochester, for helpful comments; Tom Weiss, for providing me with his worksheets on the nineteenth century labor force; Roger Ransom and Richard Sutch, for providing a CD-ROM of their 1880 sample of Southern farms; and Jon Moen, for clarifying his calculations of labor productivity in Southern agriculture. Portions of this research are supported by the National Science Foundation under a grant to the National Bureau of Economic Research.
[1] See Stanley L. Engerman, "The Economic Impact of the Civil War," *Explorations in Economic History*, 3 (1966): 176–199; Stanley L. Engerman, "Some Economic Factors in Southern Backwardness in the Nineteenth Century," in John Kain and John Meyer (eds.), *Essays in Regional Economics* (Cambridge, MA, 1971); Claudia Goldin, "'N' Kinds of Freedom: An Introduction to the Issues," *Explorations in Economic History*, 16 (1979): 8–30; Gavin Wright, *Old South, New South* (New York, 1986); and Robert A. Margo, "The South as an Economic Problem: Fact or Fiction?" in Larry Griffin and Don Doyle (eds.), *The South as an American Problem* (Athens, GA, 1995).

of wages in the South relative to the North, before and after the War. My analysis is based on wage evidence culled from various published and archival sources, reaching back into the ante-bellum period as early as the 1820s and extending (in some cases) to the end of the century.

There are several reasons why a study of the impact of the War on relative (South-to-North) wages is of value. One reason is that regional data on wages are available more frequently, in the temporal sense, than are estimates of per capita income.[2] As evidence, wage data are arguably more "direct" than are estimates of per capita income, which (for the nineteenth century) typically require strong assumptions, both in construction and interpretation. Wage data are available for different occupations and various locations, and thus can be used to assess differential effects in ways that currently available data on per capita income cannot.

The wage data assembled here shed further light on the origins of the so-called "low-wage" South. As documented by Gavin Wright, there is considerable evidence that the South ca. 1900 was a low-wage region in a generally high-wage nation.[3] However, the extent to which the low-wage label can be traced solely or even mostly to the impact of the Civil War per se – versus, say, events after the War or pre-existing conditions – is less clear. Although previous work is suggestive of a structural break in wages during the 1860s, this work is far from conclusive, being based on data for a single occupation (farm labor) for a small number of states.[4]

My principal finding is that the South did experience a pronounced decline in wages relative to the North after the Civil War. In the South Atlantic states, farm and common wages were already below levels prevailing in the North prior to the War, but this was not true for skilled labor, and was not true generally in the South Central States. The post-bellum decline was immediate, being apparent as early as 1866, occurring for skilled and unskilled labor, men and women. Within the South Atlantic and South Central regions, the declines in relative wages were more severe in the Deep than in

---

[2] For example, reasonably accurate estimates of regional per capita incomes are available for only two years during the ante-bellum period, 1840 and 1860. Various economic historians (e.g., see Roger Ransom and Richard Sutch, *One Kind of Freedom: The Economic Consequences of Emancipation* [New York, 1977]; Wright, *Old South, New South*) contend that the post-bellum decline in Southern per capita income is overstated because southern incomes were unusually high in 1860. For a contrary view, see Robert W. Fogel and Stanley L. Engerman, "Explaining the Relative Efficiency of Slave Agriculture in the Antebellum South," *American Economic Review*, 67 (1977): 275–296.

[3] Wright, *Old South, New South*.

[4] Drawing on data on farm wages for four southern states (Arkansas, Mississippi, Georgia, and South Carolina) Wright (*Old South, New South*, 76) concludes that the "relative farm wage in ... the South declined sharply over the Civil War decade." He also claims that the same was true for other states and occupations, referring readers to the "admittedly imperfect and often fragmentary wage data" in Robert J. Newman, *Growth in the American South* (New York, 1964).

the Upper South. Data for West Virginia and Virginia suggest that relative wages diverged even within states that had been divided in their loyalties during the conflict.

After the initial decline, South/North wage ratios began to revert back toward their pre-war levels. For non-farm labor this reversion was substantial, if not fully complete, by 1890. For farm labor, there is evidence of mean reversion for both the South Atlantic and South Central regions in the 1870s, and in the 1880s in the South Atlantic. However, the pace of mean reversion was slower for farm labor than for non-farm labor. Further, in the South Central states, the South/North farm wage ratio began to deteriorate again in the 1880s and in both the South Central and South Atlantic states the farm wage relatives declined in the 1890s.

Prior to the Civil War few slaves (and few free blacks) worked for wages. After the Civil War, many former slaves entered the wage labor force in the South. Suppose that former slaves who worked for wages were paid less than their white counterparts, either because of differences in skills or because of racial discrimination. The combination of wage differences coupled with the change in the composition of the wage labor force would produce a decline, on average, in the South/North wage ratio, even if there were no other wage effects of the War. This explanation is difficult to confirm or refute, because there are relatively few sources of post-bellum wage data that distinguish between black and white labor. Nonetheless, the limited evidence that is available suggests that, although racial wage gaps existed, these gaps do not appear to have been large enough to have had much effect on South/North wage ratios.

Perhaps the simplest explanation of my findings is a decline in the demand for labor in the South relative to the North, along an inelastic relative labor supply curve.[5] During the immediate aftermath of the War, the Southern economy was in a shambles due to wartime devastation and dislocation. There were, as well, many difficulties associated with the transition to a free labor force and with Reconstruction.[6] Given some short-run immobility in labor, it is not surprising to find *some* short-run decline in the South/North wage ratio. However, both the size of the decline and its seeming persistence suggests that more than purely transitory factors were at play.

---

[5] An increase in the relative supply of labor in the South could also account for the decline in relative wages. However, this does not seem to be a promising avenue to pursue, in particular because labor force participation rates of ex-slaves appear to have declined after the War; see Ransom and Sutch, *One Kind of Freedom*. Thomas Weiss's ("Estimates of White and Non-White Gainful Workers in the United States by Age Group, Race, and Sex: Decennial Census Years, 1800–1900," *Historical Methods*, 32 [1999]: 21–35) state-level estimates, for example, imply that the South Atlantic's share of the total Northern and Southern labor force declined from 18 percent in 1860 to 14 percent in 1870 (and to 13 percent in 1880). I am grateful to Professor Weiss for providing me with access to his worksheets.

[6] See Ransom and Sutch, *One Kind of Freedom*, for an extensive discussion of this issue.

Among economic historians the most prominent and most controversial explanation is due to Robert Fogel and Stanley Engerman.[7] According to Fogel and Engerman, labor productivity in Southern agriculture declined "once and for all" after the War and can be linked causally to emancipation. Fogel and Engerman fashioned their explanation to account for the decline in Southern per capita income. However, the causal mechanism at work – a decline in labor demand induced by the decline in productivity – can explain the decline in relative wages, again as long as the supply of labor was less than perfectly elastic.

To buttress the evidence that a productivity shock occurred, Section IV assembles data on agricultural prices and uses these, in conjunction with the data on farm wages, to construct time series of the real product wage in southern agriculture – wages divided by the price of output. The real product wage is the dual of the direct measure of labor productivity (output per worker). Although uses of the dual are commonplace in economic history, measuring productivity change in Southern agriculture before and after the War does rest on assumptions that, for some readers, may be overly strong. However, the use of the dual in this context is not novel per se, having been applied already by Jon Moen.[8] My calculations go beyond Moen's by refining the numerator of the productivity index (wages) and by including additional years in the computation.

Like Moen, I find a substantial decline in labor productivity in Southern agriculture after the War, comparing levels in 1870 or 1880 with levels prevailing in 1860 or (in the case of the South Atlantic) 1850. However, between 1880 and 1890 labor productivity in both the South Atlantic and South Central states recovered somewhat, reaching a level in 1890 in the South Atlantic that slightly exceeded the level in 1860. Between 1890 and 1900, productivity in both regions fell once again, although to a far smaller extent than between 1890 and 1900. The dual calculations suggest that the South experienced two productivity shocks, the first between 1860 and 1870, and the second between 1890 and 1900. However, the exact sizes of these shocks, particularly the one in the 1860s, cannot be determined with the data at hand: There are insufficient observations.

Models of regional labor demand shocks also predict changes in the regional structure of prices of non-traded goods. The same sources that provide evidence on wages also provide evidence on the cost of one such good – locally produced food. Using plausible estimates of income and price elasticities, the data on board suggest that the South experienced a decline in food

---

[7] Robert W. Fogel and Stanley L. Engerman, *Time on the Cross* (Boston, 1974); Fogel and Engerman, "Explaining the Relative Efficiency."

[8] Jon Moen, "Changes in the Productivity of Southern Agriculture Between 1860 and 1880," in R. Fogel and S. Engerman (eds.), *Without Consent or Contract: Markets and Production, Technical Papers*, Vol. 1 (New York, 1992).

prices relative to the North after the War. In all likelihood, however, the decline in the South/North ratio of food prices was smaller than the decline in the ratio of wages.

II

I assemble here a variety of data on nominal wages in the South and North before and after the Civil War. The data come from various published and archival sources. Although the sources I use do not exhaust all relevant ones, I believe my selection is broadly representative and, in any case, more comprehensive than those examined in previous work.[9] Some of the wage estimates are seasoned in that they have been available for some time and thus subject to professional scrutiny. Others are tentative – in one case, entirely novel – and may change with further work. In cases where the underlying data refer to a labor contract in which board was customarily paid along with a money wage – for example, farm labor paid a monthly stipend plus board – I use ancillary information to impute a dollar value to board. The occupations are reasonably wide-ranging – farm labor, unskilled non-farm (or "common") labor, carpenters, and female domestics.

In terms of frequency of observation and underlying geographic detail, the wage data are of two types – state-level panel data pertaining to census or other years, and annual regional time series. The various sources are collated in Table 1 as period averages of South–North wage ratios.[10] The periods shown in Table 1 are pre-1866 and various post-bellum sub-periods (or single years, depending on the type of data). Readers desiring greater temporal detail are directed to the tables contained in Appendix A, which give the underlying dollar value estimates. Data sources are described in Appendix A, and in the notes to the appendix tables.

Before turning to the results, a few caveats are in order. Other than occupation, nineteenth century sources of wage evidence usually contain little

---

[9] For additional wage data see, for example, Phillip Coehlo and James Shepherd, "Regional Differences in Real Wages: The United States, 1851–1880," *Explorations in Economic History*, 13 (1976): 203–220.

[10] In the case of the estimates based on state-level panel data, the ratios derive from regional averages of nominal wages that are weighted averages of the state-level figures. The weights are estimates of the free adult (16+) male or female (16+, used for domestics) labor force prepared by Thomas Weiss ("U.S. Labor Estimates and Economic Growth, 1800–1860," in Robert Gallman and John Wallis (eds.), *American Economic Growth and Standards of Living before the Civil War* [Chicago, 1992]; "Estimates of White and Non-White Gainful Workers"). This weighting scheme is certainly debatable, but experimentation with other weights suggests that the substantive findings would not change. The reader should bear in mind that certain estimates derive from underlying data that are less than fully comprehensive, in the sense that data are missing for some states. In particular, this is true for 1870. All estimates for 1870 derive from the extant manuscripts of the 1870 Census of Social Statistics (see Appendix A), the collection of which is ongoing.

TABLE I. *South/North Wage Ratios before and after 1866*

	S. Atlantic/North	S. Central/North
A. Average monthly wage of farm labor, board included + imputed monthly value of board		
<1866	0.78	0.98
1866–1870	0.56 [0.72]	0.70 [0.71]
1871–1880	0.61 [0.78]	0.75 [0.77]
1881–1890	0.64 [0.82]	0.71 [0.72]
1891–1900	0.59 [0.76]	0.64 [0.65]
B. Daily wage of common (unskilled) labor, board not included: State-level panel data		
<1866	0.79	0.95
1870	0.55 [0.70]	0.69 [0.73]
1880	0.66 [0.84]	0.74 [0.78]
1890	0.71 [0.90]	0.80 [0.84]
C. Daily wage of common labor, board not included: Regional time series		
<1866	0.83	1.04
1866–1870	0.51 [0.61]	0.68 [0.65]
1871–1880	0.54 [0.65]	0.72 [0.69]
D. Daily wage of carpenters, board not included		
<1866	1.00	1.28
1870	0.80 [0.80]	0.99 [0.77]
1880	0.88 [0.88]	1.09 [0.85]
E. Weekly wage of female domestics with board + imputed weekly value of board		
<1866	0.90	1.22
1870	0.64 [0.71]	0.84 [0.69]
1900	0.52 [0.58]	0.72 [0.59]

Source: See text and source notes to Appendix Table A1. Wage ratios are computed from wage rates reported in Appendix Table A1. Figures in [] are ratios of post-1866 values to pre-1866 (first row in each panel; for example, in Panel E, row 2, column 1 (0.71 = 0.64/0.90).

or no information about the human capital characteristics of wage labor.[11] Thus, for example, if one observes differences in the original data in the daily wages of common labor between, say, Iowa and Massachusetts in 1860, this

---

[11] In the data examined here, gender is revealed in the occupational title (female domestics) or in the underlying micro-data.

could be because a true geographic difference existed, or it could be because common labor in Iowa differed from common labor in Massachusetts in ways that affected wages in the two locations. Or, it could be that wage labor was compensated in kind in various ways in one location but not another, and this was not recorded in the survey, but was known (and acted on) by individuals at the time. In many of the sources wages were often quoted as being the "average" in a locality, but exactly how the average was determined, or to whom it pertained, is rarely described in the sort of detail customary in twentieth century sources. These data deficiencies are such that one would not want to place much interpretive weight on small movements, up or down, in wage levels or regional gaps.

Panels A–C of Table 1 show estimates for farm labor and common non-farm labor. Panels A and B are based on the state-level panel data, while Panel C derives from the regional time series previously noted. Levels and changes differ somewhat between the two sources of data on common wages. In particular, the regional time series suggest that the initial post-bellum decline in the South/North ratio was larger, and recovery more protracted, than the pattern indicated by the state-level panel data. However, in broad terms the substantive conclusions are the same regardless of the type of data used.

Before the Civil War, wages of farm and common labor were lower in the South Atlantic states than in the North, but the regional gap was essentially non-existent in the case of the South Central states. For both types of labor, wage ratios in the immediate aftermath of the War were considerably lower than before the War. The data by single year (see the Appendix) make it plain that this was not a pre-existing trend. Rather, Southern wages declined relative to Northern wages between 1860 and 1866. In magnitude, the immediate post-bellum decline in the wage ratio was substantial and quite similar for both types of labor and for both Southern regions, averaging about 29 percent if the state-level panel data are used.[12]

The Southern economy was in a highly chaotic state between 1866 and 1870, and one might presume that the immediate effects of the War on wages were simply that. All three panels suggest that there was a tendency for wage relatives to revert to their pre-war levels in the 1870s. According to the state-level panel data, the South/North ratio of farm wages in the South Atlantic rose from 0.56 in the immediate aftermath of the War (1866–1870) to an average of 0.61 in the 1870s and further to an average of 0.64 in the 1880s. This level for the 1880s was 82 percent of the level prevailing before the War.

There is also evidence of mean reversion for common non-farm labor. As with farm labor, mean reversion began in the 1870s. The state-level panel data indicate that reversion continued through the 1880s in both Southern regions, in contrast to the pattern for farm labor in the South Central. By

---

[12] The regional time series imply a somewhat larger immediate decline in the wage ratio, averaging 37 percent across the two southern regions.

1890, the South/North ratio of common non-farm wages had reached 90 percent of its pre-war level in the South Atlantic and 84 percent of it pre-war level in the South Central.

At present, data for the 1890s are available only for male farm labor and for female domestics (one year, see following). The data for farm labor indicate that the South/North wage ratio fell in both the South Atlantic and South Central regions in the 1890s. In the case of the South Central, the 1890s decline was a continuation of a downward trend that began in the 1880s.[13] In proportionate terms, the declines in wage ratios that occurred late in the post-bellum era were smaller than those that occurred initially. For example, in the case of farm labor in the South Atlantic, the initial decline (1866–1870 compared with pre-1866) was 28 percent [0.72 = 0.56/0.78] whereas the 1890s decline was 8 percent [0.92 = 0.59/0.64].

Panel D (Table 1) shows estimates for carpenters. In contrast to common and farm labor, wages of carpenters in the South Atlantic states before the War were identical, on average, to wages of carpenters in the North, and wages in the South Central region were 28 percent higher.[14] As was true of common and farm labor, South/North wage ratios for carpenters fell during the immediate post-bellum period. This decline, however, was proportionately smaller than that which occurred for farm or common labor. As was true for the other occupations, wage ratios for carpenters recovered in the 1870s, but had not reached parity with pre-war ratios by 1880.

Estimates of weekly wages of domestics with the value of board imputed are shown in Panel E (Table 1). As was true in the other occupations, wages in the South rose relative to the North during the 1850s, but then declined sharply relative to the North in the 1860s. The next data point for domestics pertains to 1900. It indicates an even further erosion of the South's wage position relative to the North, most likely (judging on the basis of the farm data) during the 1890s.

Panel A of Table 2 shows South/North wage ratios for farm labor distinguishing between the Deep South and Upper South states within each sub-region. The expectation is that, because of distance from the North and heavier initial reliance on slave labor, the immediate post-bellum declines in wage ratios would have been greater for the Deep South and recovery may have been more protracted. The first expectation is clearly borne out in the data in both sub-regions, whereas the second also appears to have been true

---

[13] Later in the paper I demonstrate that labor productivity in agriculture was increasing in both sub-regions in the 1880s, which suggests that the source of the 1880s deterioration in the South Central/North farm wage ratio must be found elsewhere. However, as noted in Section I, the calculations imply that labor productivity in agriculture fell in the 1890s in both sub-regions.

[14] See Robert A. Margo, *Wages and Labor Markets in the United States, 1820–1860* (Chicago, 2000), Table 3A.7, for evidence that the similar regional contrasts existed for white collar labor before the Civil War. That is, prior to the Civil War, it appears that the returns to skill were higher in the South than in the North.

TABLE 2. *The Effects of the Civil War on South/North Wage Ratios: Within-South Differences, Farm Labor*

	S. Atlantic Deep/North	S. Atlantic Upper/North	S. Central Deep/North	S. Central Upper/North
	A. Deep South versus upper South			
<1866	0.85	0.75	1.09	0.89
1866–1870	0.52 [0.61]	0.57 [0.76]	0.71 [0.65]	0.70 [0.79]
1871–1880	0.53 [0.62]	0.66 [0.88]	0.75 [0.69]	0.75 [0.84]
1881–1890	0.60 [0.71]	0.67 [0.89]	0.70 [0.64]	0.72 [0.81]
1891–1900	0.50 [0.59]	0.65 [0.87]	0.64 [0.59]	0.64 [0.72]
	Ratio of Farm Wage (V/WV)			Index (<1866 = 1)
	B. Virginia/West Virginia			
<1866	0.84			
1866–1870	0.65			0.78
1871–1880	0.74			0.88
1881–1890	0.82			0.98
1891–1900	0.79			0.95

Source: (A) see notes to Appendix Table A1. Variable is monthly wage of farm labor, board included plus imputed monthly value of board. Deep: South Atlantic: Florida, Georgia, South Carolina; South Central: Alabama, Mississippi, Louisiana, Texas. Upper consists of remaining southern states in each region.

Source: (B) 1850, 1860: computed from manuscript records of Census of Social Statistics for Virginia. Post-1866: state-level panel data, see notes to Appendix Table A1.

for the South Atlantic. Otherwise, however, the general pattern – a sharp decline immediately after the War, followed by a period of recovery, then a period of retrogression – was the same for Deep South and Upper South states.

Some states were divided in their loyalties during the War. Perhaps the most important example was Virginia: the state of West Virginia was carved out of Virginia's pre-war borders. It is straightforward to compute Virginia–West Virginia wage ratios after the War. Because I have county-level data for Virginia in 1850 and 1860, it is possible to compute these ratios before the War. The presumption, not trivial, is that had West Virginia existed as a separate political entity before the War, its geographic boundaries would have been the same as after the War. Assuming this, the results for farm labor are shown in Panel B of Table 2.

Before the War farm wages were about 16 percent higher in the counties of Virginia that ultimately became West Virginia than elsewhere in the state. This wage gap was wider during the immediate post-bellum period. In proportional terms the initial decline in the Virginia/West Virginia wage ratio was smaller than that which occurred at the regional level or within sub-regions, distinguishing between the Deep and Upper South, but still a very substantial 22 percent [0.78 = 0.65/0.84]. Recovery ensued in the 1870s that continued into the 1880s, by which point the wage ratio had reached near parity with its pre-war level. As elsewhere the wage ratio fell in the 1890s but the decline was smaller, percentage-wise, than that which occurred at the regional or sub-regional level.

In sum, data of various types for a variety of occupations suggest that there was a structural break in the North–South wage ratio associated with the Civil War. The initial declines in South/North wage ratios were substantial – 39 percent, for example, in the case of farm labor in the Deep South states of the South Atlantic, using the state-level panel data. Wage relatives recovered during the 1870s and, for some occupations and areas, during the 1880s but, in general, had not fully returned to pre-war levels by 1890.

In the case of farm labor, further erosion in South/North wage ratios occurred in the 1890s in both the South Atlantic and South Central states, the latter continuing a downward spiral that began in the 1880s. Had these late post-bellum declines in wage ratios not occurred, unskilled labor in the South Atlantic would still have been "low-wage" ca. 1900 but not to an extent appreciably different than during the late ante-bellum period. In the case of South Central farm labor, low wages ca. 1900 were a product primarily of the War and subsequent declines in relative wages after 1880.

III

Wage data from a variety of sources and occupations point to a sharp decline in the South's position relative to the North after the Civil War. Although the low-wage South did not owe its origins solely to the War, a structural break clearly did occur.

Perhaps the simplest way to explain the patterns exhibited in Tables 1 and 2 is with a regional model of relative labor demand and supply.[15] In such a model, the quantity of labor demanded in, say, region j relative to region k is a negative function of the wage in region j relative to region k. A decline in the relative demand for labor in region j occurs for some reason. In the very short run, the relative supply of labor to region j may be taken as perfectly inelastic, and thus there is no change in the allocation of labor between the two regions. However, the decline in labor demand causes the wage in region j to fall relative to the wage in region k.

What happens next depends on the size and the persistence of the shock to labor demand, as well as the costs of labor migration. If the size is small and persistence low – that is, a small transitory shock – relative to the costs of migration, there may be little or no adjustment in relative labor supply. With a transitory shock, labor demand eventually reverts, restoring relative

[15] See Olivier J. Blanchard and Lawrence F. Katz, "Regional Evolutions," *Brookings Papers on Economic Activity*, 1 (1992): 1–75.

wages back to their original level. If the shock is relatively large or persistent, however, eventually the relative supply of labor to region j should shift inward (a decrease), also causing wages in region j to rise relative to wages in region k.

I alluded to a plausible mechanism in Section I for explaining the initial decline in the demand for labor in the South relative to the North – a decline in agricultural productivity in the South caused, in the short run, by disruption and devastation associated with the War, and reinforced in the long run by emancipation. Before turning to that story, however, I wish to consider another, more mechanical explanation, one involving a change in the racial composition of the Southern labor force.

Before the Civil War the vast majority of African-Americans in the South were enslaved, and few were employed as wage laborers. When slavery ended, all labor in the South was, by definition, free labor, and some ex-slaves chose to enter the wage labor market. If former slaves were paid less than their white counterparts, some of the post-bellum regional divergence in wages might be explained mechanically by an increased proportion of African-Americans in the Southern wage labor force.[16]

How large could this compositional effect be? To answer this question, the following identity is useful:

$$W_{sj} = W_{swj} \times (1 - \beta_{sj}) + W_{sbj} \times \beta_{sj}$$

where W = average wage, j indexes the occupation, s = South, w = white, b = black, and β = proportion black. Letting W_{nj} be the average wage in occupation j in the North (n), the identity can be re-expressed in ratio form as

$$W_{sj} / W_{nj} = \phi_j \times [1 + (r_{sj} - 1)\beta_{sj}]$$

where $\phi = W_{sw} / W_n$ and $r_s = W_{sb} / W_{sw}$. Treating ϕ and r as constants, it follows that

$$\Delta(W_{sj} / W_{nj}) = \phi_j \times (r_{sj} - 1) \times \Delta\beta_{sj}$$

The left-hand side of this expression is the compositional effect.[17] The magnitude of the effect depends on (1) ϕ, the ratio of the wage of white labor in the South to the Northern average wage; (2) r, the extent of racial differences

---

[16] This is not the only potential compositional shift. In particular, if migrants from the South after the War were "positively selected" – that is, the more economically able were more likely to migrate, this could explain why wages stayed low. I am grateful to Chris Hanes for this observation. On positive selection in migration from the South, see Robert A. Margo, *Race and Schooling in the South, 1880–1950: An Economic History* (Chicago, 1990), ch. 7.

[17] The values of ϕ and r may not be constant. If they are not, there will be interaction effects involving $\Delta\beta$. As noted in the text, because we are evaluating a pure compositional story, it makes little sense to entertain changes in ϕ. However, if r declined in occupations in which $\Delta\beta$ was positive (i.e., the relative wage of black labor in the South fell in occupations that ex-slaves entered), the decomposition in the text would understate the importance of compositional change. At the present time this possibility cannot be investigated empirically.

in wages in the South; and (3) $\Delta\beta$, the change in the African-American share in occupation j associated with emancipation.

It is important to note that, if $r \geq 1$, the compositional story goes in the "wrong" direction, no matter what the values of ϕ or $\Delta\beta$. Also, because some ante-bellum free blacks, as well as slaves, worked for wages, and not all post-bellum Southern workers were black, it follows that $\Delta\beta < 1$. For common and farm labor the evidence presented in Tables 1 and 2 suggests that $\phi < 1$ in the South Atlantic states before the Civil War, and slightly greater than one in the South Central states, as a first approximation. Assume, as a point of departure for the calculation, that the true value of ϕ did not change after the War. The explanatory power of the compositional story, therefore, hinges on whether r was close to zero (a large racial wage gap) or close to one (a small racial wage gap).

There are, unfortunately, very few readily available sources of wage data for the post-bellum South that provide race-specific information that is broadly comprehensive. Perhaps the two best sources that I have found are for agriculture. Race-specific data on farm wages were collected by the United States Department of Agriculture (USDA) at the very end of the nineteenth century. The USDA data were published in the form of state averages. In addition, the sample of farms from the 1880 Census of Agriculture collected by Roger Ransom and Richard Sutch contains sufficient information to estimate a value for r, although the nature of the 1880 data is such that the estimate for 1880 should be viewed with considerable caution.[18]

Table 3 shows estimated values of r from the Ransom and Sutch sample and for the late nineteenth century USDA sample. Estimates are shown separately for the South Atlantic and South Central regions. It is immediately obvious that, regardless of the source of the data, r was less than one but relatively close to it. On average, the racial wage gap appears to have been relatively small. This is not a new finding. Robert Higgs reached a similar conclusion based, in part, on the same data.[19] There is some indication of a

[18] Ransom and Sutch, *One Kind of Freedom*. The 1880 Census of Agriculture reported the number of weeks of hired labor separately for black and white workers along with the total wage bill, that latter not separately by race. The average weekly wage is estimated as the total wage bill divided by the total number of weeks of hired labor. Before estimating the overall average across farms, I "trimmed" the data (excluded observations) of farms for which the farm-level average was deemed to be too low or too high (see the notes to Table 4). In Table 4, the weekly wage of white (black) labor pertains to farms that hired only white (black) labor. This yields a biased estimate of either the white or black wage because it excludes farms that hired both white and black workers. For these farms the data do not speak directly to racial wage differentials. Manufacturing data from early twentieth century Virginia, which do reveal racial wage differentials within integrated establishments, suggest that excluding integrated farms from the 1880 calculation may bias my estimate of r downwards; see Robert Higgs, "Firm Specific Evidence on Racial Wage Differentials and Workforce Segregation," *American Economic Review*, 67 (1977): 243.

[19] Robert Higgs, "Did Southern Farmers Discriminate?" *Agricultural History*, 46 (1972): 325–328; Robert Higgs, "Did Southern Farmers Discriminate? Interpretive Problems and Further Evidence," *Agricultural History*, 49 (1975): 445–447.

TABLE 3. *Black–White Wage Ratios, Agricultural Labor, 1880 and 1898*

	South Atlantic	South Central
Census of Agriculture, 1880 (Ransom–Sutch sample), ratio of average weekly wages	0.97	0.97
USDA, 1898, ratio of average monthly wages with value of board imputed	0.90	0.91

Sources and Notes: 1880, Ransom and Sutch sample of southern farms. Weekly wage of hired labor = total wages paid/total weeks of hired labor. Total weeks of hired labor = weeks of hired white labor + weeks of hired black labor. For each state in sample, average weekly wage of white labor is estimated for farms that hired white labor only; similarly, for each state, average weekly wage of black labor is estimated for farms that hired black labor only. Farms with average weekly wage < $2 or > $5 were excluded. Regional estimates of black and white wages are weighted averages of state estimates using sampling weights supplied by Ransom and Sutch. Figures in table above, row 1, are black/white ratios of regional estimates. 1898: weighted average of state ratios (black/white), weight equal to adult male labor force. Data pertain to monthly wages of farm labor without board. Data were also reported for daily wages but the substantive findings would not change if these data were used instead (see Higgs, *Competition and Coercion*, 64). Source is Blodgett, "Wages."

decline in r between 1880 and the end of the century which, if true, could have contributed to a continued stagnation in the North–South wage gap. However, any such decline appears to have been small and, in view of the assumptions underlying the 1880 calculation, may very well be in the range of sampling (and other) error.

Even with r in the neighborhood of 0.91 (the USDA data) and assuming that $\phi = 1$, the compositional effect was clearly less than ten percentage points (because $\Delta\beta < 1$). At ten percentage points, the compositional effect could only explain a modest portion of the post-bellum divergence in the North–South gap in farm wages. Further, this is a serious over-estimate of the upper bound, because the USDA data clearly show that ϕ was significantly less than one.[20] Put another way, white farm labor in the South earned far less than farm labor in the North, which was overwhelmingly white, after the War, than before the War (see Table 1).

While I would not pretend that the data in Table 3 settle this issue, it does not seem likely that the changed racial composition of the Southern wage labor force after the Civil War can explain much of the post-bellum decline in South/North wage ratios in the case of farm labor. Whatever was the case for farm labor, is very likely to have been true for common labor as well, insofar that there were few barriers to mobility within the South between

[20] For example, the ratio of the monthly wage of white farm labor in Alabama to the white farm wage in Ohio (both with the value of board imputed) was 0.64; see James H. Blodgett, *Wages of Farm Labor in the United States* (Washington, DC, 1903).

the farm and non-farm sectors.[21] My results do not completely preclude a compositional story, but they do suggest that the explanatory power of any such story is arguably small.

IV

The Civil War left the economy of many parts of the South in a devastated state. Physical capital had been destroyed, potential workers had been disabled or killed, and the region's government was forced to be Reconstructed. The destruction of capital and disruption of government, by themselves, may have been enough to induce an immediate decline in the demand for labor in the South relative to the North, in aftermath of the War.

If the relative supply of labor to the South had been perfectly elastic in the short run, a short-run decline in relative labor demand would not have left an imprint on relative wages. However, this does not describe the nineteenth century United States (or, for that matter, the twentieth century United States). To a first approximation, the relative supply of labor to a very small area – a town or village, perhaps – might have been close to fairly elastic over some suitably defined short run. However, the available evidence for the ante-bellum period suggests that this is not a good approximation for geographic areas as large as states, let alone entire regions.[22] But capital can, and was, re-built, and government re-established. Destruction and Reconstruction, in other words, were transitory shocks. Emancipation was a permanent shock.

As noted in Section I, Fogel and Engerman argued that a decline in labor productivity occurred in Southern agriculture after the War. This decline was permanent precisely because it was caused by emancipation. Slavery, Fogel and Engerman asserted, conferred a productivity advantage in certain crops through the use of the gang system. Because the gang system relied on extensive division of labor and labor "speed-up" to produce efficiency gains, its use was predicated on a certain minimum efficient scale in terms of numbers of slaves and, therefore, in terms of farm size. Before the War,

---

[21] See Wright, *Old South, New South*. It is possible that the compositional story has more relevance in the case of skilled or white collar labor. The limited data that exist suggest that, around the turn of the century, black workers in skilled or white collar occupations in the South earned less than their white counterparts; see Robert Higgs, *Competition and Coercion: Blacks in the American Economy* (New York, 1977) and Margo, *Race and Schooling*, ch. 4 (on teachers). However, because relatively few slaves received training in skills before the Civil War and because there were racial barriers to entering the skill trades after the War, the change in racial composition was far smaller than for unskilled labor.

[22] The Gold Rush is a good example. The discovery of gold in California resulted in an extraordinary short-run increase in wages in California relative to other locations in the country because it was costly to get to California – labor, in other words, was inelastically supplied; see Margo, *Wages and Labor Markets*, ch. 6.

free labor was apparently unwilling to work under the gang system at a wage premium that would still have made use of the system profitable. Ex-slaves were unwilling, too, to work in gangs. The abandonment of the gang system meant a loss of economies of scale and, therefore, a once-and-for-all decline in the level of labor productivity in Southern agriculture. Various studies attempting to measure the decline in productivity using direct data on output are consistent with this argument.[23]

Labor productivity can also be measured indirectly using the *dual*: wages divided by the price of output. The operative assumption is that labor is paid the value of its marginal product; if so, an index of the real product wage will track, to a first order of approximation, an index of output per worker.[24]

The dual has been used with some frequency by economic historians to measure changes in agricultural labor productivity, either because direct data on outputs and inputs are not available, or as a check on the plausibility of assumptions underlying a direct calculation.[25] To the best of my knowledge, the only previous use of the dual to track labor productivity in Southern agriculture before and after the Civil War is by John Moen, purely as a check on the robustness of direct measures of output per worker that were computed from the 1860 and 1880 censuses of agriculture.[26]

Moen calculated the dual by dividing an index of monthly farm wages in the South in 1860 and 1880 by an index of agricultural prices in the South in these same years.[27] According to the dual, labor productivity declined by about a third between 1860 and 1880. My calculation builds on Moen's

---

[23] Goldin, "'N' Kinds of Freedom"; Moen, "Changes"; James R. Irwin, "Explaining the Decline in Southern Per Capita Output after Emancipation," *Explorations in Economic History*, 31 (1994): 336–356.

[24] If the production function is Cobb–Douglas, then $w/p = \alpha Q/L$, where α = labor's share. If α is a constant, w/p will track Q/L exactly.

[25] See, for example, Paul David, "The Growth of Real Product in the United States Before 1840: New Evidence, Controlled Conjecture," *Journal of Economic History*, 27 (1967): 151–197; Winifred Rothenberg, *From Market Places to a Market Economy: The Transformation of Rural Massachusetts, 1750–1850* (Chicago, 1992).

[26] Moen, "Changes."

[27] To compute the wage index (the numerator of the dual) Moen relied on the state-level estimates of farm wages as reported in Stanley Lebergott, *Manpower in Economic Growth: The American Record Since 1800* (New York, 1964). The overall Southern wage was computed by weighting each state's wage by its share of the agricultural labor force. The price index was calculated by valuing crops in 1860 using 1860 national prices and again using 1880 prices, and taking the ratio of two values; and second, by valuing outputs in 1880 the same way and taking the ratio. Prices of various crops were taken from Marvin W. Towne and Wayne D. Rasmussen, "Farm Gross Product and Gross Investment in the Nineteenth Century," in William Parker (ed.), *Trends in the American Economy in the Nineteenth Century* (Princeton, NJ, 1960). The output data were derived from samples of farms from the manuscript records of the 1860 and 1880 censuses. The Parker–Gallman sample was used for 1860 and the Ransom and Sutch sample was used for 1880.

work by making a slight correction to the numerator of his index, and by adding more years – specifically, 1850, 1870, 1890, and 1900.[28]

To compute the denominator of the dual, the index of agricultural prices, I derived a set of weights for a fixed group of outputs produced in Southern agriculture in 1860 (i indexes the product). These weights are each product's share of the total net value of agricultural production, where "net" refers to allowances for seed, livestock feed, and so on.[29] For each crop I then computed a price index, setting the 1860 price equal to one. The overall price index is the geometric-weighted average of the crop-specific indices.[30]

The dual is the ratio of the wage and price indices. The wage indices (South Atlantic and South Central) were derived from the census year values for farm labor reported in Appendix Table A1, again setting the 1860 values equal to one. For the purposes of the calculation, I assume that the same price index prevailed in both regions.[31] For ease of interpretation, I multiply all values of the dual by 100; thus, in particular, the 1860 value is 100. The price index and the dual indices are shown in Table 4. The notes to the table list the goods included in the index and their weights. Note that, according to my calculations, agricultural prices in the South in 1880 were 6.8 percent higher on average than in 1860, slightly higher than Moen estimated (about 5 percent).

My results for 1860 and 1880 are essentially the same as Moen's. Measured by the dual, agricultural labor productivity in the South Atlantic was 30 percent lower in 1880 than in 1860. The comparable figure for the South Central was 32 percent.[32]

---

[28] As noted in note 27, Moen used Lebergott's wage estimates. These pertain to the portion of the monthly farm wage paid in money terms; they do not impute a value to board, even though the underlying data clearly pertain to labor contracts in which board was provided (and hence, such an imputation is clearly desirable). My correction, therefore, is to impute a value to board. This correction has little effect on the substantive findings.

[29] Outputs of various crops and livestock were taken as published in the 1860 Census of Agriculture, and valued by the same prices used by Moen. By net I refer to deductions for allowances for seed, consumption of corn by animals, and so on; for this purpose I relied on Dongyu Yang, "Agricultural Productivity in the Northern United States, 1860," in R. Fogel and S. Engerman (eds.), *Without Consent or Contract*; and Fogel and Engerman, *Time on the Cross*.

[30] Letting p_{it} be the price index number of the ith output in year t and δ_i be the value weight, the overall price index, P_t is a geometric-weighted average of the commodity-specific indices: $\ln P_t = \Sigma \delta_i \ln p_{it}$.

[31] It would clearly be useful to construct a regional price index to deflate wages. It would also be useful to experiment with weights from different years, or allow for shifts in weights. Both extensions are left for future work.

[32] These estimates are just shy of what Moen found for the South as a whole (33 percent, see Moen, "Changes," 348) but less than what is implied by his direct estimates based on outputs and inputs from the 1860 and 1880 censuses, unless a substantial allowance is made for a reduction in labor force participation by former slaves. In particular, allowing for a 30

TABLE 4. *The Dual Measure of Labor Productivity in Southern Agriculture,*
1850–1900

Year	Price Index	Dual, South Atlantic	Dual, South Central
1850	87.5	86.2	71.2
1860	100.0	100.0	100.0
1870	149.6	65.7	64.2
1880	106.8	69.9	68.3
1890	86.2	104.3	89.4
1900	87.5	95.4	81.7

Notes: The overall price index (column 2) is a geometric weighted average of commodity-specific price indices. Commodity prices are from Towne and Rasmussen, "Farm Gross Product." The weights are based on state-level production totals (or stocks) from the published tables of the 1860 census of agriculture, as modified by allowances for seed or (in the case of livestock) animal weights; see Fogel and Engerman, *Time on the Cross*, and Yang, "Agricultural Productivity." The same weights are used, and consequently the same price index, for the South Atlantic and South Central regions. The commodities included in the index and their weights are as follows: milk, 0.128; wheat, 0.049; corn, 0.071; rye, 0.004; oats, 0.003; peas, 0.008; Irish potatoes, 0.003; sweet potatoes, 0.025; barley, 0.0003; buckwheat, 0.0003; hay, 0.003; cotton, 0.362; tobacco, 0.039; rice, 0.0061; sugar, 0.028; molasses, 0.006; cows, 0.028; cattle, 0.072; hogs, 0.171. Dual: wage index, farm labor/price index. Wage indices are from Table 1 (Panel A), setting each region's value to 100 in 1860. 1900 figure uses wage estimates for 1899.

The calculation also reveals that the level of labor productivity in 1870 was lower than in 1880, which is consistent with a role for purely transitory factors, as well as disruptions caused by the adjustment to a free-labor system. However, productivity recovered strongly in the 1880s in the South Atlantic, so much so that the level achieved in 1890 exceeded the level in 1860. Labor productivity also increased in the South Central region in the 1880s, although not as rapidly as in the South Atlantic. In both southern regions, labor productivity in agriculture declined in the 1890s.[33]

percent reduction in the labor input of former slaves yields a decline of 33 percent in labor productivity in Southern agriculture between 1860 and 1880; see Moen, "Changes," p. 332.

[33] Ransom and Sutch, *One Kind of Freedom*, Table F.3 present estimates of the real value of crop output per capita in South Carolina, Georgia, Alabama, Mississippi, and Louisana for 1859, and on an annual basis from 1866 to 1900. Crops included in the calculation are cotton, sugar, rice, tobacco, corn, oats, Irish and sweet potatoes, rye, and wheat. Crops were valued at the average of farmgate prices over the period 1899–1908. "Per capita" means rural population, where "rural" is the opposite of "urban" and urban means the population living in incorporated towns and cities of population 2,500 or more. Rural population for years between census dates was estimated by linear interpolation. Setting the value for 1860 (actually, the 1859 crop year) to 100, the index numbers for the years shown in Table 4 are as follows: 62.1 (1870), 68.1 (1880), 76.3 (1890), and 68.3 (1899). That is, according to Ransom and Sutch's figures, agricultural output per capita declined between 1860 and 1870, rose modestly in the 1870s and 1880s, and then declined in the 1890s. This is the same pattern as in Table 4, except that my calculations suggest more rapid productivity growth in the 1880s than do Ransom and Sutch's figures.

The declines in labor productivity in the 1860s and the 1890s coincide with the declines in South/North wage ratios. However, relative farm wages in the South Central began to decline in the 1880s, at the same time that labor productivity was rising (according to the dual). Thus, although declining labor productivity in agriculture could account for the fall in relative wages in the 1860s and the 1890s, it cannot fully explain the behavior of relative wages in the 1880s.

Although the figures in Table 4 clearly support the conclusion that the South experienced reductions in agricultural labor productivity between 1860 and 1870 and again between 1890 and 1900, the data are insufficient to determine precisely how large these shocks were relative to "normal" levels of productivity. Moen compared 1860 with 1880, but this assumes that productivity in both years were "on trend" – that is, neither lower nor higher for cyclical, or other transitory reasons. With only two data points for each region before the Civil War, it is impossible to answer this question for 1860. For the post-bellum period, there is only one degree of freedom per region (three data points). Therefore, to determine the precise sizes of declines in productivity relative to trend, more data, particularly for non-census years, are necessary.[34]

Taking Table 4 at face value, one can question the meaning of the dual in the small and in the large. In the small, there is a point raised by Moen.[35] The numerator pertains to adult male labor, and wages of other types of farm labor might not have moved proportionately with it. However, as argued earlier in the paper, the wage effects of the War seem to have been approximately the same for all types of unskilled labor, which suggests that Moen's point has limited empirical relevance.

A more fundamental question is whether the dual is appropriate in theory as a measure of productivity change in an economy undergoing the transition from slavery to freedom. Appendix B sketches out a simple general equilibrium model to evaluate this question. The model's answer is a qualified "yes." The qualifications are several. First, slave labor and free labor must be perfect substitutes in the production of goods in which slavery had no inherent, special advantage. Second, slave owners might be able to use a particular technology (the gang system) to enhance the productivity of slaves in the production of some goods (cotton) but these goods do not use up all of the slave labor available in the economy. Third, labor, either slave or free, is mobile between sectors (cotton and other goods), at least in the long run. Under these conditions, the value of the marginal product of labor would be equalized between sectors and between free and slave labor, and the dual would be a reliable way to measure labor productivity.

---

[34] However, as long as both 1850 and 1860 were not far above trend levels of productivity, the data are sufficient to establish that a productivity decline took place.

[35] Moen, "Changes."

Is this a reasonable argument? On the one hand, there is no question that slaves were employed in the production of cotton using the gang system, but also in the production of many other goods that did not rely on the gang system. Free labor shunned the gang system, but free labor certainly produced cotton before the Civil War. There appears to have been no special productivity advantage to using slave labor over free labor except under the gang system. Without the gang system, slave and free labor were very close, perhaps even perfect substitutes (as the model assumes). On the other, the model presumes that the Southern economy was in long-run equilibrium before the War. The opposite could be argued – in particular, that more slaves should have been allocated to the production of cotton and other goods that made use of the gang system. However, if this were true, it would follow that the dual would understate the (true) value of the marginal product of slave labor before the War and, therefore, understate the decline in labor productivity due to emancipation.[36]

V

I have shown that the South-to-North ratio of wages fell after the Civil War, and that the decline in relative wages was greater in the short run – the years immediately following the War – than in the long run. I interpreted the movements in relative wages using a simple model of relative demand and supply. In the short run of this framework, labor is inelastically supplied to a particular region like the South, so a decline in labor demand induces a decline in relative wages. In the long run, labor demand will revert back to the extent that the negative shock is transitory or because the supply of labor to the affected region is more elastic due to out-migration.

My framework is a simplified version of Blanchard and Katz's well-known model of "regional evolutions."[37] In this model, relative wages evolve as just described in response to a negative, region-specific shock to labor demand. However, Blanchard and Katz also note that their model implies another price effect – a decline in the cost of living in the region experiencing the negative shock relative to other regions. This decline occurs, according to the logic of their model, through a decline in the price of non-traded goods. The decline in the price of non-traded goods occurs because the demand for these goods has declined, due to the decline in incomes produced by the negative shock.[38]

---

[36] As Moen, "Changes," p. 348, n.21 notes, most of his direct estimates of labor productivity imply a larger decline between 1860 and 1880 than his (or, for that matter, my) estimates based on the dual.

[37] Blanchard and Katz, "Regional Evolutions."

[38] The details can be fleshed out a bit by elaborating on the simple supply-demand model developed in the previous section. Let X represent the non-traded good, C the traded

In their empirical work, Blanchard and Katz use housing prices to measure this impact. It is known that the price of land in the South fell dramatically after the War, and the price of land is certainly a key component of the price of housing.[39] Collecting and analyzing regional data on actual housing prices before and after the War would be a major undertaking, well beyond the scope of this paper.

However, many of the same sources that contain information on wages also contain information on the cost of "board." This is the cost of food produced for local consumption, using raw materials (e.g., cornmeal or pork); capital equipment (pots and pans, a stove); some land (not much); fuel; and a little labor.[40]

Panel A of Table 5 shows estimates of the daily cost of board for the two Southern regions relative to the North. The periods shown are the same as in Table 1. Annual dollar values by region are reported in Appendix Table A3. The data clearly show a decline in the cost of board in the South, relative to the North, during the immediate aftermath of the War. As was true of farm wages, the relative decline was steeper in the short run than in the long run, and there was a further deterioration in the 1890s. In terms of magnitude, the changes in the relative cost of board were quite similar to the changes in the relative farm or common wages.

The cost of board measures expenditure on food, and expenditure is price times quantity. What I seek is the price component. If the demand for food were Cobb–Douglas, nominal expenditure on food would be a linear function of nominal income, and it would not be surprising to discover that the South/North ratio of board moved approximately "one-for-one" with the South/North ratio of wages.

agricultural good – the South's export. Assume that Southerners consume X plus an imported good M (Northern manufactures). The prices of C and M are assumed to be set in world markets, and these are also assumed – unrealistically to be sure – to be exogenous. Aggregate factor supplies (labor, capital, land) in the South are exogenous. The negative shock to the production of C reduces labor demand in the sector. This releases labor to the production of X, shifting the supply of X outward, and causing the nominal wage to decline relative to the price of C (or M). At the same time, aggregate real income declines in the South, reducing the demand for X (and, for that matter, M). A new equilibrium is reached at which the price of X is now lower relative to either the price of C or the price of M. Whether the price of the non-traded goods will fall relative to the wage is not determinate. Under realistic assumptions, however, w will decline more than the price of the non-traded goods.

[39] Moen, "Changes." For one major Northern city – New York – it is known that land prices increased dramatically after the war; see Jeremy Atack and Robert A. Margo, "'Location, Location, Location': The Price Gradient for Vacant Urban Land: New York, 1835 to 1900," *Journal of Real Estate Finance and Economics*, 16 (1998): 151–172.

[40] It is presumed that the data on board refer solely to the cost of food, not "room" and board. However, if "room" were included in some cases (that is, in some states) it would only serve to reinforce the argument.

TABLE 5. *South/North Ratios, Weekly Cost of Board and the Price of Food*

	S. Atlantic/North	S. Central/North
	A. Weekly cost of board	
<1866	0.82	1.00
1866–1870	0.61	0.73
1871–1880	0.63	0.76
1881–1890	0.73	0.72
1891–1900	0.61	0.60
	B. Implied price of food: No demand shift, income elasticity = 0.75, Own Price Elasticity = −0.4 (1860 = 100)	
<1866	100.0	100.0
1866–1870	92.4	90.8
1871–1880	87.6	87.7
1881–1890	105.4	87.2
1891–1900	86.5	73.1

Source: see text and Appendix Table A3.

Studies of nineteenth century household budgets, however, suggest that both the own-price and income elasticities of the demand for food were less than one. Panel B uses plausible values of these elasticities (see Table 5) as estimated by Michael Haines to compute changes in the South-to-North ratio of food prices before and after the War, under the assumption that there were no shifts in demand other than those induced by the decline in relative wages.[41]

The specific magnitudes in Panel B should be viewed with considerable skepticism, because they will be sensitive to the choice of elasticities and to the underlying assumption of no demand shifts except for income.[42] Given these assumptions, the calculations do imply a decline in the South/North ratio of food prices during the immediate aftermath of the War. This was not

[41] Michael Haines, "Consumer Behavior and Immigrant Assimilation: A Comparison of the United States, Britain, and Germany, 1889/1890," National Bureau of Economic Research Working Paper Series on Historical Factors in Long Run Growth, No. 6 (Cambridge, MA, 1989). Let b = board, p = price of food, q = quantity, and $b = pq$. Also, let $q = dp^{-\epsilon}w^{\delta}$. Letting "$\Delta$" indicate the change in the North–South ratio after the War and assuming d is constant, $\Delta \ln p = [\Delta \ln b - \delta \Delta \ln w]/1 - \epsilon$. In the calculations I substitute South/North values for $\Delta \ln b$ and $\Delta \ln w$.

[42] Note that I make no assumptions about the supply of food. If I assume that the supply of food is (1) upward sloping with respect to price and (2) does not shift, it can be shown that $\Delta \ln p$ and $\Delta \ln w$ will always move in the same direction, that is, they will be positively correlated. This conclusion will hold *a fortiori* if the only factor shifting the supply of produced food is the cost of labor.

a continuation of a pre-war trend, as the values for 1850 and 1860 imply rising food prices in both regions relative to the North during the 1850s.[43]

The behavior of food prices in the 1880s and 1890s is also broadly what one would expect, given changes in South–North wage ratios. For example, the calculations show declines in South/North food prices in the 1890s in both Southern regions, at the same time that South/North wage ratios were decreasing. However, the behavior of the food price relatives in the 1870s is contrary to expectations. According to the model, we would expect to see rising South/North food prices due to mean reversion in the wage ratios. Instead, however, food price ratios fell. Why this occurred is beyond the scope of the paper, but possible explanations include falling raw materials prices and improved food-distribution networks.[44]

VI

At the onset of the twentieth century the South was undeniably poor. Poverty had many faces and took many forms, but one facet that was clearly evident at the time was low wages, particularly for farm and unskilled non-farm labor. The "low-wage" South ca. 1900 might have been a product of very recent forces. It might have been a very long-standing characteristic, predating the Civil War by decades or more. It might have been a consequence, in part or whole, of the Civil War itself.

This paper has assembled a variety of data to examine how the Civil War affected the regional structure of wages. These data, to be sure, are far from ideal, but they are remarkably consistent in their implications. Prior to the War, farm and common non-farm wages in the South Atlantic region were below levels in the North, but this was not the case in the South Central region. Relative to wages in the North, wages in the South declined sharply in the immediate aftermath of the Civil War. The immediate decline in South/North wage ratios appears to have spared no occupation. It did, however, vary somewhat in severity within the South, being more pronounced in the Deep than in the Upper South.

Following the immediate decline, South/North wage ratios began to revert back to their pre-war levels. Data for non-farm labor suggest that the reversion began in the 1870s and continued at least through 1890, the last year that data currently cover. For farm labor, the data extend into the 1890s. These indicate a deterioration in South/North wage ratios in both the South

---

[43] The values of board and wages imply that the South/North ratio of food prices increased between 1850 and 1860 by 22.4 percent in the South Atlantic and by 15.3 percent in the South Central.

[44] Recall from Table 4 that the price index for Southern agricultural products fell rapidly in the 1870s.

Atlantic and South Central regions, that for the South Central being a continuation of a downward trend that began in the 1880s.

Thus, the origins of the low-wage South at the turn of the twentieth century were complex. Wages were low, in part, because of very recent adverse trends. In part, they were low in the South Atlantic because they had been low there before the Civil War. To a significant extent, however, they were low because the Civil War made them so.

The Civil War could have been responsible for the low-wage South simply by altering the racial composition of the Southern wage labor force, if black labor was paid less than white labor. On the basis of the available data, which are few and very fragmentary at present, there seems to be little question that black labor was paid less than white labor. But, for unskilled labor at least, the racial gap in wages appears to have been too small to account for more than a small portion of the decline in South/North wage ratios.

I used the wage evidence in conjunction with price data to construct dual measures of labor productivity in Southern agriculture for 1850 to 1900. The measures suggest that labor productivity in Southern agriculture declined between 1860 and 1870, and again between 1890 and 1900. The same sources that yielded regional information about wages also contain information on the cost of board. These data show that the cost of board in the South, relative to the North, declined after the Civil War. Under plausible assumptions, the data on board suggest that the price of a non-traded good – locally produced food – declined in the South relative to the North after the War.

This paper has demonstrated that the Civil War left an imprint on the regional structure of wages and has interpreted the decline in South/North wage ratios in terms of shifts in labor demand. The mystery of why the low-wage South persisted beyond the very short run, however, is as much about labor supply as it is about labor demand. To be sure, I have suggested that prices of non-traded goods in the region – a component of the cost of living – also fell relative to the North after the War, but these did so endogenously. The underlying explanation must be found in something "real" embedded in the fabric of the Southern economy and its society. Southerners elected to stay in the region despite the fact that wages, and more generally incomes, were low. The question, still an open one, is "why"?[45]

---

[45] This is not for lack of trying. Among the factors that have been suggested to explain why more Southerners did not leave the region are poverty itself (geographic mobility is expensive); inadequate schooling (the better educated are more likely to migrate); institutional factors that inhibited geographic mobility (such as "debt peonage"), and network externalities (European immigrants got "there" – the North – first). On these issues see, among others, Engerman, "Some Economic Factors"; Ransom and Sutch, *One Kind of Freedom*; Wright, *Old South, New South*; and Margo, *Race and Schooling*; and "The South as Economic Problem."

Appendix A

The state-level panel data derive primarily from four sources: (1) the 1850 and 1860 published tables of the Census of Social Statistics, and extant manuscript records for selected states of the 1870 Census of Social Statistics; (2) surveys conducted for various years by the Department of Agriculture; (3) nationally representative samples of establishments from the manuscripts of the 1880 Census of Manufactures; and (4) estimates prepared by Stanley Lebergott.[46] The unit of observation is the state, and each figure could be thought of as (in principle) as a state "average" of equally weighted observations within each state.[47] Sources (1) and (2) provide information on farm wages; sources (1), (2), and (4) on common non-farm labor and artisans; and sources (1) and (4) on female domestics. Annual values of region-specific wage rates in nominal dollars are shown in Appendix Table A1 for the various occupations used in Table 1.

In other work I have estimated annual series of nominal wages of common labor, artisans, and white collar workers by census region (Northeast, Midwest, South Atlantic, and South Central) for the period of 1820 to 1860.[48] The data derive from payroll records of civilian workers of the United States Army who were employed at various forts and other military installations throughout the country. Comparisons with purely civilian sources suggest that, by and large, the Army paid the going wage in the local labor market surrounding the fort. The ante-bellum series are derived from hedonic regressions controlling for various worker characteristics reported in the payrolls, and (in the case of common labor and artisans) are benchmarked to 1850, based on the Census of Social Statistics for that year.

Similar payroll records are also available for the post-bellum period. I am engaged in a project to collect regional samples of these with the aim of producing post-bellum series similar to my ante-bellum series. Currently the available post-bellum samples cover the period of 1866 to 1880; using these, I have produced preliminary annual series for common labor by census region. Like the ante-bellum series, these also derive from hedonic regressions, but the post-bellum series are much more frequently benchmarked than are the ante-bellum series. Being preliminary, they are subject to further revision; however, I believe that the preliminary series are sufficiently reliable for the

---

[46] The 1880 manufacturing data are described in Jeremy Atack and Fred Bateman, "U.S. Historical Statistics: Nineteenth Century Industrial Development Through the Eyes of the Census of Manufactures," *Historical Methods*, 32 (1999): 177–188; Lebergott, *Manpower*.

[47] In some cases, notably the social statistics data, the underlying data within states – again, in theory – pertain to averages for known geographic areas (minor civil divisions). The census of manufacturing data are state-level averages of establishment level data, in which each establishment is weighted by total employment.

[48] Margo, *Wages and Labor Markets*.

Year	S. Atlantic	S. Central	North	S. Atlantic/North	S. Central/North
A: Average monthly wage of farm labor with board + monthly value of board					
1850	$12.96	$15.65	$17.82	0.73	0.88
1860	17.18	21.97	20.60	0.83	1.07
1866	17.24	21.52	31.19	0.55	0.69
1869	16.89	21.10	29.46	0.57	0.72
1870	17.99	22.38	32.99	0.55	0.68
1875	16.16	19.08	26.95	0.60	0.71
1879	12.84	16.01	20.25	0.63	0.79
1880	13.40	16.66	22.27	0.60	0.75
1882	15.23	17.43	24.62	0.62	0.71
1885	15.32	16.89	24.07	0.64	0.70
1888	15.56	16.82	23.60	0.66	0.69
1890	15.33	17.06	23.86	0.64	0.72
1892	15.37	17.32	24.29	0.63	0.71
1893	13.90	15.28	23.68	0.59	0.65
1894	13.19	13.92	22.44	0.59	0.62
1895	13.16	13.74	22.81	0.58	0.60
1898	14.02	15.32	23.65	0.59	0.65
1899	14.34	15.71	25.32	0.57	0.62
B: Daily wage of common labor, board not included					
1850	$0.66	$0.75	$0.87	0.76	0.86
1860	0.83	1.06	1.03	0.81	1.03
1870	0.93	1.18	1.70	0.55	0.69
1880	0.82	0.92	1.25	0.66	0.74
1890	1.00	1.12	1.40	0.71	0.80
C. Daily wage of carpenters, board not included					
1850	$1.33	$1.66	$1.36	0.98	1.22
1860	1.64	2.18	1.63	1.01	1.34
1870	2.20	2.73	2.76	0.80	0.99
1880	1.71	2.12	1.95	0.88	1.09
D. Weekly wage of domestics with board + weekly value of board					
1850	$2.21	$2.81	$2.54	0.87	1.11
1860	2.75	3.93	2.97	0.93	1.32
1870	3.08	4.07	4.83	0.64	0.84
1900	2.74	3.77	5.25	0.52	0.72

Notes to Panel A: Sources: 1850: J. D. B. DeBow, *Statistical View of the United States* (Washington, DC, 1854); 1860: Joseph C. G. Kennedy, *Population of the United States in 1860* (Washington, DC, 1864). 1870: computed from manuscript censuses of social statistics for the following states: Arkansas, Florida, Georgia, Illinois, Indiana, Iowa, Kentucky, Louisiana, Massachusetts, Michigan, New York, Pennsylvania, Tennessee, Texas, and Virginia. 1866, 1869, 1875–1899: James H. Blodgett, *Wages of Farm Labor in the United States, Results of Eleven*

purposes of this paper. Five-year moving averages of the post-bellum series are shown in Appendix Table A2. Readers desiring further details regarding the construction of the series (the hedonic regressions) or the annual values should contact the author.

Appendix B

This appendix sketches a simple general equilibrium model of a slave economy. The purpose of the model is to evaluate the conditions under which the dual would be a reliable way to measure labor productivity.

As a point of departure, imagine that the Southern economy produced two goods, C (cotton) and X (a composite commodity). Initially, there are two types of labor, slave (S) and free (F). Cotton can be produced under two technologies. One of these, $C^S(L_{SC}, T_{SC})$, uses slave labor, and the other, $C^F(L_{FC}, T_{FC})$, uses free labor. There is a single technology to produce the composite commodity in which slave and free labor are perfect substitutes, $X(L_{FX} + L_{SX}, K)$. The factor T ("land") is specific to the production of cotton, and can be allocated freely between the two technologies, while the factor K ("capital") is specific to the production of X. The price of cotton is p_C and the price of X is one.

APPENDIX TABLE A1 *(continued)* *Statistical Investigations, 1866–1899* (Washington, DC, 1901). Data in original sources refer to monthly wage of farm labor in which board was customarily provided. 1866, 1869, and 1875–1899: Daily value of board was calculated as the difference between the daily wage of farm labor with board and daily wage without board; monthly value of board = 26 × daily value of board. 1850, 1860, 1870: daily value of board = daily wage of common labor without board − daily wage with board. Monthly value of board = 26 × daily value of board.

Notes to Panel B: 1850–70: see notes to Panel A. 1880a: computed from Atack–Bateman sample of manufacturing establishments from 1880 manuscript census of manufacturing, with a correction for Delaware based on ratio of Delaware/Maryland in Lebergott, *Manpower*, Table A-25. 1890: Using Lebergott, *Manpower*, Table A-25 and labor force weights from Weiss ("Estimates"), I estimated regional values, and from these regional values, growth rates between 1880 and 1890. These growth rates were then applied to the 1880 estimates above to generate adjusted values for 1890. I used this procedure because Lebergott's original estimates for 1880 generally exceed the levels implied by the Atack–Bateman sample, and judged against my 1880 estimates, his 1890 figures imply extraordinarily high rates of nominal wage growth, in excess of other estimates for the period. It seemed prudent, therefore, to use Lebergott's figures to calculate growth rates, and apply the growth rates to my 1880 estimates.

Notes to Panel C: 1850–70: see notes to Panel A; United States Department of Agriculture, Report of the Statistician, Annual Report of the Commissioner of Agriculture (Washington, DC, 1881), p. 145.

Notes to Panel D: Figures are from Lebergott, *Manpower*, 542. The data pertain to domestics who were paid a weekly cash wage plus room and board. The value of board is imputed at 6 × daily value of board, as described above.

APPENDIX TABLE A2. *Nominal Daily Wages, Board Not Included, of Common Labor in the South and North, Level and South/North Ratios, 1821–1880: Margo Series*

	S. Atlantic	S. Central	North	S. Atlantic/North	S. Central/North
	A. Ante-bellum: Five-year averages, 1825–1860				
1821–25	$0.64	$0.75	$0.71	0.90	1.06
1826–30	0.63	0.87	0.69	0.91	1.26
1831–35	0.55	0.87	0.75	0.73	0.93
1836–40	0.71	0.88	0.85	0.84	1.04
1841–45	0.56	0.86	0.82	0.68	1.05
1846–50	0.68	0.76	0.85	0.80	0.89
1851–55	0.69	1.00	0.91	0.76	1.10
1856–60	0.88	1.03	1.02	0.86	1.01
	B. Post-bellum: Five-year averages, 1866–1880				
1866–70	$0.93	$1.23	$1.81	0.51	0.68
1871–75	0.89	1.13	1.72	0.52	0.66
1876–80	0.71	1.00	1.30	0.55	0.77

Panel A Source: Margo, *Wages and Labor Markets*, Table 3A.5. Figures for the North are a weighted average of estimates for Northeast and Midwest; using regional occupation weights for common labor from Margo, *Wages and Labor Markets*, Appendix 5B, Table 5B.1.

Panel B Source: sample of payrolls collected by the author from *Reports of Persons and Articles Hired*, Record Group 92, National Archives. Estimates are based on hedonic regressions; dependent variable is log of daily wage (monthly wages are converted to daily wages by dividing by 26 days per month), independent variables include dummies for location of military installation, whether paid on a monthly basis, season of year, job related characteristics associated with unusually high or low wages, occupation (teamsters and watchmen), and year of employment. In some regressions sample sizes are insufficient to include single-year dummies for all years. Estimates are benchmarked in 1866, 1869, 1875, 1879, and 1880 using (1866–1879) average daily wage paid to farm labor (board not included) from Blodgett (*Wages of Farm Labor in the United States, Results of Eleven*) aggregated to regional level (as above) using free adult male labor force as weights adjusted from cross-regional distribution of common labor. Coefficients of time dummies from regression are used to measure annual change in log wage between benchmark dates, with a positive or negative adjustment to allow for trend implied by benchmark estimates. Further details available from the author on request. Figures for North are weighted average of estimates for Northeast and Midwest, weights pertain to regional distribution of common labor (available from author on request).

Assume as well that the free labor is freely mobile between X and C and – this is the key point – owners of slave labor can freely allocate slaves between the two sectors to equalize the marginal returns. The following conditions characterize an equilibrium in which L_{SX}, L_{FX}, T_{SC}, and T_{FC} are all positive:

$$p_C \, dC^S/dL_{SC} = dX/dL_{SX}$$
$$p_C \, dC^F/dL_{FC} = dX/dL_{FX}$$
$$dX/dL_{FX} = dX/dL_{SX}$$

APPENDIX TABLE A3. *Nominal Daily Cost of Board in the South and North, Level and South/North Ratios*

Year	S. Atlantic	S. Central	North	S. Atlantic/North	S. Central/North
1850	$0.18	$0.21	$0.24	0.75	0.88
1860	0.24	0.30	0.27	0.89	1.11
1866	0.28	0.35	0.45	0.62	0.78
1869	0.27	0.34	0.43	0.63	0.79
1870	0.30	0.32	0.51	0.59	0.63
1875	0.25	0.29	0.39	0.64	0.74
1879	0.19	0.23	0.28	0.68	0.82
1880	0.18	0.23	0.32	0.56	0.72
1882	0.23	0.23	0.33	0.70	0.70
1885	0.22	0.22	0.31	0.71	0.71
1888	0.22	0.22	0.29	0.76	0.76
1890	0.22	0.21	0.30	0.73	0.70
1892	0.21	0.23	0.31	0.68	0.74
1893	0.16	0.15	0.25	0.64	0.60
1894	0.15	0.14	0.25	0.60	0.56
1895	0.16	0.14	0.26	0.62	0.54
1898	0.17	0.18	0.29	0.59	0.62
1899	0.18	0.18	0.33	0.55	0.55

Source: 1850, 1860: Census of Social Statistics. Average daily cost of board = average daily wage of common labor board not included – average daily wage of common labor with board. 1866–1899: Blodgett, *Wages of Farm Labor, Results of Eleven*. Average daily cost of board = average daily wage of farm labor, board not included – average daily wage of farm labor with board.

Note that, if these equations hold, it follows that the values of the marginal products of slave and free labor are the same. On average, the gang system might make slave labor more productive than free labor in the production of C: $C^S/L_{SC} > C^F/L_{FC}$. At the margin, however, as long as some slave labor is employed in the production of X, and slave and free labor are perfect substitutes in this sector, the marginal returns to slave and free labor will be equalized. The availability of the gang system shifts more slave labor toward the production of C, compared to an economy with slave labor but no gang system. Because it is a more productive technology, this raises the aggregate level of w/p_C. When the gang system is no longer, w/p_C declines.

The Writings of Stanley L. Engerman

Books

The Reinterpretation of American Economic History, edited with R. W. Fogel, Harper and Row, 1971.

Time on the Cross (2 volumes), with R. W. Fogel, Little, Brown & Co., 1974. Co-winner Bancroft Prize in American History. Reissued, with a new afterword, by W. W. Norton, 1989.

Race and Slavery in the Western Hemisphere: Quantitative Studies, edited with Eugene Genovese, Princeton University Press, 1975.

Between Slavery and Free Labor: The Spanish-Speaking Caribbean in the Nineteenth Century, edited with Manuel Moreno Fraginals and Frank Moya Pons, Johns Hopkins University Press, 1985.

Long-Term Factors in American Economic Growth, edited with Robert E. Gallman, University of Chicago Press, 1986.

British Capitalism and Caribbean Slavery, edited with Barbara L. Solow, Cambridge University Press, 1987. Several papers published in a special issue (*Caribbean Slavery and British Capitalism*) of the *Journal of Interdisciplinary History* (Spring 1987).

Quantitative Economic History, edited with N. Crafts and N. Dimsdale, Oxford University Press, 1991. Papers previously published in *Oxford Economic Papers* (1987, 1988).

Without Consent or Contract: Technical Papers on Slavery (2 volumes), edited with Robert W. Fogel, W. W. Norton, 1992.

The Atlantic Slave Trade, edited with Joseph Inikori, Duke University Press, 1992. Several papers previously published in *Social Science History* (1990, 1991).

The Growth of the World Economy: Trade and the Industrial Revolution, 1700–1850 (2 Volumes), editor, Edward Elgar, 1995.

Cambridge Economic History of the United States, Volume I: The Colonial Era, edited with R. E. Gallman, Cambridge, 1996; *Volume II: The Long Nineteenth Century* and *Volume III: The Twentieth Century*, 2000.

The Lesser Antilles in the Age of European Expansion, edited with Robert Paquette, University Presses of Florida, 1996.

A Historical Guide to World Slavery, edited with Seymour Drescher, Oxford University Press, 1998.
Terms of Labor, editor, Stanford University Press, 1999.
Slavery: A Reader, edited with Seymour Drescher and Robert Paquette, Oxford University Press, 2001.
Finance, Intermediaries, and Economic Development, co-editor, Cambridge University Press, 2003.
The Cambridge History of Slavery (4 vols.) edited with David Eltis, Cambridge University Press, forthcoming.

Articles

"Regional Aspects of Stabilization Policy," in R. A. Musgrave (ed.), *Essays in Fiscal Federalism*, The Brookings Institution, Washington (1965), pp. 7–62. Reprinted in L. Needleman (ed.), *Regional Analysis*, Penguin Books (1968).
"The Economic Impact of the Civil War," *Explorations in Entrepreneurial History*, Second Series (Spring/Summer 1966). Reprinted in Ralph Andreano (ed.), *The Economic Impact of the American Civil War*, Second Edition, Schenkman Publishing Company (1967), and Robert W. Fogel and Stanley L. Engerman (eds.), *The Reinterpretation of American Economic History* (1971).
"The Effects of Slavery Upon the Southern Economy," *Explorations in Entrepreneurial History*, Second Series (Winter 1967). Reprinted in Irwin Unger (ed.), *Essays in the Civil War and Reconstruction*, Holt, Rinehart, and Winston (1970), Hugh G. J. Aitken (ed.), *Did Slavery Pay?*, Houghton Mifflin (1971), and Paul Finkelman (ed.), *Economics, Industrialization, Urbanization and Slavery*, Garland (1990).
"Slavery as an Obstacle to Economic Growth in the United States: A Panel Discussion," with others, *Journal of Economic History* (December 1967). Reprinted in Bobbs-Merrill Reprint Series in Black Studies, and I. Unger and D. Reimer (eds.), *The Slavery Experience in the United States*, Holt, Reinhart, and Winston (1970).
"A Model for the Explanation of Industrial Expansion During the Nineteenth Century: With an Application to the American Iron Industry," with Robert W. Fogel, *Journal of Political Economy* (May/June 1969); Reprinted in *Reinterpretation*.
"'The Antebellum South' What Probably Was and What Should Have Been," *Agricultural History* (January 1970); also in William N. Parker (ed.), *The Structure of the Cotton Economy in the Antebellum South*, Agricultural History Society (1970).
"A Note on the Economic Consequences of the Second Bank of the United States," *Journal of Political Economy* (July/August 1970).
"Human Capital, Education, and Economic Growth," in *Reinterpretation*.
"The Economics of Slavery," with Robert W. Fogel, in *Reinterpretation*.
"The Relative Efficiency of Slavery: A Comparison of Northern and Southern Agriculture in 1850 and 1860," with Robert W. Fogel, *Explorations in Economic History* (Spring 1971).
"Some Economic Factors in Southern Backwardness in the Nineteenth Century," in John Kain and John Meyer (eds.), *Essays in Regional Economics*, Harvard University Press (1971).

"The American Tariff, British Exports, and American Iron Production, 1840–60," in Donald N. McCloskey (ed.), *Essays in a Mature Economy*, Methuen (1971).

"Some Economic Issues Relating to Railroad Subsidies and the Evaluation of Land Grants," *Journal of Economic History* (June 1972).

"The Slave Trade and Capital Formation in the Industrial Revolution," *Business History Review* (Winter 1972). Reprinted in Peter Hoffer (ed.), *Africans Become Afro-Americans*, Garland (1988).

"Some Considerations Relating to Property Rights in Man," *Journal of Economic History* (March 1973). Reprinted (in Portuguese) in *Novos Estudos* (1988).

"Philanthropy at Bargain Prices: Notes on the Economics of Gradual Emancipation," with Robert W. Fogel, *Journal of Legal Studies* (June 1974). Reprinted in *Without Consent or Contract*, and in Paul Finkelman (ed.), *Slavery in the North and West*, Garland (1990).

"Comments on the Study of Race and Slavery," in Stanley L. Engerman and Eugene D. Genovese (eds.), *Race and Slavery in the Western Hemisphere*, Princeton University Press (1975).

"A Reconsideration of Southern Economic Growth, 1770–1860," *Agricultural History* (April 1975).

"Models of Immiserization: The Theoretical Basis of Pessimism," with R. M. Hartwell, in A. J. Taylor (ed.), *The Standard of Living in Britain in the Industrial Revolution*, Methuen (1975).

"Ship Patterns and Mortality in the African Slave Trade of Rio de Janeiro," with Herbert S. Klein, *Cahiers d'études africaines* (1975). Reprinted (in Portuguese) in Carlos Manuel Pelaez and Mircea Buescu (eds.), *A Moderna História Econômica* (1976).

"Some Economic and Demographic Comparisons of Slavery in the United States and the British West Indies," *Economic History Review* (May 1976). Reprinted (in French) in Sidney W. Mintz, *Esclave – facteur de production*, Punod (1981).

"The Height of Slaves in the United States," *Local Population Studies* (Spring 1976). Reprinted in Cuff and Komlos (eds.), *Classics in Anthropometric History* (1998).

"Factors in Mortality in the French Slave Trade in the Eighteenth Century," with Herbert S. Klein, *Annales* (November/December 1976). Reprinted in *Without Consent of Contract*.

"The English Slave Trade in the 1790s," with Herbert S. Klein, in Roger Anstey and P. E. H. Hair (eds.), *Liverpool, the African Slave Trade and Abolition*, Historical Society of Lancashire and Cheshire (1976).

"The Southern Slave Economy," in Harry P. Owens (ed.), *Perspectives and Irony in American Slavery*, University Press of Mississippi (1976).

"Changes in Black Fertility and Family Structure, 1880–1940," *Journal of Family History* (Summer 1977). Also in Tamara K. Hareven and Maris Vinovskis (eds.), *Family and Population in Nineteenth-Century America*, Princeton University Press (1978).

"Explaining the Relative Efficiency of Slave Agriculture in the Antebellum South," with Robert W. Fogel, *American Economic Review* (June 1977); and "Reply" (September 1980). Reprinted in *Without Consent or Contract*.

"Quantitative and Economic Analysis of West Indian Slave Societies: Research Problems," in Vera Rubin and Arthur Tuden (eds.), *Comparative Perspectives on Slavery in New World Plantation Societies*, New York Academy of Sciences (1977).

"Recent Developments in American Economic History," *Social Science History* (Fall 1977).

"Economic Perspectives on the Life Course," in Tamara K. Hareven (ed.), *Transitions*, Academic Press (1978).

"Fertility Differentials between Slaves in the U.S. and the British West Indies: A Note on Lactation Practices and Their Possible Implications," with Herbert S. Klein, *William and Mary Quarterly* (April 1978). Reprinted in Paul Finkelman (ed.), *Comparative Issues in Slavery*, Garland (1990).

"Relooking at *The Slave Community*," in Al-Tony Gilmore (ed.), *Revisiting John Blassingame's Slave Community*, Greenwood (1978).

"Marxist Economic Studies of the Slave South," *Marxist Perspectives* (Spring 1978). Reprinted in Paul Finkelman (ed.), *Slavery and Historiography*, Garland (1990).

"The Economics of Mortality in North America, 1650–1910: A Description of a Research Project," with R. W. Fogel et al., *Historical Methods* (Spring 1978).

"A Note on Mortality in the French Slave Trade in the Eighteenth Century," with Herbert S. Klein, in Henry Gemery and Jan Hogendorn (eds.), *The Uncommon Market*, Academic Press (1979).

"Recent Findings on Slave Demography and Family Structure," with R. W. Fogel, *Sociology and Social Research* (April 1979). Reprinted in Paul Finkelman (ed.), *Women and the Family in Slave Society*, Garland (1990).

"The Realities of Slavery: A Review of Recent Evidence," *International Journal of Comparative Sociology* (1979).

"New Books on the Measurement of Capital," with Sherwin Rosen, in Dan Usher (ed.), *The Measurement of Capital*, University of Chicago Press (1980).

"Economic Aspects of the Abolition Debate," with David Eltis, in Christine Bolt and Seymour Drescher (eds.), *Anti-Slavery, Religion, and Reform*, Dawson (1980).

"Changes in Income and Its Distribution During the Industrial Revolution," with Patrick K. O'Brien, in Roderick Floud and Donald McCloskey (eds.), *Economic History of Britain Since 1700*, Cambridge University Press (1981).

"Notes on the Patterns of Economic Growth in the British North American Colonies in the Seventeenth, Eighteenth, and Nineteenth Centuries," in P. Bairoch and M. Levy-Leboyer (eds.), *Regional and International Disparities in Economic Development Since the Industrial Revolution*, Macmillan (1981).

"Some Implications of the Abolition of the Slave Trade," in David Eltis and James Walvin (eds.), *Abolition of the Atlantic Slave Trade*, University of Wisconsin Press (1981).

"Economic Growth, 1783–1860," with Robert E. Gallman, *Research in Economic History*, Volume 8 (1983).

"Exploring the Uses of Data on Height: The Analysis of Long-Term Trends in Nutrition, Labor Welfare, and Labor Productivity," with R. W. Fogel and J. Trussell, *Social Science History* (Fall 1982).

"Economic Aspects of the Adjustments to Emancipation in the United States and the British West Indies," *Journal of Interdisciplinary History* (Autumn 1982).

"Contract Labor, Sugar, and Technology in the Nineteenth Century," *Journal of Economic History* (September 1983).

"Changes in American and British Stature Since the Mid-Eighteenth Century: A Preliminary Report on the Usefulness of Data on Height for the Analysis of Secular Trends in Nutrition, Labor Productivity and Labor Welfare," with R. W. Fogel

et al., *Journal of Interdisciplinary History* (Autumn 1983). Also in Robert Rotberg and Ted Rabb (eds.), *Hunger and History*, Cambridge University Press (1985).
"The Level and Structure of Slave Prices on Cuban Plantations in the Middle of the Nineteenth Century: Some Comparative Perspectives," with Manuel Moreno Fraginals and Herbert S. Klein, *American Historical Review* (December 1983). Also published (in Spanish) in *Revista de Historia Economica* (1983).
"The Demographic Study of the American Slave Population," with Herbert S. Klein, in M. L. Marcilio (ed.), *População e Sociedade* (1984, in Portuguese).
"Economic Change and Contract Labor in the British Caribbean: The End of Slavery and the Adjustment to Emancipation," *Explorations in Economic History* (April 1984). Also published in David Richardson (ed.), *Abolition and Its Aftermath in the West Indies, Volume I, The Historical Context, 1790–1870*, Frank Cass (1985).
"The Transition from Slave to Free Labor: Notes on a Comparative Economic Model," with Herbert S. Klein, in *Between Slavery and Free Labor*. Also published (in Spanish) in *Revista Latinoamerica de Historia Economica y Social* (Summer 1983).
"Slavery and Emancipation in Comparative Perspective: A Look at Some Recent Debates," *Journal of Economic History* (June 1986). Reprinted in Paul Finkelman (ed.), *Slavery and Historiography*, Garland (1990), and Lawrence B. Goodheart, Richard D. Brown, and Stephen G. Rabe (eds.), *Slavery in American Society* (3rd Edition), D. C. Heath (1992).
"Trends and Patterns in the Prices of Manumitted Slaves, Bahia, 1819–1888," with Katia M. de Queiros Mattoso and Herbert S. Klein, *Slavery and Abolition* (May 1986). Also published (in Portuguese) in João José Reis (ed.), *Escravidão e Invenção da Liberdade* (1988).
"Clio is Alive and Well in More Places than Oxford, Ohio," with Lance E. Davis, *The Newsletter of the Cliometrics Society* (April 1986). Also Published in *Historical Methods* (Summer 1987).
"From Servant to Slaves to Servants: Contract Labor and European Expansion," in P. C. Emmer (ed.), *Colonialism and Migration: Indentured Labour Before and After Slavery*, Martinus Nijhoff (1986).
"British Capitalism and Caribbean Slavery: The Legacy of Eric Williams: An Introduction," with Barbara L. Solow, in Engerman and Solow (eds.), *British Capitalism and Caribbean Slavery*, Cambridge University Press (1987).
"Methods and Meanings in Price History," with Herbert S. Klein, in Lyman Johnson and Enrique Tandeter (eds.), *Growth and Integration of the Atlantic Economy: Essays on the Price History of the Eighteenth Century Latin America*, University of New Mexico Press (1989).
"Past History and Current Policy: The Legacy of Slavery," in R. America (ed.), *The Wealth of Races*, Greenwood (1990).
"Exports and the Growth of the British Economy, from the Glorious Revolution to the Peace of Amiens," with Patrick K. O'Brien, in Barbara Solow (ed.), *Slavery and the Rise of the Atlantic System*, Cambridge University Press (1991).
"Coerced and Free Labor: Property Rights and the Development of the Labor Force," *Explorations in Economic History* (January 1992).
"The Economic Response to Emancipation and Some Economic Aspects of the Meaning of Freedom," in Seymour Drescher and Frank McGlynn (eds.), *The Meaning of Freedom*, University of Pittsburgh Press (1992).

"Expanding Protoindustrialization," *Journal of Family History* (Number 2, 1992).

"Was the Slave Trade Dominated by Men?" with David Eltis, *Journal of Interdisciplinary History* (Autumn 1992).

"Reflections on 'The Economic Approach to History'," in E. Radnitzky (ed.), *Universal Economics: Assessment of the Achievements of the Economic Approach*, Paragon House (1992).

"Seasonality in Nineteenth Century Labor Markets," with Claudia Goldin, in Thomas Weiss and Don Schaefer (eds.), *Economic Development in Historical Perspective*, Stanford University Press (1993).

"The Ranks of Death: Secular Trends in Income and Mortality," with Stephen J. Kunitz, *Health Transition Review* (Vol. 2, Supplementary Issue, 1992).

"Fluctuations in Sex and Age Ratios in the Transatlantic Slave Trade, 1663–1814," with David Eltis, *Economic History Review* (May 1993).

"Chicken Little, Anna Karenina, and the Economics of Slavery," *Social Science History* (Summer 1993).

"The Economics of Forced Labor," *Itinerario* (Number 1, 1993).

"Mercantilism and Overseas Trade, 1700–1800," in Roderick Floud and Donald McCloskey (eds.), *Economic History of Britain Since 1700* (2nd Edition), Cambridge University Press (1994).

"The Industrial Revolution Revisited," in Graeme Snooks (ed.), *Was the Industrial Revolution Necessary?*, Routledge (1994).

"The Big Picture: How (and Why and When) the West Grew Rich," *Policy Research* (1994).

"The British Standard of Living Debate," in John James and Mark Thomas (eds.), *Capitalism in Context*, University of Chicago Press (1994).

"Family and Economy: Some Comparative Perspectives," in Richard Rudolph (ed.), *The European Peasant Family and Economy: Historical Studies*, Liverpool University Press (1995).

"Emancipations in Comparative Perspective: A Long and Wide View," in Gert Oostinde (ed.), *Fifty Years Later: Capitalism and Antislavery in The Dutch Orbit*, KLTV Press (1995).

"The Atlantic Economy of the Eighteenth Century: Some Speculations on Economic Development in Britain, America, Africa, and Elsewhere," *Journal of European Economic History* (Spring 1995).

"Europe, the Lesser Antilles, and Economic Expansion, 1600–1800," in Robert Paquette and Stanley L. Engerman (eds.), *The Lesser Antilles in the Age of European Expansion*, University Presses of Florida (1996).

"The Land and Labor Problem at the Time of the Legal Emancipation of the West Indian Slaves," in Roderick A. McDonald (ed.), *West Indies Accounts: Essays on the British Caribbean and the Atlantic Economy in Honour of Richard Sheridan*, University of West Indies Press (1996).

"Slavery, Serfdom, and other Forms of Coerced Labor: Similarities and Differences," in Michael Bush (ed.), *Serfdom and Slavery*, Longman (1996).

"Prices as a Tool of Historical Analysis," with Herbert S. Klein, (in Spanish), *Boletín de América Latina en la Historia Económica* (1996).

"Trade, Technology, and Wages: A Tale of Two Countries," with Ronald W. Jones, *American Economic Review* (May 1996).

"Immigration Debates in the Past," in *Levy Economics Institute of Bard College Public Forum Proceeding* (May 1996).

"Caribbean Population, 1700–1900," with Barry Higman, in Volume III of the *UNESCO History of the Caribbean*, Franklin Knight (ed.) (1997).

"The Civil War: A Modern View," with J. M. Gallman, in Stig Förster and Jörg Nagler (eds.), *On The Road to Total War*, Cambridge University Press (1997).

"Factor Endowments, Institutions, and Differential Paths of Growth among New World Economies: A View from Economic Historians of the United States," with Kenneth Sokoloff, in Stephen Haber (ed.), *Why Did Latin America Fall Behind?*, Stanford University Press (1996).

"Cultural Values, Ideological Beliefs, and Changing Labor Institutions: Notes on their Interactions," in John Drobak and John Nye (eds.), *Frontiers of the New Institutional Economics*, Academic Press (1997).

"Labor – Free or Coerced? A Historical Reassessment of Differences and Similarities," with Robert J. Steinfeld, in Tom Brass and Marcel van der Linden (eds.), *Free and Unfree Labor*, Peter Lang (1997).

"The Standard of Living Debate in International Perspective: Measures and Indicators," in Roderick Floud and Richard Steckel (eds.), *Health and Welfare During Industrialization*, University of Chicago Press (1997).

"International Labor Flows and National Wages," with R. W. Jones, *American Economic Review* (May 1997).

"Long-Term Trends in African Mortality in the Transatlantic Slave Trade," with Herbert S. Klein, *Slavery and Abolition* (April 1997).

"The Bricks of Empire, 1415–1999: 85 Years of Portuguese Emigration," with Joao Cesar das Neves, *Journal of European Economic History* (Winter 1997).

"British Imperialism in a Mercantilist Age, 1492–1849: Conceptual Issues and Empirical Problems," *Revista de Historia Economica*, 16 (Spring 1998).

"The Lessons from Nineteenth Century Transitions from Slavery to Free Labor," in Ewa Hauser and Jacek Wasilewslci (eds.), *Lessons in Democracy*, University of Rochester Press (1999).

"The Economy of British North America: Miles Traveled, Miles to Go," with Lance Davis, *William and Mary Quarterly* (January 1999).

"Max Weber as Economist and Economic Historian," in Stephen Turner (ed.), *The Cambridge Companion to Weber*, Cambridge University Press (2000).

"A Population History of the Caribbean," in Michael Haines and Richard Steckel (eds.), *A Population History of North America*, Cambridge University Press (2000).

"Changing Views of Slavery in the United States South: The Role of Eugene D. Genovese," with Robert W. Fogel, in Louis Ferleger and Robert Paquette (eds.) *Slavery, Secession, and Southern History*, University of Virginia Press (2000).

"The Importance of Slavery and the Slave Trade to Industrializing Britain," with David Eltis, *Journal of Economic History* (March 2000).

"France, Britain, and the Economic Growth of Colonial North America," in John J. McCusker and Kenneth Morgan (eds.), *The Early Modern Atlantic Economy*, Cambridge University Press. (2000).

"Mortality on Slave Ships Compared with Those in Other Long Distance Oceanic Migrations," with Herbert S. Klein, Robert Haines, and Ralph Shlomowitz, *William and Mary Quarterly* (January 2001).

"Institutions, Factor Endowments, and Paths of Development in the New World," with Kenneth Sokoloff, *Journal of Economic Perspectives* (June 2000).

"Comparative Approaches to the Ending of Slavery," in Howard Temperly (ed.), *After Slavery*, Frank Cass (2000).

"Inequality, Institutions, and Differential Paths of Growth among New World Economies," with Stephen Haber and Kenneth Sokoloff, in Claude Ménard (ed.), *Institutions, Contracts, and Organizations*, Edward Elgar (2001).

"Labor Incentives and Manumission in Ancient Greek Slavery," in G. Bitros and Y. Katsoulacos (eds.), *Essays in Economic Theory, Growth, and Labor Markets*, Edward Elgar (2002).

"Pricing Freedom: Evaluating the Costs of Emancipation and Manumission," in V. Shepard (ed.), *Working Slavery, Pricing Freedom*, Ian Randle Press (2002).

"The Emergence of a Market Economy Before 1860," with Robert E. Gallman, in William Barney (ed.), *Blackwell Companion to American History*, B. H. Blackwell (2002).

"Changing Laws and Regulations and Their Impact on Migration," in David Eltis (ed.), *Coerced and Free Migration*, Stanford University Press (2002).

Review Articles, Published Discussions, and Book Reviews

"Discussion," Papers in Economic History, *American Economic Review* (May 1967).

"Discussion," Precis of Dissertations, *Journal of Economic History* (March 1971).

"Gary Hawke's *Railways and Economic Growth in England and Wales, 1840–1870*," *Business History* (July 1975).

"Up or Out: Social and Geographic Mobility in the United States," (a review of Stephan Thernstrom's *The Other Bostonians*), *Journal of Interdisciplinary History* (Winter 1975).

"Comments on Richardson and Boulle and the Williams Thesis," in *Revue Française d'Histoire d'Outre-mer* (October 1975). Also published in Emmer, Mettas, Nardin (eds.), *The Atlantic Slave Trade: New Approaches* (1976).

"Douglass C. North's *The Economic Growth of the United States, 1790–1860* Revisited," *Social Science History* (Winter 1977).

"Studying the Black Family: A Review of *The Black Family in Slavery and Freedom, 1750–1925*," *Journal of Family History* (Summer 1977).

"Introduction" and editor, issue of *Southern Studies* devoted to slavery in the eighteenth century Chesapeake region (Winter 1977).

"Elites and Economic Development: A Commentary," in Working Papers from the Regional Economic History Center (1978).

"Frederick Cooper's *Plantation Slavery in East Africa*," *Economic Development and Cultural Change* (April 1979).

"Comments on the Slave Family and Its Legacies," *Historical Reflections* (Summer 1979). Also in Michael Craton (ed.), *Roots and Branches*, Pergamon (1979).

"*Logic and Society* on 'Counterfactuals and the New Economic History'," *Inquiry* (1980).

"AHR Forum: Antebellum North and South in Comparative Perspective," *American Historical Review* (December 1980).

"Foreword" to Robert J. Cottrol, *The Afro-Yankees*, Greenwood Press (1982).

"Foreword" to John David Smith, *Black Slavery in the Americas*, Greenwood Press (1982).

Co-editor, Special Issue of *Social Science History* on "Secular Trends in Nutrition, Labor Welfare, and Labor Productivity," with R. W. Fogel (Fall 1982).

"Three Recent Studies of Ethnicity and Relative Economic Achievement: A Review Essay," *Historical Methods* (Winter 1983).

Comment on "Slavery in a Nonexport Economy: Nineteenth-Century Minas Gerais Revisited," with Eugene D. Genovese, *Hispanic-American Historical Review* (August 1983).

"Reconstructing English Population History: A Review Essay of Wrigley and Schofield's *The Population History of England,*" *Annals of Scholarship* (1983).

"Introduction" to Michael Plunkett (compiler), *A Guide to the Collections Relating to Afro-American History, Literature, and Culture in the Manuscripts Department of the University of Virginia Library*, University of Virginia Library (1984).

Entry on "Cliometrics" in Adam Kuper and Jessica Kuper (eds.), *The Social Science Encyclopedia*, Routledge and Kegan Paul (1985); revised for second edition (1995); also entry on "Economic History," (1995).

Comment on "Population and Labor in the British Caribbean in the Early Nineteenth Century," in *Long-Term Factors in American Economic Growth* (1986).

Entry on "Slavery" in John Eatwell, Murray Milgate, Peter Newman (eds.), *The New Palgrave*, Macmillan (1987).

Entries on "Slave Prices" and Slave Demography," in Randall M. Miller and John David Smith (eds.), *Dictionary of Afro-American History*, Greenwood (1988).

Entry on "Douglass C. North," in John Cannon, R. H. C. Davis, William Doyle, and Jack P. Greene (eds.), *The Dictionary of Historians* (1988).

Co-editor with N. F. R. Crafts and N. Dimsdale, special issue of *Oxford Economic Papers* on economic history (1987).

Co-editor with Joseph Inikori, 4 issues of *Social Science History*, 1990, 1991, on the Atlantic slave trade; "Introduction," reprinted in part in David Northrup, *The Atlantic Slave Trade*, Heath (1994).

"Foreword," to M. Plunkett, *Afro-American Sources in Virginia: A Guide to Manuscripts*, University Press of Virginia (1990).

"Comments" [on paper of Robert E. Gallman on U.S. Capital Stock] in Robert E. Gallman and John Wallis (eds.), *The Standard of Living in Early Nineteenth-Century America*, University of Chicago Press (1992).

"Robert William Fogel: An Appreciation by a Coauthor and Colleague," in Claudia Goldin and Hugh Rockoff (eds.), *Strategic Factors in Nineteenth-Century American Economic History*, University of Chicago Press (1992). Reprinted in *Two Pioneers of Cliometrics*, Cliometric Society (1993).

"Plantation Wage Labor and Urban Slavery," (in Spanish) *HISLA* (Peru), special issue on slavery (1992).

"Quantification," in *Encyclopedia of American Social History*, Charles Scribner's Sons (1992).

"Comments" [on the historical study of heights in North America and Asia] in John Komlos (ed.), *The Standard of Living and Economic Development: Essays in Anthropometric History*, University of Chicago Press (1994).

"Concluding Reflections" in Larry E. Hudson, Jr. (ed.), *Working Towards Freedom*, University of Rochester Press (1994).

"The Extent of Slavery and Freedom Throughout the Ages, in the World as a Whole and in Major Sub-areas," in Julian L. Simon (ed.), *The State of Humanity*, Blackwell's (1995).

Entry on "Eric Williams," *The Encyclopedia of Democracy* (1995).

"Introductory Remarks on 'Economic History and Old Age,'" *Journal of Economic History* (March 1996).

Entry on "Slavery (World-Wide)," Microsoft Encarta 97 Encyclopedia (1997).

Entry in John Maurice Clark, *American National Biography*, Oxford University Press (1999).

"Introduction" to Seymour Drescher, *From Slavery to Freedom*, Macmillan (1998).

"Introductory Essay: Terms of Labor: Slavery, Serfdom, and Free Labor," in Engerman (ed.), *The Terms of Labor* (1999).

AHR Forum: "Looking at Slavery from Broader Perspectives," *American Historical Review* (April 2000).

Co-editor (with Lance Davis) of special issue of *William and Mary Quarterly* (January 1999), on "The Economy of British North America."

"Comment: *One Kind of Freedom*: A Comparative Perspective," *Explorations in Economic History* (January 2001).

Entries on "Capitalism," "The Slave Trade," "Slavery," and "Economics" in Paul S. Boyer, *The Oxford Companion to United States History*, Oxford University Press (2001).

Entries on "R. W. Fogel," "Caribbean Regions: Pre-emancipation Period," and "Capitalism" (with R. M. Hartwell) in Joel Mokyr (ed.), *Oxford Encyclopedia of Economic History*, Oxford University Press (2001).

Contributors

Laird W. Bergad is professor in the Ph.D. program in History and Director of the Center for Latin American, Caribbean, and Latino Studies, Graduate Center, City University of New York.

Lee A. Craig is Alumni Distinguished Professor of Economics at North Carolina State University.

Seymour Drescher is University Professor of History and Professor of Sociology at the University of Pittsburgh.

Pieter C. Emmer is professor in the History of the Expansion of Europe at the Department of History, University of Leiden, The Netherlands.

David Eltis is professor of history at Emory University.

Elizabeth B. Field-Hendrey is professor of economics at Queens College and Graduate Center, City University of New York.

James R. Irwin is associate professor in the Department of Economics, Central Michigan University.

Herbert S. Klein is professor of Latin American history at Columbia University.

Frank D. Lewis is professor of economics at Queen's University, Canada.

Francisco Vidal Luna is professor of economics, Faculdade de Economia e Administração, Universidade de São Paulo.

Robert A. Margo is professor of economics and of history, Vanderbilt University, and research associate, National Bureau of Economic Research.

Philip D. Morgan is professor of history at The Johns Hopkins University.

David Richardson is professor in the Department of History, University of Hull, United Kingdom.

Kenneth L. Sokoloff is professor of economics at UCLA and research associate at the National Bureau of Economic Research.

Lorena S. Walsh is historian at The Colonial Williamsburg Foundation.

Index